Effective
Human Relations
In Organizations

Houghton Mifflin Company · Boston

Dallas   Geneva, Illinois   Lawrenceville, New Jersey   Palo Alto

Effective Human Relations In Organizations

Third Edition

Barry L. Reece

*Virginia Polytechnic Institute
and State University*

Rhonda Brandt

Human Resource Development Specialist

Figure Credits

Figures 5.1, 5.3, 5.5, 5.6, 5.7, 5.8, 5.9 adapted from Gerald L. Manning and Barry L. Reece, *Selling Today: A Personal Approach*, 3rd ed. (Dubuque, Iowa: Wm. C. Brown, 1987). Figure 6.3 from Frederick Herzberg, "One More Time: How Do You Motivate Employees," *Harvard Business Review*, January-February, 1968, p. 57. Copyright © 1968 by the President and Fellows of Harvard College; all rights reserved. Figure 7.1 adapted from Richard I. Evans, *Dialogue with Gordon Allport*. Published by Praeger Publishers, New York. Copyright © 1971 and 1981 by Richard I. Evans. Figure 7.2 reprinted, by permission of the publisher, from *Managerial Values and Expectations* by Warren H. Schmidt and Barry Z. Posner, p. 17, © 1982 by AMA Membership Division, American Management Associations, New York. All *(Credits continue on p. 485.)*

Total Person Insights

p. 13: William Raspberry, "Topmost Priority: Jobs," *Washington Post*, 1977. *p. 17:* Alice Sargent, *The Androgynous Manager*, p. 1; Reprinted by permission of the publisher. (New York: AMACOM, a division of American Management Associations, 1981). *p. 65:* M. Scott Peck, *The Road Less Traveled* (New York: Simon and Schuster, 1978), p. 37. *p. 85:* Joshua Liebman, from "The Best Thoughts on Self" by Eugene Raud-

sepp, *PACE*, May–June 1977, p. 37. *p. 126:* David W. Merrill and Roger H. Reid, *Personal Styles and Effective Performance* (Radnor, Penn.: Chilton Book Company, 1981), p. 2. *p. 135:* "30 Ways to Motivate Employees to Perform Better," *Training/HRD*, March 1980, p. 51. *p. 179:* Chris Lee, "Ethics Training: Facing the Tough Questions," *Training*, March 1986, p. 31. *p. 200:* Ger- *(Credits continue on p. 485.)*

Text Credits

pp. 44–45: "Gossip and the Grapevine: Understanding Informal Information Networks," by Bruce A. Baldwin. Reprint permission from PACE magazine, the Piedmont Airlines inflight magazine (Pace Communications, Inc., Greensboro, NC), and by permission of the author. *p. 48:* "Selling from the Subconscious," *The American Salesman*, November 1981. © 1981 by The National Research Bureau, Inc., 424 North Third Street, Burlington, Iowa 52601. Reprinted by permission. *p. 61:* Levering, Moskowitz and Katz, *The 100 Best Companies to Work for in America*, pp. 173, 177. © 1984, Addison-Wesley Publishing Company, Inc. Reading, Massachusetts. Reprinted with permission. *pp. 67–69, 71: Developing Attitude Toward Learning*, by Robert F. Mager. Copyright © 1968 by David S. Lake Publish- *(Credits continue on p. 485.)*

Contents

6   Identifying Your Motivations   133

7   Personal and Organizational Values   156

Part III   Personal Strategies for Improving Human Relations   187

8   Constructive Self-Disclosure   188

9   Learning to Achieve Emotional Control   213

10   The Power of Positive Reinforcement   239

Part VI You Can Plan for Success   443

17 Making Your Plan for Improved Human Relations   444

Preface

Over the ten years we have worked on the various editions of *Effective Human Relations in Organizations*, several changes have emerged in the workplace. One of the most significant developments has been the increased importance of interpersonal skills in almost every type of organization. Employers want to hire persons who can work effectively in teams and who are able to represent the employer favorably to clients, customers, and members of the public. They want employees who possess the ability to communicate clearly and in a pleasant manner. A growing number of employers are attempting to create a work environment that nurtures these important skills. They realize that how well people feel about themselves and others affects how well the company performs.

The third edition of *Effective Human Relations in Organizations* provides an expanded introduction to the human side of today's work world. This was accomplished by incorporating into the text a greater number of real-world examples obtained from a wide range of organizations. These examples have been obtained from relatively small companies such as Celestial Seasonings, as well as from large firms such as Citicorp, Dayton-Hudson, and Pitney Bowes. This edition also features many examples from government agencies and nonprofit institutions.

The "total person" approach to human relations, a feature in past editions that has been highly praised by instructors and students, has been expanded and enriched in this edition. We continue to take the position that human behavior at work is influenced by many interdependent traits such as physical fitness, values orientation, self-concept, nutrition, emotional control, and self-awareness—to name just a few. This approach focuses on those human relations skills students need to be well-rounded and thoroughly prepared for the job world. The material in this text will give students a sense of balance in terms of their career preparation.

Some aspects of the third edition have not changed. The material is presented in a nontechnical, interesting, and readable style. Students preparing for a variety of careers will find the content practical and relevant. The book is also appropriate for people who are currently employed and returning to school or continuing their education. We have tested the concepts presented in this book in over 250 seminars, workshops, and short courses for adult learners. These concepts can be immediately and effectively applied to on-the-job situations.

Chapter Organization

Effective Human Relations in Organizations is divided into six major parts. Part I, "Human Relations: The Key to Success," provides a strong rationale for the study of human relations and reviews the historical development of this field. One important highlight of Chapter 1 is a detailed discussion of the major forces influencing behavior at work. This material helps students develop a new appreciation for the complex nature of human behavior in a work setting. Another important feature of Chapter 1 is the description of seven broad themes that emerge from a study of human relations. They are communication, self-acceptance, self-awareness, motivation, trust, self-disclosure, and conflict management. The communication process, the basis for all human relations, is explained from both an individual and organizational level in Chapter 2.

Part II, "Career Success Begins with Knowing Yourself," reflects the basic fact that our effectiveness in dealing with others depends in large measure on our self-awareness and self-acceptance. We believe that by building a positive self-concept and by learning to explore inner attitudes, motivations, and values the reader will learn to be more sensitive to the way others think, feel, and act.

Part III is titled "Personal Strategies for Improving Human Relations." The chapters in this section feature a variety of practical strategies that can be used to develop and maintain good relationships with coworkers, supervisors, and managers. Chapters on constructive self-disclosure, learning to achieve emotional control, positive reinforcement, and positive first impressions discuss the importance of these concepts in the workplace and help the reader develop skills in these areas.

In Part IV, "If We All Work Together . . . ," the concepts of team building and conflict management are given detailed coverage. Because employers are increasingly organizing employees into teams, the chapter on team building takes on new importance. The chapter on conflict management describes three basic conflict management strategies and provides an introduction to the role of labor unions in today's workforce.

Part V, "Special Challenges in Human Relations," is designed to help the reader deal with some unique problem areas—coping with personal and professional life changes, prejudice and discrimination, and sexism in organizations. Each chapter in this section focuses on ways of coping with these special problems on the job.

Part VI, "You Can Plan for Success," gives support to the idea that "all development is self-development." The material in this section helps the reader design a step-by-step plan to improve or develop specific human relations skills.

Special Features

A large number of teaching/learning aids are featured throughout the book. Each chapter opens with a preview of major topic areas and an opening vignette that builds reader interest in the material. The new two-color format enhances the book's readability and visual appeal.

Numerous Thinking/Learning Starters within each chapter give students a chance to reflect on the material and relate their own experiences to the concepts discussed. A new feature in this edition is a series of Total Person Insights. These are thought-provoking quotes from a variety of authors, leaders in business, and scholars. The chapters close with a list of key terms and a series of review questions designed to reinforce the reader's understanding of important ideas. If students are interested in pursuing a particular subject in greater detail, a list of suggested readings is also offered at the end of each chapter.

Each chapter features two case problems based on actual human relations situations. Some cases focus on an employee problem within the context of a specific organization. Other cases focus on a human relations problem that may require a change in organizational policies or procedures.

A comprehensive study guide/activities manual, written by Robert Lussier and Lester Hirsch, is also available to students. This manual can be used as a home-study aid as well as an in-class learning tool.

Acknowledgments

Many people have made contributions to *Effective Human Relations in Organizations*. Throughout the years the text has been strengthened as a result of numerous helpful comments and recommendations. We extend special appreciation to the following persons:

Deborah Lineweaver
New River Community College

William Price
Virginia Polytechnic Institute and State University

Naomi W. Peralta
The Institute of Financial Education

Jack C. Reed
University of Northern Iowa

Michael Dzik
North Dakota State School of Sciences

John Elias
University of Missouri

V. S. Thakur
Community College of Rhode Island

Robert Kegel, Jr.
Cypress College

Mike Fernstead
Bryant & Stratton Business Institute

Leonard L. Palumbo
Northern Virginia Community College

Vance A. Kennedy
College of Mateo

Marlene Katz
Canada College

C. Winston Borgen
Sacramento City College

Linda Truesdale
Midlands Technical College

Burl Worley
Allan Hancock College

M. Camille Garrett
Tarrant County Junior College

J. Douglas Shatto
Muskingum Area Technical College

Carolyn K. Hayes
Polk Community College

Erv J. Napier
Kent State University

Lawrence Carter
Jamestown Community College

Roberta Greene
Central Piedmont Community College

Garland Ashbacher
Kirkwood Community College

Rhonda Barry
American Institute of Commerce

James Aldrich
North Dakota State School of Science

Sally Hanna-Jones
Hocking Technical College

We would also like to thank Dr. Denis Waitley and Mr. Charles Haefner for helping us develop a fuller understanding of human relations.

We are indebted to over 200 business organizations, government agencies, and nonprofit institutions that provided us with the real-world examples that appear throughout the text. Special recognition is given to the following organizations that allowed us to conduct interviews, observe workplace environments, and use special photographs and materials: Lowe's Companies, Inc., Allen Health Systems, Inc., Deere & Company, Delta Air Lines, Josten's Inc., O. C. Tanner Company, Marriott Corporation, Maytag Company, Pitney Bowes, Inc., Wal-Mart Stores, Inc., and Silo Inc.

B.L.R.
R.B.

Effective
Human Relations
In Organizations

I

Human Relations: The Key to Success

Chapter 1

Introduction to Human Relations

Chapter Preview

After studying this chapter, you will be able to
1. Understand how the study of human relations will help you succeed in your chosen career.
2. Explain the nature, purpose, and importance of human relations in an organizational setting.
3. Explain how the human relations movement has helped organizations see workers and managers as complex human beings.
4. Identify the reasons why human relations is receiving greater attention in the workplace.
5. Identify the major forces influencing human behavior at work.
6. Identify the seven basic themes emerging from a study of human relations.

Each decade seems to bring unique challenges and opportunities. In the 1960s Americans were experiencing strife at home and fighting in Southeast Asia. The Civil Rights movement, resistance to the Vietnam War, the women's movement, and concern for the environment were some of the issues that created tension and disharmony. Throughout the 1970s Americans seemed to grow tired of debating these issues and began withdrawing into themselves. Writer Tom Wolfe proclaimed it the "me decade." A strong desire for individual self-improvement surfaced, and people seemed less interested in social problems.

In the early 1980s we began to see a shift from social to economic issues. The economic environment became increasingly competitive, and American workers began competing for jobs, not just with each other, but with the workers of Japan, Western Europe, and the Third World. Employment started to decline in such goods-producing industries as steel, textiles, and shoes. In contrast to the decline in manufacturing jobs, the service-producing sector has been growing. This sector includes services in the areas of finance, insurance, health care, and merchandising. As one source has stated, "The times have changed, and we no longer live in Industrial America."[1]

Although some organizations have not been able to survive in this changing climate, many new firms have come along to take their places. Some of these new employers have given their workers an improved quality of work life. One such company is Federal Express Corp., the nation's leading provider of overnight, door-to-door delivery of packages and letters. This is a company that adheres to a no-layoff policy, pays good wages, offers profit sharing, and maintains excellent communications with employees. One means of improv-

Federal Express Corp. demonstrates the belief that motivated and conscientious employees will provide the professional service necessary to ensure profits and continued growth. (Photo courtesy of Federal Express Corp.)

ing employee communication at Federal Express is to schedule brown bag lunches at which top company officials regularly address groups of employees during lunch breaks. Fred Smith, founder and chairman of Federal Express, says, "We are interested in making this a good place to work, where people are dealt with as human beings rather than as some number."[2]

Federal Express does not represent an isolated success story. Organizations throughout the United States are discovering and rediscovering the benefits of encouraging employee participation and improving the quality of work life. A growing number of organizations, from hospitals to hotels, are giving greater attention to the human side of enterprise. Most of the organizations that survive and prosper over a long period of time maintain a proper balance between concern for production and concern for people.

The Nature, Purpose, and Importance of Human Relations

Many of America's best-managed organizations are going beyond being "nice to people" to genuinely helping them come alive through their work. Managers have learned that the goals of worker and workplace need not conflict.[3] They have also discovered that apparent policy or procedural problems are actually conflicts among people, or *human relations* problems. The issue may involve management-employee conflicts, poor communication, low morale, or a combination of these factors. Such problems can have serious repercussions not only on the operations of the organization, but for the individual workers themselves. This chapter focuses on the nature of human relations, its development, and its importance to the achievement of individual and organizational goals.

Human Relations Defined

The term **human relations** in its broadest sense covers all types of interactions among people—their conflicts, cooperative efforts, and group relationships. It is the story of those beliefs, attitudes, and behaviors that cause interpersonal conflict in our personal lives and in work-related situations. Knowledge of human relations does not begin in the classroom. Although this may be your first formal course in the subject, your "education" in human relations actually began with your family and friends. You learned what was socially acceptable and what was not. You tested your behavior against others, formed close relationships, experienced conflict, developed perceptions of yourself, and discovered how to get most of your needs met.

By the time you reached college age, you had probably formed a fairly complex network of relationships and had a pretty good idea of who you were.

However, experiences acquired at home or school cannot always be used as a reliable guide to human relations on the job. For example, a casual attitude about getting to work on time could limit your chances for success or advancement. Friends may accept your lack of punctuality, but a supervisor will take a dim view of an employee who cannot keep appointments or is late for an important client meeting.

The Importance of Human Relations

Technical ability is often not enough to achieve career success. Employers point out that many of the people who have difficulty obtaining or holding a job or advancing to positions of greater responsibility possess the needed technical or professional competence, but lack effective human relations skills.

As the nation's economy shifts to a concentration in the service sector, greater reliance on information creation and exchange, and new electronic technology, we will see human relations skills becoming more important. Why? Here are a few of the major reasons.

1. The work force is tending to become organized into teams in which each specialized employee plays a part. Most jobs today are interdependent, and if the people in these jobs cannot work effectively as a team, the goals of the organization will suffer.

2. Organizations are developing an increasing orientation toward service to clients, patients, and customers. As the authors of *Service America* note, we now live in a new economy, a service economy, where relationships are becoming more important than physical products. Restaurants, hospitals, banks, public utilities, colleges, airlines, and retail stores all have the problem of gaining and retaining the patronage of their clients and customers. In a service-type firm there are thousands of "moments of truth," those critical incidents in which customers come into contact with the organization and form their impressions of its quality and service.[4] Employees must not only be able to get along with customers, they must project a favorable image of the organization they represent. J. W. Marriott, Jr., president of Marriott Corporation, stated, "We have found that our success depends more upon employee attitudes than any other single factor."

3. A new breed of supervisory-management personnel will be needed to match the new generation of workers. The current generation of workers are better educated, better informed, and have higher expectations than did previous generations. (See Table 1.1.) There's a new attitude that psychologists describe as a **feeling of entitlement** among younger workers. They

Table 1.1   Changing Levels of Education in the United States

	Year	Percent of Labor Force Who Completed 4 Years*
High School	1960	46%
	1980	66
	1990	80 (projected)
College	1970	11%
	1980	17
	1990	24 (projected)

*High school data include only those work force members over age twenty-five.
Source: U.S. Bureau of Labor Statistics.

seek jobs that give not only a sense of accomplishment but also a sense of purpose, jobs that provide meaningful work.[5] Today's supervisors and managers must shift from manager-as-order-giver to manager-as-facilitator. John Naisbitt, author and consultant, notes that "we are moving from the manager who is supposed to have all the answers and tells everyone what to do, to a manager whose role is to create a nourishing environment for personal growth."[6] We must think of today's manager as teacher, mentor, resource, and developer of human potential.

4. In the 1990s and beyond, employees must be adaptable and flexible, able to achieve success within a climate of change. In addition to technical changes in the work place, we will see the creation of new jobs that do not even exist today. About 25 percent of the jobs in the 1990s will be different from the jobs of today.[7] Today, no line of work, company, or industry enjoys complete immunity from the forces of change that exist in our economy. Most of us will change jobs several times throughout our lives. It is important to develop those interpersonal skills—courtesy, sensitivity, a positive attitude, ability to cope with conflict—that are valued by all employers.

The Behavioral Science Influence on Human Relations

The field of human relations also draws on the behavioral sciences—psychology, sociology, and anthropology. Basically, these sciences focus on the *why* of human behavior. Psychology attempts to find out why *individuals* act as they do, while sociology and anthropology are concerned primarily with *group* dynamics and social interaction. Human relations differs from the behavioral sciences in an important respect. Although also interested in the why of human behavior, human relations goes further and looks at what can be done to anticipate problems, resolve them, or even prevent them from happening. In other words, the field of human relations emphasizes knowledge that can be *applied* in practical ways to problems of interpersonal relations in an organization.

Human Relations and the "Total Person"

The material in this book will focus on human relations as the study of *how people satisfy both personal growth needs and organizational goals in their personal career.* We believe, as do most authors in the field of human relations, that such human traits as physical fitness, emotional control, self-awareness, self-concept, and values orientation are interdependent. Although some organizations may occasionally wish they could employ only a person's skill or brain, all that can be employed is the whole or **total person.**[8] One's separate characteristics are part of a single system making up a whole person. Work life is not totally separate from home life, and emotional conditions are not separate from physical conditions. The quality of one's work, for example, is often related to physical fitness and nutrition.

Many organizations are beginning to recognize that if the whole person can be improved, significant benefits accrue to the firm. They are establishing employee development programs that address the total person, not just the employee skills needed to perform the job. These programs include such topics as stress management, assertiveness training, physical fitness, problem solving, and personal attitude development. A few examples follow:

Item: Hoffman-La Roche, Inc., a New Jersey-based firm, sponsors a fully developed corporate child-care program. This program was the outgrowth of a staff survey indicating that employees wanted to minimize baby-sitting arrangements as much as possible.

Item: Pitney Bowes established a career planning workshop to help employees form and chart their long-term career goals inside or outside the firm. This program enables employees to develop the skills needed to manage their careers.

Item: Adolph Coors Company, the brewer, spent $600,000 converting an adjacent supermarket into a "wellness" center for group exercise and clinics devoted to nutrition, stress management, and control of drinking, smoking, and weight.[9]

Item: Northwestern Mutual Life Insurance Company is taking care of the physical and mental needs of its employees. In the company's four-star rated cafeteria (lunch is free), the daily menu reports how many calories each item contains. More than 1,300 paintings hanging throughout the building contribute to a more human work environment.[10]

Some of the results of these programs may be difficult to assess in terms of profit and loss. For example, does the person in good physical health

Kimberly-Clark Corporation recognizes the benefits of the total-person approach to productivity enhancement. (Photo courtesy of Kimberly-Clark)

contribute more? If an employee is under considerable stress, does this mean he or she will have more accidents on the job? Specific answers vary, but most human relations experts agree that an employee's physical and mental well-being have a definite impact on job performance and productivity. Robert Pike, a noted management consultant, has stated:

> The greatest resource we have in our companies today is the human resource.... By helping people develop the tools to reduce and resolve personal conflicts, by assisting them to become more aware of what attitudes they have, and by helping them to experience the results that improved attitudes can provide, we can help build better people, a more productive company, and make a positive contribution to our community.[11]

The Need for a Supportive Environment

Not everyone is convinced that human relations work. Some people do not believe that total-person training, job enrichment, motivation techniques, or career development help increase productivity or strengthen worker commitment to the job. It is true that when such practices are tried halfheartedly or without full management support, there is a good chance they will fail. Such failures often have a demoralizing effect on employees and management alike. "Human relations" may take the blame, and management will be reluctant to try other human relations techniques or approaches in the future.

A basic assumption of this book is that human relations, when applied in a positive and supportive environment, can help individuals achieve greater personal satisfaction from their careers and help increase an organization's productivity and efficiency. In the subsequent chapters of the book, we will examine the impact of an individual's values, attitudes, appearance, motivation, and communication style on interpersonal relations in the work place. We will also take a look at group interaction and the special human relations problems that organizations encounter in today's environment.

Myths and Misconceptions

Now that you know what human relations *is*, it may be helpful to explore what it *isn't.*

It is not concerned with personality or character development in order to give you the power to manipulate people. Nor does human relations offer the ultimate formula to solve the people problems you are likely to encounter. In dealing with others, you will often find that there is seldom a clear-cut "right" or "wrong" way to handle conflict situations. In one plant, for example, the night superintendent found that workers on the first shift settled their disputes themselves. They viewed his efforts to arbitrate as an interference. The second shift, however, expected their superintendent to settle disagreements and brought him all their disputes. Their view of a good manager was someone who knew how to arbitrate.

Human relations *can* help you develop appropriate solutions to problems by giving you a good grasp of behavior concepts—both of your own behavior and that of others. Texts such as this one can provide a good grounding in the fundamentals of human relations and offer guidelines and suggestions for modifying behavior and enhancing group interaction. But human relations skills do not guarantee quick changes. Unlike characters in a movie, people in real life do not alter their behavior overnight. Even when everyone agrees a change needs to be made, it still takes time and effort. You may have experienced this fact yourself in trying to break an old habit or develop a new one. Unless people are willing to *work* at change, no solution—no matter how good—will be effective. Chapter 17 offers practical suggestions for assessing your human relations skills and making changes you feel are necessary.

It is also a popular belief among some people that human relations is nothing more than good common sense. Everyone knows that you give praise where it's due, acknowledge a job well done, and listen to what employees have to say. Yet surveys conducted by the Department of Labor, major universities, and other institutions tell a different story. These studies indicate that employees do not feel they are given adequate recognition for work well done and that management fails to listen to employees' suggestions, concerns, and grievances. Apparently, common sense is not enough to ensure good human relations on the job.

Forces Influencing Behavior at Work

A major purpose of this text is to increase your knowledge of factors that influence human behavior in a variety of work settings. An understanding of human behavior at work begins with a review of the major forces that influence the worker. Figure 1.1 shows the five forces that affect every employee, regardless of the size of the organization.

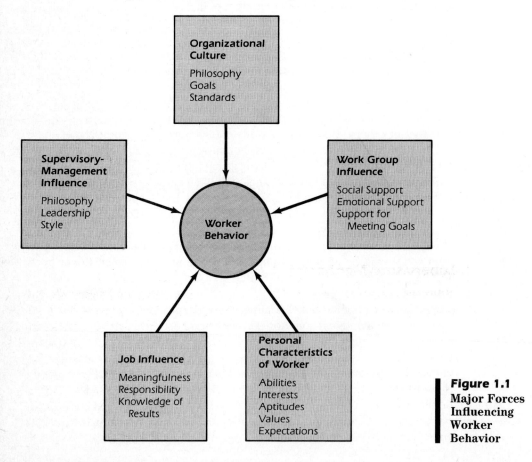

Figure 1.1
Major Forces Influencing Worker Behavior

Organizational Culture

Every organization, whether a manufacturing plant, retail store, hospital, or government agency, is unique. Each has its own culture. **Organizational culture** is a collection of beliefs, behaviors, and work patterns held in common by the workers employed by a specific firm. Most organizations over a period of time tend to take on distinct norms and practices. At Maytag Company, for example, a commitment to high quality products has been instilled in every member of the work force. Maytag machines rank at the top in industry comparisons, and this fact builds pride in the workers. Polaroid Corporation places a great emphasis on equal employment opportunity. About one out of every five of its hourly employees is a minority.

The uniqueness of an organization is an outgrowth of the philosophy and goals of those who join together to create it. Some organizations are cold and impersonal, and place major emphasis on achieving productivity goals regardless of the human costs. Other organizations are warm, friendly, and supportive of employee needs. Which organizational climate is more effective? The human-oriented climate is usually best in the long run. People tend to be more productive when they are part of an organization that inspires personal growth and development, and builds and maintains a sense of personal worth. These, after all, are the basic rewards of work.

Jay Hall, author of *The Competence Process*, says that when people lose access to the basic rewards of work, they are deprived of self-respect and become less productive. He further states that work is the context of individual competence, and the organization creates the context for work.

> People come to the organization, capable and desirous of working competently. Managers then supply them with the policies and ground rules, standards and objectives, which will characterize their work. People supply the capacity and managers supply the context. Often the two collide because the context for doing work reflects few of the reasons people work at all.[12]

Supervisory-Management Influence

Supervisory-management personnel are in a key position to influence employee behavior. It is not an exaggeration to say that supervisors and managers are the spokespersons for the organization. They establish its image in the eyes of employees. Each employee develops certain perceptions about the organization's concern for his or her welfare. These perceptions, in turn, influence such important factors as productivity, customer relations, safety consciousness, and loyalty to the firm. Effective managers are aware of the organization's basic purposes, why it exists, and its general direction. They are able to communicate this information to workers in a clear and positive manner.

"I'd like to think of you as a person, David, but it's my job to think of you as personnel." (Drawing by Vietor; © 1986 The New Yorker Magazine, Inc.)

Supervisory-management personnel hold the key to both outlook and performance. They are in a unique position to unlock the internal forces of motivation and help employees channel their energies toward achieving the goals of the organization. Today, managers need to use both logic and intuition, recognize both facts and feelings, and be both technically competent and emotionally caring.[13]

Work Group Influence

In recent years behavioral scientists have devoted considerable research to determine the influence of group affiliation on the individual worker. They are particularly interested in group influence within the formal structure of the organization. This research has identified three functions of group membership.[14] First, it can satisfy *social needs*. Many people find the hours spent at work enjoyable because coworkers provide the social support they need. Second, the work group can provide the *emotional support* needed to deal with pressures and problems on the job. Finally, the group provides *assistance in meeting goals*. A cohesive work group lends support to all individuals as they seek to meet the goals of the work unit. An effective work group is often described as one that maintains a balance between group productivity and the satisfaction of individual needs.

Job Influence

Some workers find their jobs to be a source of enormous personal satisfaction. Charles Jordan, director of design for General Motors Corporation, is

Total Person Insight	. . . Jobs do a lot more than merely provide income. They provide the opportunity to learn and enhance skills, to have some control over one's fate and, perhaps most important, to gain a sense of self-worth, a sense of carrying one's own weight.
William Raspberry	

one of these people. He has been quoted as saying, "I've got the best job in the world. I love cars and I'm living in the future." In reference to his position, he says, "It never quite seems like work!"[15] Unfortunately, not everyone receives this much satisfaction from work. Many workers perceive their jobs to be meaningless and boring because there is little variety to the work. Some autoworkers complain that their work is noisy, dirty, and monotonous. In some southern textile plants, workers still labor in the heat on dirty, greasy equipment to produce cotton cloth and other materials. And many electronic data processing terminal operators say the tedious work causes them physical and mental anguish.

Job satisfaction tends to increase when there is compatibility between the wants and needs of the employee and job characteristics. To be completely satisfying, a job must provide three experiences for a worker: meaningfulness, responsibility, and knowledge of results.[16] Throughout the past two decades, there has been a gradual increase in job satisfaction among American workers. One factor that appears to be contributing to this positive trend is improved organizational practices dealing with human relations.

Personal Characteristics of the Worker

Every worker brings to the job a combination of abilities, interests, aptitudes, values, and expectations. Worker behavior on the job is most frequently a reflection of how well the work environment accommodates the unique characteristics of each worker. For more than half a century, work researchers and theorists have attempted to define the ideal working conditions that would maximize worker productivity. These efforts have met with partial success, but some unanswered questions remain.

Identifying the ideal work environment is difficult because the work force is gradually changing. The challenge is to monitor changes closely and attempt to respond to the evolving needs of workers. Today many management and union leaders fail to realize that a philosophy and organization of work that was appropriate for the 1960s and 1970s may not be appropriate for the 1980s.[17] Coming into the workplace today is a new generation of workers with value systems and expectations about work that are very different from those of previous generations. Today's better educated and better informed workers value identity and achievement. They also have a heightened sense of their rights.

This review of the five major forces that influence employee behavior at work helps us understand the complex nature of interpersonal relations. It also helps us develop greater awareness of why people-oriented problems surface with such frequency in organizational settings.

Development of the Human Relations Movement

Problems in human relations are not new. All cooperative efforts carry the potential for people-oriented conflicts. However, it is only within the past few decades that management, researchers in behavioral sciences, and industry experts have recognized that human relations problems can have considerable impact on organizational productivity. Since the late 1800s, the human relations movement has matured into a distinct and important field of study.

Although it is difficult to pinpoint exactly when the human relations movement began, most researchers and historians agree that it emerged in about the mid-1800s. In the beginning, the focus was mainly to improve efficiency, motivation, and productivity. But over time, human relations research became more involved with a redefinition of the nature of work and the gradual perception of workers as complex human beings. The change reflected a shift in values from a concern with things to a greater concern for people.

Impact of the Industrial Revolution

Prior to the Industrial Revolution, most work was performed by individual craftworkers or members of craft guilds. Generally, each worker saw a project through from start to finish. Skills such as tailoring, carpentry, or shoemaking took a long time to perfect and were often a source of pride to an individual or a community. Under this system, however, output was limited.

The Industrial Revolution had a profound effect on the nature of work and the role of the worker. Previously, an individual tailor could make only a few items of clothing in a week's time; factories could now make hundreds. Employers began to think of labor as another item in the manufacturing equation, along with raw materials and capital. Individuals no longer worked for themselves but sold their labor in the marketplace. As farmers and other rural workers sought employment in the factories and shops, cities became congested urban centers where the labor supply was cheap and plentiful.

Employers at that time did not realize how workers' needs affected production. As a result, few owners or managers gave any thought to working conditions, health and safety precautions, or worker attitudes and motivation. Hours were long and the pay was low.

Taylor's Scientific Management

Around the turn of the century, Frederick Taylor and other researchers interested in industrial problems introduced the concept of **scientific management.** They believed that productivity could be improved by breaking a job down into isolated, specialized tasks and assigning workers to each of those tasks. The development of scientific management coincided with the revolutionary concept of mass production. Needless to say, Taylor's theories became immensely popular among business owners and managers. Eventually, they helped pave the way for the assembly line.

Taylor's work was sharply criticized by those who felt it exploited more than helped the workers. More than ever, employees were treated as a commodity, as interchangeable as the parts they produced. Taylor originally felt that by increasing production, the company would end up with a larger financial pie for everyone to share. Management would earn higher bonuses; workers would take home more pay. He did not foresee that his theories could be applied in ways that dehumanized the workplace even further.

Testing and the Emerging Individual

As scientific management gained wide acceptance, employers and managers found themselves assessing each worker's unique capabilities to match the right person with the right job. Some workers seemed skilled at intricate, detailed work, whereas others could handle heavy machinery. Still others showed a knack for supervising work crews and achieving company goals. If managers could test for the specific skills they needed, they could improve their hiring practices and increase efficiency and output. Many employers believed they had found the answer to their production problems. The concept of testing for skills and abilities made scientific management seem even more "scientific."

But the popularity of testing as a way to solve labor-management problems had an interesting and unexpected side effect. As more and more organizations developed and administered tests, evidence began to accumulate that an individual's performance was influenced by the level of personal motivation. In addition, workers' job performances did not always match their test scores. Some exceeded their potential, and others fell consistently below it. Apparently something more complex influenced people's performance on the job.

The Hawthorne Studies

Elton Mayo and his colleagues accidentally discovered part of the answer while conducting research in the mid-1920s at the Hawthorne Western Electric plant located near Chicago. Their original goal was to study the effect of illumination, ventilation, and fatigue on production workers in the plant. Their research became known as the **Hawthorne Studies** and has become a landmark in the human relations field.

The Hawthorne Studies paved the way for experiments that demonstrated the powerful effect human relations has on worker productivity. (Photo reproduced with permission of AT&T)

For one part of their research, Mayo and his colleagues selected two groups of employees doing similar work under similar conditions and kept output records for each group. After a time, the researchers began to vary the intensity of light for one group while keeping it constant for the other. Each time they increased the light, productivity rose. To determine if better illumination was responsible for the higher outputs, they began to dim the light. *Productivity continued to rise.* In fact, one of the highest levels of output was recorded when the light was scarcely brighter than the full moon! The researchers realized some other influence was at work.

In talking with employees, Mayo made two important discoveries. First, all the attention focused on the test group made them feel more important. For the first time, they were getting feedback on their job performance. In addition, test conditions allowed them greater freedom from supervisory control. Under these circumstances, morale and motivation increased and productivity rose. Mayo repeated his experiments over several years, always with the same results. Group morale and motivation seemed to override the effects of fatigue, illumination, and ventilation.

Second, Mayo found that the interaction of workers on the job created a network of relationships called an **informal organization.** This organization exerted considerable influence on workers' performance and could, in some cases, countermand orders handed down through the formal or managerial structure. For example, if management wanted to increase production, the workers could decide among themselves not to speed up the work. Thus, the informal organization could affect the rate of output substantially.

Mayo's research helped change the way management viewed workers. The assembly line had streamlined the work, and testing procedures could isolate and identify some abilities and skills. But studies such as Mayo's revealed that the average worker was a complex combination of needs, values, and attitudes.

From the Depression to the 1980s

For a brief time during the Depression, interest in human relations research waned. During that period, unions increased their militant campaigns to organize workers and force employers to pay attention to such issues as working conditions, higher pay, shorter hours, and protection for child laborers. When Congress passed the Wagner Act, businesses were required by law to negotiate contracts with union representatives. Other labor laws passed in the 1930s outlawed child labor, reduced the hours women worked, and instituted a minimum wage for many industries.

Through World War II and the years of postwar economic expansion, interest in the human relations field was revived. Countless papers and research studies on efficiency, group dynamics, organization, and motivational methods were published. Douglas McGregor introduced his Theory X, a rather pessimistic, authoritarian view of human behavior, and Theory Y, a more positive, optimistic view. Abraham Maslow, a noted psychologist, devised a "hierarchy of needs," stating that people satisfied their needs in a particular order. Both theories had considerable influence on the study of motivation and will be explored in detail in Chapter 6.

Since the 1950s, theories and concepts regarding human relations have focused more and more on an understanding of human interaction. Eric Berne in the 1960s revolutionized the way people think about interpersonal communication when he introduced transactional analysis with its "Parent-Adult-Child" model. At about the same time Carl Rogers published his work on personality development, interpersonal communication, and group dynamics. In the early 1980s, William Ouchi introduced the Theory Z style of management, which is based on the belief that worker involvement is the

---

Total Person Insight

Alice Sargent

As concern for people inches toward parity with concern for getting the job done, managers will have to exercise greater skills in dealing with people. They will need to express and accept emotions, nurture and support colleagues and subordinates, and promote interactions between bosses and subordinates and between leaders and members of the work team. These behaviors are desirable not only for their own sake, but because they can increase organizational effectiveness and efficiency.

key to increased productivity. We will explore these and other concepts throughout the book.

Thinking/Learning Starters

1. As the nature of work changed in the 1800s, how did this affect the individual worker?
2. What was the major purpose of Frederick Taylor's work?
3. List the principal conclusions of Mayo's research. Do you feel these conclusions hold true today? Why or why not?

Major Themes in Human Relations

Several broad themes emerge from a study of human relations. They are communication, self-acceptance, self-awareness, motivation, trust, self-disclosure, and conflict management. These themes reflect the current concern in human relations with the twin goals of personal growth and development and the satisfaction of organizational objectives. To some degree, the themes overlap and may be discussed in more than one chapter.

Communication

Human relations is founded on good **communication.** Communication is the means by which we come to an understanding of ourselves and others. In order to continue to grow and develop as persons, we must communicate. John R. Diekman, author of *Human Connections*, says that "... if we are going to do anything constructive and helping with one another, it must be through our communication."[18] Communication is the *human* connection. That is why the subject is covered in more than one section of this book. Chapter 2 explores both personal and organizational communication processes. In Chapter 5 we will focus on communication styles, a person's pattern of behavior when relating to others. Chapters 8 and 9 offer ways to improve communication with others.

Self-Acceptance

The degree to which you like and accept yourself is the degree to which you can genuinely like and accept other people. **Self-acceptance** is crucial, not only for your relationships with others, but for setting and achieving your own goals. The more you believe you can do, the more you are likely to accomplish. Chapter 4 deals with the concept of self-acceptance.

Self-Awareness

Do you fully understand how your behavior influences others? Are you fully aware of your attitudes toward others? Do you know what is most important to you in life? How do you evaluate your ability to handle conflict? **Self-awareness** means gaining a better understanding of who you are and how your behavior influences other people.

On and off the job, your decisions regarding what is appropriate behavior are based in large part on your self-awareness. As you learn more about the impact of your behavior on other people, you can make more appropriate decisions. Part Two discusses the concept of self-awareness and suggests ways you can increase yours.

Motivation

Human relations researchers no longer talk about **motivation** simply in terms of reward and punishment but rather as the drive to satisfy needs. Most employees tend to work best when they feel the organization is meeting their needs for growth and development. As a result, motivation is likely to be high where employees and management support and influence one another in positive ways.

Chapter 6 will explore the complex drives of human beings and examine the theory and practice of motivation techniques. Chapter 7 will help you identify the priorities and values in life that motivate you. In addition, Chapter 10 discusses how worker performance can be influenced by positive reinforcement.

Trust

Good relationships, whether among coworkers or between employer and employee, are based on **trust.** Without trust, most human relationships will degenerate into conflict. William Ouchi, author of *Theory Z,* a best-selling book about how American business can meet the Japanese challenge, recognizes trust as a key to long-term personal and organizational success. He said, "To trust another is to know that the two of you share basic goals in the long-run so that left to your own devices, each will behave in ways that are not harmful to the other."[19] When a climate of trust is present, frank discussion of problems and a free exchange of ideas and information are encouraged. The concept of trust is discussed in Chapters 8 and 12.

Self-Disclosure

Self-disclosure and trust are two halves of a whole. The more open you are with people, the more trust you build up. The more trust in a relationship, the safer you feel to disclose who you are. Self-disclosure is also part of good communication and helps eliminate unnecessary guessing games. Managers who let their subordinates know what is expected of them help those employees fulfill their responsibilities. Chapter 8 emphasizes the need of individuals to verbalize the thoughts and feelings they carry within them.

Conflict Management

Conflict management in human relations refers primarily to conflicts *within* an organization, although it can also mean disputes among organizations or between an organization and the public. It is true that whenever people work together, some conflict is inevitable. But disputes, personal clashes, and disagreements left unresolved can hurt an organization's operations and reduce its effectiveness as a provider of goods or services. Conflict tends to obstruct cooperative action, create suspicion and distrust, and decrease productivity. The ability to anticipate or resolve conflict can be an invaluable skill.

Chapter 13 deals specifically with the issue of conflict managment. However, the chapters on team building, achieving complementary transactions, and communication should also give you a better understanding of how conflict can be handled constructively.

Thinking/Learning Starter

Now that you have had an opportunity to review the seven themes of human relations, what do you consider your strongest areas? In which areas do you feel you need improvement? Why?

Human Relations: Where to Begin

Right now you may be thinking: "Human relations is an important subject, but can it really be *taught?* Isn't getting along with others a matter of experience, something you learn through trial and error?" Experience is undoubtedly an important part of the learning process, but as a teaching method it has certain drawbacks. After all, you can learn an important lesson by being fired, but you will have to find another job before you can apply your new-found knowledge.

A basic course in human relations cannot give you a foolproof set of techniques for solving every people-oriented problem that might arise. It can, however, give you a better understanding of human behavior in groups, help you become more sensitive to yourself and others, and, it is hoped, enable you to act more wisely when problems occur. You may even be able to anticipate conflicts or prevent small problems from escalating into major ones.

Many leaders feel that courses in human relations are important because fewer workers on the job are responsible to themselves alone. They point out that most jobs today are interdependent. If people in these jobs cannot work effectively as a team, the efficiency of the organization will suffer. Many young, inexperienced workers, leaving school for the first job, are surprised to learn that their attitudes, behavior, and personality matter just as much if not more than their technical or business skills.

Summary

Human relations is the study of how people fulfill both personal growth needs and organizational goals in their careers. Many organizations are beginning to realize that an employee's life outside the job can have a significant impact on work performance, and some are developing training programs in human relations that address the total person. Increasingly, organizations are discovering that many forces influence the behavior of people at work.

Human relations is not a set of foolproof techniques for solving people-oriented problems. Rather it gives people an understanding of basic behavior concepts that may enable them to make wiser choices when problems arise, to anticipate or prevent conflicts, and to keep minor problems from escalating into major ones.

The development of the human relations movement has involved a redefinition of the nature of work and the gradual perception of managers and workers as complex human beings. Two landmarks in the study of motivation and worker needs are Frederick Taylor's work in scientific managment and Elton Mayo's Hawthorne studies. Many industry leaders predict an increased emphasis on human relations research and application. The reasons for this trend include higher educational levels of employees and managers, worker organizations pressing for attention to employee concerns, a weakening of the traditional work ethic, and increased federal legislation affecting organizations.

Seven major themes emerge from a study of human relations: communication, self-acceptance, self-awareness, motivation, trust, self-disclosure, and conflict management. These themes reflect the current concern in human relations with the twin goals of personal growth and the satisfaction of organizational objectives.

Key Terms

human relations	communication
feeling of entitlement	self-acceptance
total person	self-awareness
organizational culture	motivation
scientific management	trust
Hawthorne Studies	self-disclosure
informal organization	conflict management

Review Questions

1. Define *human relations* in your own words.
2. List some of the myths and misconceptions about human relations.
3. Each individual brings a unique set of skills, experiences, and goals to the job. Why does this often create human relations problems?
4. Why is the total-person approach to employee development becoming more popular?
5. List and describe the five major forces influencing human behavior at work.
6. In what ways can training in human relations benefit an organization?
7. How did Taylor's work help usher in the modern assembly line? Why was his work criticized by some researchers and not by others?
8. Mayo's research indicated that workers could influence the rate of production in an organization. What discoveries did he make that led to this conclusion?
9. List four reasons why human relations skills are becoming more important in the work place.
10. What seven themes emerge from a study of human relations? Describe each one briefly.

Case 1.1

The Human Factor at Delta[20]

Several years ago, three Delta Air Lines stewardesses announced that they and other Delta employees had pledged nearly $1,000 each to buy a $30 million Boeing 767 jet for the airline. "We just wanted to say thanks for the way Delta has treated us," one of the women explained.[21] Delta, a nonunion company except for its pilots and dispatchers, has weathered a number of economic storms without a single layoff.

It maintains a fifty-year-old business philosophy that emphasizes a strong belief in good employee relations and customer service. Delta has a no-furlough policy (no permanent employee has been let go during the past two decades) and an open-door policy for all personnel regardless of position. The company holds regular meetings with its employees to keep them well informed and allows workers to question or criticize company policies. Delta has also been a pioneer in employee benefits and follows a policy of promoting from within. In summary, each of the 36,000 employees is treated as a person, not a number.

Questions

1. Delta appears to have a loyal work force. What aspects of this company's culture contribute to this loyalty?
2. Will the policies and practices at Delta work in other large organizations? Small organizations? Why or why not?

Case 1.2

The New Manager

Andy Baldoni, the new manager of data processing, was the youngest person ever hired to head a department at McReddy & Cresap, a management consulting firm. He had a brilliant record in the computer field, and his ambition was to build the finest data processing department in the business. The data processing personnel had heard of Andy's reputation and were looking forward to working with him.

However, at the first department meeting, Andy presented a complete development plan for the coming year. His staff of programmers and systems analysts resented being left out of the planning process—after all they had good ideas too. When arguments arose over various stages in the plan, Andy used his authority as department head to end any conflict. "There's only one captain of the ship—me," he said. "Just follow the steps I've outlined, and you'll see I'm right."

Unfortunately, he had trouble communicating instructions. His mind worked so rapidly that he often skipped steps, assuming his staff could fill in the missing information. Time after time they had to come back to him to clarify various points. He became increasingly impatient with what he saw as the staff's inability to follow simple procedures.

As something of a workaholic, Andy often stayed after five o'clock and assumed that his assistant, Ella Tuskey, would do the same. She explained that she had classes two nights a week; she was fulfilling a lifelong ambition to become a computer programmer. If she finished her courses, the company would reimburse the $483 tuition. Andy promised she would have those nights free, but all too often projects started during the day lasted well into the evening. After a month, Ella had to drop her class because she had missed too many sessions. Andy noticed only that she seemed more difficult to get along with and less motivated.

Finally, without realizing it, Andy tended to favor the younger workers, those in their twenties and early thirties. Since they were closer to his own age, he felt they would be able to grasp his ideas more quickly. Although never putting the thoughts into words, he also believed that workers in their forties were not as up-to-date on the latest advances in technology. After all, they had received their training in the 1950s and early 1960s.

After six months, the mood in the department could best be described as "mutinous." Andy's immediate boss heard about the problems and called Andy in to talk about them. He summarized the situation by saying, "You devised a brilliant plan for the department, but forgot one thing: the human factor. You have to work *with* people, not just *through* them. To run an efficient operation, you need to have good human relations skills."

Questions

1. Across the top of a sheet of paper, write down the seven human relations themes. List the human relations problems in Andy's department that correspond to the appropriate theme.
2. How would you rate Andy's level of self-awareness? Give reasons for your rating.
3. How could training in human relations make a difference in this situation?

Notes

1. Karl Albrecht and Ron Zemke, *Service America* (Homewood, Ill.: Dow Jones-Irwin), 1985, p. v.
2. Robert Levering, Milton Moskowitz, and Michael Katz, *The 100 Best Companies to Work for in America* (New York: New American Library), 1985. pp. 110–115.
3. Perry Pascarella, *The New Achievers* (New York: The Free Press), 1984, p. x.
4. Albrecht and Zemke, *Service America*, p. 31.
5. Craig Brod, *Technostress* (Reading, Mass.: Addison-Wesley), 1984, p. 35.
6. John Naisbitt, "New Way of Doing Business Looming for U.S. Industry," *The Charlotte Observer*, January 6, 1985, p. 60.
7. John J. Leach and B. J. Chakiris, "The Dwindling Future of Work in America," *Training and Development Journal*, April 1985, pp. 5–6.
8. Keith Davis, *Human Behavior at Work* (New York: McGraw-Hill), 1981, p. 12.
9. "America's Fitness Binge," *U.S. News and World Report*, May 3, 1982, p. 60.

10. Levering, Moskowitz, and Katz, *The 100 Best Companies to Work for in America*, pp. 250–251.
11. Robert W. Pike and Frank Plasha, "Total Person Training," *Personnel Administrator*, April 1975, p. 35.
12. Jay Hall, *The Competence Process* (The Woodlands, Texas: Teleometrics International, 1980), p. 39.
13. Alice G. Sargent, *The Androgynous Manager* (New York: AMACOM, a division of American Management Associations, 1980), p. viii (introduction by Elsa Porter).
14. D. R. Hampton, C. E. Summer, and R. A. Webber, *Organizational Behavior and the Practice of Management* (Glenview, Ill.: Scott, Foresman, 1973), p. 215.
15. "Tabletop Production Line," *Road & Track*, October 1982, p. 122.
16. Roy W. Walters, "Improving Man/Machine Interface for Greater Productivity," *BNAC Communicator*, Summer 1982, p. 13.
17. "American Productivity: Prescription for Success," *Training and Development Journal*, May 1982, p. 12.
18. John R. Diekman, *Human Connections* (Englewood Cliffs, N.J.: Prentice-Hall), 1982, p. xii.
19. "William Ouchi on Trust," *Training and Development Journal*, December 1982, p. 71.
20. Based on personal interviews.
21. Levering, Moskowitz, and Katz, *The 100 Best Companies to Work for in America*, p. 74.

Suggested Readings

Albrecht, Karl, and Ron Zemke. *Service America*. Homewood, Illinois: Dow Jones-Irwin, 1985.

Editors of *Harvard Business Review*. *Harvard Business Review—On Human Relations*. New York: Harper and Row, 1979.

Hall, Jay. *The Competence Process*. The Woodlands, Texas: Teleometrics International, 1980.

Levering, Robert, Milton Moskowitz, and Michael Katz. *The 100 Best Companies to Work for in America*. New York: New American Library, 1985.

Naisbitt, John. *Megatrends—Ten New Directions Transforming Our Lives*. New York: Warner Books, 1982.

Naisbitt, John, and Patricia Aburdene. *Re-inventing the Corporation*. New York: Warner Books, Inc., 1985.

Pascarella, Perry. *The New Achievers*. New York: The Free Press, 1984.

Peters, Thomas, and Robert Waterman, Jr. *In Search of Excellence: Lessons from America's Best-Run Companies*. New York: Harper and Row, 1982.

Sargent, Alice G. *The Androgynous Manager*. New York: American Management Associations, 1980.

Chapter 2

Improving Personal and Organizational Communication

Chapter Preview

After studying this chapter, you will be able to

1. Distinguish between information-giving and communication.
2. Understand the communication process and the filters that affect communication.
3. Define the responsibilities of both sender and receiver in the communication process.
4. Describe the formal and informal channels of communication in an organization and understand their strengths and weaknesses.
5. Identify some of the ways to improve communication in organizations, including the development of good listening skills.
6. Understand the need for cross-cultural and bilingual training in organizations today.

When John G. Smale became head of Procter & Gamble several years ago, he discovered a tedious communication process that seemed to be slowing down the company's progress. All decisions were made at top levels of management, and one-page memos were the chief way to send information to the top. Instead of meeting to discuss proposals, top-level managers often required multiple revisions of the memos. Mid-level managers were spending more of their time rewriting memos than focusing on the content of their proposals.

Although it forced managers to sharpen their proposals, some said the process put more emphasis on grammar and writing style than on expediting good ideas. A former manager recalled spending a month tinkering with a memo because no one could agree on which of the three points to list first.

Today, the memo has been replaced with the "talk sheet," an informal outline. Managers from several organizational levels meet weekly and quickly refine proposals. The result? A faster, more open communication process that allows decisions to be made with input from several levels. One advertising manager estimates the difference between the old memo and the new talk sheet to be "a week and a half and fifteen rewrites."[1]

Communication within organizations is changing faster than even John Naisbitt, author of *Megatrends*, ever imagined. With satellites, electronic mail, and computer terminals at almost every desk and in many homes, it's a wonder we have time to read all the data available to us, let alone interpret and act upon the new information. The hectic pace of today's life and the rapid flow of information sometimes cause communication breakdowns.

Communication breakdowns are a prime factor in organizational problems ranging from low productivity through employee turnover to the failure of subordinates to carry out responsibilities properly. It has been calculated that if each of the country's 100 million workers made just one $10 mistake a year because of poor communication skills, it would cost the economy more than $1 billion annually.[2] Unfortunately, the reality is far worse. Poor communication also takes its toll in employee injuries and deaths, particularly in industries where workers operate heavy machinery or handle hazardous materials.

Good communication, which is essential for the smooth functioning of the organization, depends on the orderly exchange of information. Managers need clear lines of communication to transmit orders and policies, build cooperation, and unify group behavior. Employees must be able to convey their complaints or suggestions and feel that management has heard what they have to say. Clear communication among coworkers is vital to good teamwork and to problem solving and conflict management. In short, effective human relations is founded on good communication.

Communication breakdowns are inevitable. However, when we reduce communication to its simple elements of speaking, writing, reading, and listening, the task of communicating effectively becomes more manageable. How would you rate your own communication skills? Are you a good lis-

Total Person Insight Paul R. Timm	"Communication breakdown" has just about taken the place of original sin as an explanation for the ills of the world—and perhaps with good cause. As our world becomes more complex and we spend more time in organized activities, the need for interpersonal understanding has never been greater. And just as important, the cost of failure has never been higher.

tener? Can you get your ideas across clearly and concisely? This chapter examines the nature of the communication process, ways of improving your skills as a speaker and a listener, and how communication works in an organization.

The Communication Process

Most people take communication for granted. When they speak or listen to others, they assume that the message given or received is being understood. In reality, most messages are distorted, incomplete, or lost on their way from one person to another. As a result, it's important to understand something about the process of how we communicate with one another.

Communication Versus Information-Giving

We often use the word *communication* when we really mean *information giving*. When we use such words as "impart," "transfer," or "transmit," we are talking about a one-way **information-giving** process. This method is used to present facts, instructions, and the like. In an organization, memos, letters, computer printouts, manuals, or bulletin boards are quick, easy ways to "get the word out." However, people receiving the information have no opportunity to ask the sender any questions or to clarify vague or confusing wording.

For true **communication** to take place, the message must be understood by the person receiving the information in the same way the person sending it intended. Such words as "share," "exchange," "interact," and "interchange" reflect two-way communication, as opposed to one-way information giving. In two-way communication, some type of **feedback,** or response, is necessary to make sure the message has been understood. Communication is a dialogue during which people can share their thoughts and feelings. In an organization, dialogues can take place in meetings, over the phone, in face-to-face interviews, and in discussions.

Sam Walton, head of Wal-Mart Stores, Inc., the nation's second largest discount store chain with over 800 stores and approximately 90,000 employees, relies on face-to-face communication as a way of staying in touch with Wal-Mart branches throughout the United States. Walton and his top executives try to visit six to twelve stores each week. Walton chats with staffers—hundreds of whom he knows on a first-name basis—to find out what items and promotions are popular. He also helps managers exchange ideas and solve problems. On Fridays and Saturdays, he is back at headquarters attending merchandise meetings and listening to plans for weekly and monthly sales budgets and promotional programs. His "hands-on" communication style has helped boost company earnings and has kept the firm growing even through recessions.

Effective communication takes time. Many companies use information-giving methods instead of true communication because it is a faster way to convey what needs to be said. The speed and quantity of information-giving has increased tenfold through the use of computers. Corporate headquarters often send information to their branch offices through their computer networks. Yet some types of information, such as price changes, inventory figures, product shipping information, and so forth, can be better sent by computer than other types of information. The announcement, "The Southeast Division has broken all sales records for the previous month," can be transmitted by computer without problems. Everyone gets the same information at the same time, and no immediate feedback is necessary for the message to be completely understood. Yet announcing through the computer system, "The Northeast Division will be closed in 30 days," could generate enormous problems. Computers can be invaluable when it comes to information giving; but they cannot replace the two-way communication process when feedback and discussion are necessary.

The computer is an effective tool for information-giving. But sometimes a manager can have too much information. In any organization, someone must read all the computerized information and implement the necessary strategies based on that information. Lee Iacocca, president of Chrysler Corporation, says people who visit his office are often surprised that he doesn't have a computer terminal on his desk. "The biggest problem facing American business today is that most managers have too much information. It dazzles them, and they don't know what to do with it all."[3] When organizations realize it takes humans relating effectively with one another to get the job done, they realize information-giving is not enough. Effective communication is the basis for success in every organization.

Sender—Message—Receiver

Effective communication is composed of three basic elements: a **sender,** a **receiver,** and an understood *message.*[4] To illustrate, suppose you are a clerk in a purchasing department, ordering parts from a manufacturer. You phone in the order to the warehouse clerk, who repeats it back to you to

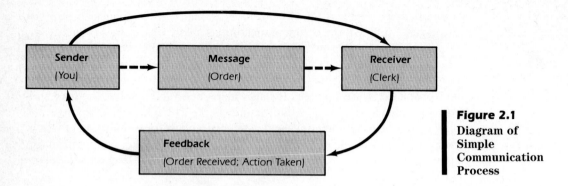

Figure 2.1
**Diagram of
Simple
Communication
Process**

make sure all the details are correct. Later, a document confirming the order is sent, indicating number, price, and delivery date. A simplified diagram of this process would look like Figure 2.1.

Now suppose you are explaining to your supervisor why a new procedure she wants to try will not work. The communication process becomes much more complicated, as shown in Figure 2.2. The sender's message must pass through several "filters": semantics, emotions, attitudes, nonverbal cues, and role expectations (that is, how people expect others to act on the basis of their roles as supervisor, employee, and the like).

The supervisor may interpret your objections as resistance to change. In fact, you are pointing out a vital step that she has forgotten. You, on the other hand, may feel she is trying to get more work out of everyone, while she may feel her procedures will actually make the job a little easier.

Most communication processes look like the diagram in Figure 2.2. Considering how many filters messages must pass through, it's surprising that

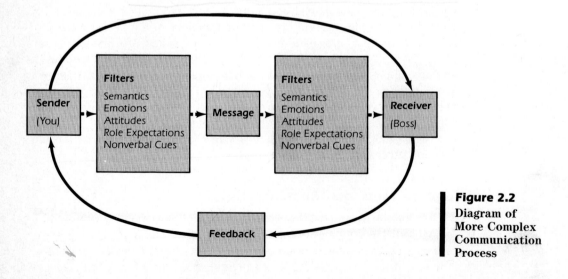

Figure 2.2
**Diagram of
More Complex
Communication
Process**

two people ever understand one another. Nor does it always help to have similar backgrounds. Some of the biggest communication problems are between members of the same family!

Who Is Responsible for Effective Communication?

The sender and the receiver both share the responsibility for effective communication. The communication loop, as shown in Figure 2.2, is complete when the receiver understands, feels, or behaves according to the message of the sender. If this does not occur, the communication process has broken down.

Organizations can improve their human relations by basing all of their communications on a simple premise: The message *is* the message received. If the receiver hears a different message from the one the sender intended, the communication loop has not been completed. The message the receiver hears is, in effect, the only message that exists. If the discrepancy between what the sender intended to say and what the receiver heard is serious, disagreements or even fights can occur. When emotions calm, it doesn't help for the sender to say, "But that's not what I meant. You misunderstood!" By then, human relations between the sender and receiver have already been damaged.

When the sender accepts complete responsibility for sending a clear, concise message, the communication process begins. However, the receiver must accept full responsibility for receiving the message as the sender intended. Receivers must provide senders with enough feedback to ensure that an accurate message has passed through all the filters that might alter it.

Thinking/Learning Starters

1. Explain the difference between information-giving and communication.
2. Think back to a time when someone was explaining a new procedure to you. Did you understand everything that was said? How would you rate the person who gave the explanation? What would you do differently if you could replay the situation?

Communication Filters

Messages are filtered through semantics, emotions, attitudes, role expectations, and nonverbal cues. Each of these filters affects communication.

Momma

By Mell Lazarus

(Courtesy of Mell Lazarus and News America)

Semantics

Most people are so accustomed to using words when they communicate that they give **semantics,** the meanings and the changes in meanings of words, little thought—and that can be a problem. We naturally assume that the words we use mean the same things to others, but this is not always true.

Words are not things but labels that stand for something. The meanings of words—or semantics—lies within us. We have agreed that particular words will have associated meanings and usage. We can easily understand what words like *typewriter, computer,* or *envelope* mean. But more abstract terms, such as *job satisfaction, upward mobility,* or *word processing,* have less precise meanings and will be interpreted by different people in different ways. The more abstract the term, the less likely it is that people will agree on its meaning.

The meaning of words can be altered by the context in which they are used. For example, *centimeter* represents a fixed unit of measure. To an engineer constructing two spans of a bridge that must meet in the middle, a one-centimeter deviation from plan is almost negligible. But to a hybrid circuit engineer who works in thousandths of a centimeter, one centimeter represents a vast scale of measurement. The word is the same, but the context in which it is used changes the way each person understands it.

People's internal context—that is, their attitudes, background, experiences, and interests—also affect how they interpret what they hear. For example, a salesperson dictates an order to a clerk in the shipping department and tells her to send a customer's order "right away." Since most orders are placed weeks, even months in advance, to her, "right away" means within the next two or three days. The following afternoon, an angry salesperson discovers that his client's order still hasn't been sent. To him, "right away" means "immediately"!

Not only are the meanings of words subject to different interpretations, but words themselves are constantly changing. Words can be dropped from common usage or acquire additional meanings, and new words can be created as society changes.

Emotions

Emotions are perhaps the most powerful communication filter over which we have limited control. Strong emotions can either prevent people from hearing what a speaker has to say or make them too susceptible to a speaker's point of view. If they become angry or allow themselves to be carried away by the speaker's eloquence, they may "think" with their emotions and make decisions or take action they regret later. They have shifted their attention from the *content* of the message to their *feelings* about it.

You may have had the experience of being called by an angry customer who demands to know why the wrong order was delivered. If you allow the customer's anger to trigger your own, the call quickly deteriorates into an argument. The real issue—what happened to the order and what is to be done about it—is lost in the shouting match. Detaching yourself from another's feelings and responding to the content of the message is often difficult. Yet many jobs require that employees remain calm and courteous regardless of a customer's emotional state.

Attitudes

Attitudes are beliefs backed up by emotions. They can be a barrier to communication in much the same way emotions can, by altering the way people hear a message. The listener may not like the speaker's voice, gestures, mannerisms, dress, or delivery. Perhaps the listener has preconceived ideas about the speaker's topic. Negative attitudes create resistance to the message and can lead to a breakdown in communication. On the other hand, overly positive attitudes can also be a barrier. They can lead a listener to hear what he or she wants to hear. Biased in favor of the message, the listener may fail to evaluate it effectively.

Attitudes can also facilitate communication, however. If listeners are impressed by a speaker's expertise, character, and good will, they are likely to be more receptive to the message. The quality of communication between supervisor and employee, for example, is heavily influenced by the level of openness and trust that exists between them. More will be said about acquiring and forming attitudes in Chapter 3.

Role Expectations

Role expectations are how people expect themselves—and others—to act on the basis of the roles they play such as boss, customer, employee, and so on. These expectations can distort communication in two ways. First, people may identify others too closely with their roles. In such cases, they may discount what the other person has to say. "It's just the boss again, saying the same old thing." Or they may not allow others to change their roles and take on new ones. This often happens to employees who are promoted from within the ranks of an organization and move from subordinate to management positions. Others may still see them as a secretary instead of a supervisor, as "old Chuck" from accounting, rather than the new department head. Other employees may not take them seriously in their new roles or listen to what they have to say.

Second, role expectations can affect good communication when people use their roles to alter the way they relate to others. This is often referred to as "position power." For example, a manager may expect employees to accept what he or she says simply because of the authority invested in the position. Employees are not allowed to question decisions or make suggestions of their own, and communication becomes one-way information giving. A manager who is called on to relate to others outside the role may find it difficult to establish communication.

Nonverbal Messages: The Language of the Body

When we attempt to communicate with another person, we use both verbal and nonverbal messages. Nonverbal communication has been defined as "messages without words" and "silent messages." These are the messages we communicate via facial expressions, gestures, tone of voice, appearance, posture, and other non-linguistic means. In this chapter we will limit our discussion of nonverbal communication to **kinesics,** or what is more commonly referred to as *body language.*

Kinesic - body language

Many people believe that by watching a person's gestures, eye contact, and use of personal space they can tell what the other person is really thinking and feeling. Although there is some truth in this belief, no one gesture or posture will always mean the same thing. Remember that body language is part of people's total social interaction; be careful not to read too much into someone's nonverbal cues.

Yet research indicates that nonverbal messages carry five times as much impact as verbal messages.[5] Generally, when people's words and body language are consistent, they give others the impression that they can be trusted and that what they say reflects what they truly believe. When the two contradict each other, there is usually a breakdown in communication. Listeners become confused about which message to believe. Given a choice, most people tend to believe an individual's nonverbal cues. Intuitively, they feel such cues are not easily controlled and reveal more of a person's true thoughts and feelings.[6]

Body language can be discussed in terms of the use of proxemics, eye contact, and gestures.

Body language can be a strong nonverbal cue as to what a person is really thinking and feeling in a certain situation. (Photo by Christopher Morrow, Stock Boston, Inc.)

proxemics-
study of
personal
space

Proxemics Until the 1960s, social scientists resisted the idea that human beings have a sense of territory just as animals do. Since then, research has provided ample evidence that people use the space around them to define relationships and to establish either close or distant communication.[7] This study of personal space is called **proxemics.** Dr. Edward T. Hall, professor of anthropology and author of several books on personal space, lists four zones, or **circles of intimacy,** in which people operate: intimate, personal, social, and public distances.[8] These are shown in Figure 2.3.

As you might expect, *intimate distance* is for your closest friends and loved ones. Hall estimated this distance could be "close," that is actually touching, or "far," from 6 to 18 inches. *Personal distance* ranges from close—1½ to 2 feet—to far, 2 to 4 feet. At this distance you may touch the other person if you like or maintain a certain privacy around yourself. In either case you are close enough for a personal conversation.

Social distance varies from 4 to 7 feet up to 7 to 12 feet. Generally people carry on impersonal business from this distance, such as shopping at the grocery store or meeting a new client. *Public distance* is the farthest extension of personal territory and may reach anywhere from 12 to 25 feet and beyond. It is suitable for such events as informal gatherings, public meetings, or an address by the head of an organization to employees.

It is important to remember that different cultures have different rules about personal space. As organizations become more international, executives and employees will need to be aware of these customs. Many Euro-

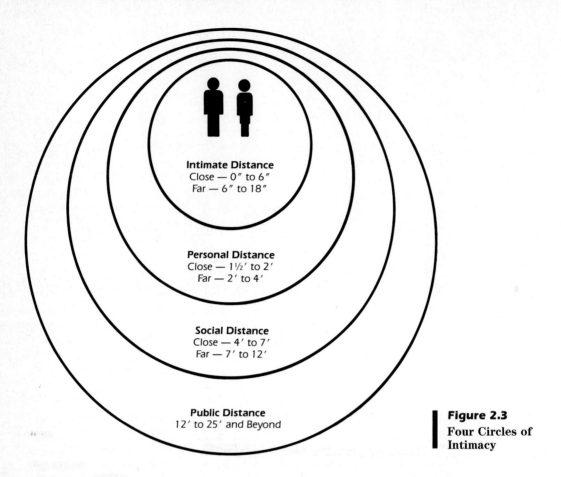

Intimate Distance
Close — 0″ to 6″
Far — 6″ to 18″

Personal Distance
Close — 1½′ to 2′
Far — 2′ to 4′

Social Distance
Close — 4′ to 7′
Far — 7′ to 12′

Public Distance
12′ to 25′ and Beyond

Figure 2.3
Four Circles of Intimacy

peans, for instance, have a personal distance of 9 to 10 inches. Asians and Latin Americans prefer about 12 inches. Unaware of these cultural differences, some Americans might interpret this proximity as an intrusion into their personal space of 24 to 36 inches and become uncomfortable and hostile. At the same time, the person of another culture might interpret the American as cold and standoffish. In both cases, the differences in spacial comfort zones can make conducting business awkward.

At a recent international conference, observers noted that when Americans met and conversed, they stood about 2 to 4 feet from each other and remained in the same place while talking. However, when a Japanese person spoke with an American, the two slowly began to move around the room. The Japanese person, with the smaller 10-inch personal zone, continually stepped forward to adjust to his spatial needs. This invaded the American's intimate space, causing him to step backward. Video recordings of this encounter played at high speed give the impression that both individuals are dancing around the conference room with the Japanese leading.[9]

Eye Contact   Eyes transmit more information than any other part of the body. Because **eye contact** is so revealing, people generally observe some unwritten rules about looking at others. A direct prolonged stare between strangers is usually considered impolite, even potentially aggressive or hostile. People entering elevators or other crowded areas will glance at others briefly—acknowledging their presence—then look away.

In business, however, direct eye contact is considered important. Salespeople usually build trust with prospects by looking them steadily in the eye while describing a product or service. In addition, interviewers tend to put great weight on an applicant's ability to make good eye contact. However, relying on this trait as a means of judging character has its drawbacks, particularly for those who interview and hire people from different cultures. One interviewer complained that a young man with excellent qualifications would not look him in the eye during the interview. A colleague discovered the young man was Puerto Rican and explained that Puerto Rican youth are taught to look down as a mark of respect when speaking with adults. "For him, looking you straight in the eye would have been as rude as putting his feet up on your desk."

As a general rule, people communicating in an organizational setting should focus their eyes on the triangle formed by the person's two eyes and the center of the forehead. To build good rapport, your gaze should meet the other person's about 60 to 70 percent of the time. Staring makes people just as uncomfortable as no eye contact at all.

Gestures   Did you know you are sending a nonverbal message every time you place your hand over your mouth, clench your hands together, cross your legs, or grip your arms? These **gestures** send constant messages to people about how you are reacting to them and to the situation in which you find yourself. No one gesture will mean the same thing all the time, but your gestures can reflect what you are thinking and feeling in a particular instance.

Dr. R. L. Birdwhistell, one of the researchers who has helped develop the science of body language, believes that gestures also indicate whether people are open or closed to communication, who is the true leader of a group, and how comfortable people are with physical contact.[10] For example, employees usually "elect" a leader from their own ranks while outwardly acknowledging the supervisor or manager as boss. One researcher noted that in a company's department meetings, whenever the manager proposed a change in work procedures, employees would glance at their own "leader" to watch his reaction. Often they unconsciously imitated the way he was sitting or his facial expression as he listened to the manager. This **mirroring** is a nonverbal means by which people can signal agreement. By imitating another's postures and gestures, a person is saying, "As you can see, I think the same as you."

Perhaps the most powerful way to use body language is to make sure your messages are being received. If your receiver is nonverbally telling you that your message is not getting through, you can identify the problem before communication completely breaks down.

Item: If you are speaking to a group and several people put their hands over their mouths, you can infer that they have objections or questions about what you are saying. By asking for the receivers' comments, you can answer any questions and make sure that objections are brought into the open.

Item: If your receivers begin to rub their ears, they may have heard enough and want to speak. You should allow them the opportunity.

Item: If receivers begin to lose interest in a speaker, they may rest their heads in their hands. You can ask them a question or change the subject to regain their attention.

Item: If your receiver has crossed arms with hands gripping the biceps, he or she may be restraining a negative attitude toward your message. By handing the receiver a document or object to break the position, you can give your message a better chance of getting through.

Item: When your receiver has crossed arms and legs, he or she has probably withdrawn from the conversation. You can ask probing questions to uncover the person's objections.

Books such as Albert Scheflen's *Body Language and Social Order*, Julius Fast's *Body Language*, and Allan Pease's *Signals: How to Use Body Language for Power, Success and Love* offer literally hundreds of hints on how to use body language effectively. If you would like to study this subject in greater detail, we suggest you investigate these books. They will offer hints not only on proxemics, eye contact, and gestures, but also on the way to arrange your office furniture, how to position yourself around a conference table or an authority figure's desk, and so forth.

Body language can provide valuable insights into people's feelings and thoughts. However, you should avoid making any hard and fast judgments on the basis of nonverbal cues. Different cultural and ethnic groups will have different customs regarding gestures, eye contact, and personal space. In general, it takes close observation and considerable experience to be able to use your knowledge of nonverbal cues correctly.

Thinking/Learning Starters

1. Have you ever misunderstood what another person said to you because of your attitude toward that person? Explain.
2. Can you recall a time when you relied on body language to determine what someone really thought or felt? Was your interpretation of the person's posture or gestures correct? Explain.

Communication Channels

The healthy functioning of any organization—large or small—depends on cooperation. Good communication helps build cooperation by permitting a two-way exchange of information and unifying group behavior. People need to know their job responsibilities, the purpose of the organization, and the accepted channels through which communication flows.

The communication process in organizations is roughly the same as the diagram in Figure 2.2. That is, there is still a sender, a message, and a receiver. But the number of people involved may vary anywhere from 1 to 1,000 depending on the size of the organization. The more people you add to the process, the more difficult it is to communicate effectively.

Organizations establish formal channels or structures through which communication travels. In most organizations, however, the informal channel, the grapevine, offers the real communications link. In order for an organization to function smoothly, everyone needs to know how to utilize both communication channels.

Formal Channels

Figure 2.4 presents the **formal channels** or structure of a large hospital. This type of diagram is called an organization chart and outlines formal reporting relationships among the various levels of management and employees. The larger an organization, the "taller" it becomes, that is, the more layers of management it acquires. This makes it difficult to transmit information and to provide channels for feedback to ensure accurate communication.

Smaller organizations also have their communication problems, but such problems are offset by the fact that in many cases misunderstandings can be cleared up fairly quickly. In some instances, it may involve a short walk down the hall to the manager's office or a quick phone call to the warehouse. In a complex, multilayered organization, locating the sender of a memo to clarify facts may be extremely difficult. The communications chain may be so long and involved that tracing a message back to its source is nearly impossible. Communication in an organization generally moves along vertical and horizontal lines. Horizontal communication occurs between departments, divisions, managers, or employees on the *same* organizational level. Vertical channels carry messages from the top executive levels down to the lowest level in the organization.

Vertical Channels As shown in Figure 2.4, communications moving via **vertical channels** from top management levels reach a great many people down through the organization and carry considerable force. In general, if the level of trust between management and employees is fairly high, these messages will usually pass through the organization effectively. Messages

40

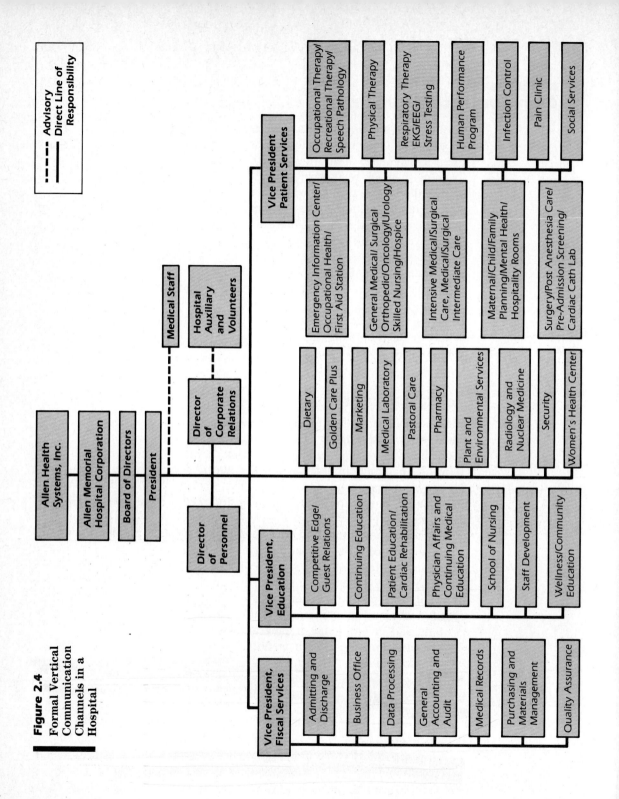

Figure 2.4
Formal Vertical Communication Channels in a Hospital

will be understood, believed, accepted, and acted on. If there is a low level of trust in the organization, however, workers will tend to put more faith in information passed on by word of mouth, even if such information consists mainly of rumors.

Many managers find that a brief phone call to their staff is much less expensive and more effective than sending memos; also, phone calls allow for immediate feedback. Studies show that upper management often prefers written communication. Middle and line managers—and those under them—prefer oral communication. Talking with a manager or employee offers both sides the chance to ask questions, clarify instructions, and give an immediate response. This type of communication is not simply an exchange of facts or directives but a true exchange of ideas and opinions.

Also, sensitive matters are best handled face to face. If someone is denied a promotion, has a personal problem that is affecting the person's work, or needs to be disciplined in some way, the manager can explain the situation in person rather than rely on a memo or letter. Written communications in such cases can be easily misunderstood. Talking things over not only allows for feedback but can give the manager an opportunity to stress a worker's strengths once the negative information has been conveyed.

Although communicating down the vertical channel is fairly routine, communicating back up is usually more difficult. Top managers sometimes perceive themselves as the senders and their subordinates as the receivers of their messages. In some workplaces, unions help establish regular channels for communicating up the vertical structure, particularly in organizations where employees have failed repeatedly to get upper management to listen to their concerns. Union representatives and officials usually have access to high-level executives and can bring employees' issues to their attention.

In other workplaces, **quality circles** (sometimes referred to as employee participation groups, project task forces, or systems refinement teams) pro-

Quality circles can be a source of valuable information for the organization interested in solving problems and improving productivity. (Photo courtesy of General Electric Co.)

vide the vehicle through which employees can provide feedback up through the organization. A quality circle is a small group of employees (usually six to eight people) who volunteer to meet regularly to solve work-related problems such as quality control, productivity, waste, and so forth. Employees in a quality circle can be from the same department or from different departments and levels within the organization. They usually decide which problem to address at a given meeting and follow a set of guidelines and procedures to solve the problem.

This cost-effective communication system has become extremely popular since American management teams began studying the success of Japanese corporations. Over 400 major companies including Ford Motor Co., Control Data Corp., and General Electric Co. now encourage teams of employees to meet for an hour or so each week, on company time, to discuss organizational problems. Since 1979, more than 80 quality circles in manufacturing and engineering departments have developed at Martin Marietta's Michaud Division in New Orleans. One noted authority indicates that an organization's profits can be boosted by as much as 30 to 40 percent by improving lines of communication from the bottom to the top.[11] Some companies claim production increases of as much as 50 percent due to quality circles. Honeywell reports a cost reduction of several million dollars as a result of quality circles.[12]

Upward communication is valuable in any organization. The opportunity for such communication encourages employees to contribute valuable ideas that can lead to substantial savings for the organization. But there are intangible benefits as well. When employees can participate in decisions that directly affect their work, they feel as if they are a part of the organizational community, not just an individual collecting a paycheck. "The effective organization has a feeling of community. . . . Productivity, involvement, shared ownership, intimacy, and a feeling of participation are important aspects of the feeling that 'we are living in a community.' "[13]

Horizontal Channels   People on the same level of authority, such as the buyers and store managers in Figure 2.5, communicate with one another across **horizontal channels**. Some of these channels are formal: regular staff meetings, memos, planning sessions, and the like. Others are informal: managers may talk over lunch, pick up ideas from employees and pass them on, or decide among themselves how formal work plans are to be carried out. Horizontal channels work as well for secretaries as they do for management. For example, when a new clerical position opens up, the support staff is likely to pass the word among themselves before the position is advertised outside the organization.

In some situations, horizontal channels may cut across vertical authority lines. Project teams, brought together for a specific task, may be composed of vice presidents, line managers, supervisors, and middle management. The team leader may be giving orders to someone who is officially higher up the

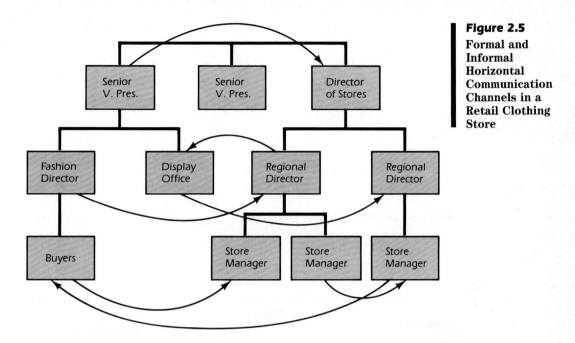

Figure 2.5
Formal and Informal Horizontal Communication Channels in a Retail Clothing Store

organizational ladder. This type of communication can either help break down the rigid barriers of formal reporting lines or put a strain on an otherwise normal relationship between executive and subordinate.

Improving Formal Channels of Communication Horizontal communication lines in an organization effectively keep people informed about what others in similar positions are doing. Many organizations complement these lines with an in-house newsletter that informs all personnel about the accomplishments of other divisions. When used effectively, these newsletters help keep employee morale high, open channels of communication among vertical and horizontal levels of the organization, and provide a medium for communication. Messages that are slowed down by bottlenecks may never reach their intended receiver. By asking the newsletter editor to include their message, managers can bypass bottlenecks, reach people through an alternative medium, and increase the chances of their message being understood.

Integrated Genetics Inc., a $5 million bioengineering firm in Framingham, Massachusetts, suggests another way for opening vertical and horizontal communication. Integrated Genetics employs 100 scientists and 30 administrative employees. Each Friday, one of the scientists gives a presentation to the entire company on subjects ranging from his or her own in-house work to a new development in biotechnology. Once a month, an employee from sales, marketing, or administration takes a turn speaking to the scientists on anything from finance to strategic planning. The company also runs a weekly in-house seminar called "Science for Non-Scientists," in which scientists explain their work in detail to about 20 administrative employees. "The formation of separate cliques, with their own little cultures, is a danger at companies like ours," says Pat Connoy, Vice President of Sales and Marketing.[14]

Informal Channels: How Things Really Get Done

The cartoon on page 45 may be only a slight exaggeration. Top executives are often amazed at how quickly and, in many cases, how accurately information passes along **informal channels**. If these channels were filled in on the organization chart shown in Figure 2.4, the result would be a maze of lines resembling a web.

Informal channels can work horizontally *and* vertically. A message, often referred to as gossip, may pass from a vice president's secretary to someone in the mailroom, or from a division head's assistant to the assistant in another division.

"I Heard It Through the Grapevine" Perhaps the best-known informal communications channel for gossip (the message) is the organization's **grapevine.** It serves several functions for employees. The grapevine satisfies social needs, provides a way to clarify orders that come through formal channels, and acts as a safety valve, particularly if upward communication is blocked or ineffective. Many officials have come to respect the grapevine's ability to convey even semisecret information quickly. William R. Thurston, head of GenRad, Inc., a worldwide manufacturer of electronic systems and instruments, says of his company:

> We probably have the most precise and accurate grapevine in existence. When we come out with a major reorganization, it's usually known and understood, approved or disapproved, before the memo gets out. I used to think of it as a nuisance, but somebody told me it was an indication of good internal communication. Employees are the primary constituents of the corporation, and if you don't have them as good constituents, you can't have good customers.[15]

However, at times, messages that move through the grapevine may be distorted, abbreviated, exaggerated, or completely inaccurate. Many managers have found through personal experience how difficult it is to correct information that has been garbled by the grapevine.

Grapevine networks are both powerful in their impact and subtle in their working. Here are some basic principles that can help you to understand grapevines and their influence on your professional life.[16]

1. You cannot hide from the grapevine. The grapevine usually knows some of the truth although not all of it.

"Miss Johnson, I have a message of great importance for all employees. Please connect me with the grapevine." (Copyright © 1975. Reprinted by permission of AMACOM and Henry Martin.)

2. In the absence of clear and credible positive information, the grapevine tends to interpret events in a negative fashion.
3. Grapevine gossip tends to travel down from centers of power within the organization to the less powerful, or it travels horizontally among levels within an organization.
4. Severe social sanctions and distrust are directed toward individuals who consistently pass negative information about others through a grapevine network.
5. There are many grapevine networks in any organization. Each network is a community of individuals bound by shared experiences or concerns.
6. In any particular grapevine network, relatively few individuals communicate most of the information.
7. Your reputation is produced by the grapevine. Grapevine information can create a mindset in those who deal with you that is quite difficult to change once established.
8. The grapevine consistently confronts the individual with real-life moral and ethical dilemmas that help clarify personal values and decision-making processes.

Grapevines exist in all organizations. These informal channels of communication can be positive or negative. Understanding how they work and how you participate in them can be a decided advantage as you learn the true communication lines within your organization.

Thinking/Learning Starters

1. Describe the strengths and weaknesses of formal and informal channels of communication in an organization.
2. Have you ever experienced negative or positive results from grapevine communications? Explain.

How To Improve Organizational Communication

Now that you understand formal and informal communication channels within organizations, you can help improve your communication skills within these channels by sending clear messages, providing feedback, and listening.

Send Clear Messages

Become a responsible sender by always sending clear, concise messages with as few filters as possible. (See Figure 2.2.) As you formulate your messages, keep in mind how filters creep into all messages from both the sender's and receiver's vantage points.

Use Repetition When possible, use parallel channels of communication. For example, send a memo and make a phone call. The sender not only gains the receiver's attention through dialogue but also makes sure there is a written record to refer to in case specific details need to be recalled. Repetition, or redundancy, has been shown in many studies to be an important element in ensuring communication accuracy. Redundant forms ensure that a back-up message can be sent if part of a message is lost.

Use Words Carefully Try to use concise words that are not vague or confusing. Avoid buzz words, or complex, official language. Tailoring the message to the receiver by using words effectively will help ensure your message is understood.

This principle is equally important when using written communication within an organization as well as with clients or prospective customers. According to some estimates, more than two-thirds of the letters, memos, and reports written in industry fail to meet their stated objectives.[17] Some companies are now sponsoring business writing courses for their employees. Honeywell offers a number of courses in business English and effective memo and report writing. The results have been gratifying. Lengths of letters and reports have been reduced 45 percent, readability raised 27 percent, persuasiveness up 76 percent, and overall effectiveness increased 46 percent. New York Life Insurance Company has introduced an extensive company-wide program to improve correspondence. Company chairman R. Manning Brown, Jr., states: "We're known by the letters we write. In this age of the computer, letter writing is still one of the few personal ways we have for staying in touch with policy owners."[18]

As another example, a federal judge in New York recently ordered the United States government to rewrite Medicare benefit form letters into plain English instead of "bureaucratic gobbledygook"; recipients of the letters couldn't understand what they said. And during the past few years, high-ranking military personnel have initiated lists of technical terms that are to be eliminated from all military documents because the terms no longer have any meaning.

Despite these efforts, the use of clear language has become far less common. Buzz words, usually developed by relatively small, specialized groups, are often used to impress or to exclude outsiders. Although some buzz words can be useful, such as "competent failure" (an understandable failure experienced after a worthwhile effort) or "mousemilking" (undue effort for a small return), more often they simply confuse. New words to describe advances in technology are being created so rapidly that Webster's publishes a special supplement each year. But before you start using these new words with any frequency, be sure that everyone is working with the same vocabulary. As one communication specialist advises, "Spend long words and money very, very carefully."

Time the Message   Keep in mind that most employees, particularly at the managerial level, are flooded with messages every day. An important memo or letter may not get attention simply because it is competing with more pressing problems facing the receiver. Some organizations solve the problem by establishing standard times for particular messages to be sent and received. Important financial information, for example, may be sent on the second Thursday of every month. Other organizations send press releases to the media and to employees' computer screens simultaneously at 11 A.M. every Monday. Timing the delivery of your message will help ensure that it is accepted and acted upon.

Provide Feedback

Feedback allows the sender to find out how a message was actually interpreted by the receiver. There are formal and informal ways of gathering feedback. Informally, you can ask questions, watch facial expressions and other body language, and be alert for other signs that indicate how the listener is receiving the message. More formal means may involve written questionnaires, memos, reports, or meetings to gather feedback and make sure the message is being understood. Remember that communication is most effective when it is two-way. Be sure to offer feedback to others, just as you expect them to provide feedback to you. Suggestions for giving good feedback are covered in Chapter 3.

We cannot overestimate the power feedback has in effective organizational communication. Without it, communication does not exist. The more effective the feedback, the more effective the communication.

Listen

Research performed at Ohio State University indicates that the amount of time we spend on different parts of the communication process is divided: listening, 45 percent; speaking, 30 percent; reading, 16 percent; writing, 9 percent.[19] Most of us spent first grade learning to write, and we have continued to write throughout our academic careers. In second grade, the entire year focused on teaching reading. Every year thereafter has provided constant practice in reading. Perhaps we took a speech course in high school or college. Yet schools rarely offer a course in listening. This skill is taught the least, yet it is used the most according to the Ohio study. It's no wonder most of us spend our time thinking about what we are going to say next instead of truly listening to what another person has to say. People speak at approximately 150 words per minute. Our listening capacity is 450 words per minute. Since the message is usually much slower than our capacity to listen, we have plenty of time to concentrate on all aspects of the message. Why, then, are messages lost between the sender and the receiver?

All too frequently, hearing is confused with listening. To hear is simply to perceive sounds by the ear. To listen, however, is to make a conscious effort to hear something and to blend it with reason and understanding. We may not be able to improve our hearing, but we can improve our listening skills. Communication expert John T. Samaras of the University of Oklahoma points out six signs of poor listening habits:

1. Thinking about something else while waiting for the speaker's next word or sentence.
2. Listening primarily for facts rather than ideas.
3. Tuning out when the talk seems to be getting too difficult.
4. Prejudging, from a person's appearance or manner, that nothing interesting will be said.
5. Paying attention to outside sights and sounds when talking to someone.
6. Interrupting with a question whenever a speaker says something puzzling or unclear.[20]

Several years ago, J. Paul Lyet, chairman and chief executive officer of Sperry Corporation, discovered that when customers talked, few of his employees were really listening. The result—a sizeable amount of lost business. He also found that the problem was not unique to Sperry. It was costing other companies billions of dollars in lost revenues.

Lyet began to stress communication skills—particularly good listening habits—in company training programs. His first aim was to train those employees who have contact with customers. Sperry turned for help to Dr. Lyman K. Steil, a communication expert who believes that "... listening is a human behavior, a set of skills that flows from attitudes and knowledge you can measure, observe, test, and improve."

The workers' response to the program has been gratifying. Now other organizations are requesting Sperry's help in setting up listening seminars of their own. Among them are AT&T, the Department of Labor, and the U.S. Senate![21]

Listening, speaking, writing, and reading—these are the four basic skills of communication that everyone should learn early in life. According to many studies, we don't learn them well. We need to accept the fact that listening is a skill. It can be taught, and it can be learned. Most of all, it needs to be practiced. Dr. Steil and other communication experts offer some general guidelines for teaching people to be better listeners.

1. *Don't anticipate.* Resist the temptation to finish a speaker's sentences or jump to conclusions when only part of the message has been given. Give the speaker time to find the right words and to finish the message. Too often, the conclusions we jump to are the wrong ones.
2. *Avoid prejudging the speaker.* A poor listener usually decides in advance that the topic is dull and tunes out the message after the first few sentences. A good listener may not be any more impressed with the topic but will still attempt to evaluate the concepts to determine if any can be used. In addition, a poor listener will be distracted by the speaker's delivery or appearance. A good listener focuses on the content and on learning what the speaker knows about the subject. On a one-to-one basis, a critical listener can bring a conversation to a quick end. Good listening means creating a climate of trust, mutual respect, and warmth.
3. *Eliminate distractions.* A good listener creates a quiet, comfortable environment for listening. Closing a door, turning off noisy machinery, moving closer to the speaker, or changing to a quieter location can ensure that both sender and receiver can communicate well.
4. *Ask for clarification; restate important points.* Good listeners make sure they understand the terms and concepts the other person is using. One must not only be aware of the everyday meaning of words but also realize that each person has his or her own unique definitions associated with them. If there is confusion about what the speaker means, the listener can ask questions or restate what has been said until the points are clear.

5. *Be ready to give feedback.* When asked, a listener should give feedback as soon as possible. The response should be specific and framed in "I" statements. Instead of saying, "Your thinking is fuzzy here," the listener must pinpoint what needs to be done or changed. "I feel an important step has been overlooked. I suggest you check with inventory before planning that large an order."

Thinking/Learning Starters

1. Has the use of a buzz word ever had a positive or negative effect on your communication with someone? Explain.
2. Think of some people you know who are good listeners. How do they listen? What qualities make them good listeners?

Communication and International Business

The growing integration of international trade and business is creating additional communication problems and challenges for the modern corporation. More firms are opening branch offices abroad or entering into joint ventures with foreign corporations.

Yet all too often the American going overseas has little knowledge of the language and culture of the host country. There are many subtle communication traps for the unwary.[22]

Item: In Mexico, you should always inquire about a man's wife and family. In Saudi Arabia, you should never inquire about a client's family.

Item: In Japan, small gifts are almost obligatory in business situations. In China, gifts to individuals are prohibited in business situations.

Item: In Latin America, people are usually late. In Sweden, you must be prompt to the second.

Item: In the United States, "tabling" something means postponing it. In England, "tabling" means discussing it now.

Item: In the United States, the most important items usually receive attention first. In Ethiopia, high-priority items are postponed.

Item: "America" means the United States to people in this country. It includes Canada, Central America, and South America to the rest of the world.

The trend toward multinational business presents communication challenges for all organizations and employees involved. (Photo © Sandra Johnson 1982)

Companies are sending more employees abroad. They are also employing more foreign-born workers domestically. This trend means that supervisors and managers must have the communication skills to manage a multilingual, multicultural work force. On the other hand, foreign workers may be equally confused and dismayed by aspects of our culture, such as women occupying positions of authority, or top executives working with their own hands or being challenged in meetings by younger managers.

In the face of such problems at home and abroad, many multinational companies are establishing their own cultural and language training facilities for their employees. The cost can range from $3,900 to over $5,700 for four to six weeks of training. These courses, however, may not always prepare employees for the subtleties of culture and custom or the multitude of idioms and accents that abound in any language. Since transferring an employee abroad costs companies at least $138,000 per person, a high failure or turn-over rate can be an expensive proposition.[23]

The international business community is growing more complex and interconnected each year. Consequently, the need to communicate across language and cultural barriers is more pressing now than ever before. As one executive noted, "Americans have had a bad reputation for imposing our way of doing business on others abroad. This is no longer acceptable. Those who cling to the outdated notion that we have the only way are doing themselves and their clients a disservice."[24]

Summary

While information-giving is a one-way process, communication involves a two-way exchange in which the receiver understands the message in the same way the sender intended it. Responsibility for effective communication is shared equally by the sender and receiver.

Communication is often filtered through semantics, emotions, attitudes, role expectations, and nonverbal cues. Body language conveys information about people's thoughts and feelings through gestures, eye contact, and use of personal space, or proxemics. In addition, language itself is constantly changing as words are created, changed, or dropped. Context also affects how you interpret what you hear.

Communication in organizations unifies group behavior and helps build cooperation. To be effective, a message must be understood, believed, accepted, and acted upon. Communication moves along formal and informal channels. Formal channels follow the structure of the organization and can be vertical or horizontal. Informal channels, such as the grapevine, are vertical and horizontal. They may transmit information more rapidly and accurately than formal channels.

Improving communication in organizations involves sending clear messages, providing feedback, and listening. Good listening skills are rarely taught but can be learned. Five general guidelines for improving listening skills are (1) don't anticipate the speaker's message; (2) avoid prejudging the speaker; (3) eliminate distractions; (4) ask for clarification and restate important points; and (5) be ready to give feedback.

The integration of international trade and business means that companies must train their employees to be able to communicate in spite of language and cultural differences.

Key Terms

information-giving	circles of intimacy
communication	eye contact
feedback	gestures
sender	mirroring
receiver	formal and informal channels
message	vertical and horizontal channels
semantics	quality circle
kinesics – body language	grapevine
proxemics – study of personal space	

**Review
Questions**

1. Describe the difference between communication and information-giving. Explain the communication process in your own words.
2. Why is feedback essential to good communication?
3. What are the responsibilities of both sender and receiver in the communication process?
4. Describe the various communication filters and how they affect communication.
5. How can you make sure that you are being understood or that you understand others? Explain.
6. Are nonverbal cues always a reliable clue to a person's true feelings and thoughts? Why or why not?
7. What functions do formal communication channels serve in an organization?
8. Describe the strengths and weaknesses of informal channels.
9. Explain the difference between horizontal and vertical channels. What functions do each of these channels serve?
10. List some of the ways organizations can improve communication. What are some of the guidelines for improving your listening skills?

Case 2.1

Railroad Merger Derails Communication[25]

When the Norfolk and Western Railway merged with Southern Railway, workers at Western's Roanoke Shops were told that more jobs would be created at the shops. Yet, not long afterwards, production was stopped—something that had never happened in the hundred years the shops had operated.

Due to merger agreements made twenty years earlier, many workers felt their jobs were protected. But they, too, were laid off, along with men with 20 to 40 years' seniority.

Ed Hollandsworth, who spent 38 years at Western as a pattern-maker, says, "A lot of people have no idea what's going on." So many rumors had run through the place that the workers felt the shops would not open again. J. W. Medley, chairman of the local union, reinforced this idea, saying: "We got everything through the grapevine. There's a lot of questions, but management won't tell me (what's going on). They won't tell anybody."

Among other things, workers would like to know why there are large sums of money for advertising but none for needed maintenance or repair work.

Ed Hollandsworth doesn't understand. There is plenty of work to do, yet men are being let go. None of it makes any sense.

Questions

1. How could the company have handled the situation differently?

2. If the company were to explain the situation to employees, what method of communication do you think would be the most effective in this case: face-to-face meetings with groups of workers, a general meeting with all workers present, a memo explaining the changes being made, or personal letters to each employee explaining the changes? Explain your answer.

3. What principles of good communication is management violating in this situation?

Case 2.2

Not What You Say, But How You Say It

Frank Catham slumped wearily into a chair opposite the production manager's desk and handed him the production sheets for the past week. His crew had just finished assembling over a thousand small motors in record time.

"I'll tell you, I wouldn't want to do a job like that again," Frank said.

His boss, Ron Navarez, barely glanced up at him. Instead, still making corrections to a memo, he shoved next week's production schedule across the desk.

"Well, you better get ready for another one," Ron said, "because the top brass wants this new production run in four days."

Frank sat upright. "Four days!" he said in disbelief. "Hey, look, the guys are dead on their feet. Come on, Ron, can't you get us some extra time?"

Ron leaned back and folded his arms across his chest. "This run is very important to the big wheels in research and development. There's a lot of money riding on this product and they want results."

"They're always in a sweat about every bright idea they get. Some of my crew have been putting in twelve-hour days for ten days straight. I can't ask them to go another week like that."

Ron turned back to his memo. "I don't have any choice in the matter, Frank. *How* you do it is up to you. Just do it."

Frank snatched the production order off Ron's desk and strode angrily out of his office.

Questions

1. Discuss how each man's attitudes, role expectations, emotions, and non-verbal cues affected his communication.
2. How could Ron have presented the new production order to Frank in order to gain his cooperation?
3. Could Frank have done anything differently to get his message across and persuade Ron to extend the production deadline?

Notes

1. Jolie Solomon and John Bussey, "Pressed by Its Rivals, Proctor & Gamble Co. Is Altering Its Ways," *Wall Street Journal*, May 20, 1985, p. 22.
2. Susan Mundale, "Why More CEO's Are Mandating Listening and Writing Training," *Training/HRD*, October 1980, pp. 37–41.
3. David Abodaher, *Iacocca: America's Most Dynamic Businessman* (New York: Zebra Books, 1985), p. 59.
4. Sy Lazarus, *Loud & Clear* (New York: AMACOM, 1975), p. 3.
5. Allan Pease, *Signals: How to Use Body Language for Power, Success and Love* (New York: Bantam, 1984), p. 15.
6. Albert E. Scheflen, *Body Language and Social Order* (Englewood Cliffs, N.J.: Prentice-Hall, 1972), pp. xii–xiii.
7. Ibid., pp. 3–9.
8. Edward Hall, "Proxemics—A Study of Man's Spatial Relationships," in *Man's Image in Medicine and Anthropology* (New York: International Universities Press, 1963).
9. Allan Pease, *Signals*, p. 33.
10. "The Anatomy of a Message," *Ford's Insider*, 1981, pp. 4, 9.
11. James Brassil, "Communication in Business: Encouraging Upward Communication," *Pace*, November/December 1984, p. 39.
12. Charles Hall, "A Staff Meeting by Any Other Name," *Supervisory Management*, June 1984, p. 31.
13. Jack R. Gibb, *Trust—A New View of Personal and Organizational Development* (Los Angeles: The Guild of Tutors Press, 1978), p. 199.
14. John Persinos, "Communication—Getting Together," *INC.*, June 1985, p. 116.

15. Mundale, "Why More CEO's," pp. 40–41.
16. Bruce A. Baldwin, "Gossip and the Grapevine: Understanding Informal Information Networks," *Pace*, November/December 1983, pp. 11, 14, 16.
17. Mundale, "Why More CEO's," pp. 40–41.
18. Ibid.
19. Thomas Koziol, "Listening . . . A Lost Skill?", *The Hot Buttoneer*, August 1984, p. 1.
20. *American Salesman*, November 1981, p. 17.
21. Mundale, "Why More CEO's," pp. 37–41.
22. Lennie Copeland, "Training Americans to Do Business Overseas," *Training*, July 1984, p. 23.
23. Dick Schaef, "The Growing Need for Cross-Cultural and Bilingual Training," *Training/HRD*, January 1981, pp. 85–86.
24. Ibid.
25. James A. Bacon, "Laid-Off NW Workers Feel Confused, Betrayed, Bitter," *Roanoke Times & World News*, November 7, 1982, pp. A-1, A-14.

Suggested Readings

Copeland, Lennie. "Cross-Cultural Training: The Competitive Edge." *Training*, 1985.

Diekman, John R. *Human Connections.* Englewood Cliffs, N.J.: Prentice-Hall, 1982.

Fast, Julius. *Body Language.* New York: Simon & Schuster, 1970.

Johnson, Bonnie McDaniel. *Communication: The Process of Organization.* Boston: Allyn and Bacon, 1977.

Montgomery, Robert L. *Listening Made Easy.* New York: AMACOM, 1981.

Munter, Mary. *Guide to Managerial Communications.* Englewood Cliffs, N.J.: Prentice-Hall, 1982.

Pease, Allan. *Signals: How to Use Body Language for Power, Success and Love.* New York: Bantam, 1984.

Scheflen, Albert E. *Body Language and Social Order.* Englewood Cliffs, N.J.: Prentice-Hall, 1972.

Tubbs, Stewart L., and Sylvia Moss. *Human Communication—An Interpersonal Perspective.* New York: Random House, 1974.

II

Career
Success
Begins
with
Knowing
Yourself

Chapter 3

Your Attitudes

Chapter Preview

After studying this chapter, you will be able to

1. Understand the impact of employee attitudes on the success of an organization.
2. List and explain the ways people acquire attitudes.
3. Discuss the three major factors that influence people to change their attitudes.
4. Understand how others' attitudes can be influenced by providing nonthreatening feedback.
5. Identify the skills needed to help change your attitudes.

Listed as one of the one hundred best companies to work for, Johnson Wax is one of those dream companies that has never had a layoff; gives employees an opportunity to express their views; and provides a flexible health plan, recreational facilities, extensive insurance, and retirement and profit-sharing plans. The attitudes and morale of the employees reflect a strong commitment to the success of the organization. They feel they are part of a family.

While attending a meeting of the company's British plant near London, Samuel Johnson, chairman of the company, found that some of the employees were concerned about their future. Even though the British employees participate in a generous profit-sharing plan and work in comfortable, attractive facilities, they wondered how they fit into the big American company. Since Johnson Wax does 60 percent of its business outside the United States, Mr. Johnson recognized that something needed to be done to solidify the attitudes of these people. He wanted to prove to them they were part of the "family."

He chartered a Boeing 747 jet and flew the entire British work force—480 people—to the United States. They were first taken to corporate headquarters in Racine, Wisconsin, where they stayed in hotels, toured the company's facilities, shopped, and were feted at a company banquet. On one night, employees in Racine took a British guest home for dinner. Before flying back to Britain, they spent two days in New York City sightseeing and were treated to a complimentary dinner at the World Trade Center.[1]

Needless to say, the attitudes of the British workers greatly improved. And the American work force was inspired by how their company continues to instill confidence in all of its employees worldwide. The power of such attitudes is often not measurable. But the correlation between positive attitudes and high performance, low turnover, and increased productivity exists in most organizations.

What Is an Attitude?

Most psychologists define an **attitude** as any strong belief or feeling toward people and situations. We have favorable or unfavorable attitudes toward ethnic groups, rich people, poor people, homosexuals, and other groups. We have strong or moderate attitudes toward welfare, labor unions, religion, politics, and other social issues. Attitudes are not quick judgments we make casually and can easily change. As we acquire them throughout our lives, they are deeply ingrained in our personality. We are very much in favor of those things toward which we have a positive attitude. And we are very much against those things toward which we have a negative attitude.

Dr. Jerome Kagan, Harvard professor and author, explains, "It is this 'for' or 'against' quality that distinguishes attitudes from more superficial and less influential opinions."[2] The point of view that more women seem to be entering the management level in organizations is an opinion. However, the belief that women should have equal pay and equal access to top-level jobs is an attitude with strong emotional ties.

Attitudes represent a powerful force in any organization. An attitude of trust can pave the way for improved communication and greater cooperation between an employee and a supervisor. A caring attitude displayed by an employee can increase customer loyalty and set the stage for repeat business. An attitude of respect for safety rules and regulations can result in fewer accidents.

What people see and hear is usually shaped by their attitudes. A sincere effort by management to improve working conditions, when screened through attitudes of suspicion and cynicism, may have a negative impact on employee-management relations. These same actions by management, screened through attitudes of trust and hope, may result in improved worker morale.

How you feel about something is usually no secret to friends and acquaintances. Others will interpret your attitudes by your behavior. The office worker who turns out letters filled with typographical errors will no doubt be viewed as someone who just doesn't care. The salesperson who always meets or exceeds the established quota will very likely be seen as ambitious and conscientious. It is difficult to conceal an attitude.

People possess both positive and negative attitudes. And it is generally agreed that in the area of interpersonal relations positive attitudes bring positive results just as negative attitudes bring negative results. People who are optimistic about their future and display a positive attitude toward others are usually surrounded by friends who possess similar attitudes. Those who are pessimistic and have a negative attitude toward other people usually have few friends, and those few are apt to be negative thinkers as well. Remember, attitudes are contagious—are yours worth catching?

How Do You Acquire Attitudes?

The society into which we are born begins to influence us almost from the moment of birth. As you develop from child to adult, you interact with your parents, family, teachers, and friends. From all of these people, you learn the language of your culture, how to behave toward other people, and how to express or conceal your emotions. You learn what you and your family value and what your society considers right and wrong. This process through which children are integrated into a society by exposure to the actions and opinions of others is called **socialization**.[3] Dr. Kagan identifies several elements of socialization that contribute to the formation of our attitudes.[4]

1. *Looking and listening during early childhood.* Children often feel that statements made by parents are the "proper" things to believe. For example,

the mother who repeatedly tells her three-year-old child "never eat food without first washing your hands" will likely instill an early attitude toward personal hygiene. If the mother washes her own hands before each meal, the child will see this behavior as an acceptable practice. This is especially true if the mother is admired and respected by the child.

2. *Reward and punishment.* During early childhood, attitude formation is often related to reward and punishment. Parents, teachers, and others with some authority over the child will generally encourage certain attitudes and punish the person for holding others. Naturally, an individual will tend to develop attitudes that minimize punishments and maximize rewards. A child who is praised for sharing toys with playmates is likely to repeat the behavior.

Rewards and punishments can also shape the attitudes of adults in an organizational setting. The Liebert Corporation, a Columbus, Ohio based manufacturer, uses rewards to improve employee attendance. The company gives hourly employees three shares of company stock for each year of perfect attendance and two free movie tickets for each unblemished quarter.[5] Flexcan Company, a specialty paper firm located in Spencer, Massachusetts, is using rewards to help employees quit smoking. The third Thursday of every month, the company puts $30 gift certificates into the pay envelopes of workers who quit smoking or who are nonsmokers and did not start. The company also gives $15 certificates to employees who reduce their smoking. Many employees have quit smoking or cut down as a result of the program.[6]

3. *Identification.* Most young people would like to have more power, status, and popularity. These goals are often achieved through identification. Young children are most likely to identify with their parents. During later stages of development, television stars and sports heroes may replace the parents as role models. As you might expect, such people can exert considerable influence—for better or for worse—on a child's developing attitudes.

Throughout life we adopt new role models and discard old ones. A high school student may prefer a model who "thinks" young and is physically attractive. Later in life, as an employee, this same person may identify more readily with an older employee who is respected by coworkers. More will be said about models later in this chapter.

4. *Cultural influence.* **Culture** can be defined as the arts, beliefs, institutions, and transmitted behavior patterns of a community or population. In a general sense, culture is everything around us that is made by human beings. People acquire a way to define themselves in every culture. And the definition varies from culture to culture. If you ask an adult living in Japan, "Who are you?" that person is likely to respond, "I'm an employee of Sony Corporation." In Japanese culture, people are likely to be defined by the organization for which they work. In the United States, your job and employer are somewhat less likely to be your major source of identity.

Today, what people believe is more likely to define their identity. A young woman who spends hours each week trying to improve the environment may define herself as an environmentalist. The fact that she works as a department supervisor at a local supermarket may be incidental to how she defines herself.

Attitudes may be very persistent. Yet they are not always consistent with the information available because of the emotions involved. Some attitudes reflect the effects of socialization and conformity to our peers and culture. We sometimes form attitudes without ever considering evidence that might change our beliefs. When we receive information that conflicts with our attitudes, we try to find ways to hold on to them. For instance, you and your coworkers may be convinced that Sam Malone is the best possible candidate for president in the upcoming union election. The local newspaper prints an editorial proving Sam is guilty of taking bribes from corporate officials. Because of your attitude, you may dismiss the editorial as gossip, convince yourself that the newspaper is biased against Sam, or forget the article and pretend it never existed. Some psychologists have concluded that the most remarkable thing about our attitudes is the amount of inconsistency we manage to tolerate.

Thinking/Learning Starters

1. Recall at least one childhood attitude you developed as a result of reward or punishment. Has this attitude changed?
2. At age sixteen, did you identify closely with an actor or actress, sports figure, or musician? Is this person still your idol?
3. Identify one or two attitudes about yourself or other people or things that you have changed during the past year. What factors caused you to change?

Changing Attitudes

People do not easily adopt new attitudes or discard old ones. It is difficult to break the strong emotional ties. Yet attitudes can be changed.

The socialization process does not stop when you become an adult. You are constantly placed in new situations with people from different backgrounds and cultures. Each time you go to a new school, take a new job, get a promotion, or move to a different neighborhood, your attitudes are exposed to change. During this continuous socialization process, you may find your-

Total Person Insight	It is only through a vast amount of experience and a lengthy and successful maturation that we gain the capacity to see the world and our place in it realistically, and thus are enabled to realistically assess our responsibility for ourselves and the world.
M. Scott Peck	

self consciously or subconsciously changing your attitudes in order to work more effectively with others. Knowing how to change your attitudes intentionally can be essential to your success in an organization.

Throughout the remainder of this chapter, we will focus on the factors within organizations that can influence employees' attitudes. These factors are feedback, conditions and consequences, and role modeling. As you study this information, keep in mind that these techniques can be used to alter your own attitudes; they can also be used to help your fellow employees alter theirs.

Feedback

Feedback often stimulates us to adopt new attitudes. It is information that helps us understand how we are perceived by others. Feedback offers the opportunity to change attitudes that might influence the productivity of the organization. When we learn to give positive feedback to others, they will respond with positive behaviors. Consider the following conversation:

Diane: I can't believe that man! Every time I turn around, Jim tells me another way to close a sale. Doesn't he know I've been selling longer than he has? I can't stand people who try to tell me what to do and how to do it. I don't want anything to do with him.

Judy: Yes, Jim is aware of your sales experience and has a great deal of respect for you. But did you know that our boss, Mr. Connors, sent Jim to an expensive sales seminar that focused on closing the sale? Since Mr. Connors could afford to send only one person, he asked Jim to share the information he learned with the rest of us. The company needs us to increase our "close" ratio. Jim is only doing what he was told to do.

Diane: Well, why didn't someone tell me? Let's go find Jim and learn more!

This kind of feedback helped defuse a potentially damaging relationship within the organization. Of course, feedback is more apt to influence our attitudes when it is given in a helpful, nonthreatening manner. We are less

Feedback should be given in a helpful, nonthreatening manner to avoid putting the person being evaluated on the defensive. (Photo © Richard Kalvar, Magnum Photos, Inc.)

likely to develop defensive attitudes when given feedback that meets one or more of the following guidelines.

1. *Good feedback is a balance of positives and negatives.* Frances Meritt Stern, director of the Institute for Behavior Awareness, suggests that a useful rule of thumb is to give two positives for each negative.[7] Feedback is more effective when you maintain a balanced view, praising the person's strengths as well as evaluating his or her weaknesses. Totally negative feedback produces negative results.

2. *Focus feedback on the behavior rather than the person.*[8] Concentrate on what a person does, not on the person's competence or character. "You were really careless today" attacks the person and will evoke a negative response. Instead say, "There were several mistakes in today's budget report. Do you want me to sit down with you and help figure out what went wrong?" Focus on what can be changed: People don't change, behaviors do.

3. *Avoid feedback that includes judgments.*[9] A **judgment** is an evaluation of good or bad, or right or wrong. When a wife says to her husband, "You look awful. That suit looks as if you slept in it," you can bet his attitude is anything but positive the rest of the day. Instead, use words that describe the situation. "It looks as if your suit needs to go to the cleaners. Will you take it or shall I?" Good feedback avoids emotion-laden, biased words.

4. *Focus feedback on specific situations.* The nurse who says to an aide, "Your records are sloppy," is not being helpful. Feedback should specify what was done improperly and how to correct it. The nurse will get better results if she says, "I reviewed the morning report you completed yesterday and found an error. Here, let me show you the mistake." People are more likely to accept feedback that pinpoints specific problems and suggests ways to change them.

5. *Provide feedback at the appropriate time and place.*[10] Feedback often triggers emotional reactions, so exercise sensitivity about the best time to give it. Appropriate feedback presented at an inappropriate time may do more harm than good. An employee who has a serious accident on the job should not be given a lecture on safety immediately after the traumatic experience.

Feedback, when given in the proper way, can have a positive influence on attitude development. The key is to meet the needs of the other person rather than satisfy some need of your own. If you are offering criticism and your feelings are hostile, anxious, or punitive, they are bound to color your remarks. A negative attitude is difficult to conceal, and the other person is apt to react to your emotional attitude rather than to the substance of your words.

Thinking/Learning Starters

1. Can you recall receiving or giving feedback at work that focused on the *person* rather than *performance*? Give at least two examples.
2. Think about the feedback you give others. Do you present a balance of positives and negatives? Give an example.

Conditions and Consequences

Attitudes can often be changed by altering conditions and consequences. Most people have trouble recalling exactly how they developed many of their attitudes. For example, if you love classical music and hate mathematics, can you pinpoint when you began to feel this way? Robert Mager, a nationally known authority in the field of training and development, conducted a study designed to identify the most favored and least favored school subjects of selected students.[11] Once these subjects were identified, each person was asked a series of questions to determine how these attitudes developed. The results of the study were quite interesting.

"I'm giving you a 'marginal' on your attitude toward constructive criticism." (Kaser, *Phi Delta Kappan*)

Almost every person was able to identify subjects they really liked or strongly disliked. Once the most favored and least favored subjects were identified, Mager followed up with this question: "How did it get to be that way?" Here the results were somewhat unexpected. He found that few people understood how they came to favor certain subjects over others. The response was often general: "I always liked science."

When people were asked about the subject they liked least, the story was often quite different. They could easily recall the events or conditions that made them want to avoid the subject. Here is a sampling of interview summaries:

Case 1
Favorite subject: Music

How it got that way: I've always liked music. It was just a personal liking. No events had anything to do with it.

Least favored subject: English

How it got that way: None of the teachers could get down to a level where the students could understand what they were trying to get across. They didn't know how to make the subject interesting.

Case 2
Favorite subject: Art

How it got that way: I've always liked art. Mother encouraged art by providing lots of materials. In high school the instructor was very good. Had a good sense of humor, and worked with students. He encouraged us to participate in contests. I still use my art knowledge in my work.

Least favored subject: Mathematics

How it got that way: I was skipped to third grade after completing only half of second grade. I missed considerable background and felt lost. The third grade teacher was very impatient and did not believe in individual instruction. She ridiculed me in front of the class. I was above average in all other subjects, but I failed in accounting in college.[12]

Mager summarizes his study by saying

... a favorite subject tends to get that way because the person seems to do well at it; because the subject was associated with liked or admired friends, relatives, or instructors; and because the person was relatively comfortable when in the presence of the subject or activity. A subject least favored tends to get that way because the person seems to have little or no aptitude for it, because the subject is associated with disliked individuals, and because being in the presence of the subject is often associated with unpleasant conditions.[13]

Thus, the *conditions* that surround a subject and the *consequences* associated with it are of major importance in forming your attitudes.

These findings are not limited to the field of education. Conditions and consequences also shape attitudes in an organization.

Conditions   If you want to develop a favorable attitude toward a task or duty, try to accentuate the positive **conditions** surrounding it. Monique Hilliston, age sixteen, quit her first job in disgust. Five weeks ago she had started working at a nearby fast-food restaurant to earn money for some new clothes.

Monique began her new job with a good attitude. She wanted to be successful and was determined to do her best. But from the first day, she found the job frustrating. The manager simply didn't seem to care whether she succeeded or failed. He spent about five minutes going over the proper way to process a customer's order and then assigned her to a counter station. Soon she found the customers asking questions she couldn't answer and had trouble operating the cash register. Other workers were too busy to be of much help. At the end of her shift, the manager said, "If you don't get with it, I'm going to replace you. We only give instructions once around here."

Monique finally learned how to handle orders quickly, but she found other aspects of the job to be unpleasant. There was little cooperation among the workers. The people who worked on her shift did not work as a team. Also, the people she worked with, including supervisors, did not take pride in their work. She finally decided to quit.

It is interesting to note that all the conditions that made work unpleasant for Monique could be changed. The manager could have displayed a caring attitude toward her. Someone could have given her adequate training before she actually began working with customers. Feedback concerning her performance could have been given in a more effective manner.

Managers can never be sure a new worker will obtain satisfaction from performing the duties assigned. However, they may be able to get rid of conditions that are undesirable and help employees develop positive attitudes toward work. Most employers can create a positive, productive, working climate by

1. Providing an orientation to the job and adequate training.
2. Replacing equipment that is out of date or worn out.
3. Encouraging workers to help new employees feel at home.
4. Avoiding tactless comments that reduce the employee's self-esteem.
5. Providing periodic feedback so workers are kept informed of their progress.

Consequences When your contact with an activity or event is followed by positive **consequences** you will probably repeat the activity. By the same token, you tend to avoid things that are followed by negative consequences.

Assume that you are at a staff meeting called by your immediate supervisor. She announces the need for a 10 percent cut in operating expenses. She says that suggestions from the staff are important and encourages everyone to express their views. Soon a person seated across the table speaks up and says, "I think we can all reduce the length of our long-distance telephone calls. I know I talk too long to established customers." The supervisor smiles, nods her head approvingly, and writes down the suggestion. It is clear that the boss really wants and appreciates input from the staff. Soon everyone is eager to share their ideas.

Suppose this supervisor had reacted differently to the first person's suggestion. What if she had frowned, pushed her chair back, and said, "Look, we've talked about that problem before. I'm looking for fresh ideas!" Chances are members of the group would be reluctant to speak up. If the risk of encountering negative consequences is too great, they will avoid sharing their ideas.

Managers, supervisors, and anyone else involved in shaping attitudes should keep this simple rule in mind: Whenever an experience is followed by positive consequences, it is more likely to be repeated in the future. If you want people to arrive for work on time, reward this behavior in some way. If operating expenses are too high, look for ways to encourage workers to cut costs, and reward those who manage to reduce expenses. As a rule, people will avoid doing things that bring about negative consequences for themselves.

One final word regarding positive and negative consequences. Look at consequences through the eyes of the person you are trying to influence. Mager says:

> It doesn't matter what I might seek out or avoid: it is what is positive or aversive to the person whose behavior I am trying to influence that counts. And this, incidentally, is one reason we don't succeed more often than we do in the area of human interaction. We try to influence others by providing consequences that are positive to us but not to them.[14]

Most organizations are becoming more aware of the impact of negative consequences on worker attitudes and are taking steps to reduce boredom, physical discomfort, frustration, and anxiety. This subject is discussed at greater length in Chapter 6.

Thinking/Learning Starters

1. Think about your first job and try to list at least two positive and two negative experiences during the first week. What conditions created these experiences? Could these conditions have been avoided?
2. Assume you are working at a large Sears, Roebuck mail-order store. The manager assigns each new employee to work closely with an experienced employee during the first week. A new employee started work on Monday and was instructed to work closely with you. What can you do to ensure that this person develops a positive attitude toward work?

Role Modeling

Role models at home, at school, and at work shape many of our attitudes. We acquire many of our attitudes by observing the behaviors of parents, teachers, fellow workers, and supervisors. The term *role* comes from the field of sociology. It can be defined as a pattern of behavior expected of a person in activities involving others. Each role calls for different types of behavior. People view a police officer's role differently from that of a nurse working in a hospital. You expect police officers to act in a certain way, and your attitudes toward law enforcement are shaped by how they conduct themselves. Every police officer is a potential role model for others.

When you want to learn how to behave in an unfamilar situation, you usually turn to **role models.** Think about your first job. How did you deter-

Role models can have considerable influence on employee attitude development. (Photo by Peter Southwick, Stock Boston, Inc.)

mine correct behavior? You very likely watched to see what others did and then imitated their actions. People tend to learn by imitation.[15] Bankers Trust of New York recruited several young candidates into their fast-track management training program, promising trainees that they would be at the first level of management within one year or they would leave the company. The key to this program's success is that each management trainee is assigned to a bank officer for the year. "They were our boss, our counselor, and our evaluator," reported Alan Woods, one management trainee. "Having a good boss meant a better chance of success. A good boss was one who encouraged us to be creative, open, and questioning. The bosses who were able to carry this training into their role as models 'were the best.' "[16]

In the work environment, an employee may have several role models. The new machinist in a factory may look to the department supervisor, the union steward, and a highly skilled senior employee for clues about correct and incorrect behavior.

In an organizational setting, role models can have a major influence on new employee attitude development. The new salesperson in the menswear department wants help in adjusting to the job. So does the new dental hygienist and the recently hired auto mechanic. These people will pay special attention to the behavior of coworkers and managers. For example, if a worker leaves the job early and no negative consequences follow, other employees may decide that staying until quitting time is not as important as they had thought. If an employee is rude to customers and suffers no negative consequences, the new employee may imitate this behavior.

In most organizations, supervisory and management personnel have the greatest impact on employee attitudes. The supervisor's attitudes toward safety, cost control, accuracy, dress and grooming, customer relations, and the like become the model for subordinates. Employees will pay more attention to what their supervisors do than to what they say.

> Many of us do not recognize ourselves as role models, yet we project behavior which people use as a pattern for their own conduct. Everyone who serves as a role model also teaches, since the followers first learn behavior or ideas and then manifest them in their own lives.[17]

If supervisors want to shape employee attitudes, they must demonstrate the kind of behavior they want others to develop. Albert Schweitzer, the French philosopher and Nobel Peace Prize winner, was right on target when he said, "Example is not the main thing in influencing others, it is the only thing."

Thinking/Learning Starters

1. Try to recall an unfamiliar situation where it was necessary to rely on a role model for guidance and direction. How much influence did this person have on you? Was the influence long lasting?
2. We have said that if a role model says one thing and models something else, we will pay attention to the person's behavior and ignore what the person says. Can you recall a situation where someone's behavior conflicted with the person's words?

Job Enrichment

Research findings indicating that conditions and consequences can shape attitudes in a positive direction have prompted many organizations to establish **job enrichment** programs. The major goal of job enrichment is to make routine jobs more challenging and interesting. Companies that have adopted some form of job enrichment include Maytag, Prudential Insurance, Corning Glass Works, IBM, Motorola, and Texas Instruments.

Job enrichment may involve something as simple as giving the receptionist responsibility for ordering supplies, or it may mean redesigning an assembly line to provide production workers with more challenging and interesting work experiences. Many jobs, though quite specialized, can be redesigned so the worker performs less routine tasks. One company that has achieved considerable success in the area of job enrichment is IBM. Many years ago, the company began experimenting with ways to enlarge jobs so that workers exercised greater judgment, had more control over the flow of work, and performed a variety of tasks. These changes resulted in increased worker morale and efficiency.

Volvo, the Swedish car manufacturer, initiated a major job enrichment program in the early 1970s. When a new assembly plant was built at Kalmar, Sweden, Volvo rejected the traditional conveyor assembly line in favor of special carriers that move automobiles in various states of completion among small assembly departments. The movement of carriers is worker controlled. Within each department, a team of 15 to 25 workers is free to structure its tasks in any way its members see fit, provided their assigned output is achieved.[18] Has this departure from the auto industry's traditional practices influenced workers' behavior at the Kalmar plant? Yes, says Volvo's management, who point to reduced absenteeism, reduced turnover, and better quality automobiles.

Some attempts at job enrichment, however, have not been successful. Programs sometimes fail because management does not prepare workers for a change in their jobs. The way in which a new program is introduced is of critical importance. If workers perceive the change as a gimmick developed by management, the program will likely not be a success. In addition, the introduction of a job enrichment program may have a negative impact on the morale of workers who have learned to cope with a lack of challenge and do not possess a strong desire to become involved in nonroutine work. Some employees value the security of a routine job and minimal responsibility more than the opportunity for variety in their work and greater responsibility.

How to Change Your Attitudes

If you begin to notice that successful people will not associate with you, that you've been overlooked for that promotion you thought you should have had, or that you go home from work each night depressed and a little angry at the world, you can almost always be sure you need an attitude adjustment. It helps to realize that outside elements, such as the economy, your supervisor, the traffic, and the weather, are out of your control. At the same time, one thing you *can* control is your attitude. Others may influence your attitudes, but you are ultimately in control of your thoughts. Your mind is like a computer: You only get out what you put in. If you allow yourself to dwell on negative thoughts or attitudes, you can expect negative, self-destructive behaviors. When you screen your thoughts to accentuate the positive, you will find your world a much more pleasant place to be. When people are happy and feel in control of their lives, other people enjoy working with them. Being in control of your attitudes is a powerful human relations skill. Here are some helpful hints to help you change your attitudes.

1. *Become aware of your negative attitudes toward people and situations.* Decide if they are valid or if you have been socialized into holding those beliefs.

2. *Think for yourself.* Determine your own attitudes and reasons for having them. Peer pressure and family ties are strong influences, but you can be in control when and if you choose to be.

3. *Realize that there are few, if any, benefits to harboring negative attitudes.* If negative attitudes, such as holding grudges, can only be harmful, then why continue to hold on to them?

4. *Keep an open mind.* We often make decisions and then refuse to consider any other points of view. In refusing to consider other viewpoints, we may miss a valid point.

William James, the famous Harvard psychologist, for generations has been known for this discovery: By changing the inner attitudes of your mind, you can change the outer aspects of your life. Each generation seems to rediscover this for themselves. You can begin *now* to change your life in a positive direction by gaining control of your attitudes.

Summary

An attitude is defined as any strong belief toward people and situations. It is a state of mind backed up by feelings. People possess hundreds of attitudes about work, family life, friends, coworkers, and the like.

Attitudes represent a powerful force in every organization. If the persons employed by a service firm display a caring attitude toward customers, the business will likely enjoy a high degree of customer loyalty and repeat business. If the employees of a manufacturing firm display a serious attitude toward safety rules and regulations, fewer accidents are likely to occur.

According to Jerome Kagan, people acquire attitudes in several ways: looking and listening during early childhood, rewards and punishment, identification, and cultural influence. Although many factors can influence the formation of an attitude, people do not easily adopt new ones or discard old ones. People often hold attitudes that are inconsistent with available information. In some cases, people change their attitudes through feedback from others. When they discover that something they do bothers others, they may be motivated to change a particular attitude or behavior. Self-awareness can increase as the result of nonthreatening feedback.

Healthy attitudes can be instilled through feedback that is a balance of positives and negatives, focuses on the behavior rather than the person, avoids judgments, and relates to a specific situation.

The conditions that surround an experience and the consequences following it may also create a change in attitude. If you want to develop a favorable attitude toward a task or duty, try to accentuate the positive conditions surrounding it. Be sure that positive consequences follow the task or duty.

Role modeling represents another way to change attitudes. People often form attitudes toward their work by observing fellow employees and supervisory or management personnel.

Research indicates that conditions and consequences can positively shape attitudes. As a result, many companies have initiated job enrichment programs to help make routine jobs more interesting for workers. Job enrichment is sometimes successful, and employees become happier and more efficient. It can also fail if management does not prepare employees for change or if enrichment is forced on employees who are happy with their jobs as they are.

Many conditions within an organization are out of the average worker's control. Individuals must take responsibility for changing their own attitudes. When you want to change an attitude, become aware of your negative attitudes, think for yourself, realize that there are few benefits to harboring negative attitudes, and keep an open mind.

Key Terms

attitude	conditions
socialization	consequences
culture	role models
feedback	job enrichment
judgment	

Review Questions

1. Provide a concise definition of the term *attitude.*
2. It has been said that "attitudes represent a powerful force in any organization." What examples can you give to support this statement?
3. Describe how rewards and punishment can shape the attitudes of employees in an organization. Give at least one example.
4. How does feedback contribute to attitude change?
5. Why is it important to focus feedback on behavior rather than the person?
6. Robert Mager says the conditions that surround a subject can play an important role in shaping our attitudes. Provide at least one example to support Mager's statement.
7. Explain how consequences can influence the shaping of attitudes in an organization.
8. Describe how role models influence attitude formation. Give at least one example.
9. Describe job enrichment and give one example of a company that has adopted this approach.
10. Describe the benefits of being in control of your attitudes.

Case 3.1

Worker Involvement: Is It Worth It?[19]

Iggesund, a Swedish supplier of pulp, paper, lumber, chemicals, and steel, was selected to participate in a national research project attempting to assess the value of worker participation in the development of a new company plant. The project was organized so that worker representatives would serve with managers on various planning committees. The representatives, paid for the time spent in committees, were involved in the evaluation of different machines, the need for tools, and the layout of the work area. When the project began, Iggesund had no prior experience with worker participation in management planning, nor had it experimented with job enrichment. Today, both parties are proud of the results and agree that the plant is different from what it would have been without the workers' involvement. The chief difference is the attention to personnel facilities and environmental controls, including enclosures to reduce machinery noise and a ventilation system to remove dirt and grease. Iggesund found, however, that worker participation increased the planning expenses by 46 percent and increased the total project cost by 7 percent. The additional meeting time added 3 months to the project.

Questions

1. As an executive, you want your firm to consider employee participation in the development of a new plant. Your colleagues have handed you the statistics on increased expenses and project delays given above. How would you counter these statistics to reaffirm your position?
2. What are the long-range benefits that might result from the changes implemented by the employee representatives?
3. What influence might national attention have had on the personnel involved in the study?

Case 3.2

Maintaining Staff Morale

One year ago, Maria Vargas assumed the duties of administrator of the Marion County Hospital. She inherited a well-trained professional staff, but the physical plant was seriously run down and in need of repair. Also, much of the equipment was out of date and needed to be replaced. With the aid of resident physicians, maintenance personnel, supervisors, and nurses, and advice from a firm specializing in hospital architecture, Maria developed a two-year plan to modernize the hospital. The plan included replacing windows and doors that were not energy efficient, worn-out floor covering, and several pieces of equipment, as well as moving some walls to provide more space in selected areas and repainting the entire hospital.

The plan received approval of the hospital board two weeks ago. Maria was very pleased with the support she received from the board, but she now felt uneasy about the future. The hospital would soon be invaded by an army of carpenters, painters, plumbers, and other workers who would create daily barriers to the efficient operation of the hospital. Just keeping it clean enough would be a major challenge. What would happen to staff morale? Would patient service suffer? Would the resident physicians be willing to work under the temporarily adverse conditions?

Questions

1. Based on your knowledge of conditions and consequences, what steps can Maria Vargas take to ensure that staff morale and patient service do not suffer during the lengthy remodeling period? Be specific as you suggest ways to maintain the current positive attitudes of the staff.
2. Based on your knowledge of role modeling, what advice would you give Maria Vargas and the nursing supervisors?

Notes

1. Robert Levering, Milton Moskowitz, and Michael Katz, *The 100 Best Companies to Work for in America* (New York: New American Library, 1985), pp. 173–177.
2. Jerome Kagan, *Psychology: An Introduction* (New York: Harcourt Brace Jovanovich, 1984), p. 558.
3. Ibid., p. 548.
4. Jerome Kagan, "The Psychology of Attitudes," *Forum*, Spring/Summer 1973, pp. 4–5.
5. "Attendance Required," *INC.*, June 1985, p. 115.
6. "Cash for Clean Lungs," *INC.*, October 1984, p. 149.
7. "Getting Good Feedback—and Giving Back in Kind," *Training/HRD*, April 1982, p. 34.
8. David W. Johnson, *Reaching Out—Interpersonal Effectiveness and Self-Actualization* (Englewood Cliffs, N.J.: Prentice-Hall, 1981), p. 23.
9. Ibid.
10. Hendrie Weisinger and Norman M. Lobsenz, *Nobody's Perfect—How to Give Criticism and Get Results* (Los Angeles: Stanford Press, 1981), p. 75.
11. Robert F. Mager, *Developing Attitude Toward Learning*, (Belmont, Calif.: Fearon-Pitman, 1968), p. 33.
12. Ibid.
13. Ibid.
14. Ibid., p. 47.
15. Bernard L. Rosenbaum, "Back to Behavior Modeling," *Training and Development Journal*, November 1984, p. 88.
16. Patricia Galagan Hurley, "Supervising the Supergrad," *Training and Development Journal*, March 1983, p. 56.
17. Barbara A. Meyer, "Role Modeling: Rewards and Responsibilities," *Delta Kappa Gamma Bulletin*, Vol. XLVIII–2, Winter 1982, pp. 46–50.

18. Knut Haganäes and Lee Hales, "Scandinavian Models of Employee Participation," *S.A.M. Advanced Management Journal*, Winter 1983, pp. 23–24.

19. Ibid., pp. 24–26.

Suggested Readings

Buscaglia, Leo. *Living, Loving, and Learning.* New York: Holt, Rinehart, and Winston, 1982.

Clinard, Helen Hall. *Winning Ways to Succeed with People.* Houston: Gulf Publishing Company, 1985.

Dyer, Wayne. *Gifts from Eykis.* New York: Simon & Schuster, 1983.

Mager, Robert F. *Developing Attitudes Toward Learning.* Belmont, Calif.: Fearon-Pitman, 1968.

Weisinger, Hendrie, and Norman M. Lobsenz. *Nobody's Perfect—How to Give Criticism and Get Results.* Los Angeles: Stanford Press, 1981.

Chapter 4

Building a Positive Self-Concept

Chapter Preview

After studying this chapter, you will be able to

1. Define *self-concept* and discuss how it is developed.
2. Explain why a positive self-concept is essential for effective human relations and success at work.
3. Understand the impact of workers' self-concepts in an organizational setting.
4. Understand the power of expectations.
5. Identify ways to help build a positive self-concept.

When Peter Ueberroth was only in his mid-twenties, he formed an air-shuttle company to provide service between Los Angeles and the Spokane, Washington World's Fair. Within a year, due to a drop in the demand for charter service, his company failed and he was $100,000 in debt.

Nevertheless, Ueberroth did not give up. He established another transportation company the following year. This new company provided central reservation services for the smaller hotels, airlines, and passenger ships that did not have their own representatives. Though he started with only $5,000 and one employee, this time Ueberroth's business grew. In 1967, he began selling stocks publicly. During the next ten years, Ueberroth's name and financial success became well known. Ueberroth took over several failing travel agencies and formed First Travel Corporation as a holding company for his properties. In 1980, it was the second-largest travel company in the country.

When Ueberroth was asked to head the organizing committee for the 1984 Los Angeles Olympic games, the committee was already in debt for $300,000. Because of city and state restrictions, the committee was unable to depend on governmental subsidies; the games had to be financed solely by private funding. Accepting the position would have been an enormous challenge for anyone—it would also mean a 70% cut in Ueberroth's yearly salary. Confident that he could succeed and eager for the challenge, Ueberroth accepted the position.

A less-confident person probably would have quit the first week on the job. He was locked out of his office because the Olympic committee had not paid the rent; he had no employees; and he had no bank account until he opened one with $100 of his own money. Still, Ueberroth persisted.[1] Some people had trouble with Ueberroth's forceful and decisive style. Others found him to be the perfect manager—flexible and diplomatic when he needed to be, unwavering when he felt he was right.[2] The 1984 summer Olympic games are history now, and so is the $215 million surplus Ueberroth created.

Once again out of a job, Ueberroth accepted the job of commissioner of baseball, another challenging position. Why would he accept another such difficult job? The answer is simple. He is confident that he can succeed. Despite setbacks that would stop most people, his self-confidence remains stronger than ever. And while he acknowledges the potential for failure, he expects—and achieves—success. This winner's edge, a strong, positive self-concept, is the basis for high achievers in any organization.

Self-Concept Defined

"Love thy neighbor" is one of the world's greatest human relations principles. Yet most people forget that the phrase ends "as thyself." Those last two words are the foundation for accomplishing the first three. When your self-concept is positive, you will feel confident, free to express yourself without being overly concerned with others' reactions. You can work to fulfill your needs for achievement, strength, recognition, independence, and appreciation—to reach your greatest potential. If your self-concept is negative, you will tend to be plagued by doubts and anxieties that will limit your ability to achieve success.

Some social scientists believe that self-concept is closely connected to students' performance in school: Students with negative self-concepts tend to do less well than students with positive self-concepts.[3] And some believe that a negative self-concept can cause more serious problems throughout life. The California State Assembly recently voted to create a Self-Esteem Commission to promote self-esteem in individuals after hearing testimony that people with negative self-concepts are more likely to exhibit violent behavior, discriminate against others, abuse drugs and alcohol, and feel powerless and lethargic.[4] Although some researchers are finding that generalizations about self-concept and success can't be made as easily for females as they can for males,[5] and others are beginning to challenge the correlation between poor self-concept and delinquency,[6] it is clear that a negative self-concept can create barriers between friends, family, and business associates, leading to an inevitable breakdown in effective human relations. It's no wonder that Alfred Adler, a noted psychologist, has stated, "everything begins with self-esteem, your concept of yourself."[7]

Your **self-concept** is the organized, consistent set of ideas, attitudes, and feelings you have about yourself that influences the way you relate to others. Your self-concept comes from the roles you play in life, such as friend, brother or sister, daughter or son, employee or employer, student, researcher, athlete, leader, and so on. It includes the personality traits you believe you have, such as honesty, creativity, assertiveness, flexibility, and many more. Often, your self-concept is built on your physical characteristics along with your skills and abilities. Are you tall, slender, short, or heavy? Do you like what you see in the mirror? Are you good at writing, fixing appliances, researching topics, mathematics, or some other skill?

All of these components make up your self-concept. Although a positive self-concept is the basis for a healthy personality, it does not mean becoming egotistical, that is, thinking and acting with only your own interests in mind. Someone with such an orientation to the world sees everything and everyone in terms of their usefulness to the person's own aims and goals. Such egotism undermines good human relations; people become objects to be manipulated or used.

In an insurance office with five agents, a manager, and two secretaries, workers help one another to achieve personal and company goals. Everyone gets along well with everyone else—until the number one salesperson walks in each day. He has such a self-centered view of his work and himself that he expects other people in the office to drop everything and help him first. He'll leave a stack of letters on the secretary's desk and tell her, "I need

"HEY! C'MON, MAN! I'm 'arrogant, rude and smug' because I got LOW SELF-ESTEEM." (Reprinted by permission of Newspaper Enterprise Association, Inc.)

these typed by five." He ignores the fact she is already hard at work on correspondence for three other agents. He tells the manager how an important client should be handled even though the manager has known the client for over ten years. He may or may not speak to the other agents—they are not as successful, and he has important calls to make, so why waste time? This person's self-concept has passed beyond the bounds of healthy confidence and has become a negative, egotistic personality. In terms of human relations, he has become a liability to the company, even though he is successful as a salesperson.

An individual with a positive self-concept realizes the value of other people and the role they play in his or her success. Recognizing the difference between a positive self-concept and an egotistic personality is important in developing and maintaining good human relations.

How Your Self-Concept Is Formed

A Sunday school teacher once asked her class of small children, "Who made you?" Instead of giving the expected reply, an insightful child responded, "I'm not finished yet!" You are not born knowing who and what you are. You acquire your self-concept over time by constantly receiving messages about yourself from the people closest to you and your environment. Your natural abilities also play a part in developing your self-concept.

Childhood Your family is the earliest source of information about yourself that you receive. You heard your parents and others in the family describe your personal characteristics and actions. They told you that you were smart, good, talented, lovable—or that you were lazy, thoughtless, clumsy, irritating. Later, friends, teachers, and others outside the family added to the picture you were forming of yourself. In most cases, you probably did not stop and analyze these messages; you simply accepted them as true. As a result, your subconscious mind gradually developed a picture of yourself, whether accurate or distorted, that you came to believe as real.

> Everyone was once a child. Our experience today is filtered through the events and feelings of childhood, recorded in detail. We cannot have a feeling today that is "disconnected" from similar feelings recorded in the past, the most intense of which occurred to us in the first five years of life. This does not mean that today's feelings are not real, or that we are to discount them by claiming "they're just an old recording." We are today who we once were.[8]

The type of family discipline you grew up with probably had considerable effect on your self-concept. Interestingly enough, some psychologists have found that children brought up in a permissive environment tend to develop a *lower* self-concept than those raised in a firmer and more demanding home. Parental discipline is one way of telling children the parents care about them and what they do. When someone cares about you, you tend to think more positively about yourself.

The power of that early self-concept can have far-reaching effects in the course of a person's life. Irene Carpenter, the first woman elected a senior vice president in the ninety-year history of Citizens and Southern National Bank in Atlanta, recalls of her childhood: "My parents raised us to believe we could do anything we chose to do.... Many women in management do not start out with that concept of themselves. It has enabled me to overcome many of the obstacles I've encountered in the banking industry."[9]

The self-concept formed in childhood lays the foundation for your attitudes toward work, success, personal abilities, and the roles you play.

Adolescence The ages of twelve to twenty are among the most crucial in developing and consolidating your self-concept. During these years, you are moving away from the close bond between parent and child and are attempting to establish ideals of independence and achievement.[10] You must also deal with physical changes; relationships with peer groups; an emerging, often confusing identity; and the loss of childhood and assumption of some adult responsibilities. Is it any wonder that your self-concept seemed to

Total Person Insight	Many people go throughout life committing partial suicide—destroying their talents, energies, creative qualities. Indeed, to learn how to be good to oneself is often more difficult than to learn how to be good to others.
Joshua Liebman	

change not only day by day but hour by hour? In fact, many people never move beyond the self-image they gain in high school. Outwardly successful, they may still be trying to prove to their old classmates that they can "make it." For this reason, adolescent problems should not be underestimated, for it is in the resolution of these problems and conflicts that the self-concept of the adult is born.

It is also during these years that you are likely to have your first job experiences. Probably, you were extremely sensitive to what your boss and coworkers had to say about you—both the criticism and the praise. Henry Kaiser, founder of Kaiser Aluminum & Chemical Corporation, was told as a young stock boy that he would have to learn how to listen to orders better if he wanted a business career. His supervisor pointed out that he had good leadership potential, but as any top executive would advise, a good leader has to learn how to follow orders first. By comparing Kaiser with a top executive, his supervisor helped build the young man's self-concept as someone with leadership ability. And by pointing out a weakness Kaiser needed to correct, his supervisor helped ground that self-concept in the real world.

Adulthood By the time you reach your early twenties, your self-concept has been fairly well molded by your childhood and adolescent experiences. You are now concerned with achieving some of the goals you have identified earlier in your life. Also, you are expanding the roles that you play, taking on, perhaps, the role of wife, or husband and even parent. Work experiences and your relationships with your coworkers and supervisors can have a major impact on your attitude toward yourself. Doing a job well and being respected as a competent worker enhances your self-concept. On the other hand, a difficult work situation that provides few opportunities to experience success can diminish your self-respect and inhibit your ability to learn and develop your skills. Thus, spouses, coworkers, friends, and professional colleagues are among those who will continue to influence your self-concept throughout your life. In some cases, they may reinforce an already negative self-concept, whereas in others they may reaffirm the positive images you have built or help you correct an outmoded picture of your abilities and potential.

Dr. Denis Waitley, psychologist for the U.S. Olympic teams and well-known author and public speaker, discusses his changing self-concept.

> I've had my own struggles with a poor self-image. Even though my parents told me I was special, my peer group in grammar school and junior high told me different. They offered me such labels as "buzzard beak," "beaver teeth," "Waitley Come Lately.". . . During my plebe year at Annapolis the superlatives were, "Mr. Waitley, you couldn't lead a one-cadet parade," "You're so dense you couldn't lead a silent prayer!" or, "If your eyes were any closer together, we'd call you Cyclops." As I began to wear the labels others pinned on me, I began to play my own games. . . . In response to a birthday gift I would say, "You shouldn't have gone to all this trouble for ME." In response to a compliment, "Don't mention it. It was nothing." In response to a compliment on a great golf shot, "Yeah, bet I won't do that again!" After a seesaw career as a young adult, I finally learned to stop associating myself with external labels, negative self-talk, and humiliating self-presentation. In my early thirties, I began to talk affirmatively about my accomplishments and goals. I began to say "thank you" when other people would bestow any value upon me. I began to accept myself as a changing, growing, and worthwhile human being, imperfect but capable of becoming a Double Winner. And I began to feel good about myself.[11]

As an adult, you will be constantly adjusting your self-concept to the real world around you. It is important to be aware of how other people have influenced and will continue to influence your beliefs about yourself. You will need to learn how to protect your self-concept against those who try to diminish or limit your potential and how to listen to those who will encourage and challenge you. Such knowledge can help you distinguish between what is helpful and what is destructive, what is true and what is false in your current self-concept, and help you expand the range of what you believe you can be and do in the future.

Thinking/Learning Starters

1. Can you recall two or three people from your childhood or adolescence who had a positive effect on your self-concept? What did these people say or do? Were there any who had a negative effect on you? What did they say or do?
2. List all the roles you play in life—son, daughter, student, worker. Indicate how you feel about yourself in each role by putting a plus or minus sign after each one. Why do you feel the way you do about yourself in these roles?

Chuck Yeager is a good example of the power of a positive self-concept. Sick to his stomach the first few times he flew in a plane, he persevered and became the first pilot to fly faster than the speed of sound. (Photo © 1986 Anthony Loew)

A Positive Self-Concept and Success at Work

Your self-concept is a powerful factor influencing your choice of career and how well you progress in that career. According to Richard Grote, president of Performance Systems Corporation in Dallas, "People take you at the value you put on yourself. If you believe in your own power, other people will believe you and treat you with the respect you've provided for yourself."[12]

In an organizational setting, workers with positive self-concepts tend to do more than what is strictly required on the job. They are more receptive to new experiences, meeting new people, accepting responsibility, and making decisions. People who accept themselves usually have a greater ability to accept others, tolerate differences, share their thoughts and feelings, and respond to the needs of others. Such people contribute to the well-being and productivity of a group and can explore the opportunities offered by an organization.

On the other hand, workers with a negative self-concept can cause problems on several levels. They can affect the efficiency and productivity of a group because they tend to exercise less initiative, hesitate to accept responsibility or make decisions on their own, and may ask fewer questions and take longer to learn procedures. They often have trouble relating well to others. A self-rejecting person generally has a pessimistic view of human nature and may always be on the lookout for an insult or "attack" from someone else, an attitude that can cause interpersonal conflicts. Also, their lack of self-confidence can be misinterpreted by coworkers as unfriendliness. They may require more supervision because they are afraid of making a mistake or appearing ignorant if they ask questions. Even when offered a chance to receive training or career development courses, they may feel they are being singled out as workers who need more instruction than other employees.

Your Self-Concept Influences Your Behavior

When you accept what others say about you during your early years, these comments are "programmed" into your subconscious mind. You form a mental picture of yourself, which influences your behavior. Your subconscious mind does not evaluate what is put into it; it merely acts on the information it receives—good or bad.

Most people do not realize that this aspect of their mind represents a powerful creative capacity within their control. By controlling what goes into your subconscious mind, you can change your self-concept. This awareness can be used for positive or negative ends. For example, if you see yourself as a failure, you will use your creative capacity to find some way to fail. William Glasser, author of *Reality Therapy* and other books on human behavior, calls this the **failure syndrome.** No matter how hard you work for success, if your subconscious mind is saturated with thoughts and fears of failure, it will make your success impossible. On the other hand, if your subconscious has been intentionally or unintentionally programmed with positive thoughts to help you succeed, you will be able to overcome many barriers, even those considered handicaps, such as age or a disadvantaged background.

The late Colonel Harland Sanders of Kentucky Fried Chicken fame began his franchise business at an age when most people start collecting Social Security. He had been a moderately successful businessman but had little to show for it beyond the belief that people would buy his fried chicken prepared according to his secret recipe. All the conventional wisdom of the business community was against him. They told him he was too old; people wanted hamburgers, not chicken; his recipe was too spicy; the franchise market was already flooded with fast-food items; and he could never make it on his own.

But Colonel Sanders did not see himself settling down in a retirement home and sitting on the sidelines for his remaining years. He was so confident of his own judgment that he took the risk and started his own business. Within a few short years, his name was as familiar to consumers as McDonald's golden arches. Eventually, the colonel sold his franchise business for several million dollars.[13]

Although physical appearance, talents and abilities, background, and education all play a part in our success, *what we believe about ourselves* is the controlling factor that can override or undermine all the rest. This principle was vividly demonstrated by the work of the noted plastic surgeon Dr. Maxwell Maltz in his book, *Psycho-Cybernetics.* Throughout his twenty-five years of practice, Maltz operated on soldiers wounded in war, accident victims, and children with birth defects. Many of these individuals saw only their defects and could not believe they would ever be successful in life. In many cases, after he removed a scar or corrected some type of physical deformity, dramatic and sudden changes in personality resulted. Improving the person's physical image seemed to create an entirely new individual.

Yet, curiously, not all patients responded this way. Dr. Maltz discovered that for some, corrective surgery did little to change their low self-concept. The deformity continued to exist in the patient's mind. Further, some people came to see him who did not need plastic surgery at all. Their "deformity" was in their mental picture of themselves.

Maltz soon realized that if people could not reprogram their subconscious minds and change what they believed about themselves, plastic surgery would not help them. Once they understood how to use the creative power of their subconscious minds, their physical appearance became less important. The real change happened within; they began to believe in themselves.[14]

The Power of Expectations

Your thoughts about yourself are often expressed in terms of expectations— how far you believe you can go and what you feel you can do. Many behavioral psychologists agree that people's expectations about themselves have a significant impact on their performance and how much risk they are willing to take. If you set out to learn a new skill and expect to master it, chances are you will succeed. If you secretly believe you will fail, that expectation is also likely to come true. Once you have acquired an idea about your abilities and your character, you will tend to live up—or down—to your expectations.

Your Expectations

People tend to behave in a way that supports their own ideas of how successful or incompetent they are. This somewhat mysterious power of expectations is often referred to as the **self-fulfilling prophecy.** Your career successes and failures are directly related to your expectations about your future.

In looking over applications for an M.B.A. program, an admissions director noticed that some students had answered questions about their future plans with phrases such as, "I *plan* to . . ." or "I *will* . . ." Other students had written "I *hope* to . . ." The words used by the first group represented a statement of belief that they could achieve specific goals. Not surprisingly, their academic records and outside accomplishments showed that these students set and reached high performance levels. The second group of students had lower expectations and less confidence in their ability to accomplish their goals.[15]

The effect of self-fulfilling prophecies can be dramatic in terms of employees' career aspirations and personal development. More than one manager has witnessed the phenomenon of capable, talented employees refusing promotions or being afraid to move out of the positions they have occupied for a time. On the other hand, managers have also seen average employees become motivated to succeed. These workers achieve far more than their personnel records or the opinions of their coworkers indicated they could accomplish.

Joan would like to be promoted to assistant supervisor in her department. She has often thought about the position and what it would mean in terms of more responsibility, greater use of her skills, and an increase in salary. However, every time she starts to apply for the promotion, her self-doubts take over. Maybe she doesn't have enough power—what if she gave an order and someone refused to follow it? The competition is awfully tough. Company politics play a big part in who is promoted, and she doubts anyone would be willing to support her. Her self-fulfilling prophecy is, "Even if I got the job, which I doubt, I wouldn't be able to do it." As a result, Joan turns in her application for promotion, but "forgets" to fill out an important section. The application is refused. Her self-fulfilling prophecy keeps her in the same subordinate position she has filled for six years.

Positive expectations can lead to positive results. Natalie wanted to become a field representative for a computer hardware company, but lacked self-confidence and the ability to mix easily with other people. She finally decided that she could learn to become more outgoing and self-assured, just as she had learned the company's products inside and out. She enrolled in sales courses, practiced overcoming her shyness and reserve, watched and imitated other people who had the skills she wanted to cultivate, and acted as if she were confident even when inwardly nervous. At some point along the way, she began to *enjoy* talking with clients. She didn't have to worry about what to say or how to introduce herself.

Not long afterward, a field representative position in the company became available, and Natalie applied. When she was offered the position a week later, one of the interviewers commented on her "self-confidence and ability to relate well with others." She was launched on her new career.

The Expectations of Others

The self-fulfilling prophecy reflects a connection between your own expectations for yourself and your resulting behavior. But people can also be greatly influenced by the expectations of others. The influence of others, called the **Pygmalion Effect,** sometimes causes people to become what others expect them to become.

This term was first used by Dr. Robert Rosenthal, a professor at Harvard University, and is based on a Greek legend about Pygmalion, the king of Cyprus. In the legend, the king longs for an ideal wife. Since no mortal woman meets his expectations, he fashions a statue of his ideal woman out of ivory and eventually falls in love with his creation. His desire to make the statue his wife is so intense that his belief brings it to life.

Zig Ziglar, author and motivational speaker, tells his own Pygmalion story in his book, *See You at the Top*. Early in his career, Zig attended a sales training session conducted by P. C. Merrill. When the training session was over, Mr. Merrill took Zig aside and quietly told him, "You know, Zig, I've been watching you for two and a half years, and I have never seen such a waste. You have a lot of ability. You could be a great salesman and maybe even one of the best in the nation. There is no doubt in my mind if you really went to work and started believing in yourself, you could go all the way to the top."[16]

Zig described himself as an "average" person as far as intelligence or ability was concerned. He did not suddenly acquire a new set of skills that day, nor did his I.Q. jump 50 points. Zig admired and respected Merrill. When the man told him, "You can be a great salesman," Zig believed him and started seeing himself as a top salesperson. He began to think, act, and perform like one. Before the year was over, Zig ranked number two in a company of over seven thousand sales personnel. By the next year, he was one of the highest paid managers in the country and later became the youngest division supervisor in the nation. P. C. Merrill's image of Zig helped him see himself as someone special who had something to offer others. Merrill was Ziglar's Pygmalion.

Organizations are beginning to realize the impact of management expectations on employee performance. Many companies are redesigning their training programs to provide a supportive or enabling environment to foster and encourage positive expectations in employees. For example, in one company, data processing trainees were regularly told that it would take them three weeks to master the program and that they would be able to program about two hundred cards per hour. Not surprisingly, employees met those expectations precisely. They learned the program in three weeks and could process only two hundred cards per hour.

Then a new personnel director was hired, who scrapped the old training sessions, hired new trainers, and set up a program oriented toward increasing management expectations of employees. New recruits were told only that they could master the program quickly and were not given any limits on the number of cards per hour they could process. The new recruits learned the program in less than a week and by the end of the training session were programming five hundred cards per hour. The management realized the value of setting open expectations rather than limiting productivity in view of past performance. The self-fulfilling prophecy can have a powerful negative or positive effect.

Mentors

Mentors are people who have been where you want to go in your career and who are willing to act as your guide and friend. They take you under their wing and show you how to get to the next step in your career. They act as sponsors, teachers, devil's advocates, and coaches.

As sponsors, mentors will create opportunities for you to prove yourself. In an organization, this might mean they will ask you to help them on a project, analyze a problem, or make a presentation to higher levels of management. As teachers, mentors will present you with hypothetical situations and ask you, "What would you do?" An important part of the teaching responsibility is to explain both the written and unwritten rules of the organization. As devil's advocates, mentors challenge you and confront you to give you practice in asserting your ideas and influencing others. You can learn a variety of ways to gain acceptance of your ideas and tremendous self-confidence. Mentors can act as coaches, supporting your dreams, helping you find out what's important to you and what skills you have.

Although mentors are not mandatory for success, they certainly help. Research indicates that business executives with a mentoring relationship earn larger salaries, engage in more formal education, and are more likely to follow a systematic career path. They are also happier with their careers and derive more satisfaction from their work.[17]

At W. L. Gore & Associates, new employees are included in a "sponsor" system. A more experienced associate takes personal interest in the contributions, problems, and goals of the new associate. Everyone at Gore has a sponsor. President Bill Gore says, "As the number of associates grew, we had to find a way to help people get started and then to follow their progress." Ultimately, new associates in turn become sponsors for someone else, passing along the benefits they received from their own sponsors.[18]

Mentoring is an important part of the Management Readiness Program (MRP), a six-month career development program established at Merrill Lynch. One important goal of this program is to build bridges between high-level managers and employees. It helps participants learn about the firm's culture and career opportunities. Mentors at Merrill Lynch are department or higher-level managers who volunteer to serve as a counselor/advisor to four individuals during a six-month period. They agree to meet with these persons once a month in either group or individual meetings.[19]

There may be a person in your life who encouraged you to enter the business world. Chances are they didn't just say, "You should study business in college." They probably identified your strong points and helped you visualize yourself as a career person in business.

There will always be days when you feel nothing you do is right. Your mentor can help repair a damaged self-concept and encourage you to go on. With the power of another person's expectation reinforcing your own native abilities, it's hard to fail!

Thinking/Learning Starters

1. How have your expectations for yourself helped or hindered your development? Try to recall specific examples of thoughts that may be contributing to or detracting from your growth and development.
2. Can you identify a person in your life who has acted as a mentor? How did that person help you?

Building a Positive Self-Concept

Now that you are aware of the power your self-concept has over your life, can you take the next step—examining the image you have of yourself and identifying what might need to be changed? You wouldn't think of trying to fix a machine until you attempted to understand something about how the machine was supposed to work. On the other hand, you don't need to understand the machine completely before you try to make improvements. The same goes for your self-concept. Even though you may not be totally aware of your current self-concept and how it was formed, you can begin making plans for improving it.

It isn't easy to meet yourself face to face or to discuss your feelings about your inner self with others. But bringing your present self-image out into the open is the first step in understanding who you are, what you can do, and where you are going.

Each day can mean another step toward a more positive self-concept. The person you will be tomorrow has yet to be created. Most people continue to shape that future person in the image of the past, repeating the old limitations and negative patterns without realizing what they are doing. The development of a new, positive self-concept will not happen overnight, but it *can* happen. Such a change is the result of a slow evolution that begins with the desire to overcome a negative self-concept. Many people have proven that it is never too soon or too late to begin.

Peter Ueberroth, commissioner of baseball, has experienced both success and failure in his life. A positive self-concept has helped him rise up the ladder of success. (AP/Wide World Photos)

Characteristics of a Positive Self-Concept

When several leaders were asked about the qualities exhibited by people with positive self-concepts, they pointed out the following characteristics:

1. *They are future oriented and not overly concerned with past mistakes or failures.* They learn from their errors and are not immobilized by them. Every experience has something to teach—if you are willing to learn. A mistake can show you what doesn't work, what not to do. One consultant, asked whether he had obtained any results in trying to solve a difficult problem, replied, "Results? Why man, I've had lots of results. I know a hundred things that won't work!" The same principle applies to your own progress. Falling down does not mean failure. Staying down does.

2. *They are able to cope with life's problems and disappointments.* Successful people have come to realize that problems need not depress them or make them anxious. It is their attitude toward problems that makes all the difference. In his autobiography, Lee Iacocca recalls many disappointments. At the top of his list was the experience of being fired as president of Ford Motor Company after the firm had recorded two years of record profits. After being fired by Henry Ford he moved to Chrysler Corporation and brought the ailing company back from the brink of failure. Years later,

he recalled the loss of his job at Ford: "A lot has happened since July 13, 1978. The scars left by Henry Ford, especially on my family, will be lasting, because the wounds were deep. But the events of recent years have had a healing effect. So you move on."[20]

3. *They are able to feel all dimensions of emotion without letting those emotions affect their behavior in a negative way.* This characteristic is one of the major reasons people with a positive self-concept are able to establish and maintain effective human relations with the people around them. They realize emotions cannot be handled by repressing them or giving them free rein and lashing out at other people. You may feel better after such an explosion, but the people around you will not. While you may not be able to stop feeling what you feel, you can control your thoughts and actions while under the influence of a particularly strong emotion. Robert Conklin, author of *How to Get People to Do Things,* suggests keeping the following statement in mind: "I can't help the way I feel right now, but I *can* help the way I think and act."[21] Remembering this principle can help you bring an emotionally charged situation under control.

4. *They are able to help others and accept help.* People with a strong self-concept are not threatened by helping others to succeed nor are they afraid to admit weaknesses. If you are not good at dealing with figures, you can bring in an accountant who will manage the records. If you see someone whose abilities are not being used to their fullest, you can suggest ways in which the person will be able to develop his or her talents. An old adage in business goes, "First-rate people hire first-rate people. Second-rate people hire third-rate people." Individuals with a secure self-concept realize that in helping others succeed, they benefit themselves as well.

5. *They are skilled at accepting other people as unique, talented individuals.* People with good self-concepts learn to accept others for who they are and what they can do. A relationship built on mutual respect for one another's differences and strengths can help both parties grow and change. It is not a relationship that limits or confines either person. Acceptance of others is a good indication that you accept yourself.

Accepting the Past, Changing the Future

The first step toward a better self-concept is to accept yourself as you are now. The past cannot be changed, but the future is determined by how you think and act. Various techniques and theories have been developed to help people build a positive self-concept. None of these approaches offers a quick, easy route for changing your picture of yourself. You developed your present self-concept over many years; it will take time to change it. But the results can be well worth the effort. Some of the basic principles common to all approaches are summarized here.

Developing A Better Self-Concept:

Identify and Accept Your Limitations Part of building a positive self-concept is learning to tolerate limitations in yourself. This step reflects the process of becoming more realistic about who you are and what you can and cannot do. Demanding perfection of yourself can make you less tolerant of others' faults as well as your own. Also, failures and mistakes will take on undue importance, and you will be unable to put them in perspective as learning experiences.

Some women in business, such as Marcie Schorr Hirsch, director of career planning at Brandeis University, have decided they no longer want to live up to the "superwoman" image, juggling home, family, and career. They realize their time and energy are limited, and they are adjusting their schedules to accommodate those realities. She states: "I'm concerned about the quality of my existence. I'm willing to work hard; but I don't want to work so hard at everything that nothing gets done well, and I end up feeling like a failure."[22]

If you have a bad habit or some personal trait you dislike and wish to change, hate the activity but not yourself. Hating yourself tends to make the habit worse. If you condemn yourself for being weak, how can you muster the strength to change? However, if you become an "observer" and view the activity as separate from yourself, you leave your self-concept intact while you work on changing the behavior. Acting as an observer and detaching yourself from negative thoughts and actions can help you break the habit of rating yourself according to some scale of perfection and enable you to substitute more positive and helpful thoughts.

Visualize the Results You Want The power to visualize is in a very real sense the power to create. We often visualize ourselves succeeding or failing in some enterprise without knowing that such mental pictures can affect our behavior.

Peter Egan, Senior Editor of *Road and Track* magazine, recalls the point in his life when he decided to become a race-car driver. He didn't own a race car, had little money, but started to visualize himself driving a race car. His first step was to spend $99.95 on a Nomex driver's suit. He explains why he purchased the suit: "This was a bold move for a guy who didn't own a racing car and was then dragging down, easily, two figures per week as an assistant rain gutter installer and backyard mechanic. Nevertheless, I drove home from Elkhart Lake, hung the driver's suit on the back of the closet door where I couldn't miss seeing it every day and began to look for a racing car."[23] Several months later, Peter Egan purchased a race car and went racing.

Olympic star Mary Lou Retten mentally rehearses before each gymnastic event. She visualizes the perfect performance in her imagination then steps onto the mat to carry out the routine just as she had imagined it. Salespeople often close the sale in advance. Some hosts plan the party in advance. When it comes time for the actual performance, the mentally rehearsed events have become habits. Your concept of yourself is no exception. Visualize the be-

Recognized as one of the nation's most determined and successful teachers, Marva Collins opened her own inner city school where very high standards are demanded from students. (UPI/Bettmann News Photos)

haviors you want to exhibit. When you consciously decide to build a positive self-concept, you are harnessing the mind's creative force to work for you. You are constructing an image of your ideal self and imagining all the qualities and skills you would like to have. Although it sounds like an exercise in fantasy, it is an accepted fact that mental practice has improved the performances of salespeople, executives, and others in the business community.[24] These individuals visualized themselves meeting new clients, talking in front of groups, improving their business skills, and becoming more relaxed and confident.

Set Goals Just Out of Reach, But Not Out of Sight   A person without goals is like a football team without a game plan. Can you imagine the Dallas Cowboys running onto the field, hoping that someone else would show them how to get the ball into the end zone. By visualizing who you want to be, you have already begun your life's game plan. The secret to goal setting is very simple: Establish clearly defined goals, write them down, then dwell on them morning and night with words, pictures, and emotions. Break down long-term goals into several attainable short-term goals. The feeling of success you will gain from achieving those goals will spur you on to set and attain even higher ones.

Richard Grote recommends that at the beginning you set moderate goals for yourself. "Set reasonable objectives for each hour, each day, each week.

Keeping long-term sights in mind is important, but don't put unnecessary obstacles in your way by setting objectives too high. People who don't reach those high goals many times feel like failures."[25]

It often helps to internalize these goals by writing **affirmations** for each of your goals. Affirmations are short statements declaring qualities you want to develop. They need to be formed with a first-person pronoun, a present-tense verb, and a vivid picture of the end results you want to achieve. For instance:

▶ I keep the commitments I make.
▶ I am feeling healthier every day.
▶ I am slim and trim.
▶ I feel confident.
▶ I am an effective and assertive salesperson.

Write affirmations for every facet of your personal and professional life. Put them on three-by-five-inch index cards and attach them to your bathroom mirror, refrigerator, car dashboard, desk blotter, and so on. Another technique for absorbing these thoughts rapidly is to record your affirmations on a blank cassette tape while quiet, one-beat-per-second music (largo) is playing in the background.[26] Play the tape repeatedly, especially when you are in a relaxed state, for example, just before you fall asleep at night, before you get up in the morning, or while you are driving on a boring interstate highway. Your brain is like a computer. It will "put out" exactly what you "put in." Put positive affirmations in and positive behavior will result.

Make Decisions Psychologists have found that children who were encouraged to make their own decisions early in their lives have a stronger self-concept than those who were kept dependent on their parents for a longer period of time. Making decisions helps you develop confidence in your own judgment and enables you to explore options.

At age thirty, Mary Boone is one of the most successful art dealers in the United States. Her galleries are showplaces. But she can recall a time when her self-confidence was conspicuously lacking. "In a family of three girls," she states, "I was the oldest and homeliest." Her mother helped develop her artistic abilities, but Boone found she had more talent for organizing other students' shows than for her own painting.

After a few years as an assistant art dealer in New York, she made the decision to open a gallery of her own. "I had a great ambivalence about making art a business. But I realized that [art] dealing had become important to me. Not knowing what you're going to do is like not knowing who you are," Boone says. "When I opened the gallery, I'd found my place in life."

The painters whose work she exhibits agree. As one commented, "In a business like this, clients are as much buying the vision of the dealer as they're buying the work. They look into her eyes and they think . . . 'she really believes what she's saying.' "[27]

Take every opportunity you can to make decisions both in setting your goals and in devising ways to achieve them. Organizations with supportive management personnel encourage decision making at the lowest level in order to develop more employee initiative and self-management skills. Along with making decisions, be willing to accept the consequences of your actions, positive or negative.

Develop Expertise in Some Area Developing "expert power" not only builds your self-concept but increases the value of your contribution to the organization. Identify and cultivate a skill or talent you have whether it is a knack for interviewing people, a facility with math, or good verbal skills. Alice Young, a resident partner in the law firm of Graham & James in New York, developed an expertise in her youth that she didn't know would be a major asset in her career. "I speak Japanese, Chinese, French, and English," she says. "I have a knowledge of Asian cultures that I developed before trade with the East opened up." She has been able to capitalize on her expertise to help American and Asian companies do business with one another and to smooth over many cultural differences that would otherwise make negotiations difficult if not impossible. She advises others to "use what you know to benefit yourself and your company."[28]

Developing expertise may involve continuing your studies after completing your formal education. Some professions offer advanced courses to enable people to advance in their careers. For example, the Institute of Financial Education conducts courses for persons employed by financial institutions.

Steps Organizations Are Taking

Organizations are beginning to include information on building a positive self-concept in their employee and management training sessions. R. J. Reynolds, Deere & Company, IBM, Shell Oil, and Calgon, to name just a few, realize the impact of self-concept on a worker's ability to learn and grow.

Employees at all levels, from secretaries to janitors to management trainees, are given the opportunity to look at themselves and remove some of the self-limiting barriers to using their abilities. They are encouraged to consider new areas of work and responsibility as well as to acquire new skills. William J. Rothwell, a special services officer in the Illinois Office of the General Auditor, has found that one of the main reasons people seek training is the desire to increase their self-esteem. He sees this as an opportunity for management to encourage workers to build their self-concept. "We can emphasize to participants the strengths of training as a means of unlocking creativity and hidden potential."[29]

Research clearly shows that the highly skilled high-tech employees of the future will need more than training and high salaries to maintain their high self-esteem.[30] Today, organizations are adopting long-range plans for investing in their people as well as their physical plants. They realize that employees with high self-esteem are more creative, more energetic, and more committed to both the work and the organization. While boosts to self-esteem may come from technical achievements, they must also come from other sources, such as increased opportunities for decision making and more personalized management-employee relationships.

Effective organizations are demonstrating to employees that their opinions and views matter and their ideas are being implemented in significant ways. They make sure that each person feels cared about through warm, empathic relationships and open two-way communication that expresses feelings as well as facts. Organizations need to help employees feel they are accomplishing their own goals while helping the organization reach its highest productivity. By constantly reinforcing these visible and recognized goals, organizations will be able to meet the self-esteem needs of their employees.

Summary

Self-concept is the organized, consistent set of ideas, attitudes, and feelings you have about yourself. It includes the roles you play and your personality traits, physical appearance, skills, and abilities. A healthy and positive self-concept is the foundation for a successful life and good human relations. Organizations are beginning to recognize the impact of employees' self-concepts on their ability to learn and contribute to the organization's productivity.

People acquire and build their self-concept every day of their lives from the day they are born. Parents, friends, associates, and professional colleagues all influence the development of a person's self-concept. Most of this process takes place in the subconscious mind; people do not objectively evaluate the information they take in. As a result, their self-concept may represent an accurate reflection of their true abilities or a negative and distorted image.

A positive self-concept is essential for success in an organization. People's self-concepts are often expressed in terms of expectations—how much or how little they believe they can do. These expectations can become self-fulfilling prophecies. The power of other people's expectations can result in a Pygmalion Effect in which an individual lives up to the image another has of him or her. Mentors can strengthen a person's self-concept by expressing belief in that individual's abilities and talents. They can act as sponsors, teachers, devil's advocates, and coaches. Managers in organizations can act as Pygmalions and mentors to employees and provide a supportive or enabling environment for strengthening workers' self-concepts.

Building a positive self-concept is important both personally and professionally. People who have a positive self-concept tend to be future oriented, able to cope with problems creatively, handle their emotions, give and receive help, and accept others as unique, talented individuals. Although there are many approaches to changing a negative self-concept into a positive one, such as making positive affirmations, certain underlying principles are common to all. These principles include identifying and accepting personal limitations, visualizing positive results, setting goals, making decisions, and developing an expertise in one area.

Key Terms

self-concept   Pygmalion Effect
failure syndrome   mentors
self-fulfilling prophecy   affirmations

Review Questions

1. What is a positive self-concept? Why is the development of a positive self-concept important in a person's life?
2. What influences help shape a person's self-concept?
3. How do the expectations of yourself and others affect your self-concept? Give examples from your own life.
4. What are some of the qualities that you feel people with positive self-concepts exhibit?
5. Why are organizations concerned about employees' self-concepts? In what ways are they helping workers build positive images of themselves?
6. Do you believe you can change your self-concept once you reach adulthood? If so, what actions can you take to make your self-concept more positive?
7. Do you agree with the statement, "People tend to take you at the value you put on yourself; if you believe in your own potential abilities, so will others"? Explain your answer.
8. Look over the basic principles of building a positive self-concept. Which ones would be the easiest for you to achieve? Why? Which ones would be the most difficult? Why?
9. What role does the subconscious mind play in developing and changing a person's self-concept?
10. How can visualization help change a person's behavior and self-concept?

■■■■■■■
Case 4.1

Unmanagement at W. L. Gore & Associates[31]

When Bill Gore founded his company, he "set out to recreate the sense of excited commitment, personal fulfillment, and self-direction" for his employees that he had in his own work life. His company is organized around a "lattice" system of management in which there are no titles, orders, or bosses. Everyone who works there deals directly with everyone else, crossing over traditional horizontal and vertical lines of authority.

Associates, as all Gore employees are called, choose an area in the company that they feel best matches their interests, skills, and abilities. Then they are urged to develop their potential to the fullest. "We don't manage people here," Bill Gore says, "people manage themselves. We organize ourselves around voluntary commitments."

Gore found that the lattice system worked well until the number of associates reached about two hundred. At that point, human relations and worker satisfaction began to suffer, and the group became less cooperative. Instead of adding layers of management to the company, however, Gore opened another plant. As the number of associates dropped to one hundred and fifty, morale lifted and workers felt part of the team again. Each time the number of associates exceeded two hundred, Gore opened another plant. He has opened a total of twenty plants, including the first, and has seven more under construction.

How is the system working? Sales have neared $125 million, and the company is profitable. Customers state that the lattice management system leads to trouble with day-to-day operations at times, but they admit they have "seen at Gore remarkable examples of people coming out of nowhere and excelling."

For the employees, the lattice is difficult to describe; it's "a feeling, a state of mind." And if that means a sense of excitement and personal growth, that, as much as anything, is what Bill Gore set out to create.

Questions

1. List some of the ways that employees at Gore are encouraged to develop and expand a positive self-concept.

2. Bill Gore found that when the company grew too large, it had a negative effect on workers. Besides making employees feel more anonymous, why would size tend to affect workers negatively? What impact might it have on their self-concepts?

3. What would you say are Bill Gore's expectations about the people who come to work for him?

Case 4.2

When Stepping Up Means Speaking Out

Last year Ms. McKenzie, marketing director for Thornberg Department Stores, suggested to Michael Wilson that he apply for a transfer from the Thornberg advertising division into her merchandising display department. She had seen some of Michael's creative ideas for window displays and felt he could be a valuable asset to the department.

Michael respected Ms. McKenzie's opinion and had often daydreamed about being the head of a display department himself. But he had never taken his dreams seriously until now. His father and two brothers were all in sales and advertising; they considered the display area too "lightweight" to be a real career field.

Michael talked to his manager about transferring to Ms. McKenzie's department. He was not encouraging. "Moving from advertising into display could be seen as a step down," he told Michael. "It could hurt your career chances later on. Besides, are you really sure you have the ability? One bad display can really hurt the store's image." By the end of the conversation, Michael had dropped the idea of transferring.

He went back to his regular duties, but he could not get over the feeling that he had given in too quickly. It seemed he had always heard other people say, "You can't do that." Why couldn't he speak for what *he* wanted? He resented the advertising manager's negative evaluation of his abilities. Soon his attitude toward his coworkers became sullen and withdrawn.

A month after Ms. McKenzie's words of encouragement, Michael's productivity is down, and he is frequently late for work. His motivation to achieve personal and company goals is at an all-time low.

Questions

1. Describe Michael's basic self-concept. How is that self-concept affecting his performance and relationships at work?
2. What part could Ms. McKenzie play in Michael's life? What part does his manager seem to be playing?
3. What would you advise Michael to do at this point? Outline the options he has and the actions he could take to renew his career development.

Notes

1. *Current Biography*, April 1985, p. 37.
2. Ibid., pp. 38–39.
3. William Watson Purkey, *Self-Concept and School Achievement* (Englewood Cliffs, N.J.: Prentice-Hall, 1970), pp. 14–17.
4. "Trouble in Paradise," *Training and Development Journal*, December 1984, p. 12.
5. Purkey, *Self Concept and School Achievement*, pp. 14–17.

6. Judy Folkenberg, "Delinquency and Self-Dislike," *Psychology Today*, May 1985, p. 16.

7. A. H. Maslow, "A Theory of Human Motivation," in *Psychological Foundations of Organizational Behavior*, ed. Barry M. Staw (Santa Monica, Calif.: Goodyear Publishing, 1977), pp. 7–8.

8. Amy Bjork Harris and Thomas A. Harris, *Staying OK* (New York: Harper and Row, 1985), p. 24.

9. Sue Baugh, "Cool Path to the Top," *NABW Journal*, January-February 1982, pp. 28–30.

10. Margaret Hennig and Anne Jardin, *The Managerial Woman* (New York: Anchor Books, 1977), pp. 106–107.

11. Denis Waitley, *The Double Win* (Old Tappan, N.J.: Revell, 1985), pp. 76–77.

12. "How to Gain Power and Support in the Organization," *Training/HRD*, January 1982, p. 13.

13. Zig Ziglar, *See You at the Top* (Gretna, La.: Pelican Publishing, 1975), p. 99.

14. Maxwell Maltz, *Psycho-Cybernetics* (New York: Pocket Books, 1972), pp. 6–7.

15. Natasha Josefowitz, *Paths to Power* (New York: Addison-Wesley, 1980), pp. 66–67.

16. Ziglar, *See You at the Top.*

17. Breda Murphy Bova and Rebecca R. Phillips, "Mentoring as a Learning Experience for Adults," *Journal of Teacher Education*, May/June 1984, p. 17.

18. Lucien Rhodes, "The Un-Manager," *INC.*, August 1982, p. 38.

19. Caela Farren, Janet Dreyfus Gray, and Beverly Kaye, "Mentoring: A Boon to Career Development," *Personnel*, November/December 1984, p. 22.

20. Lee Iacocca with William Novak, *IACOCCA* (New York: Bantam Books, 1984), p. 137.

21. Robert Conklin, *How to Get People to Do Things* (Chicago: Contemporary Books, 1979), p. 69.

22. Anita Shreve, "Careers and the Lure of Motherhood," *New York Times Magazine*, November 21, 1982, pp. 38–43, 46–52, 56.

23. Peter Egan, "Return of the Bugeye, Part I," *Road and Track*, June 1985, p. 192.

24. Albert Ellis and Robert A. Harper, *A New Guide to Rational Living* (North Hollywood, Calif.: Wilshire Book Company, 1975), pp. 210–215.

25. Richard Grote, "Make Sure Training Builds Self-Esteem and Peer Acceptance," *Training/HRD*, December 1981, p. 13.

26. Sheila Ostrander and Lynn Schroeder, *Superlearning* (New York: Dell Publishing, 1979), pp. 87–109.

27. Maggie Pale, "Mary Boone: A Confident Vision," *Savvy*, July 1982, pp. 62–67.

28. Cheri Burns, "The Extra Edge," *Savvy*, December 1982, p. 42.

29. "Make Sure Training Builds Self-Esteem," p. 13.

30. Pete Bradshaw and Sandra Shullman, "Managing High-Tech Employees Through Self-Esteem," *Infosystems*, March 1983, pp. 111–112.

31. Rhodes, "the Un-Manager," pp. 34–46.

Suggested Readings

Dyer, Wayne W. *Your Erroneous Zones*. New York: Funk & Wagnalls, 1976.

Ellis, Albert, and Robert A. Harper. *A New Guide to Rational Living*. North Hollywood, Calif.: Wilshire Book Company, 1975.

Gray, James, Jr. *The Winning Image*. New York: AMACOM, 1982.

Jongeward, Dorothy, and Dru Scott. *Women as Winners*. Menlo Park, Calif.: Addison-Wesley, 1979.

Jongeward, Dorothy, and Philip Seyer. *Choosing Success: Transactional Analysis on the Job*. New York: Wiley, 1978.

Maltz, Maxwell. *Psycho-Cybernetics*. New York: Pocket Books, 1972.

Waitley, Denis. *The Winner's Edge: How to Develop the Critical Attitude of Success*. New York: Times Books, 1980.

Chapter 5

Understanding Your Communication Style

Chapter Preview

After studying this chapter, you will be able to

1. Understand the concept of communication style bias and its effect on interpersonal relations in organizations.
2. Realize the personal benefits derived from an understanding of communication styles.
3. Discuss the major elements of the communication style model.
4. Identify your preferred communication style.
5. Avoid communication style bias through style flexing.

Ted Turner is a freewheeling Southern entrepreneur who has been described as Atlanta's "town character." In a city where gentle manners and discretion are valued in the conduct of business and public life, Turner displays a brash and confrontational style. He is bold, entertaining, and envied for his ability to accept challenges and win them. After his father's suicide in 1963, he took over the family's struggling billboard business and parlayed it into a sports and communication empire that is today worth millions of dollars.[1] In the late 1970s, he polished his yachting skills so that he and his crew were able to successfully defend the America's Cup. In 1980 he gambled nearly everything he was making from his Atlanta-based television station to launch the 24-hour Cable News Network. Although CNN lost money for several years, it is today nearly in the black.

In 1985, Ted Turner raised the curtain on what would become one of the most dramatic takeover bids in America's history. He announced that he would try to take over Columbia Broadcasting System, then the country's top-rated TV network.[2] (This never did come to pass, however.) In recent years Turner has toned down his brash, outspoken manner in an effort to gain the support of Wall Street's conservative money lenders. He is "flexing" his communication style in order to gain greater acceptance from others.

Communication Styles: An Introduction

Have you ever wondered why it seems so difficult to talk with some people, and so easy to talk with others? Can you recall a situation where you met someone for the first time and immediately liked the person? Something about the individual made you feel comfortable. You may have had this experience when you started a new job or began classes at a new school. A major goal of this chapter is to help you understand the impact your communication style has on the impression you make on others.

Communication Style Defined

The impressions that others form about us are based on what they observe us saying and doing. They have no way of knowing our innermost thoughts and feelings, so they make decisions about us based on what they see and hear.[3] The name we will give to the patterns of behaviors that others can observe is **communication style.**

Each person has a unique communication style. By getting to know your style, you can achieve greater self-awareness and learn how to develop more effective human relations with your coworkers.

It is sometimes difficult for us to realize that people can be different from us and yet not be inferior. Understanding other people's communication styles improves working relationships by increasing one's acceptance of other people and their way of doing things. Ted Turner is a bold, assertive person who frequently voices strong opinions. The person who is less assertive, more reserved, and less inclined to express strong views may find Turner's style difficult to cope with.

In recent years, thousands of people have sought to improve their interpersonal relationship skills through the study of communication styles. They seek not only greater awareness of their own style but greater sensitivity to and tolerance for other persons' styles. And they learn how to use their style to advantage in organizational settings.

Fundamental Concepts Supporting Communication Style Theory

This is very likely your first opportunity to study communication styles, so a review of a few basic principles that support communication style theory will be helpful. Some of these principles follow:[4]

1. *Individual differences exist and are important.* Length of eye contact, use of gestures, speech patterns, facial expressions, and the degree of assertiveness people project to others are some of the characteristics of a personal communication style. Findings from behavioral science research indicate that these factors form a unique image of the speaker that others perceive. For example, every person's voice has a distinct tone, pitch, tempo, and volume. When a friend or acquaintance calls you on the telephone, you can often tell almost immediately who it is by the voice.

Janet Elsea, in her book entitled *The Four-Minute Sell*, explains in detail how we nonverbally communicate impressions to those we come into contact with.[5] Voice patterns, eye movement, facial expression, and posture are some of the components of our communication style. Additional characteristics will be discussed later in this chapter.

2. *Individual style differences tend to be stable.* The basics of communication style theory were established by the famous Swiss psychiatrist Carl Jung. In his classic book, *Psychological Types*, he stated that every individual develops a primary communication style that remains quite stable throughout life. Each person has a relatively distinctive way of responding to people and events.[6] Some people find this hard to believe. They say, "I'm a different person every day," or "I act differently when I'm with parents than with my friends." From day to day you may feel differently about yourself and act differently around other people, but your basic communication style nevertheless remains stable throughout your life.

Lee Iacocca, president of Chrysler Corporation, provides a good example of someone who has displayed remarkable consistency in his communication style. He is a strong-willed and assertive person who projects a serious attitude. He uses firm hand gestures, earthy language, and a tone of voice that communicates the message, "I'm in charge!" In 1961, taking a major gamble with his career, he sold Henry Ford on the idea of producing the Mustang—

Lee Iacocca fits the description of the director communication style. He expresses strong opinions and projects the image of someone who wants to take charge. (Photo courtesy of Chrysler Corp.)

a move that would pay off in record sales and help edge him up to the presidency at Ford. Later, as president of Chrysler, he persuaded Congress to approve a $1.2 billion federal loan that helped save the ailing auto company.

Carol Burnett's acting career has spanned many years. This well-known television and movie personality is outspoken, enthusiastic, and very stimulating. She tends to develop social relationships quickly and feels comfortable in an informal atmosphere. Throughout her long acting career, she has expressed her opinions dramatically and impulsively.

Our communication style is based on a combination of hereditary and environmental factors. At the time of birth, the style we inherit is already partially formed. It takes on additional uniqueness during the first three to five years of our life. As a child, you may be encouraged to make most of your own decisions and become a self-reliant person. On the way to becoming an independent person, you might learn that considerable assertiveness is necessary to achieve your goals. Once developed, this personal trait is likely to be part of your communication style throughout life.

3. *There are a limited number of styles.* Jung observed that people tend to fall into one of several behavior patterns when relating to the world around them. Those in the same behavior category tend to display similar traits. One of Jung's categories was labeled "thinking." The thinker places a high value on facts, figures, and reason. This person is not apt to leap to conclusions but likes to "sleep on it." He or she tends to follow an orderly approach to task completion. Very often the thinker is seen by others as cautious, structured, and rigid. On the positive side, the thinker is viewed as precise, deliberate, and well disciplined.

4. *Everyone makes judgments about others based on their communication styles.* As we noted earlier, when people meet you for the first time, they form an immediate impression. This impression tends to influence how the other person will react to you. In the book, *Contact: The First Four Minutes,* Leonard and Natalie Zunin contend that the pattern of communications in the first few minutes is critical. A first impression is often formed in less than four minutes. If you enter a restaurant and the hostess greets you with a smile and a pleasant "Hello," you will no doubt experience a positive feeling toward this person and, in a more subtle sense, toward the restaurant. Assuming the food and service are also pleasant, chances are you'll want to return.

Although style is stable, you can learn to work cooperatively with people who have different styles. Also, by understanding your own style, you can learn to adapt it to fit other persons' needs. This is called "style flexing," which will be discussed later in this chapter.

Learning to Cope with Communication Style Bias

Several forms of bias exist in our society. People over forty sometimes complain that they are victims of age discrimination. Sex bias problems have made headlines for several years. And members of minority groups—blacks, Hispanics, and native Americans—say that racial and ethnic bias is still a fact of life today. Communication style bias represents another common form of prejudice.

Almost everyone experiences **communication style bias** from time to time. The bias is apt to surface when you meet someone who displays a style distinctly different from your own. For example, a quiet, reflective person may feel overwhelmed by an individual who displays a dynamic, outgoing style.

However, if the person receiving your message has the same communication style as yours, you will probably have a much better chance of understanding each other. The message is less likely to be misunderstood.[7] Using the analogy of radio, you are both on the same wave length.

At this point, you may be saying to yourself, "But in the world of work, I

To improve communication, it is often necessary to adjust your own style to meet the needs of others. (Photo by Barbara Alper, Stock Boston, Inc.)

don't have a choice—I have to get my message across to all kinds of people no matter what their communication style is." Office receptionists must deal with a variety of people throughout each day. Bank loan officers cannot predict who will walk into their offices at any given time.

How can you learn to cope with communication style bias? First, you must develop awareness of your own unique style. As we noted in Chapter 1, self-awareness is a major key to developing good human relations. Knowledge of your communication style can give you a fresh perspective and set the stage for improved relations with others. Second, you must learn to assess the communication style of those people with whom you have contact. Through careful observation and listening, you can pick up enough clues to identify the communication style of the other person. Third, you can adjust your own style to accommodate another's needs. The material that follows will help you develop these skills.

The Communication Style Model

In this section you will be introduced to a model that encompasses four basic communication styles. This simple model is based on research studies conducted over the past fifty years and features two important dimensions of human behavior: dominance and sociability.

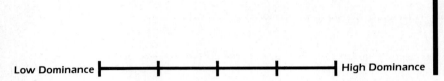

Figure 5.1
Dominance Continuum

Source: Gerald L. Manning and Barry L. Reece, *Selling Today: A Personal Approach*

The Dominance Continuum

In study after study, those "differences that make a difference" in interpersonal relationships point to dominance as an important dimension of style.* Dominance is defined as the tendency to display a "take charge" attitude. Every person falls somewhere on the **dominance continuum,** illustrated in Figure 5.1. David W. Johnson, in his book *Reaching Out*, states that people tend to fall into two dominance categories.[8]

1. *Low dominance*. These individuals are characterized by a tendency to be cooperative and eager to assist others. They tend to be low in assertiveness and are more willing to be controlled by others.

2. *High dominance*. These people give advice freely and frequently initiate demands. They are more assertive and tend to seek control over others.

The first step in determining your most preferred communication style is to identify where you fall on the dominance continuum. Do you tend to be low or high on this scale? To answer this question, complete the dominance indicator form in Figure 5.2. Rate yourself on each scale by placing a checkmark at a point along the continuum that represents how you perceive yourself. If most of your checkmarks fall to the right of center, you rank high in dominance. If most fall to the left of center, you are someone who is low in dominance.

Another way to assess the dominance dimension is to ask four or five people who know you well to complete the dominance indicator form for you. This approach may provide a more accurate indication of where you fall on the dominance continuum. It is often difficult to stand outside ourselves and make accurate observations. Self-assessment alone is sometimes inaccurate because we often do not see ourselves objectively.[9] Once you

---

*The dominance factor was described in an early book by William M. Marston, *The Emotions of Normal People* (New York: Harcourt, 1928). Research conducted by Rolfe La Forge and Robert F. Suczek resulted in the development of the Interpersonal Check List that features a dominant-submissive scale. A person who receives a high score on the ICL tends to lead, persuade, and control others. The Interpersonal Identity Profile, developed by David W. Merrill and James W. Taylor, features a factor called "assertiveness." Persons classified as being high in assertiveness tend to have strong opinions, make quick decisions, and be directive when dealing with people. Persons classified as being low in assertiveness tend to voice moderate opinions, make thoughtful decisions, and be supportive when dealing with others.

I Perceive Myself as Somewhat

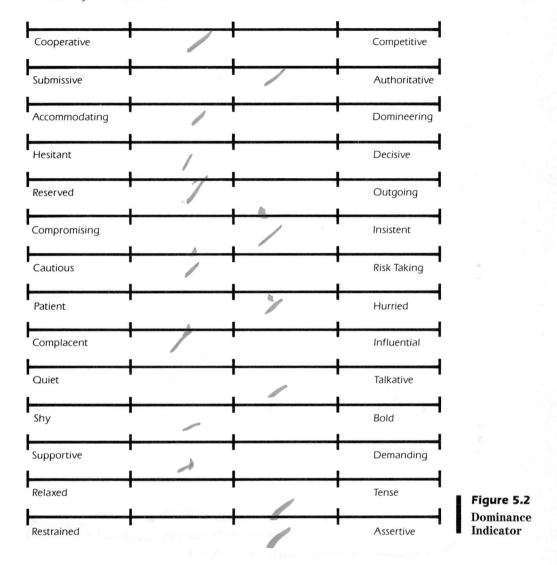

Cooperative				Competitive
Submissive				Authoritative
Accommodating				Domineering
Hesitant				Decisive
Reserved				Outgoing
Compromising				Insistent
Cautious				Risk Taking
Patient				Hurried
Complacent				Influential
Quiet				Talkative
Shy				Bold
Supportive				Demanding
Relaxed				Tense
Restrained				Assertive

Figure 5.2
Dominance
Indicator

have received the forms completed by others, try to determine if a consistent pattern exists. (Note: It is best not to involve parents, spouses, or close relatives. Seek feedback from coworkers or classmates.)

The Dominance Factor in an Organizational Setting

Is there any best place to be on the dominance continuum? Not really. Successful people can be found at all points along the continuum. However, there are times when we need to act decisively in order to influence the adoption of our ideas and communicate clearly our expectations. This means that someone low in dominance may need to become more assertive temporarily in order to achieve an objective. New managers who are low in dominance must learn how to influence others without being viewed as aggressive or manipulative. The American Management Associations offer a course entitled "Assertive Training for Managers," which is designed for managers who want to exercise a greater influence on others, get their proposals across more effectively, and resolve conflict situations decisively, yet diplomatically.[10] Persons low in dominance may need to learn how to be responsive to others without giving up their own convictions.

Persons who are high in dominance must sometimes curb their desire to express strong opinions and initiate demands. A person who is perceived as being extremely strong willed and inflexible may fail to establish a cooperative relationship. In an organizational setting, it is important to learn how to get the job done without stepping on toes.

Thinking/Learning Starters

1. On a sheet of paper, list the names of two people you know who are low in dominance. These persons will be characterized by a tendency to be quiet, reserved, and accommodating. Then list the names of two people who are high in dominance. These persons will be characterized by a tendency to be outspoken, assertive, and demanding.
2. Complete the dominance indicator form shown in Figure 5.2 for each of the people you have listed.

The Sociability Continuum

Have you ever met someone who was open, talkative, and seemed easy to get to know? An individual who is friendly and expresses feelings openly can be placed near the top of the **sociability continuum.*** The continuum is illustrated in Figure 5.3. Sociability can be defined as one's tendency to seek and enjoy social relationships with others.

---

*The research conducted by La Forge and Suczek resulted in identification of the hostile/loving continuum, which is similar to the sociability continuum. Their Interpersonal Check List features this scale. L. L. Thurstone and T. G. Thurstone developed the Thurstone Temperament Schedule that provides an assessment of a "sociable" factor. Persons with high scores in this area enjoy the company of others and make friends easily. The Interpersonal Identity Profile developed by Merrill and Taylor contains an objectivity continuum. A person with low objectivity is seen as attention seeking, involved with the feelings of others, informal, and casual in social relationships. A person who is high in objectivity tends to be indifferent toward the feelings of others. This person is formal in social relationships.

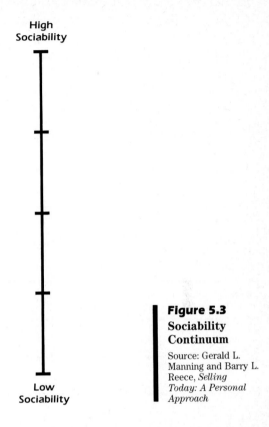

Figure 5.3
Sociability Continuum

Source: Gerald L. Manning and Barry L. Reece, *Selling Today: A Personal Approach*

Sociability can also be thought of as a measure of whether you tend to control or express your feelings. Those high in sociability will usually express their feelings freely, whereas people low on the continuum tend to control their feelings. The person who is classified as being high in the area of sociability is open, talkative, and likes personal associations. The person who is low in sociability is more reserved and formal in social relationships. Charles Margerison, author of *How to Assess Your Managerial Style*, says that high sociability is an indication of a person's preference to interact with other people. He says low sociability is an indicator of a person's desire to work in an environment where you have more time to yourself rather than having to make conversation with others.[11]

The second step in determining your most preferred communication style is to identify where you fall on the sociability continuum. To answer this question, complete the sociability indicator form shown in Figure 5.4. Rate yourself on each scale by placing a checkmark at a point along the continuum that represents how you perceive yourself. If most of your checkmarks fall to the right of center, you are someone who is high in sociability. If most fall to the left of center, you are low in sociability.

I Perceive Myself as Somewhat

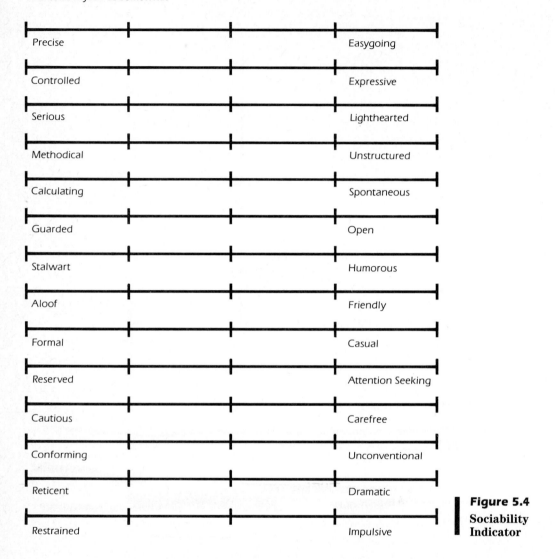

Precise				Easygoing
Controlled				Expressive
Serious				Lighthearted
Methodical				Unstructured
Calculating				Spontaneous
Guarded				Open
Stalwart				Humorous
Aloof				Friendly
Formal				Casual
Reserved				Attention Seeking
Cautious				Carefree
Conforming				Unconventional
Reticent				Dramatic
Restrained				Impulsive

Figure 5.4
Sociability Indicator

The sociability indicator form is not a precise instrument, but it will provide you with a general indication of where you fall on the scale. You may also want to make copies of the form and distribute them to friends or coworkers for completion. Remember, again, it is best not to involve parents, spouses, or close relatives in this feedback exercise.

The Sociability Factor in an Organizational Setting

Where are successful people on the sociability continuum? Everywhere. *There is no best place to be.* People at all points along the continuum can achieve success in an organizational setting. However, there are some common sense guidelines that need to be followed by persons who fall at either end of the continuum.

A person who is low in sociability is more apt to display a no-nonsense attitude when dealing with other people. This person may be seen as impersonal and businesslike. Behavior that is too guarded and too reserved can be a barrier to effective communication. Such persons may be perceived as unconcerned about the feelings of others and interested only in getting the job done.

Persons who are high in sociability openly express their feelings, emotions, and impressions. They are perceived as being concerned with relationships and therefore are easy to get to know. At times, emotionally expressive people need to curb their natural exuberance. Too much informality can be a problem in some work relationships. Later in this chapter, we will discuss the importance of adapting your style to accommodate the needs of others.

Thinking/Learning Starters

1. On a sheet of paper, list the names of two people you know who are low in sociability. These persons will be characterized by a tendency to be serious, restrained, and somewhat formal in social relationships. Then list the names of two people who are high in sociability. These persons will be characterized by a tendency to be open, talkative, and informal in social relationships.
2. Complete the sociability indicator form shown in Figure 5.4 for each of the people you have listed.

Four Basic Communication Styles

The dominance and sociability continuums can be combined to form a rather simple model that will tell you more about your communication style. The **communication style model** will help you identify your most preferred style. Dominance is represented by the horizontal axis and sociability by the vertical axis. The model is divided into four quadrants, each quadrant representing a particular communication style: emotive, director, reflective, or supportive.

Emotive Style   The upper right-hand quadrant combines high sociability and high dominance. This is characteristic of the **emotive style** of communication (Figure 5.5).

You can easily form a mental picture of the emotive type by thinking about the phrases used earlier to describe high dominance and high sociability. A good example of the emotive type of person is comedian Bill Cosby. Carol

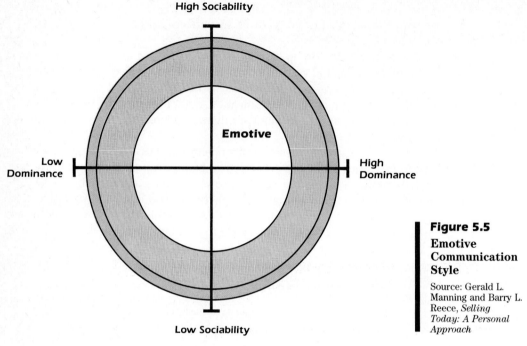

Figure 5.5
Emotive
Communication
Style

Source: Gerald L.
Manning and Barry L.
Reece, *Selling
Today: A Personal
Approach*

Burnett, as noted earlier, also projects an outspoken, enthusiastic, and stimulating style. Maria Shriver, a popular television news personality, displays the emotive style. She is animated, frequently laughs at herself, and has been described as "lithe and lively" by one interviewer.[12] Here is a list of verbal and nonverbal clues that identify the emotive person:

1. *Displays action-oriented behavior.* The emotive person seems to be constantly on the go. He or she is likely to talk rapidly and express views with vigorous hand gestures.

2. *Likes informality.* This person usually likes to operate on a first-name basis. Emotive-type people often share personal points of view soon after meeting you.

3. *Possesses a natural persuasiveness.* Combining high dominance and high sociability, this person finds it easy to express his or her point of view dramatically and forcefully.

Director Style   The lower right-hand quadrant represents a communication style that combines high dominance and low sociability—the **director style** (Figure 5.6). Television interviewer Barbara Walters, former President Richard Nixon, and England's first female prime minister, Margaret Thatcher,

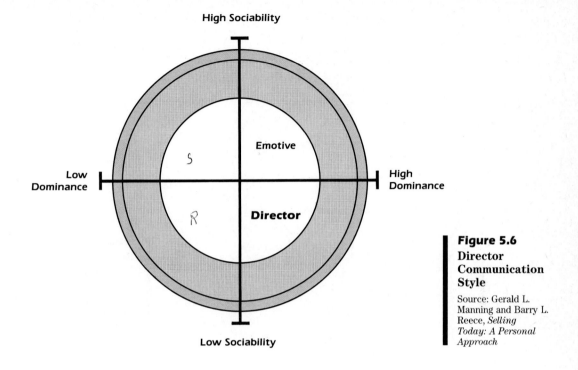

**Figure 5.6
Director
Communication
Style**

Source: Gerald L.
Manning and Barry L.
Reece, *Selling
Today: A Personal
Approach*

project the director style. Lee Iacocca is a director. The late Vince Lombardi, successful coach of the Green Bay Packers for many years, easily fits the description of this communication style. All of these people have been described as frank, demanding, assertive, and very determined. Some behaviors displayed by directors include the following:

1. *Projects a serious attitude.* Mike Wallace, one of the stars of the popular television show "60 Minutes," usually communicates a no-nonsense attitude. As a director, he often gives the impression that he cannot have fun. This businesslike attitude tends to conceal moments of happiness.

2. *Expresses strong opinions.* With firm gestures and a tone of voice that communicates determination, the director projects the image of someone who wants to take control.

3. *May project indifference.* It is not easy for the director to communicate a warm, caring attitude. He or she does not find it easy to abandon the formal approach in dealing with people.

Reflective Style The lower left-hand quadrant of the communication style model features a combination of low dominance and low sociability. This is the **reflective style** of communication (Figure 5.7).

orderly
preoccupied
formal.

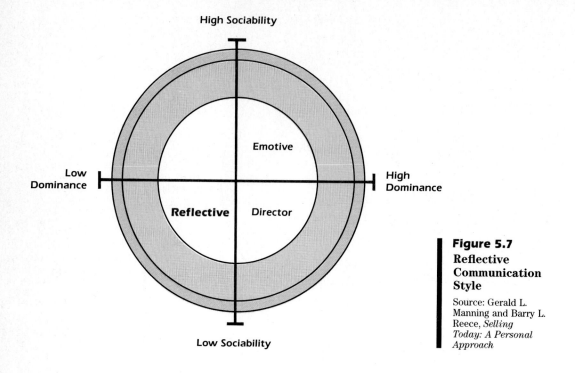

Figure 5.7
Reflective Communication Style

Source: Gerald L. Manning and Barry L. Reece, *Selling Today: A Personal Approach*

This person is usually quiet, enjoys spending time alone, and does not make decisions quickly. The late physicist Albert Einstein fits this description. He once commented on how he liked to spend idle hours:

> When I have no special problem to occupy my mind, I love to reconstruct proofs of mathematical and physical theorems that have long been known to me. There is no *goal* in this, merely an opportunity to indulge in the pleasant occupation of thinking.[13]

Former CBS newscaster Eric Sevareid, former president Jimmy Carter, and Dr. Joyce Brothers also display the characteristics of the reflective communication style. Some of the behaviors characteristic of this style are listed below:

1. *Expresses opinions in a formal, deliberate manner.* The reflective person does not seem to be in a hurry. He or she will express measured opinions. Emotional control is a common trait of this style.

2. *Seems to be preoccupied.* The reflective person is rather quiet and may

A reflective person enjoys reviewing details and making decisions slowly. (Photo by Hazel Hankin, Stock Boston, Inc.)

often appear preoccupied with other matters. As a result, he or she may seem aloof and difficult to get to know.

3. *Prefers orderliness.* The reflective person will prefer an orderly work environment. At a meeting, this person will appreciate an agenda. A reflective person enjoys reviewing details and making decisions slowly.

Supportive Style   The upper left-hand quadrant combines low dominance and high sociability—the **supportive style** of communication (Figure 5.8). People who possess this style are sensitive, patient, and good listeners.

The supportive person is reserved and usually avoids attention-seeking behavior. Some additional behaviors that commonly characterize the supportive style include the following:

1. *Listens attentively.* Good listeners have a unique advantage in many occupational settings. This is especially true of loan officers, sales personnel, and supervisors. The talent comes naturally to the supportive person.

2. *Avoids the use of power.* The supportive person is more apt to rely on friendly persuasion when dealing with people. They like to display warmth in their speech and written correspondence.

3. *Decisions are made and expressed in a thoughtful, deliberate manner.* Supportive people appear low key in a decision-making role. Dinah Shore, Perry Como, and John Denver display characteristics of this style.

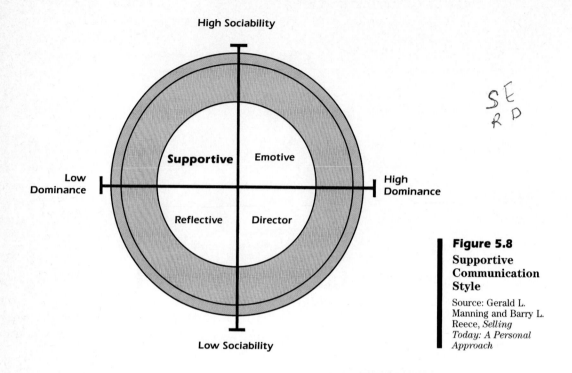

Figure 5.8
Supportive
Communication
Style

Source: Gerald L.
Manning and Barry L.
Reece, *Selling*
Today: A Personal
Approach

Determining Your Communication Style

You should now have enough information to tentatively identify your own communication style. If your location on the dominance continuum was right of center and your position on the sociability continuum was below the center mark, you fall into the director quadrant. If your location on the dominance continuum was left of center and your position on the sociability continuum was above the center mark, then your most preferred style is supportive. Low dominance matched with low sociability forms the reflective style. High dominance matched with high sociability forms the emotive communication style.

Some people feel a sense of frustration when they first identify their communication style. Paula Burgess, supervisor of a data processing center at a large insurance company, asked four associates at work to evaluate her personal traits by completing the dominance and sociability indicator forms. The results were surprising. She thought of herself as an emotive person. Others viewed her as reflective.

Paula was confused because she had always considered herself a warm, outgoing person. She took time to review both forms carefully and compare herself with other people. Finally she decided that the picture of her communication style developed by others was quite accurate. Furthermore, she began to take pride in her style. After all, what is wrong with a person who can be described as serious, deliberate, and orderly?

Variation Within Your Communication Style

Communication styles also vary in intensity. For example, a person may be either moderately or strongly dominant. Note that the communication style model features zones that radiate outward from the center, illustrated in Figure 5.9. These dimensions might be thought of as *intensity zones*.

Zone 1 People who fall within Zone 1 will display their unique behavioral characteristics with less intensity than persons in Zone 2. This means that it may be more difficult to identify the preferred communication style of people in Zone 1. They will not be as obvious in their gestures, tone of voice, speech patterns, or emotional expressions. You may have trouble picking up the right clues to identify their communication style.

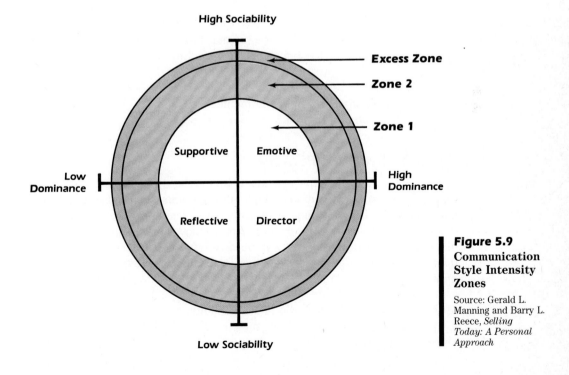

**Figure 5.9
Communication
Style Intensity
Zones**

Source: Gerald L. Manning and Barry L. Reece, *Selling Today: A Personal Approach*

Zone 2   People who fall within Zone 2 will display their behavioral characteristics with greater intensity. For example, on the dominance continuum below, Sue, Mike, Harold, and Deborah each falls within a different zone.

Low dominance	Sue	Mike	Harold	Deborah	High dominance

In terms of communication style identification, it will probably be easier to distinguish between Sue and Deborah than between Mike and Harold. Of course, the boundary line that separates Zone 1 and Zone 2 should not be viewed as a permanent barrier. Under certain conditions people will abandon their preferred style temporarily, a process we call "style flexing."

You can sometimes see style flexing when a person is upset or angry. For example, Sue above is a strong supporter of equal rights for women. At school she hears a male student say, "I think a woman's place is in the home." At that point she might express her own views in the strongest possible terms. This will require temporarily abandoning the comfort of her low dominance style to display highly assertive behavior.

Excess Zone   The excess zone is characterized by a high degree of intensity and rigidity. It might also be labeled the "danger" zone. When people occupy this zone they become inflexible and display a lack of versatility. Extreme intensity in any quadrant is bound to interfere with good human relations.

People often move into the excess zone when they are under stress. A person who feels threatened or insecure may also move into the excess zone. Table 5.1 lists some of the behaviors displayed by people who occupy this zone.

Even a temporary excursion into the excess zone should be avoided if at all possible. Inflexible and rigid communication styles are likely to lead to a breakdown in human relations.

Strength/Weakness Paradox

As we have noted previously in this chapter, there is no "best" communication style. Each style has its unique strong points. Supportive people are admired for their easy-going, responsive style. Directors are respected for the thoroughness and determination they display. The stimulating, personable style of the emotive person can be very refreshing. And finally, the emotional control and industrious nature of the reflective person is almost universally admired.

Problems arise when people overextend or rely too much on the strengths of their style. The director who is too demanding may be viewed by others as "pushy." The supportive person may try too hard to please others and be viewed as "wishy washy." An emotive person may be viewed as too excitable or not serious enough in a business setting. The reflective person who can't

Table 5.1   Behaviors Displayed in the Excess Zone

Supportive Style	Attempts to win approval by agreeing with everyone
	Constantly seeks reassurance
	Refuses to take a strong stand
	Tends to apologize a great deal
Director Style	Determined to come out on top
	Will not admit to being wrong
	Very cold and unfeeling when dealing with others
	Tends to use dogmatic phrases such as "always," "never," or "you can't"
Emotive style	Tends to express highly emotional opinions
	Outspoken to the point of being offensive
	Seems unwilling to listen to the views of others
	Gestures and facial expressions are very exaggerated
Reflective Style	Tends to avoid making a decision
	Seems overly interested in detail
	Very stiff and formal in dealing with others
	Avoids displaying emotion

seem to make a decision without mountains of information may be viewed as too cautious and inflexible.

Some people rely too heavily on established strengths and fail to develop new skills that will increase their versatility. Jeff Walker, buyer of sporting goods for a small chain of sporting goods stores, has a strong emotive communications style. He didn't have any trouble getting along with Tom Leslie, vice president in charge of merchandising, because Tom was also an emotive communicator. However, when Tom Leslie resigned to accept a position with another company and was replaced by Richard Greenbaum, a reflective person, the trouble began. Jeff was unable to curb his stimulating, promotional style and soon became viewed as "unstable" by the new vice president.

Versatility: The Third Dimension

In the early stages of this chapter we described two important dimensions of the communication style model: dominance and sociability. You will recall that these dimensions of human behavior are independent of each other. Now we are ready to discuss versatility, an important third dimension of human behavior.

Total Person Insight	When we speak of interpersonal relationships (an interaction involving at least two people), we contend that no one can do much about what another person says or does, but each of us _can_ do something about what _we_ say and do. And because dealing with others is such a major aspect of our lives, if we can control what _we_ say and do to make others more comfortable, we can realistically expect our relationships to be more positive, or effective, ones.
David W. Merrill Roger H. Reid	

Persons who can create and maintain interpersonal relations with others, regardless of their communication style, are displaying versatility. We can define **versatility** as acting in ways that earn social endorsement. Endorsement means simply that people approve of our behavior. People give us their endorsement when they feel comfortable and nondefensive when they deal with us.[14]

The dimension of versatility is independent of style. This means that the emotive style is no more or less likely to be versatile than the reflective style. Communication style remains relatively stable throughout life whereas versatility is changeable.

Versatility is something we do to ourselves, not something we do to others. Versatile people recognize that they can control their half of relationships and that it's easier to modify themselves than it is to modify others. The versatile person asks, "What can I do to make it easier for the other person to relate to me?"[15]

Achieving Versatility Through Style Flexing

Style flexing can be described as a deliberate attempt to change or alter your style in order to meet the needs of the other person. It is a temporary effort to act in harmony with the behavior of another person's dominant communication style. Style flexing is communicating in a way more readily understood by and more agreeable to persons of other styles.[16] As we noted earlier in this chapter, you can learn to adapt your style to accommodate others.

To illustrate how style flexing can be used in an organizational setting, take another look at the problem faced by Jeff Walker, buyer of sporting goods. What might Jeff do to improve communication with the new vice president in charge of merchandising? Jeff is naturally a more open, impulsive communicator. During meetings with a reflective person, he should appear less spontaneous, slow his rate of speech, and avoid the use of dramatic gestures. He should try to appear more reserved.

The reflective admires orderliness, so Jeff should be sure he is well prepared. Prior to each meeting, he should develop a mental agenda of items that he wants to cover. At the beginning of the meeting he might say: "Mr. Greenbaum, there are three things I want to discuss." He would then describe each item in a concise manner. Information would be presented slowly and systematically. This businesslike approach will be appreciated by the reflective vice president.

How can a reflective use style flexing to accommodate the needs of the emotive? The reflective person should avoid appearing too stiff and formal. During the initial meeting, the reflective should try to avoid being "all business." (The emotive person doesn't object to small talk during meetings.) The reflective communicator might also be more informal about starting and ending meetings exactly on time. They may allow the emotive to depart from the agenda now and then or bring up an item spontaneously. The reflective should try to share feelings, hopes, and concerns more openly in the presence of an emotive.

If your most preferred communication style is supportive, how might you use style flexing to develop rapport with a director? First, remember that directors find too much support annoying. Don't agree with everything or you will be viewed as a weak and incompetent person. Be a good listener, but be prepared to discuss *your* views openly and frankly. You must temporarily move to the right on the dominance continuum to be closer to the position of the other person. A good rule of thumb is to be friendly but firm. When you meet a director, be sure to use a firm handshake and maintain good eye contact during the conversation. Display as much self-confidence as possible.

If your most preferred style is director and you wish to develop rapport with a supportive, move to the left on the dominance continuum. The supportive will feel uncomfortable in the presence of a person who is too domineering. Be willing to negotiate differences of opinion. Curb your natural tendency to take charge. Friendliness is appreciated by supportives. An all-business approach is apt to make the supportive uneasy. Take time to develop a social relationship before you talk about business matters. Don't be too preoccupied with conserving time. The supportive person enjoys conducting business in a relaxed environment. Don't be pushy.

Strategies for Adapting Your Style

Once you have identified the dominant style of the other person, begin thinking of ways to gain social endorsement. Remember, you can control your half of the relationship. What can be done to meet the interpersonal needs of the other person? What follows are a few general style adaptation strategies.

Emotive Style

▶ Take time to build a social as well as a business relationship. Leave time for relating and socializing.

▶ Display interest in the person's ideas, interests, and experiences.

▶ Do not place too much emphasis on details. Emotives like fast-moving, inspirational kinds of activities.

Director Style

▶ Be specific, brief, and to the point. Use time efficiently.
▶ Present the facts logically and be prepared to provide answers to specific questions.
▶ If you disagree, take issue with the facts, not the person.

Reflective Person

▶ Appeal to the person's orderly, systematic approach to life. Be well organized.
▶ Approach this person in a straightforward, direct manner. Get down to business quickly.
▶ Be as accurate and realistic as possible when presenting information.

Supportive Style

▶ Show a sincere interest in the person. Take time to identify areas of common interest.
▶ Patiently draw out personal views and goals. Listen and be responsive to the person's needs.
▶ Present your views in a quiet, nonthreatening manner. Don't be pushy.

Style Flexing: Pitfalls and Possibilities

Will you be viewed as a phony if you flex your style and attempt to meet the other person's needs. The answer is yes and no. As a general rule, you should flex your style whenever it is needed to establish and maintain mutually productive relationships.[17] Continuous style flexing, however, will very likely mask your own style. If you fail to express your own personality, the other person may view you as artificial. Worse yet, you may not be trusted.

In an organizational setting it is usually best to flex your style when something important is at stake. Let's assume that you are head of a major department in a large hospital. Tomorrow you will meet with the hospital administrator and propose the purchase of new x-ray equipment that will cost a large amount of money. This is a good time to think about the administrator's communication style and make decisions regarding style flexing strategies.

Is style flexing just another way to manipulate others? The answer is yes if your approach is insincere and your only objective is to get something for yourself. Any method designed to improve communication can be used to manipulate people.[18] The choice is yours. If your objective is to build an honest and constructive relationship, then style flexing can be a valuable aid.

Coping with Change

In an age of accelerating change it is important that you develop a high degree of versatility. As one source noted, "Never before in history have people been required to interact with so many other people."[19] The adaptive, resourceful ways of the versatile person enable him or her to cope with changing conditions. Generally, the more-versatile person has a competitive edge over the less-versatile person. Just as a person can become technically obsolete in knowledge and skills, the less-versatile person can become obsolete from the standpoint of interpersonal skills.[20]

Summary

Communication style bias is a common problem in organizations and should be viewed as a major barrier to good human relations. Communication style tends to be stable throughout a person's lifetime. Each person has a distinctive way of responding to people and events.

The communication style model is formed by combining two important dimensions of human behavior: dominance and sociability. Combinations of these two aspects create four communication styles—emotive, director, reflective, and supportive. With practice you can learn to identify other people's communication styles. You can also adjust your own style to meet the needs of others—a process called style flexing.

Key Terms

communication style
communication style bias
dominance continuum
sociability continuum
communication style model
emotive style

director style
reflective style
supportive style
versatility
style flexing

Review Questions

1. How would you define communication style bias?
2. What are the four principles that establish a foundation for understanding communication styles?
3. How will someone employed in an organization benefit from an understanding of communication styles?
4. Explain the difference between the dominance continuum and the sociability continuum.
5. What are the four communication styles? Provide a description of each.
6. What are the characteristics of the reflective who drifts into the excess zone? The emotive?
7. What are some nonverbal clues that might help you identify a person's most preferred communication style?
8. Explain why there is no "best" communication style. Feel free to use examples from your personal life to support your answer.
9. Explain the meaning of the strength/weakness paradox.
10. Define the term *versatility*. Explain the meaning of style flexing.

Case 5.1
A Matter of Style

Betty Westmoreland is a sales representative for the World Travel Agency, a firm that specializes in packaged tours to foreign countries. She has spent two months training for this position and is now working with customers. Betty is an expressive person who is very enthusiastic about her job. She possesses all the characteristics of the emotive communication style. She is outspoken, excitable, and very personable. Betty is always attractively dressed and groomed.

Monday morning Betty has an appointment with Raymond L. Fitz, III, executive director of an association made up of bank loan officers. Raymond wants to arrange a package tour to England for about fifty persons that will include transportation, hotel accommodations, meals, and tickets to special events. He is classified as reflective in terms of communication style. People who know him well view him as industrious, cautious, and well organized. He is all business when it comes to representing the bankers' association.

Questions
1. At the initial meeting, do you anticipate that communication style bias will surface? If so, why?
2. What will be Raymond's primary communication needs?
3. How should Betty speak and act throughout the meeting in order to develop an effective business relationship with him?

Case 5.2
Hiring Financial Counselors

The First National Bank recently decided to offer customers a wider range of investment services. The bank will offer money market investment accounts and stock and bond brokerage services to customers for the first time. Full-page newspaper advertisements, soon to be released, will feature the headline "Wall Street No Longer Has a Corner on the Market." Three new financial counselors will be hired to handle the anticipated new business. These new employees will provide assistance to investors and help market the new services. Reed McConnlly, vice president in charge of marketing, is responsible for hiring the financial counselors. Recently he met with Michael Valento, director of personnel, to discuss the hiring process.

Valento: The advertisement announcing the openings will appear in local papers beginning tomorrow. What qualities will you be looking for in the applicants?

McConnlly: I hope we can hire people who are knowledgeable in the area of financial counseling and possess a strong desire to succeed. These people must aggressively promote and sell our services.

Valento: I agree we must hire people who are self-starters, but I feel we should be looking for people who possess good counseling skills.

McConnlly: What do you mean?

 Valento: If I were seeking financial counseling, I would want to deal with someone who asks plenty of questions and then listens to my answers.

McConnlly: Mike, you must keep in mind that investments is a very competitive field these days. We have to hire people who are aggressive and able to present the services we offer in a convincing manner. I want people who can sell our services.

 Valento: Many of our customers are conservative in terms of money matters and will, in my opinion, be turned off by a presentation that is made in an aggressive manner.

Questions

1. Do you agree or disagree with McConnlly's point of view?
2. Is it possible to be an effective financial counselor and still present the new bank services forcefully and enthusiastically?

Notes

1. William E. Schmidt, "Unpredictable, Outspoken 'Ted' Has Become a Folk Hero," *Roanoke Times and World-News*, July 28, 1985, p. F–1.
2. "Captain Outrageous Opens Fire," *Time*, April 29, 1985, pp. 60–61.
3. David W. Merrill and Roger H. Reid, *Personal Styles and Effective Performance* (Radnor, Pa.: Chilton Book Company, 1981), p. 7.
4. Ron Zemke, "From Factor Analysis and Clinical Psychology: Better Ways to Help Train People," *Training/HRD*, August 1976, p. 13. Reprinted with permission from the August 1976 issue of *Training*, The Magazine of Human Resources Development. Copyright Lakewood Publications, Minneapolis, Mn. (612) 333–0471. All rights reserved.
5. Janet G. Elsea, *The Four-Minute Sell* (New York: Simon and Schuster, 1984), p. 7.
6. Zemke, p. 13.
7. George F. Truell, "Communication Styles: The Key to Understanding Others," *Personnel Administrator*, March 1978, p. 48.
8. David W. Johnson, *Reaching Out—Interpersonal Effectiveness and Self-Actualization* (Englewood Cliffs, N.J.: Prentice-Hall, 1981), pp. 43–44.
9. Hugh J. Ingrasci, "How to Reach Buyers in Their Psychological 'Comfort Zones,'" *Industrial Marketing*, July 1981, p. 60.
10. American Management Associations, *Course Catalog* (New York: American Management Associations, 1986), p. 22.
11. Charles Margerison, *How to Assess Your Managerial Style* (New York: AMACOM, 1979), p. 49.
12. Dotson Rader, "The Kennedys," *Parade*, January 12, 1986, p. 5.
13. "On the Human Side," *Time*, February 19, 1979, p. 75.
14. Merrill and Reid, p. 88.

15. Wilson Learning Corporation, *Growth Through Versatility* (Eden Prairie, Minn.), p. 4.

16. Robert Bolton and Dorthy Grover Bolton, *Social Style/Management Style* (New York: American Management Associations, 1984), pp. 53–55.

17. Ibid., p. 56.

18. Ibid., p. 58.

19. Ibid., p. 6.

20. Wilson Learning Corporation, p. 6.

Suggested Readings

Bledsoe, John L., "Your Four Communicating Styles: Why, When, and How to Use Each One." *Training/HRD*, March 1976, pp. 18–21.

Bolton, Robert, and Dorthy Grover Bolton. *Social Style/Management Style.* New York: American Management Associations, 1984.

Carson, R. C. *Interaction Concepts of Personality.* Chicago: Aldine, 1969.

DeVille, Jard. *Nice Guys Finish First.* New York: Morrow, 1979.

Mehrabian, A. *Silent Messages.* Belmont, Calif.: Wadsworth, 1971.

Merrill, David W., and Roger H. Reid. *Personal Styles and Effective Performance.* Radnor, Pa.: Chilton Book Company, 1981.

Truell, George F. "Communication Styles: The Key to Understanding Others." *Personnel Administrator*, March 1978, pp. 46–48.

Zemke, Ron. "From Factor Analysis and Clinical Psychology: Better Ways to Help Train People." *Training/HRD*, August 1976, pp. 12–16.

Chapter 6

Identifying Your Motivations

Chapter Preview

After studying this chapter, you will be able to
1. Understand the relationship beween needs and motivation.
2. Identify the steps in the motivational cycle.
3. Describe Maslow's hierarchy of needs.
4. Describe Herzberg's motivation-maintenance model.
5. Compare and contrast the theories of Herzberg and Maslow.
6. Summarize McGregor's Theory X and Theory Y of human behavior.
7. Summarize Ouchi's Theory Z.
8. Discuss management approaches to worker motivation and the use of motivational techniques.

When Dr. Norman Vincent Peale talks about motivation, he frequently mentions Mary Crowe. As a youngster, she was one of eight children living in poverty. There was seldom enough food on the family table, and everywhere that Mary Crowe turned, she was confronted by the symbols of poverty. As Dr. Peale notes, "The Great Depression had the country by the throat." Despite these depressing surroundings, she was not an unhappy girl. In her mind she pictured an attractive college campus with beautiful green lawns and ivy-covered buildings. She also visualized herself receiving a diploma on graduation day. Years later, her dreams turned to reality when she entered college.

Once in college she began thinking about a career. She decided to become an insurance salesperson. She visualized herself as a successful salesperson helping buyers whose lives would be more secure because of the insurance. After graduation, she applied for a job at one of the largest insurance agencies in the city. The man in charge of hiring turned her down. In those days there were almost no women selling insurance, and he wasn't about to take a chance with Mary. She went away, but returned the next day and again requested a job. Again she was turned down. She returned several times and was finally given a job. She soon became the number one salesperson for the company and later became a member of the Million Dollar Round Table—the exclusive group of insurance agents who sell more than one million dollars' worth of insurance in a single year. From early childhood, she was motivated by the desire to achieve her goals.[1]

Learning what motivates you can be an essential part of knowing yourself, of finding out what is important to you. The information on motivation and needs presented in this chapter will provide some useful insights into your own needs and aspirations. If you know what you want out of a job, you are in a better position to plan your career. The material in this chapter will also contribute to your knowledge of human relations. Knowing what motivates others is basic to establishing and maintaining effective relations with them.[2] This chapter also examines management's responsibility in motivating workers. Although you may not be planning to become a supervisor or manager at this time, it will be helpful to understand how management approaches the problem of employee motivation.

The Complex Nature of Motivation

Human beings are motivated by many different kinds of needs. People have basic needs for food, clothing, and shelter, but they also need acceptance, recognition, and self-esteem. Each individual will experience these needs in different ways and to varying degrees. For some, basic needs may be most important, whereas for others, the need to be accepted is strongest. To make matters more complicated, people will be motivated by different needs at different times in their lives. We now know that adults, like children and

Total Person Insight

What motivates people? No question about human behavior is more frequently asked or more perplexing to answer. Yet knowing what motivates another person is basic to establishing and maintaining effective relations with others

adolescents, continue to develop and change in significant ways throughout life. Patterns of adult development have been described in such popular books as *Passages* and *Pathfinders* written by Gail Sheehy and *Seasons of a Man's Life* by Daniel Levinson. No one approach to motivation will work for everyone or for the same person all the time.

Motivation Defined

Motivation can be defined as the internal drive to accomplish a particular goal.[3] In a work setting, motivation is what makes people *want* to work. Employees and managers alike need to understand what strengthens or weakens their motivation on the job in order to fulfill both organizational and personal goals. Although some managers still subscribe to the theory that fear is the best motivator, modern management's thinking now leans toward a more positive approach. Over the long run, people will work harder to gain recognition or job satisfaction than they will to avoid negative consequences such as being terminated or disciplined in some way. In addition, there has been a shift in the traditional work ethic. As we noted earlier in this text, many of today's better educated and better informed workers possess a heightened sense of their rights and are more likely to demand responsive and equitable treatment from the organization. They want to be treated as valued persons, and they display less tolerance for an authoritarian style of management. Although some managers may dismiss these workers as "prima donnas," failure to take their needs seriously can result in motivation-related problems such as poor morale, high turnover, and low productivity.

The work of various psychologists and social scientists has added greatly to the knowledge of what motivates people and how motivation works. The basic problem, as many leaders admit, is knowing how to apply that knowledge in the workplace.

The Motivational Cycle

The **motivational cycle** describes how individuals go about satisfying a felt need. If your need is strong enough, such as acute hunger or thirst, you will be unable to concentrate on anything else until that need has been taken care of. Mahatma Gandhi reportedly said, "Not even God can talk to a hungry man."

There are five steps in the motivational cycle (see Figure 6.1). A sufficiently strong need creates tension, which in turn makes a person take action to satisfy the need. Once the goal has been achieved, there is a sense of satisfaction and reduction in tension. For example, suppose you have a report due in two weeks, one that others are counting on to help them make a crucial decision. The tension builds, and your activities become focused on completing the report—your highest felt need at the time. You may work evenings and weekends, turning down invitations to go out with friends. After several days of hard work, you achieve your goal: the report is finished. You experience an enormous sense of relief from the tension that has kept you at the job. Now you are free to relax and satisfy your other needs.

The motivational cycle begins only when you feel the need is important to you. For instance, your boss may decide to institute a cost-control program in your department, whereas you feel the company should spend *more* money on your area. Chances are you will not be highly motivated to follow the boss's cost-control guidelines very carefully. There is no felt need on your part to cut down on expenditures. Similarly, some students may enter college because their parents feel higher education is important. But if the students aren't motivated by the same need, they will have a hard time completing the required course work. People are the most strongly motivated by those needs they *feel within themselves.*

> ### Thinking/Learning Starter
>
> Look over Figure 6.1 and apply the motivational cycle to your own experience. Choose an example from work or school, and fill in the steps below.
> 1. Need:
> 2. Buildup of tension:
> 3. Behavior activities:
> 4. Goal:
> 5. Satisfaction and tension reduction:

Motivation and the Nature of Needs

What happens when you have more than one need operating at the same time? How do you choose between them, or is there some process within you that does the selecting? What impact does culture have on people's needs?

Generally, even though you feel more than one need at a time, one of those drives will be stronger than the rest, and you will be motivated to satisfy it first. If you are extremely hungry and thirsty, you will probably satisfy your

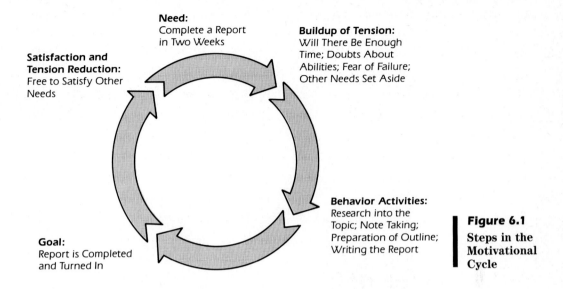

Need:
Complete a Report
in Two Weeks

Buildup of Tension:
Will There Be Enough
Time; Doubts About
Abilities; Fear of Failure;
Other Needs Set Aside

**Satisfaction and
Tension Reduction:**
Free to Satisfy Other
Needs

Behavior Activities:
Research into the
Topic; Note Taking;
Preparation of Outline;
Writing the Report

Goal:
Report is Completed
and Turned In

Figure 6.1

**Steps in the
Motivational
Cycle**

thirst and then eat. Someone who collects old phonograph recordings may forgo buying a pair of new shoes or some other practical item if the person comes across a rare recording that will complete the collection.

Cultural conditioning also affects what people perceive as needs. In Japan, for example, more business firms are committed to lifetime employment for their workers.[4] This management philosophy, in part, satisfies the worker's need for job security.

In the United States, a great deal of emphasis is placed on a good education, a sound family base, a job that pays well, and some type of group affiliation, perhaps a church or social group. Most people will seek to fulfill these needs during their lifetime. The typical American is also influenced by advertising and marketing campaigns that tell them they "need" a power mower, a new high-performance car, or the latest kitchen appliance. Given this influence, it is not difficult to see how essential needs and more artificial needs can become confused.

If you are uncertain about your own needs, you may find it difficult to determine what truly motivates you. You may be unhappy with your job and feel that the solution is an increase in salary. But with each pay raise, you find your dissatisfaction remains. Your real need may be for more responsibility, greater recognition of your work, or more authority to do the job as you see fit. Managers who can discover employees' true needs are more likely to motivate their workers effectively.

Maslow's Hierarchy of Needs

Abraham Maslow, a noted psychologist, found that people tend to satisfy their needs in a particular order—a theory he called the "hierarchy of needs."[5]

In Japan, customer courtesy and respect are given high priority. Here we see a retail employee greeting customers. (Photo by J. P. Laffont, Sygma)

Maslow's theory rests on two assumptions: (1) People have a number of needs that require some measure of satisfaction, and only unsatisfied needs motivate behavior, and (2) the needs of people are arranged in a hierarchy of prepotency, which means that as each lower level need is satisfied, the need at the next level demands attention.[6] Basically, human beings are motivated to satisfy physiological needs first (food, clothing, shelter), then the need for safety and security, followed by social and self-esteem needs. Finally, they seek to realize their potential, what Maslow called "self-actualization." Maslow's theory is illustrated in Figure 6.2. It is not difficult to see how this theory can be applied to motivation on the job.

Physiological Needs The need for food, clothing, sleep, and shelter, or **physiological needs,** were described by Maslow as survival or lower order needs. In most work environments, this basic need rarely dominates because it is reasonably well satisfied. During the Great Depression, however, many people worked solely to ensure their own and their families' survival. In most cases, they were not concerned with the type of work they did or whether they liked it.

Safety and Security Needs People's desire for some sort of order and predictability in the world is reflected in **safety and security needs.** In general, people tend to look for security in the known and familiar and avoid what they don't know or understand. They like to know that they won't lose

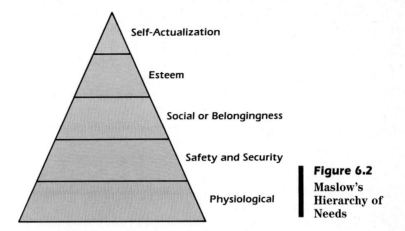

Figure 6.2
Maslow's Hierarchy of Needs

their jobs, that they can provide for their families, and that they will have enough money and resources to take care of themselves in sickness or old age. During the recession in the early 1980s, massive lay-offs put employees in a state of limbo. Even those not laid-off wondered from day to day if they would have a job the next week. This insecurity often affected productivity and strained human relationships at home and at work.

Organizations recognize the need for security by offering employees pensions, profit sharing, and insurance plans. Workers are not simply earning a paycheck but protecting themselves against injury and laying aside money for retirement. Several American companies have made a major effort to avoid layoffs. Job security is given a very high priority at such companies as Hallmark Cards, Johnson Wax, Federal Express, and Worthington Industries.

Safety needs usually focus on protection from physical harm. On the job, this means a guarantee of safe working conditions. Unions or employee groups can make sure employers maintain safety standards and reduce the risk of accident or injuries resulting from environmental hazards. Congress established the Occupational Safety and Health Act (OSHA) to help reduce deaths and injuries on the job.

Safety needs are also satisfied in other ways outside work. Advertisements for additional life or medical insurance, smoke detectors or burglar alarms, or guaranteed savings programs all appeal to people's need for safety and security.

Social Needs   While the first two needs deal with aspects of physical survival, **social needs** deal with emotional and mental well-being. Dennis Bourque, a vice president at Northern Electric in Watertown, New York, has coffee and donuts with a different group of employees each week. The "Donuts with Dennis" program not only improves communication but meets the social needs of many workers.

Research has shown that people's needs for affection, a sense of belonging, and identification with a group are as important to their health as are food and safety.

Although social needs are felt throughout childhood, they may become more intense during adolescence, when the need to belong to a group becomes more important than family ties or what parents think. As adults, the need for belonging may take the form of joining various organizations—professional associations, church groups, amateur sports, or social clubs. Special uniforms or membership privileges reflect the desire to feel part of a group in which individuals share the same interests, values, and goals.

Many people's social needs are also satisfied on the job. People form attachments with coworkers and may join the company sports teams, take part in company picnics or outings, and get together after work. In many cases, friendships developed at work may function like a "second family." This is not surprising when you consider that many employees spend more time with people on the job than they do with their own family members.

Many people are more highly motivated when they work as members of a team. Celestial Seasonings, the smallest company listed in *The 100 Best Companies to Work for in America*, attracts people from larger companies who like the teamwork that exists in this firm. Frank Boruff, the plant manager, came to Celestial Seasonings after 10 years at General Foods, a much larger company. He likes the team effort that has evolved at this small company.[7]

Managers have found that when employees have a strong sense of being a part of the team, they are likely to be more productive. Chapter 12 will focus on team building as an important factor in productivity and worker satisfaction.

Esteem Needs   Self-esteem is a term that describes how you feel about yourself at any given time. It may be positive or negative. **Esteem needs** refer to one's self-respect and to the recognition and respect of others. How important is the achievement of self-esteem in the life of a typical worker? Arthur Witkin, chief psychologist for Personnel Sciences Center, offered the following advice to managers: "Perhaps the single most important thing is to be aware of a worker's need for self-esteem. Everyone needs to feel good about himself; if he doesn't, he'll not only turn in a poor job performance, he'll keep others from doing their best."[8]

Esteem needs can be satisfied in many ways. You may set your sights on winning the top salesperson of the year award, work to build a reputation as a highly skilled and reliable employee, or volunteer to chair a committee for the annual charity drive. Often, managers miss opportunities to reinforce the self-concept of their workers. For most people, a word of appreciation or praise is a strong motivator. One employee stated, "It's such a simple thing, but hearing the boss say I did a great job makes me feel that all the work I put into a project was worth it. I go away wanting to work even harder on the next one."

Self-Actualization Needs   The four needs just described motivate people by their absence, that is, when people feel a *lack* of food, social relationships, safety, or esteem. **Self-actualization needs,** on the other hand, represent the need for growth and motivate people by their *presence.* Self-actualization is fulfilling one's potential or realizing one's fullest capacities as a human being.

Maslow used *self-actualization* in a very specialized sense to describe a rarely attained state of human achievement. Because of the uniqueness of each person, the form or content of self-actualization is a very individual thing.[9] Most of us are never truly "self-actualized" but are always finding new goals and new means of expression. The achievement of one goal stimulates the search for new challenges. It is like being on a fascinating journey where the goal is not the end of the road but the journey itself.

Each person's journey toward self-actualization will be individual and unique. It may be difficult to satisfy this need on the job, since most jobs are limited in scope and have their duties fairly clearly defined. However, this is not to say that people haven't found ways to change their jobs, create new positions for themselves, or set new goals year after year. George Guzewicz took a $15,000 pay cut to leave Xerox Corporation, the company he had worked seventeen years for, to enter a sales job.[10] (He had never sold a product or service before!) Feeling that his job at Xerox was not challenging enough, he went to work for Lambda Electronics, a manufacturer of power regulators and semiconductors. After only a few months in the new position, Mr. Guzewicz was achieving success and feeling a new sense of accomplishment. He was already setting his sights on another position within the company that would offer an even greater challenge.

The self-actualizing person may not only create his or her own job, but may have two or three careers in one lifetime. A retired elementary school teacher learned Braille at age sixty-five and taught blind children for fifteen years. In another case, a printer turned his carpentering skills into a side business and began manufacturing grandfather clocks. He kept at his "hobby" until well into his eighties.

Meeting employees' self-actualization needs on the job requires a combination of creativity, imagination, and a management willing to be flexible.

Maslow's Theory Reconsidered   Maslow based his concept of the hierarchy of needs on two observations. First, people will satisfy their needs systematically, starting with the most basic and moving up the ladder. Second, lower order needs take precedence over higher order needs.

In general, these observations hold true. But the theory should not be accepted too literally. Human beings are motivated at any one time by a complex array of needs and may satisfy several of them through one activity. Perhaps the most familiar example is the business lunch. Not only are you conducting business with a client, you are also satisfying your need to eat and drink, to engage in social activities, and to feel important in your own eyes and, you hope, the eyes of your client.

People will sacrifice lower order needs to satisfy higher order needs if the drive is strong enough. When individuals take up a dangerous sport such as sky-diving or mountain climbing, they are placing self-actualization needs over security or safety. A young lawyer may decide to open a store-front office to serve the poor rather than enter the security of an established law firm.

Despite these reservations, Maslow's contribution to the theory of motivation remains a landmark in the field. He pointed out that lower order needs, when satisfied, no longer act as motivators. Usually, people do not keep eating after they are full; they wait until they are hungry again. Since higher order needs are never completely satisfied—one goal leads to another—they will be the strongest motivators over the long run.

Herzberg's Motivation-Maintenance Model

In the 1950s, psychologist Frederick Herzberg proposed another theory of motivation called the hygiene theory, or the **motivation-maintenance model.** The word *hygiene* is a medical term referring to factors that help maintain, but do not necessarily improve, health. According to Herzberg, two conditions or factors affect individual behavior on the job: maintenance and motivational factors.

Maintenance (Hygiene) Factors These factors do not act as motivators; but if they are withdrawn, they create dissatisfaction and may result in lower productivity. Herzberg's list of maintenance factors includes salaries and some fringe benefits, working conditions, social relationships, supervision, and organizational policies and administration. People take these factors for granted as part of the job.

Suppose, however, that the organization decides to cut costs by reducing the amount of medical or life insurance offered employees. Suddenly, fringe benefits become the focus of employee dissatisfaction. Once the coverage is reinstated, dissatisfaction disappears and workers return to a more neutral position. The medical plan does not motivate employees to be more productive, but the loss of it can cause workers to look for another organization that provides the necessary coverage. At the least, the lack of maintenance factors will hurt employee morale.

Maintenance factors, then, represent the basic benefits and rights people consider essential to any job.

Motivational Factors These factors motivate employees when they are *present;* but according to Herzberg, their absence does not necessarily cause dissatisfaction. The relationship between satisfaction and dissatisfaction, and maintenance and motivational factors is illustrated in Figure 6.3.

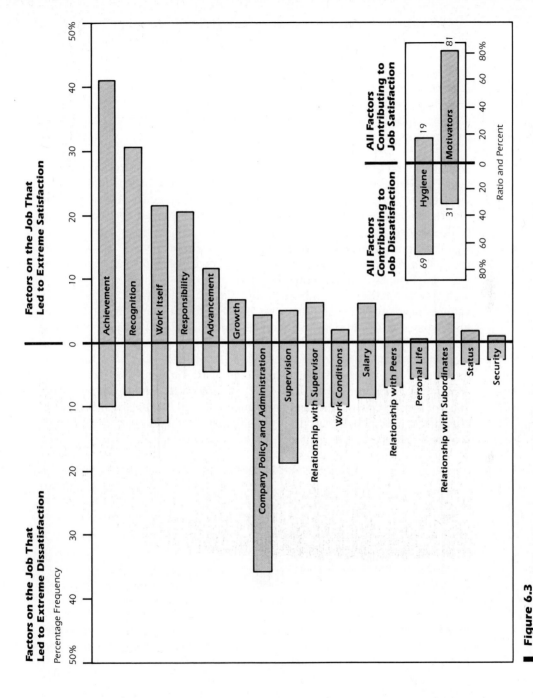

Figure 6.3

Relationship Between Satisfaction/Dissatisfaction and Motivational/Maintenance Factors

Source: Frederick Herzberg, *Harvard Business Review*

143

Herzberg's list of motivational factors parallels, to some degree, Maslow's higher order needs. The list includes:

1. Responsibility
2. Recognition
3. Achievement
4. The job itself
5. Opportunities for advancement

When these factors are present, they tend to motivate employees to achieve higher production levels, feel more committed to their jobs, and find creative ways to accomplish both personal and organizational goals. Herzberg found that their absence does not necessarily mean that workers will be unhappy or dissatisfied.

Motivational factors are those *benefits above and beyond the basic elements of a job.* When they are lacking, maintenance factors tend to become more important. Employees like to feel they are getting something beyond a paycheck for the time and effort they put into their work. If their motivational needs are not met, they may begin to ask for more fringe benefits, higher pay, better physical surroundings, or more liberal policies regarding sick leave or vacation time. Although these factors may increase satisfaction momentarily, they will not motivate workers over the long run. Each new maintenance factor quickly becomes part of the normal job benefits. For example, a Christmas bonus may start out as a motivational factor, particularly if it is based on individual performance. But if it is awarded every year regardless of employee output, it ends up as merely another fringe benefit offered by the organization.

Thinking/Learning Starter

What experiences at work have had a marked effect on increasing your feelings of job satisfaction? What experiences at work have had a marked effect on increasing your feelings of job dissatisfaction? Have feelings of job satisfaction affected your job performance?

A Final Comment on Herzberg Critics of Herzberg's theory have pointed out that he assumes most, if not all, individuals are motivated only by higher order needs. A complex, challenging, and independent job *is* motivating to those who would ordinarily seek out that type of position. However, other people may prefer more routine, predictable types of work and may be motivated more by the security of a regular paycheck than by the prospect of advancement.

Table 6.1 Comparison of the Herzberg and Maslow Theories

	Herzberg	Maslow
Motivational Factors	Work itself Achievement Responsibility	Self-actualization
	Recognition Advancement Status	Self-esteem
Maintenance (Hygiene) Factors	Interpersonal relations Supervision-technical	Love (belonging and affiliation)
	Company policy and administration	Safety and security
	Job security Working conditions Salary Personal life	Physiological needs

Perhaps the motivation-maintenance model can best be understood if you remember that the *employee's* perception of what is a motivating or maintenance factor is far more important than a *manager's* perception of it. A pay raise may strongly motivate an employee just out of college, but may simply be a routine part of the job for someone who has been in the work force for many years. Likewise, managers who believe that a more liberal vacation policy will motivate all their workers to be more productive may be in for a big disappointment.

Comparing Herzberg and Maslow

Overall, you will find that the theories of Herzberg and Maslow largely support each other. As shown in Table 6.1, satisfiers or motivators relate to Maslow's higher order needs, while dissatisfiers or maintenance factors correspond to lower order needs.

However, the theories differ in one important respect. Maslow believes that an appeal to *any* level of need can act as a motivator. For example, someone saving to buy a house will be attracted to a high-salaried job, even if the work itself is not appealing. If the person takes on more financial obligations, such as starting a family, salary will continue to be a motivating factor. Herzberg, on the other hand, contends that only appeals to higher level needs are truly motivational.

Both Maslow and Herzberg agree that higher order needs are more motivating in the long run. The sense of personal satisfaction in one's work, an opportunity to learn new skills, the feeling of being important seem to be lifelong motivating factors. On the other hand, salary, fringe benefits, and the like are at best short-term motivators.

McGregor's Theory X and Theory Y

In most organizations, day-to-day operations are significantly influenced by the relationship between workers and management. Douglas McGregor, management consultant and author, accepted the concept of a needs hierarchy, but he felt that management has failed to do so.[11] In his influential book, *The Human Side of Enterprise,* he outlined a set of assumptions that he says influence the thinking of most managers. He divided these assumptions into two categories: Theory X and Theory Y.

Theory X: A Pessimistic View

Theory X represents a pessimistic view of human nature. According to this theory, people do not really want to work—they have to be pushed, closely supervised, and threatened with some type of punishment. Since they have little or no ambition, workers prefer to avoid responsibility and will seek security as their major goal.

Theory X reflects the "carrot and stick" philosophy, combining punishment and rewards to motivate employees. This approach has two major drawbacks. First, managers who accept Theory X as valid tend to use the stick more than the carrot. "If I ever fall behind in my quota," one worker said, "you can bet I hear about it. But if I break my back to get a job done, not a word." The general belief of management under this theory is that workers are paid to do a good job; management's function is to supervise the work and correct employees if they go off course.

Second, the carrot and stick image itself creates a negative attitude toward workers. The supervisor or manager who views others as lazy, incompetent, reluctant to accept responsibility, and interested only in a paycheck will often treat subordinates with distrust, suspicion, and little respect, and will practice a form of supervision wherein fault finding, blaming, and reprimands are frequent.[12]

Theory Y: An Optimistic View

Theory Y reflects an optimistic view of human behavior. According to this theory, work is as natural to people as play or rest. People's attitudes toward work depend on their previous job experiences and the conditions surrounding the work itself. If employees are able to understand and relate to an organization's goals, they will tend to be somewhat self-directed and will not need to be threatened or coerced into working. When given the proper encouragement, people will seek responsibility rather than avoid it; and they will often exercise considerable imagination and creativity in carrying out their responsibilities.

Managers who accept Theory Y as valid are more likely to try to understand what motivates their subordinates, and in turn become better motivated themselves. They are fulfilling their own need for self-expression and achievement. A healthy, two-way relationship can create a work climate in which employees *want* to give more. A Theory Y manager will make a continuing effort to stress how important employees' efforts are to the organization as a whole.

Bill Moog, president of Moog, Inc., a company that manufactures electrohydraulic control products, is someone who takes an optimistic view of his employees. When you join this company located near Buffalo, New York, you receive an employee handbook that starts with the following statements: "Our philosophy at Moog is a simple one. We believe in the people who work for us. We believe work can be a more rewarding and satisfying experience for everyone in an atmosphere of mutual trust and confidence." This is a company without time clocks, a company that relies on each employee to report his or her performance. Moog does not have floor inspectors to check every product because employees are expected to check their own work.[13] Theory Y seems to be alive and well at Moog, Inc.

Ouchi's Theory Z

UCLA management professor William Ouchi has spent years studying the major corporations in Japan. He formulated Theory Z to describe characteristics common to certain successful Japanese and American companies. Following the Japanese tradition of treating employees like family, **Theory Z** assumes that the best management involves workers at all levels. Organizations dedicated to this management style generally have a lifetime employment policy. Even when sales are down, employees know they will not be laid off and thus have good reason to feel that their own long-term fate is tied to the company's. Workers are likely to perform job tasks conscientiously and enthusiastically in order to achieve a perfect final product. There is open communication, both vertically and horizontally, with complete trust among groups and individuals, because all employees have the same goal: the good of the company. This sense of employees as a family, pulling together for the good of the organization, seems to be the basis for the success of Theory Z. It satisfies lower-level motivational needs by being parental— looking after everyone's welfare.

In Theory Z organizations, employees also gain a psychological sense of belonging because all decisions are made in groups. In Japan, these groups may be as large as 60 to 80 people. It takes time to make final decisions with this process; yet the advantage of this **collective compromise** is that once an agreement has been reached, no one in the group will try to sabotage it. Getting dozens of American executives to build a decision by collective compromise might tie an American company in knots. Yet Intel Corporation has encouraged a collective approach by dividing employees into project teams; Proctor & Gamble uses partially self-governing work groups in some of its plants; and Hewlett-Packard kept worker turnover down during economic slumps by making sure that all employees—not just those at lower levels—had to give up some working hours and privileges.[14] Participating in decisions helps employees satisfy their higher-level motivational needs. Obviously, one of the reasons Theory Z works is because it tries to satisfy needs on all levels.

Internal Versus External Motivation

At the beginning of this chapter, we defined *motivation* as an internal drive to accomplish a particular goal. In a work setting, this definition may suggest that all motivation is the result of internal rewards that a person receives while performing the job. However, motivation at work can be triggered by rewards that occur apart from the job itself. These rewards are referred to as external motivation. Motivation, therefore, is two-dimensional; it can be internal or external.

Internal Motivation

An **internal motivation** is an intrinsic reward that occurs when a duty or task is performed. If a nurse enjoys caring for a patient, the activity is in itself rewarding, and the nurse will be self-motivated. Frederick Herzberg said that motivation comes from an internal stimulus, resulting from job content, not job environment. He suggested that jobs be enriched in order to provide responsibility, opportunity for achievement, and individual growth. Herzberg used the term **vertical job loading** to describe attempts to enrich an employee's job and thereby trigger internal motivation.[15] Table 6.2 describes several principles of *vertical job loading.* Note that each principle increases the worker's personal contribution.

One way organizations are encouraging job enrichment is through **intrapreneurship,** or encouraging employees to pursue personal ideas as company projects by giving them the money, equipment, and time. For instance, 3-M permits employees to spend 15 percent of company time experimenting with their own ideas. This practice resulted in the development of Post-it

Table 6.2 **Principles of Vertical Job Loading**

Principle	Motivators Involved
Removing some controls while retaining accountability	Responsibility and personal achievement
Increasing the accountability of individuals for own work	Responsibility and recognition
Giving a person a complete natural unit of work (module, division, area, and so on)	Responsibility, achievement, and recognition
Granting additional authority to an employee in his or her activity; job freedom	Responsibility, achievement, and recognition
Making periodic reports directly available to the worker rather than to the supervisor	Internal recognition
Introducing new and more difficult tasks not previously handled	Growth and learning
Assigning individuals specific or specialized tasks, enabling them to become experts	Responsibility, growth, and advancement

Source: Frederick Herzberg, *The Managerial Choice: To Be Efficient and To Be Human* (Salt Lake City, Utah: Olympus Publishing, 1982), p. 131.

notes, the highly successful yellow pads with the gentle adhesive. Arthur Fry, Post-it notes creator, won "3M's Nobel Prize" and was promoted to senior scientist for his efforts. Hewlett-Packard's Charles House pursued an idea for an advanced picture tube despite a management order to kill the project. The tube was eventually used as a monitor in a space flight. House's persistence won him Hewlett-Packard's "Medal of Defiance" award.[16]

Many organizations are realizing that these "corporate tinkerers" can turn their hobbies into big businesses for their employers. Employees, in turn, see intrapreneurship as a way to inject excitement and urgency into otherwise dull jobs. Rosabeth Moss Kanter, an authority on organizational change, states, "The idea that, yes, you can take action inside large companies—that you can run your own show—is very appealing."[17] The potential of being an intrapreneur may be a highly motivating factor for the workers of the future.

External Motivation

External motivation is initiated by another person and usually involves rewards or other forms of reinforcement. The reward or reinforcement is recognized as a motivational force because the worker will respond in ways that will ensure the receipt of the reinforcement. Typical external rewards in a work setting include money, paid vacations, sick leave, medical plans, awards, and the like. Some organizations are using **incentives** to encourage workers to develop good work habits and to repeat behavior that is beneficial to themselves and the organization. The incentive may take the form of cash awards, bonuses, certificates, or some type of prize. Another form of external motivation is the expectation of the supervisor or manager. When employees perceive that others expect them to succeed, they are more likely to believe that they will succeed and behave accordingly.

A Balanced Approach

Most authorities on motivation agree that organizations should attempt to provide a mix of external rewards and internal satisfaction. External rewards are rarely enough to motivate people on an ongoing basis. Most employees need to obtain internal satisfaction from their jobs as well. Ideally, an organization will provide an appropriate number of external rewards while permitting employees to experience the personal satisfaction that comes from a challenging job.

Thinking/Learning Starters

1. In what ways could a supervisor motivate you?
2. Have you, or someone you know, had experience with some form of vertical job loading? If so, describe the changes made by management and the results of these changes.
3. In places where you have worked, would you say managers believed in Theory X, Theory Y, or Theory Z? Give specific examples to support your answer.

Summary

Motivation is an internal drive to accomplish a particular goal. In a work setting, it can be defined as what makes people *want* to work.

People are motivated by different needs. The motivational cycle describes how an individual goes about satisfying a felt need. In general, people tend to satisfy their needs in a particular order. According to Maslow's theory, physiological needs will come first; followed by safety and security needs; then social, esteem, and self-actualization needs. Although Maslow believed that any need can be a motivator, only higher order needs will motivate people over the long run.

Frederick Herzberg developed the motivation-maintenance model to describe individual motivational behavior. Herzberg found that maintenance

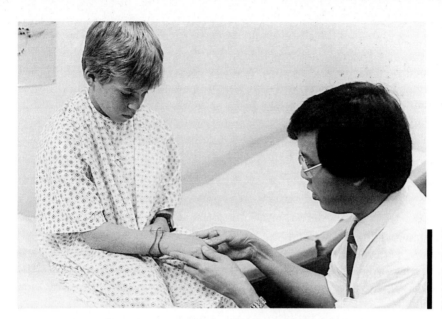

Many people are self-motivated by the satisfaction they derive from the job itself. (Photo by Nancy Lutz, The Picture Cube)

factors do not motivate workers, but will cause dissatisfaction if they are withdrawn. Motivational factors, on the other hand, motivate workers when they are present; however, their absence will not necessarily create dissatisfaction. According to Herzberg, if there are few motivational factors in a job, maintenance factors will take on greater importance.

Managers must accomplish their goals through and with other people, and they are primarily responsible for motivating their subordinates. McGregor's Theory X and Theory Y reflect a pessimistic and optimistic view of human behavior, respectively. Theory X managers are likely to adopt a carrot and stick attitude toward employee motivation. On the other hand, Theory Y managers will attempt to understand what truly motivates employees and will give them due respect and consideration.

Theory Z managers treat everyone in the organization as part of a family. Job security and group decision making make this Japanese management style very popular among workers.

Current research acknowledges that motivation is two dimensional; it can be internal or external. Internal motivation is an intrinsic reward that a person feels when performing a job. A job that is enriched to provide responsibility or opportunity for achievement will often trigger internal motivation. External motivation is initiated by another person and usually involves rewards such as incentive pay, awards, and praise. Most authorities on motivation recommend that organizations attempt to provide a mix of external rewards and internal satisfaction.

Key Terms

motivation
motivational cycle
physiological needs
safety and security needs
social needs
esteem needs
self-actualization needs
motivation-maintenance model
Theory X

Theory Y
Theory Z
collective compromise
internal motivation
vertical job loading
intrapreneurship
external motivation
incentives

Review Questions

1. How would you define motivation?
2. Why is the motivational cycle activated only by a felt need? List the steps in the cycle.
3. In what ways do Maslow's and Herzberg's theories differ? How are they similar?
4. Describe the needs listed in Maslow's hierarchy. How do organizations attempt to meet these needs?
5. Explain the difference between a motivational and a maintenance factor.
6. Will both of these factors motivate workers? In what way?
7. Who is the best judge of what is and what isn't a motivating factor for employees? Explain.
8. Describe McGregor's Theory X and Theory Y. What are the drawbacks of the carrot and stick approach?
9. What are some of the ways a Theory Y manager might motivate workers? What approach is a Theory Z manager likely to use?
10. What needs seem to be the strongest motivating factors over the long run? How can organizations meet these needs?

Case 6.1

Japan in Cleveland?[18]

Cleveland's Lincoln Electric, manufacturers of arc-welding equipment, remains one of the best-managed companies in the United States. In 1958, management made the commitment that employees who stay with Lincoln more than two years would never be laid off. They have held to that commitment.

All production personnel are paid on a piecework basis. At the end of each day, the supervisor informs each worker how much he or she has earned for the day. These workers are expected to be self-motivated. If they can arrange their work space or tasks to get a job done faster, they are free to do so and will earn more money for it. The worker will get richer, and so will the company.

Some workers quit after a few days, complaining that the factory is a "sweatshop." But the turnover rate is only 6 percent a year, about one-sixth the rate for electric manufacturing in general. What is the secret of Lincoln's success? Is it the fringe benefits? Employees once voted down a dental insurance plan, fearing it might cut into corporate profits. For the same reason, they do not challenge the lack of air conditioning. In peak years, employees accept mandatory overtime, in slow years, workers accept other job assignments, sometimes at a lower rate of pay than their original tasks. And there are no seniority rights. What Lincoln has found is that cash is an unbeatable fringe benefit in attracting a dedicated work force. Since 1934, all employees have received annual bonus checks, generally exceeding their annual income. In 1981, for instance, each employee received a bonus check averaging $44,000! A company spokesperson says, "We feel every job in our company is an important job. We treat all our employees with dignity and respect. Our workers want responsibility. They expect a fair share in the company's profits. We provide all that."

Questions

1. Identify the factors that motivate Lincoln employees.
2. People who leave Lincoln after a few days appear to be motivated by different forces than those who remain at Lincoln. What might those forces be?
3. Better than 80 percent of Lincoln Electric stock is controlled by employees, retirees, or family heirs who sometimes offer shares to the company at below-market prices for resale to employees. What might motivate this action?

Case 6.2

Motivating Employees

When Ciel Alperin took over the ladies' handbag department at R. H. Macy & Company's New York department store, she established several important goals. One was to increase sales without increasing the number of salespeople or the way they were paid. She also wanted to improve customer service and employee satisfaction. Unlike some retail supervisors, Ms. Alperin was not in a position to use commissions to reward improved performance. All her employees were paid a straight wage without a commission, and all members of the staff were unionized.

Her first step was to give all full-time employees their own counter area and their own line of merchandise. She also increased the responsibility of the sales staff for managing their own inventory and their own line of merchandise. Any salesperson who needed information or simply wished to offer the buying staff suggestions was encouraged to talk with the buyer of handbags. Previously, the sales staff felt they were not supposed to talk to buyers.

Every week, Ms. Alperin brings the staff together for a meeting. At these meetings, she emphasizes the importance of customer service and reviews any changes in departmental policies and procedures. She also encourages employees to discuss their own problems and ask questions. These meetings provide Ms. Alperin with an opportunity to publicly recognize the accomplishments of employees.

Questions

1. What motivational needs did Ms. Alperin satisfy for her full-time employees?
2. Is Ms. Alperin a Theory X, Theory Y, or Theory Z manager?
3. Ms. Alperin achieved significant productivity gains because of the complete change in employees' attitudes. What motivational strategies did she use to achieve this success?

Notes

1. Norman Vincent Peale, "Imagine Your Way to Success," *National Association for Professional Saleswomen*, October 1983.
2. "30 Ways to Motivate Employees to Perform Better," *Training/HRD*, March 1980, p. 51.
3. Fred Luthans, *Organizational Behavior* (New York: McGraw-Hill, 1973), p. 392.
4. "Eastern and Western Management: Different Worlds," *Training and Development Journal*, August 1982, p. 11.
5. A. H. Maslow, *Motivation and Personality* (New York: Harper and Row, 1954).
6. H. C. Kazanas, *Effective Work Competencies for Vocational Education* (Columbus, Ohio: National Center for Research in Vocational Education, 1978), p. 12.
7. Robert Levering, Milton Moskowitz, and Michael Katz, *The 100 Best Companies to Work for in America* (New York: New American Library, 1985), p. 39.
8. "How Bosses Get People to Work Harder," *U.S. News and World Report*, January 29, 1979, p. 63.
9. "Maslow's Term and Themes," *Training*, March 1977, p. 48.
10. "Eight Who Switched to Selling—Thanks to Hard Times," *Sales and Marketing Management*, September 13, 1982.

11. David J. Rachman and Michael H. Mescon, *Business Today*, 4th ed. (New York: Random House, 1985), p. 235.

12. John Nirenberg, "Constraints to Effective Motivation," *Supervisory Management*, November 1982, p. 27.

13. Levering, Moskowitz, and Katz, p. 231.

14. Christopher Byron, "An Attractive Japanese Export: The XYZ's of Management Theory Challenge American Bosses," *Time*, March 2, 1983, p. 74.

15. Frederick Herzberg, *The Managerial Choice: To Be Efficient and To Be Human* (Salt Lake City, Utah: Olympus Publishing, 1982), p. 130.

16. Eric Berg, "Intrapreneurs: These Mavericks Shake Up Stodgy Firms," *Roanoke Times and World News*, April 21, 1985.

17. Ibid.

18. William Baldwin, "This Is the Answer," *Forbes*, July 5, 1982, pp. 50–51.

Suggested Readings

Eddy, William B., and W. Warner Burke. *Behavioral Science and the Manager's Role.* San Diego, Calif.: University Associates, 1976.

Gellerman, Saul W. *Motivation and Productivity.* New York: AMACOM, 1978.

Herzberg, Frederick. *The Managerial Choice: To Be Efficient and To Be Human.* Salt Lake City, Utah: Olympus Publishing, 1982.

Herzberg, Frederick, Bernard Mausner, and Barbara Bloch Synderman. *The Motivation to Work.* New York: Wiley, 1959.

McGregor, Douglas. *The Human Side of Enterprise.* New York: McGraw-Hill, 1960.

Maslow, Abraham H. *Motivation and Personality.* New York: Harper and Row, 1954.

Maslow, Abraham H. *The Farther Reaches of Human Nature.* New York: Viking Press, 1971.

Pinchot, Gifford, III. *Intrapreneurship*, New York: Harper and Row, 1985.

Quick, Thomas L. *Understanding People at Work.* New York: Executive Enterprises Publications, 1976.

Vroom, Victor. *Work and Motivation.* New York: Wiley, 1964.

Chapter 7

Personal and Organizational Values

Chapter Preview

After studying this chapter, you will be able to

1. Explain the nature of values and how they influence behavior.
2. Discuss the importance of personal and organizational values and how they are formed.
3. Understand the difference between terminal and instrumental values.
4. List some of the major values motivating managers.
5. Understand how values affect human behavior in organizations.
6. Discuss some of the value and ethical conflicts that exist today in American organizations.

Frank Lautenburg, fifty-eight-year-old founder of Automatic Data Processing, a computer services firm, took a look at himself one day and decided that someone with his experience and business knowledge should be in government. When he ran for his first U.S. Senate term, he spent a record $3.4 million and defeated veteran Millicent Fenwick to become the junior senator from New Jersey. He had a dual motivation for leaving a successful firm and entering politics: the need for a new challenge and the painful memory of his father's death from cancer at the age of forty-three. He would like to help prevent other people from going through the same ordeal. As a result, Lautenburg says he will be working on health-oriented legislation.[1]

When Corning Glass Works decided to close one of their plants after nineteen years in operation, they didn't just give two weeks notice to their employees and then shut their doors. Instead, they quietly went about assisting former employees through a program called the Corning Community Fund. For a year after the plant was closed, former workers drew on this $125,000 fund as they eased into the transition to unemployment or lower-paying jobs. The fund helped some workers stay in training programs or school. It assisted others in making payments for fuel oil, home mortgages, cars, and other crucial bills. About seventy families were helped by the fund.[2]

Fashion designer Calvin Klein's ads are intended to shock. Ever since fifteen-year-old Brooke Shields seductively announced to a television audience that "nothing" came between her and her Calvins, the public has come to expect a similar shock from his ads. Klein has lived up to his reputation. In recent years, his ads have become even more blatantly sexual, and some of his newest ads are downright kinky. For instance, a recent ad in a fashion magazine pictures two men and a woman, wearing only the tiniest of briefs, sleeping together on a bed covered with towels. The lack of a caption or explanation allows readers to fill in the details as they like. According to Klein, who relies on instinct to create his own ads, the ads aren't meant to offend anyone. But they are meant to be ambiguous, and they do catch the eye. The appeal of his ads depends on continually pushing the boundaries of what is considered acceptable.

The decisions in each of these examples were based on personal or organizational values. Whether we are aware of it or not, values lie at the core of our personality and our organizations. On the basis of our value system, we determine what is important, which people to trust, what goals are worth pursuing, how we adapt to change, and what moral and ethical choices to make. Yet few people know consciously what their values are or what values guide the organization they work for. As a result, even though values represent the motivating force behind much of what is done, they remain a hidden, silent power.

In this chapter, we examine the importance of values, how they are formed, their influence, and the role they play in organizational life.

The Nature of Values

Values are the worth or importance we assign to an object or idea, and our **value system** is the set of standards by which we live. Values are so deep-seated in our personality that they are never actually "seen." What we "see" is the way in which values manifest themselves through attitudes, opinions, behavior, and the like.[3] For example, an individual may stay overtime to help a customer trace a lost order. The *attitude* displayed here is a willingness to help a customer solve a problem. The *value*, which serves as a foundation for this attitude, may be that of service to others or of loyalty to organizational policies. These are values that apply in many situations.

Values are more enduring than your attitudes or opinions. They represent deep preferences that motivate you. During your study of Chapter 6, you examined motivational strategies that organizations implement to achieve maximum productivity. This chapter will help you to discover what it is that motivates you. This discovery can only be made through a careful examination and clarification of your personal value system. Once you clarify your values, you can pursue the career and organization that best fits your value system.

Most successful organizations are based on a well-established value system. Tom Peters and Robert Waterman, authors of *In Search of Excellence*, doubt that a company can be excellent without clarity of values.[4] Values provide direction for the countless decisions made each day, at all levels of the organization. Choices or options that run counter to those values are either rejected or simply not considered. The Dayton-Hudson Corporation, a diversified retailing company, provides a good example of a corporation that has made a strong commitment to maintaining an organizational value system. The following information appears in their statement of philosophy:

> The policy of the corporation is to maintain a consistently high standard of business conduct, ethics and social responsibility. Individual employees are expected to demonstrate high levels of integrity and objectivity, unencumbered by conflicting interests in all decisions and actions affecting the corporation.[5]

As organizational values develop, they may be expressed in slogans, mottos, or creeds that communicate to the outside world what the organization stands for. Examples include Westinghouse Electric's "Progress Is Our Most Important Product," or Zenith's "The Quality Goes In Before the Name Goes On." These slogans, however, may simply be well-meaning platitudes; the true test of its values lies in the quality of the relationships between the organization and its environment—including customers, other companies, government, and suppliers—and between employees and management.

Values are equally important in understanding human behavior, since they

Quality is Job 1

"Teamwork helps us do a better job."

Michael Duncan
Fender Fitter
Kansas City, Missouri
Assembly Plant

Everybody talks about quality, Ford people make it happen.

Many stages in the building of a car need the attention of more than one person. Like the fitting and securing of front fenders, which Michael Duncan does as part of his team on the assembly line.

There is a commitment to teamwork throughout Ford Motor Company, among employees, management, union and suppliers. **This teamwork is paying off with a 48% average improvement in quality over 1980 models as reported by new car owners.**

Visit a Ford or Lincoln-Mercury dealer and see for yourself what quality teamwork can achieve.

At Ford Motor Company, Quality is Job 1.

Ford

Ford
Mercury
Lincoln
Ford Trucks
Ford Tractors

The slogans used in this advertisement express Ford Motor Company's organizational values. (Ad courtesy of Ford Motor Company)

so strongly influence people's actions. If people of different races, ethnic groups, religions, and backgrounds understand one another's value systems, they may be more appreciative and tolerant of others' behavior. Similarly, work problems might be handled more effectively if management and labor have a better understanding of each other's values. As business becomes more international, gaining a knowledge of different nations' value systems is essential. Such knowledge can prevent breakdowns in relations caused by misunderstanding the priorities and preferences of members of different cultures. It can also establish a common ground for international relations and trade.

How Values Are Formed

It has been said that although values cannot be taught, they can be learned. To a large degree, this assertion is true. We acquire our values more by watching the behavior and attitudes of others than by listening to what people *say* about values. This fact holds true whether it is one individual learning from a family or workers learning from an organization.

Acquiring Your Personal Values

Psychologists agree that individual values are formed early in life and are acquired from a variety of sources, as shown in Figure 7.1. In the early years, parents are the dominant influence in shaping your values. They teach you what behavior is acceptable and unacceptable and which character traits are to be encouraged or changed. Later, personal experiences, friends, teachers, and others outside the family will help shape your value system. Morris Massey, a noted psychologist, describes the powerful process of *modeling—* basing your behavior on people you admire—in establishing personality and values. The heroes and heroines you discover in childhood and adolescence help you form a "dominant value direction" that complements your basic personality.[6] In organizations, mentors can serve as value models. They not only teach younger workers job skills, but they transmit the values of the organization to their protégés.

Finally, changes in society will influence your value system. What was unacceptable yesterday may be commonplace today. As a result, differences in value systems constitute a major part of what has been described as the generation gap between those born in one decade and those born two or three decades later.

For generations, movies have had a powerful impact on personal values. During World War II, movies portrayed tough John-Wayne heroes and a romanticized version of war. During the Vietnam War, however, movies portrayed the futility of war with heroes such as Jane Fonda and John Voight. The post-Vietnam generation sees Rambo, portrayed by Sylvester Stallone, as the indestructible, romantic hero fighting for what he believes.

Each generation is influenced by different events and different models. A corporate manager of the 1950s and the manager of a food co-op in the 1980s will use some of the same organizing skills but for different purposes. Value differences account for much of the conflict between younger workers and

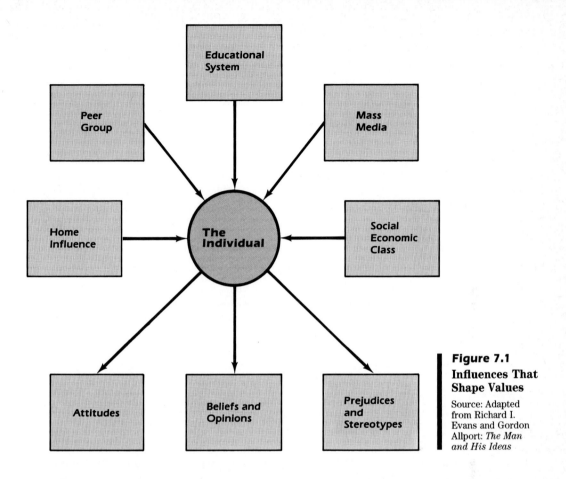

Figure 7.1

Influences That Shape Values

Source: Adapted from Richard I. Evans and Gordon Allport: *The Man and His Ideas*

older managers. Figure 7.2 shows some of the people and events that have influenced the value system of each generation in the past sixty-five years.

Terminal and Instrumental Values Throughout your life your basic values may not change, but you may rearrange them in some sort of order or priority. Your priorities change as you mature and your needs and goals change. For example, early in your career, education may be given priority over earning money. After acquiring a full-time job, achieving material success and being accepted by coworkers are likely to be more important.

Some values—such as security, family relationships, and spiritual growth—will continue to have high priority all through a person's life. Milton Rokeach calls these **terminal values**, representing goals you will strive to accomplish before you die. Other values will reflect the way you prefer to behave. Rokeach calls these **instrumental values**.[7] Each individual will determine which values are instrumental and which are terminal. A list of some of these values is shown in Table 7.1 (on page 164).

World War I		Great Depression		World War II		Korean War
Prohibition		Breadlines		Rosie the Riveter		Television
	Radio		The New Deal		MacArthur	Dr. Spock
Flappers		Charles Lindburgh		Eisenhower		Baby Boom
Women Vote				A-bomb		

```
|——————————————|————————————————|————————————————|————————
1919           1929             1939             1949
```

Rath's Values Test How can you know if you truly value something? One rule of thumb is to notice how strongly you react when the value is challenged or questioned. Yet such reactions could also be simply the result of adopting the values of parents or friends. For years, Arlene's mother and grandmother had emphasized that competition was unladylike. In her present job, Arlene had never applied for a promotion because it meant competing with other employees for the position. Finally, a friend persuaded her to put in an application for department supervisor. During the interviewing process, Arlene discovered that she had a strong competitive drive that she had been suppressing. She had never thought to question the value that women should not compete.

Louis Rath, a well-known authority in values clarification, offers a step-by-step process—a **values test**—by which you can determine if you really value something. Test your terminal and instrumental values against Rath's seven steps.

1. *Did I choose this value freely, with no outside pressure?* To be meaningful to an individual, a value must be freely selected.

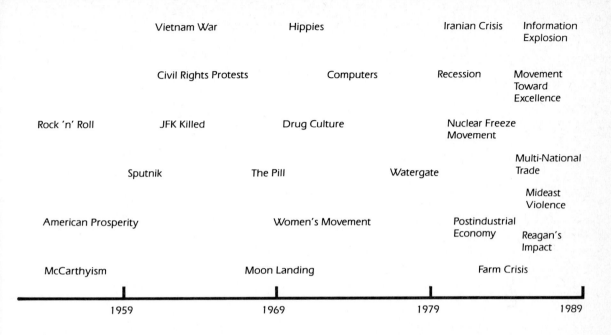

Figure 7.2
People and Events That Have Influenced the Formation of Values

Source: Adapted from Warren H Schmidt and Barry Posner, *Managerial Values and Expectations*

2. *Did I choose this value from several alternatives?* Values are the result of the choices people make.

3. *Did I consider the consequences of my choice?* Values are selected after careful consideration of the consequences of the alternatives offered.

4. *Do I like and respect this value?* Values are prized; they are the motivational mainspring of our actions.

5. *Will I defend this value publicly?* Are you willing to affirm your choice even if others diagree with you? If you value something privately and deny it publicly, chances are it is not something you truly value.

6. *Will I base my behavior on this value?* Does the value influence your actions?

7. *Do I find this value is persistent throughout my life?* Is the value consistently applied in life situations? Does it have a lasting influence on you?[8]

People, Ideas, or Things?   Your activities, attitudes, and behavior often indicate whether your value system is oriented mainly toward people, ideas, or things. Someone who enjoys working with machinery, equipment, or other

Table 7.1 Terminal and Instrumental Values

Terminal Values	Instrumental Values
Comfortable, prosperous, stimulating life	Ambitious and hard working
Sense of lasting contribution and accomplishment	Capable, competent, and effective
	Cheerful, creative, courageous
Equal opportunity for all	Honest, sincere, truthful
Family security, loved ones taken care of	Independent, self-reliant, self-controlled
Freedom of choice and independence	Loving, affectionate
	Respectful, obedient, forgiving
Enjoyable, leisurely life	Responsible and dependable
Self-respect	Neat and tidy
Social respect and admiration	Polite and well-mannered

objects will have values that are oriented toward *things*. Other people may love to work with ideas and concepts, devising strategies or creating solutions to complex problems. They may be more interested in the theoretical than the practical approach to problem solving. They are *idea* oriented. Still others are more comfortable working with people and find their greatest satisfaction in group activities, reflecting a value system that is *people* oriented.

You probably will not identify totally with any one category, but will tend to prefer one of these three value groupings. When people with different value orientations work together, conflicts can arise.

In the 1980s, American Telephone and Telegraph Company (AT&T) had to adjust to a more competitive, deregulated environment, which meant shifting from a somewhat passive sales and service approach to a more aggressive posture. One management faction, oriented toward products, wanted to make the switch quickly. Employees, they said, could be trained to sell services and equipment to the public in short seminars. But another faction, oriented more toward people, was concerned about the impact such a change would have on employees. They called in a research firm which found that an abrupt shift in company goals and values from "universal service" to "universal selling" would be a psychological shock to employees who had been oriented toward service, not sales. They recommended that the company build in the new values as carefully and thoughtfully as they had instilled the old ones in workers. It took many years for the AT&T culture to develop. Any attempt to make rapid changes in established policies and procedures might have negative consequences.

Thinking/Learning Starters

1. Using the list of terminal and instrumental values given in Table 7.1 as a guide, list your own values—those representing goals you would like to accomplish before you die and those representing standards of behavior you feel are important.
2. Can you identify the value models in your own life? Are those of your childhood and adolescence still important to you now? What values did these models exemplify?
3. Is your value system oriented toward people, ideas, or things? How do you express these values in your work or activities?

Development of Organizational Values

Like personal values, organizational values are forged over a number of years and are strongly influenced by key people in the organization as well as by events and conditions in the environment, as shown in Figure 7.3. For example, changes in the competitive or legal environment will cause changes within the organization as management responds to new conditions. Yet such responses do not take place haphazardly. Each organization has developed its own particular guidelines.

Basically, every organization has a "culture" of its own, guided by its value system that acts as a standard for behavior, goal setting, and strategic decision making. In a turbulent environment, values provide a sense of direction amid conflicting views and demands. They also indicate which matters will receive the most attention—public relations, cost cutting, research and development—and what kind of information is taken seriously—"number crunching" by financial analysts, the experienced judgment of older workers, the advice of outside consultants, and so on.

Values also have considerable impact on human relations within the organization. They determine who will be the most respected—engineers or marketers or financial types. And they play an important role in determining who rises to the top. If research and development is the overriding value, then scientists, engineers, and technicians will tend to be promoted and occupy the top jobs. If service is an important value, field service and sales personnel will have the strongest support. The organization reinforces the primary values by promoting the greatest number of people in these jobs.

Many successful companies, such as Procter & Gamble, point to their strong set of values as one of the bases of their success. In the case of Procter & Gamble, the founders did not sit down to design a value system but developed it by testing what did and did not work in the marketplace.

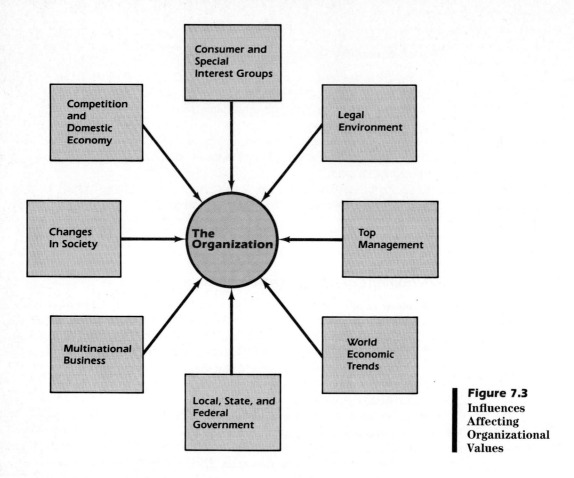

Figure 7.3
Influences Affecting Organizational Values

Procter & Gamble is a tightly disciplined organization dedicated to high performance. To achieve its high standards, P&G believes that the corporation's interests must be inseparable from those of its employees. The company carefully nurtures its employees, hiring at the entry level and promoting strictly from within. And throughout its history, P&G has been a leader in employee benefits.

▶ In 1885, P&G began giving its employees Saturday afternoons off, with pay.
▶ In 1887, the company instituted a profit-sharing plan.
▶ In 1915, P&G was one of the first companies in the nation to adopt comprehensive sickness, disability, and life insurance programs.
▶ In 1923, P&G guaranteed that production people who consistently performed well would have regular employment of not less than 48 weeks per year. (Employees who loaf, however, are fired.) This policy remains in effect today.

▶ In 1980, P&G ranked in the top 4 percent in terms of benefits paid to employees, according to a survey of 983 companies conducted by the U.S. Chamber of Commerce.[9]

Another strong value at P&G is the commitment to innovation and risk-taking. Harley Procter, cousin to one of Procter & Gamble's founders, continually sought ways to reach consumers and increase sales. He was among the first to use display advertising, radio commercials, and an independent sales force. His innovative use of new technology and consumer trends kept the company at the top of its field. To this day, P&G is always first in advertising expenditures.

While P&G is committed to the value of taking care of its employees, their tremendously high sales volume is a direct result of their recognition of the consumer's importance. P&G developed many of its products and a good part of its reputation by paying attention to consumer needs.

The Risks of Developing Strong Organizational Values

There are times when having a strong value system may be a problem as well as a source of organizational unity and strength. Management needs to be aware of some of the risks involved in building a strong set of values.

Obsolescence   Changes in the environment may make an organization's value system obsolete. AT&T's current difficulties in moving from a service to a sales orientation is a case in point. Newer companies such as MCI Communications Corporation and GTE Sprint Communications have moved quickly to capture part of AT&T's market. Their value systems are already geared toward offering competitive consumer products tailored for use in small offices and for commercial long-distance phone calls.

Resistance to Change   New or expanding markets may challenge an organization's traditional values as it tries to change from one method of operation to another. Within recent years, Sears, Roebuck and Company tried to become a merchandiser on the model of a department store such as Macy's. The new venture quickly faltered. Employees, trained to deliver value to middle-income consumers, did not know how to run a Macy's-style operation. The strategy, although potentially promising, had to be abandoned.

Inconsistency   Management must adhere to the values they intend to promote. Executives cannot emphasize to employees the value of improving customer service and at the end of the year place financial performance over customer service. If they reward departments that improved their cost-profit picture and penalize departments that spent money to upgrade customer relations, they will confuse employees and undermine the organizational value system.

One organization that maintains a high level of consistency is McDonald's Corp. Throughout the world, from Australia to Europe to Japan, the high standard of cleanliness and consistency of service at every McDonald's restaurant is impressive. Not everyone likes the product, but the kind of quality assurance McDonald's has achieved worldwide is truly extraordinary.[10]

Thinking/Learning Starters

1. Think about the values of the school you attend or the company you work for. What values seem to be expressed by the organization's attitude and behavior toward products and people?
2. In what ways do the actions and values of top management influence organizational values?

Values and the Manager

The values of management, particularly top executives, set the tone for the entire organization. In addition, managers must be flexible and sensitive enough to supervise people whose value systems and expectations differ from their own. Yet the stereotype of the typical American manager is that of a tough-minded pragmatist who makes decisions based on hard facts and who keeps personal feelings out of the decision-making process. Given a choice, so the stereotype goes, the manager would choose the organization over every other consideration, including the family.

What is frequently overlooked is that managers like everyone else are driven by their personal value systems. Managers must make such value-laden choices as how to balance immediate consumer needs against the long-term benefits of the organization, how to divide time between family and job, what information to examine or ignore, and what employee behavior to reward or discourage. The values of managers are open to influence from experience, the environment, the organization, and other people.

Shifts in Personal Values

Managers of yesterday, products of the post-Depression era, were driven by a strong work ethic and placed a premium on the security of their jobs and incomes. Today's highly educated managers tend to place a high premium on work that allows for self-actualization. Some of them reject their parents' aspirations of upward mobility and dedication to work in favor of a lifestyle that leaves them time to pursue leisure activities. Using Rokeach's table of

Today's managers are more likely to make family life a high priority. (Photo by Janice Fullman, The Picture Cube)

instrumental and terminal values, they tend to list ambition far below responsibility and honesty.[11]

For generations, managers were expected to put their company priorities over family concerns. This just isn't the case any more. Even Lee Iacocca refuses to work weekends. He believes it is important to spend time with his family, and he has been known to reprimand his executives who claim they have no time for a vacation. Managers at Wal-Mart stores nationwide do not open their doors on Sunday until noon to allow their employees to attend church with their families.

In recent years we have seen an apparent shift in the values of women who rise to management positions. Sixty percent of the women managers surveyed in one study found greater satisfaction in their careers than in home

Table 7.2 **Changing Management Values**

Past Value	Current and Future Values
1. A business manager's sole responsibility: to optimize stockholder wealth; operational management dominant	1. Profit still dominant but modified by the belief that a business manager has other social responsibilities
2. Business performance measured solely by economic standards	2. Performance measured by economic and social standards
3. Emphasis on quantity of products	3. Emphasis on quality as well as quantity of products
4. Authoritarian management	4. Permissive/democratic management
5. People subordinate	5. People dominant
6. Financial accounting	6. Financial, human resources, and social accounting
7. Short-term intuitive planning	7. Long-range comprehensive, structured planning
8. Little concern for the social costs of production	8. Increasing concern for internalizing social costs of production
9. Centralized decision making	9. Decentralized and small-group decision making
10. Entrepreneurs who prosper by concentrating on exploiting opportunities they perceive in the environment	10. Entrepreneurs who are able to innovate but who also understand political, technical, social, human, and other forces influencing their organizations
11. Business standing aloof from government	11. Business-government cooperation and convergence in planning

Source: Adapted with permission of Macmillan Publishing from *Management Policy and Strategy* by G. A. Steiner, J. B. Miner, and E. R. Gray. Copyright © 1982 by Macmillan Publishing Company, p. 54.

life, compared to 37 percent of the males. The women surveyed were more willing to relocate, to work longer hours, to accept job promotions, and to give up outside activities. They also seemed more confident that they would fulfill their life's ambitions and were more likely to feel that their values were compatible with those of their organization.[12]

Like the shifts in personal values over the past six decades, management values have also been influenced by changes in society. Table 7.2 shows some of the major value shifts that have occurred in the past few years. The new management values reflect the change in public awareness and concern about the environment, the impact of equal employment opportunity and antidiscrimination laws, the liberal movements of the 1960s and 1970s, and the growing trend toward interdependence and worldwide economic markets. Although still upholding the traditional values of the "rugged entrepreneur," American managers seem to realize that the entrepreneur works within a highly interdependent, complex environment.

Thinking/Learning Starters

1. What would you say are your value priorities between home life and career, personal interests and organizational demands, concern for people and your own ambitions?
2. What do you think are the most important values a manager should have? The least important? How do they match up with' the management values listed in Table 7.2?

Organizational Values and Human Relations

So far we have seen how values determine the direction and purpose of organizations. In this section, we look at how they affect human relations. Within an organization, values can be a source of both unity and conflict.

Harmonizing Personal and Organizational Values

It is natural to assume that the values of management and the organization are closely aligned. What is less well understood is that in many highly successful firms, most employees—from line workers to clerical personnel to supervisors—also share the basic values of the organizations.

Shared values are perhaps the strongest bond among workers in an organization. They come to think of themselves as "Motorolans," "IBMers," or "Pepsi-Cola people," not simply as employees who happen to work for a particular organization. Shared values are developed in two ways.

First, management bears the major responsibility for transmitting the organization's value system to employees through training and orientation sessions, personal example, group policies, and continual evaluation and feedback. Barry Posner and J. Michael Munson of the University of Santa Clara (California) underscore the importance of values in managing employees: "Knowing something about an individual's value system is essential in designing effective motivators. . . . Employers must be sure that the rewards they offer are actually rewards."[13] Posner and Munson are convinced that value testing, using instruments like the Rokeach test, should be as much a part of matching employees to jobs as administering vocational-interest tests. They have found that subordinates with values similar to those of their manager establish better personal and working relationships than do those whose values differ from their superiors'.

Second, as individuals better understand and clarify their own personal values, they can choose the career and organization that best suits their needs. For example, if you have a strong value orientation toward helping others, you might choose to work in a nonprofit service organization rather than a manufacturing plant. Also, in many cases, individuals find that they can identify their personal goals with those of the organization. If you value self-development and your organization is committed to developing the skills and talents of its employees, you probably will feel that your personal and corporate values are in harmony. When the values of employees are expressed in the work they do and the organization they work for, they are likely to feel more competent and fulfilled. In this regard, shared values are built by the employees' dual commitment to individual and corporate interests and expectations.

Collective or shared values also determine "how things are done" in an organization. Workers have guidelines for their behavior and a system of rewards and penalties reinforcing the standards. People work a little harder simply because they are more dedicated. Similarly, managers can make better decisions because they are guided by these shared values. If the organization's dominant concern is productivity, managers will make choices that favor productivity. Managers and others tend to give their strongest attention to whatever is stressed in the organizational value system.

Organizations with strongly shared values resemble the now-famous Japanese style of management. In the Japanese system, the collective sense of responsibility for the work and success of the company serves as the foundation for worker-management relations. This value expresses the belief that everything important in life happens as a result of teamwork or collective effort. They put little emphasis on rewarding individual effort or in singling out individuals for special recognition.[14] Although this value still seems foreign to Americans, the concept of teamwork is becoming widely recognized as a motivating force in organizations.

However, Rosabeth Moss Kanter makes an interesting qualification to this approach in her book, *The Change Masters*. "Shared philosophy—family feelings—can't be stimulated or imposed artifically because top management wants to create a Japanese-style organization; it has to derive from the way work is done.[15] Kanter identified the typical organizational culture as overly centralized in terms of power, authoritarian, resistant to change, and extremely compartmentalized with respect to work units. American companies will need to change their structure if they wish to institute shared value systems that emphasize teamwork.

It may be that as more companies examine the success of organizations like IBM, Delta, Motorola, and others, they will recognize the power of shared values and focus greater attention on the value system within their own corporate cultures.

The collective sense of responsibility for work and the success of the company serves as the foundation for worker-management relations in most Japanese organizations. (Photo by J. P. Laffont, Sygma)

Values and Conflict

If values can unite, they can also divide. One of the major causes of conflict in the organization is a clash in values. **Value conflicts** can arise within an individual or between individuals. Dr. Don Beck, a leading proponent of value system analysis, points out that when it comes to values:

> People *are* different. These differences pop out in offices, factories ... anywhere and anytime people get together.... They prefer different jobs, work environments, learning systems, social relationships, and other expressions of their uniqueness.[16]

In fact, many observers suggest that organizations look for value conflicts when addressing the problem of declining productivity. The trouble may lie not so much in work schedules or production routines as in the mutual distrust and misunderstanding brought about by clashes in workers' and managers' value systems.

Internal Value Conflicts   Value conflicts within an individual usually force the person to choose between strongly held values. Eric is the director of training and development for a large corporation, a job he considers to be a step along the road to administrator of office services. When he took over the job six months ago, he noticed that employees promoted to management positions from within the company were not given adequate management training and support. Some of them failed in their new jobs and left the company. Eric feels a strong sense of responsibility to such people and has proposed an in-house management development program.

Upper management does not want to invest time and money in such a program. Their attitude seems to be "let the new managers sink or swim."

Eric's immediate boss, the man he will replace when the latter retires next year, counsels Eric to forget the program. He will only make things difficult for himself and could endanger his promotion if he is too insistent. Lately, two employees have come to Eric asking his advice about applying for supervisory positions. He knows that with proper training the two would probably succeed. Without it, they could fail. Should he continue to press for the management development program, perhaps jeopardizing his career? Or should he take his boss's advice, keep quiet about the lack of support, and encourage the employees to apply?

You may experience many kinds of value conflicts on the job. As a manager, you may be torn between loyalty to the workers and loyalty to upper management. As an employee you may find yourself in conflict between fulfilling family obligations and devoting the time and energy required to succeed at work. Whatever value proves to be the stronger over time is the one that will determine which choice you make. How you resolve these internal value conflicts will greatly affect your attitude toward yourself, your career, and the people close to you.

Value Conflicts with Others   Some of the most common interpersonal value conflicts arise between workers of different generations, races, cultures, ethnic, or religious backgrounds; between men and women; and between supervisors and workers. Older and younger employees may clash over different interpretations of the work ethic and the priorities of job and personal life. Older workers and managers wonder why younger workers seem to believe that the world owes them a living. Middle-aged workers battle mid-life crises and worry about the meaning of their lives. Younger workers, who have learned to be suspicious of big business and the government, vow to avoid burnout and search for jobs that will let them do their own thing.[17] Women may find that even though they achieve management status, they are still being placed in support positions away from corporate power centers. Minority workers may feel that one set of standards is used to judge the performance of whites and another standard is used to judge their own performance.

Value conflicts between workers and management can often be traced to a lack of communication. Yet to work effectively together, employees and managers must learn to appreciate each other's perspective on work and life. Given differences in attitudes, values, and lifestyles, is it any wonder that communication between younger and older workers, let alone between younger managers and older subordinates, occasionally breaks down?

Managers can influence workers more effectively if they understand the value systems of those around them. Also, managers must make sure that organizational systems and procedures are compatible with employees' strongest values. Too many organizations focus attention on such factors as physical surroundings and fail to consider employees' desires for self-worth and job satisfaction.

Value conflicts based on racial, ethnic, gender, or religious differences often provoke deep emotional reactions within workers. Unless such conflicts are handled skillfully, confrontation can make the situation worse, not better. The Fiber Industries subsidiary of Celanese Corporation in Charlotte, North Carolina, developed a ten-session training program to teach employees how to deal with such value conflicts.[18] The first session outlined the issues to be resolved, which ranged from racial distrust to on-the-job discrimination experienced by women. In bringing up their value conflicts, workers were encouraged to talk about the kind of workplace they wanted. This strategy focused their attention on improving the quality of life for everyone, not just for one group. The remaining sessions helped employees discover the common ground they shared and provided methods for solving their differences.

At the end of the workshop, employees felt they had forged a set of values that reflected more clearly their own expectations and needs. For example, managers were surprised to learn how strongly workers valued knowing more about the "whys" of business. All levels of employees were impressed by the commonality of their work values and their standards for personal relationships. Through the techniques and methods provided in the workshop, employees learned firsthand the value of using compromise, nonjudgmental attitudes, and mutual respect and understanding in handling value conflicts.

Thinking/Learning Starters

1. Can you recall a time when you shared a common value system with a group or organization? What were the values expressed? How did they influence your attitudes and behavior?
2. What value conflicts have you experienced within yourself? With others? What were the values involved? How did you resolve these conflicts?

Corporate Values and Ethics

It is in the area of corporate ethics that one can see clearly how the values of top management set the course for the organization. **Ethics**, as distinguished from values, is the study of right and wrong behavior, usually based on a moral or religious doctrine. Most managers believe that unethical behavior is largely dependent on the organizational climate—especially the actions of one's immediate boss. The issue of corporate ethics is receiving increasing attention from the public, various levels of government, and business itself.

The Problem of Corporate Crime

One state antitrust prosecutor observed that managers with an exclusive profit and economic values orientation were more likely to consider illegal shortcuts when the market was tight. In recent years, the media has carried headlines concerning organizations involved in corporate crime.

Item: The E. F. Hutton Group Inc. pleaded guilty to 2,000 counts of wire and mail fraud for excessive, illegal overdrafts. The scheme resulted in millions of dollars in interest-free loans obtained from the illegal "float." E. F. Hutton ordered the practices halted and ultimately agreed to pay a fine of $2 million and to reimburse the banks for the interest they lost.

Item: Federal courts ruled that Exxon Corp. unjustly reaped huge profits by interpreting the provisions of the 1973 Emergency Petroleum Allocation Act to Exxon's advantage. Exxon was ordered to pay more than $2 billion for overpricing crude oil during the energy crisis of the 1970s. As it was impossible to assess the damages done to refineries, jobbers, manufacturers, and consumers, the $2 billion was placed in a special government account and disbursed to all fifty states to fund energy conservation programs.

Item: General Electric Co. pleaded guilty to making false claims and statements that defrauded the U.S. Air Force. The fradulent billings involved a $47 million contract to refurbish the Minuteman Mark-12A intercontinental ballistic missile. The company paid fines totaling $1 million and reimbursed the Air Force $800,000.

Item: Jacob Butcher, former chairman of the United American Bank and the key person behind the Knoxville, Tennessee, World's Fair, pleaded guilty to misuse of bank funds that led to the downfall of eight Butcher banks. He was sentenced to twenty years in prison.

These items represent only a small fraction of the corporate crime that goes on today. The majority of executives involved are rarely caught or brought to trial. What would you do if your organization asked you to do something you know is illegal or dishonest? This question led Henry Makow, a part-time professor at the University of Manitoba, Canada, to design a game called "A Question of Scruples." There are no right or wrong answers to this game and very few rules. The point of the game is the conversation sparked by questions such as, "In the supermarket, you send a dozen packages tumbling into the aisle. No one sees you. Do you walk away?" One corporate executive commented, "After I played it [Scruples] with my attorney, I told him 'I don't think I want to do business with you anymore.' "[19] Even the Harvard Business School is beginning to offer classes concerning ethics and personal responsibility. Candid discussions with your peers and clarification of your value system will offer you invaluable guidance when you are faced with moral, ethical, and legal conflicts in your organization.

Table 7.3 **Dayton-Hudson Corporation Statement of Philosophy**

Ethical Standards and Business Conduct

The policy of the corporation is to maintain a consistently high standard of business conduct, ethics and social responsibility. Individual employees are expected to demonstrate high levels of integrity and objectivity, unencumbered by conflicting interests in all decisions and actions affecting the corporation.

Corporate policies governing the business conduct of employees will serve as a minimum standard of performance. Premier status requires exemplary behavior and attitudes—conduct befitting premier employees.

Source: Dayton-Hudson Corporation. Reprinted by permission.

Emphasizing Corporate Ethics

Yet more companies than ever are promoting strong business ethics and incorporating humanistic values into corporate planning. In many industries, companies have adopted codes of ethics, such as the Dayton-Hudson Corporation's statement of philosophy shown in Table 7.3. These companies also provide training sessions to make the codes a reality in corporate policy and practice. International Paper Company sponsors a film, *The Price*, that warns employees of the dangers of price fixing. Allied Corporation of Virginia requires that a statement of proper business practices must be read and signed by all executives each year.[20] And Sears, Roebuck has announced that it will not enter into financial dealings with the government of South Africa because of that country's racial policies.

Many business executives see greater emphasis now being placed on corporate values and ethics by top management. According to George Coombe, executive vice president and general counsel of the BankAmerica Corp., "the situation is very different today from what it was in the past. Most major corporations now have a law-compliance mechanism in effect, and more boards of directors are personally addressing this question than ever before."[21] Clearly, the challenge of forging an effective value and ethical system is an important, ongoing concern.

Values and Ethics in International Business

If the situation is complex on the domestic scene, values and ethical issues become even more complicated at the international level. The subject is too broad to treat in detail in this chapter, but we can provide an overview of some of the conflicts that exist in international business.

Foreign Corporate Ethics   In many countries, bribery, under-the-table payments, kickbacks, and other practices considered illegal in the United States are part of everyday business. Many managers are underpaid and look

Total Person Insight Chris Lee	All organizations have a stake in the way their employees behave, and the way those actions may be interpreted by customers, government regulatory agencies and the courts, after the fact. Recent scandals in the defense and financial industries probably have done more to focus public consciousness on business ethics than any events since Watergate.

to these additional "revenue" sources to supplement their incomes. An American firm that wants to do business in these countries may find itself at a serious competitive disadvantage if it does not conform to the local value system.

Foreign Corporate Cultures   The nations of the world are becoming interdependent. Each culture has its own human relations "language" that, when understood by foreigners, can enhance respect for other countries' value systems. This understanding can increase the chances of effective human relations. Here are some rules of protocol that exist in various countries:[22]

Japan   Trade between the United States and Japan has increased tremendously since the end of World War II. As Americans complete business transactions with the Japanese, they are identifying value differences that could destroy the American–Japanese relationships. For instance, Japanese never say *no* in public. "Naniwabushi," getting on close personal terms with someone so that she or he will have to do you a favor, is a standard business procedure. As a result, accepting lavish gifts from Japanese business acquaintances can lead to potentially awkward obligations. In addition, the Japanese value system stresses teamwork, not individualism. Employees feel that they are part of the "family." In American organizations, people who stand out for their high achievements are rewarded. In Japan, however, they are reprimanded.

France   The French get down to business matters immediately, but are slow to make decisions. They also display an endless fascination with details. Whether good news or bad, they state their intentions unambiguously. The French operate within a highly bureaucratic culture. Their management styles tend to be impersonal and standardized, with rigid procedures and centralized hierarchies.

Germany   A technological, paternalistic culture dominates, with functional "empires" and considerable interdepartmental competition. The typical manager is a technician. Men walk and sit to the left of all women and men of senior business rank, and men rise when a woman leaves or returns to the table. Germans are offended if you don't know that West Germany is officially called the Federal Republic of Germany, and East Germany the German Democratic Republic.

Great Britain Emotions are rarely vented and adherence to protocol is a must. Business is usually relegated to the office, while lunch, dinner, and weekends are set aside for socializing. The British keep engagement calendars and frown upon spur-of-the-moment invitations.

People's Republic of China The Chinese are sensitive to status and title. Never rely on "Mr." to take the place of a person's proper title, such as "Committee Member," "General," "Factory Manager," or "Bureau Chief." The Chinese often show regard for members of their own sex by publicly holding hands or by some other physical contact; however, opposite sexes rarely make any public show of affection.

In joint ventures between nations where value differences are recognized, both sides will need to spend time and effort building mutual respect and understanding. Figure 7.4 offers a diagram of the multinational complexities of the auto industry. Imagine the problems that could result if everyone involved ignored the value systems of the other countries!

The True "Transnational" Company As more firms do business in other nations, they are realizing the importance of reflecting this international trend not only on the balance sheet but in the board room. Ciba-Geigy Corp., a Swiss company, has put a foreign director on its executive board and conducts its meetings in English. Other companies, such as Coca-Cola, which does business in over 135 countries, will likely follow suit. Such practices can increase understanding of one another's value systems and help develop a more uniform system of international business ethics.

Summary

Values are the personal worth or importance people assign to an object or idea. People's value systems serve as the foundation for their attitudes, preferences, opinions, and behavior.

Personal values are formed early in life and are influenced by parents, the process of living, and changes in society's values. Values can be categorized as terminal or instrumental. Louis Rath's seven-step test can determine whether a value is an important, influential one in a person's life. Most people's value systems are oriented toward ideas, people, or things. Corporate values act as standards for behavior, goal setting, and strategic decision making. They are strongly influenced by top management.

The personal value systems of modern managers have undergone a major shift. Changes in corporate values have helped alter managers' values also.

Shared values unify employees in an organization by providing guidelines for behavior and decisions and by fulfilling workers' most important expectations and needs. On the other hand, most conflicts in organizations can be

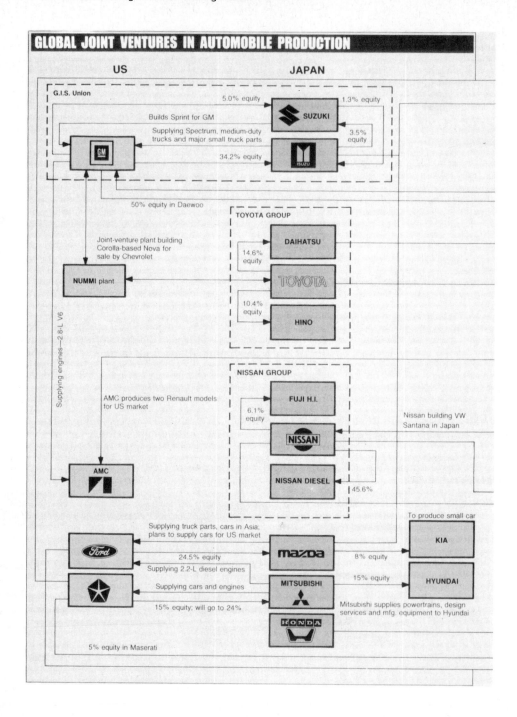

GLOBAL JOINT VENTURES IN AUTOMOBILE PRODUCTION

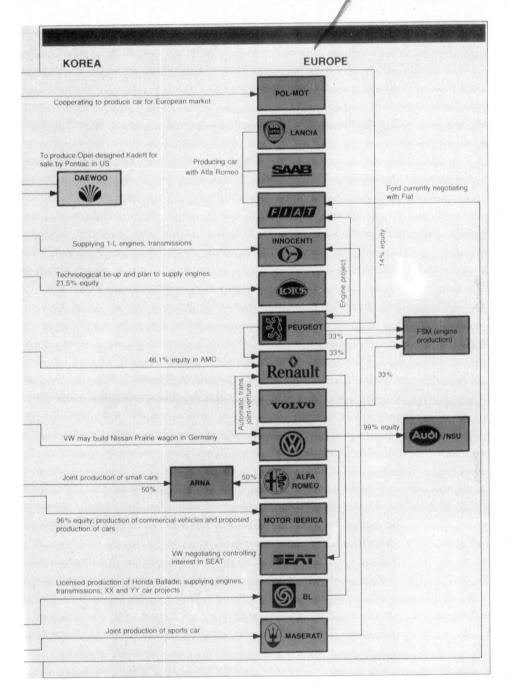

Figure 7.4
Global Joint Ventures in Automobile Production
Source: Chart courtesy of *Automotive Industries*, September, 1985.

traced to value clashes. Internal value conflicts involve choices between strongly held values. Value conflicts based on age, racial, religious, gender, or ethnic differences often require skilled intervention before they can be resolved.

Corporate values and ethics on both the domestic and international levels are receiving increasing attention. Top management, governments, and the public are holding organizations more accountable for their actions.

Key Terms

values
value system
terminal values
instrumental values

values test
shared values
value conflicts
ethics

Review Questions

1. How do values differ from attitudes, opinions, or behavior?
2. Define terminal and instrumental values. How can clarifying these values help you in your choice of a career?
3. Test one of your values against Louis Rath's seven criteria listed in this chapter. Is the value one you have chosen yourself or simply adopted from others?
4. Who has had the most influence on your value system? Which values did he or she influence the most?
5. Explain some of the ways management values are changing. What factors seem to be influencing these changes?
6. What functions do values serve in an organization?
7. How do top management values affect the purpose and direction of an organization?
8. What are some of the most common types of value conflicts in organizations? Why do they often need skilled intervention to be resolved?
9. How can knowing something about employees' value systems help a manager?
10. In your opinion, is a company ever justified in engaging in unethical behavior? Explain your answer.

Case 7.1

Tandem's Golden Rules of Management[23]

Tandem Computers Inc. is considered a "far out" company even by California standards. Started twelve years ago, the company already earns $300,000,000 per year. Its success is credited not only to a product that has captured a sizeable share of the market, but also to a remarkable management value system promoted by founder-president James G. Treybig.

Treybig feels his company "represents the convergence of capitalism and humanism," and his management philosophy emphasizes the twin goals of corporate growth and the development of human potential. It is based on five golden rules:

1. All people are good.
2. People, workers, management, and company are all the same thing.
3. Every single person in a company must understand the essence of the business.
4. Every employee must benefit from the company's success.
5. You must create an environment where all of the above can happen.[24]

New employees are given extensive orientation sessions that explain the entire company operation and their part in it. Everyone has ready access to top management, and any manager who does not treat employees with respect risks being fired. The rich opportunities for promotion, learning, and initiative give employees a sense of developing their maximum potential. Additionally, all employees receive stock options in the company. The result? Tandem's productivity levels are among the highest and its turnover rate among the lowest of the frontline computer companies.

Questions

1. List some of the dominant values that guide Tandem managers.
2. Evaluate Tandem's five golden rules of management. With which ones do you agree or disagree? Explain your answer.

Case 7.2.

Honesty Tests

Many organizations administer paper-and-pencil honesty tests. Companies who use these tests claim that they contribute significantly to the overall performance of a company by reinforcing the personnel director's ability to select potential employees who will deliver a high measure of performance.

According to companies who sell the tests, the dishonesty of just one employee can undermine the performance of an entire department or company. A dishonest attitude can be, if not outright infectious, certainly disruptive as honest employees begin to question the value of their own efforts and lower their commitment to doing their own jobs well. Since honest employees work more conscientiously, with less turnover and fewer discipline problems, selecting honest employees is essential to high performance and productivity. Some companies who administer the tests claim that they can actually boost the morale of honest employees.

Critics of the test claim that "failing" scores are too easy to obtain. Some of the questions focus on the use of marijuana and other drugs. Yet some conscientious and productive employees, claim the critics, use marijuana after work hours. These employees are penalized if they answer the test questions honestly.

Questions

1. How would you feel about taking an honesty test during a job interview? Explain.
2. If you were a personnel director, would you use honesty tests? Why or why not?

Notes

1. "Dad Would Be Proud," *Forbes*, January 17, 1983, p. 81.
2. Chuck Burress, "Corning Glass Works Stands by Workers," *Roanoke Times & World News*, September 29, 1985, p. 2.
3. Warren H. Schmidt and Barry Z. Posner, *Managerial Values and Expectations* (New York: AMACOM, 1982), pp. 12–14.
4. Thomas Peters and Robert Waterman, Jr., "Values: At the Heart of Corporate Excellence," *Roanoke Times & World-News*, May 29, 1983.
5. Dayton-Hudson Corporation, *Statement of Philosophy*, Minneapolis, Minn. p. 10.
6. Morris Massey, *The People Puzzle* (Reston, Va.: Reston Publishing, 1979).
7. Milton Rokeach, *The Nature of Human Values* (New York: Free Press, 1973).
8. Louis Rath, Merrill Haron, and Sidney Simon, *Values and Teaching* (Columbus, Ohio: Charles Merrill, 1976).
9. Robert Levering, Milton Moskowitz, and Michael Katz, *The 100 Best Companies to Work for in America*, (New York: New American Library, 1984), pp. 288–289.
10. Thomas J. Peters and Robert H. Waterman, *In Search of Excellence* (New York: Harper and Row, 1982), p. xix.
11. Benson Rosen and Thomas Jerdee, "Helping Young Managers Bridge the Generation Gap," *Training*, March 1985, pp. 43, 44.
12. Schmidt and Posner, *Managerial Values and Expectations*, pp. 27–28, 54–56.
13. "Value Studies Are a Clue to Organizational Behavior," *Training/HRD*, March 1981, p. 13.
14. William Ouchi, *Theory Z* (Reading, Mass.: Addison-Wesley, 1981), pp. 40–45.
15. Rosabeth Moss Kanter, *The Change Masters: Innovation for Productivity in the American Corporation.* (New York: Simon and Schuster, 1982), p. 32.
16. Don Beck, as quoted by Will Lorey, "Values System Analysis Theory," *Training/HRD*, January 1981, pp. 38–39.

17. Rosen and Jerdee, "Helping Young Managers Bridge the Generation Gap," p. 44.
18. Charles M. Kelly, "Confrontation Insurance," *Training/HRD*, August 1981, pp. 91–94.
19. Lisa Belkin, "Morality Becomes Party Game with A Question of Scruples," *Roanoke Times & World-News*, September 22, 1985, p. E-6.
20. "Corporate Crime: The Untold Story," *U.S. News and World Report*, September 6, 1982, pp. 25–29.
21. Ibid., p. 29.
22. Research Institute of America, "Do's and Don'ts for the Traveling Executive," *Personal Report*, October 5, 1985, p. 5.
23. Myron Magnet, "Managing by Mystique at Tandem Computers," *Fortune*, June 28, 1982, pp. 84–91.
24. Ibid., p. 87.

Suggested Readings

Buskirk, Richard H. *Modern Management and Machiavelli*. New York: CBI Publications, 1974.

Deal, Terrence E., and Allan A. Kennedy. *Corporate Cultures: The Rites and Rituals of Corporate Life*. Reading, Mass.: Addison-Wesley, 1982.

Gellerman, Saul W., "Why Good Managers Make Bad Ethical Choices," *Harvard Business Review*, July-August, 1986.

Ouchi, William *Theory Z*. Reading, Mass.: Addison-Wesley, 1981.

Scott, William G., and David K. Hart. *Organizational America*. Boston: Houghton Mifflin, 1979.

Smith, Maury. *A Practical Guide to Value Clarification*. La Jolla, Calif.: University Associates, 1977.

III

Personal Strategies for Improving Human Relations

Chapter 8

Constructive Self-Disclosure

Chapter Preview

After studying this chapter, you will be able to

1. Explain how constructive self-disclosure contributes to improved interpersonal relationships within an organization.
2. Understand the specific rewards you can receive from self-disclosure.
3. Identify the major elements of the Johari Window model.
4. Explain the criteria for appropriate self-disclosure.
5. Understand the barriers to constructive self-disclosure.
6. Apply your knowledge and practice self-disclosure.

An outpouring of national grief was triggered by the loss of the space shuttle *Challenger*. The shuttle explosion evoked powerful feelings, especially among those who could identify closely with the lost crew. In the words of one psychiatrist, "The shuttle explosion left a psychological wake that rippled from those closest to the astronauts and NASA out to the entire American people."[1]

Nowhere was the sense of loss and grief more pronounced than in Concord, New Hampshire. One of the astronauts, Christa McAuliffe, had lived and taught school in this community. On the day of the tragedy, students and faculty members cried openly as they confronted their sadness and disbelief over the death of their colleague and teacher. The day after the accident, twenty-five psychologists, guidance counselors, and therapists went into the public schools to help students deal with their grief. They encouraged the children to talk about their feelings and to accept them, rather than try to explain them away or change the way they feel.

In other parts of America, school personnel scheduled class discussions to allow students to talk openly about the accident. Parents were encouraged to talk to their children about the shuttle explosion. Many children said they felt better after such discussions. A 10-year-old Indiana girl said: "I felt very sad. I talked to my parents about it. It made me feel better to talk." A thirteen-year-old New York City girl said: "I was sad and shocked. We talked about it a lot in school and it helped."[2]

Self-Disclosure: An Introduction

"We talked about it a lot in school and it helped." These words, spoken so eloquently by the young girl from New York City, provide testimony to the effectiveness of self-disclosure. The open sharing of feelings, which was encouraged in this school setting, provided an outlet for the anxiety, guilt, and feelings of grief that surfaced after the national tragedy.

Should the disclosure of feelings be encouraged in organizations? Alice Sargent, author of *The Androgynous Manager*, says yes. She states that organizations should encourage openness in expressing feelings and emotions.[3] Although you may not fully share Sargent's view, you will probably agree that much of the growth and satisfaction we experience on the job is an outgrowth of open communication with coworkers and supervisors. You enjoy working in an environment where ideas, recommendations, and concerns can be exchanged freely. A spirit of openness often results in higher morale and increased productivity.

As a general rule, relationships grow stronger when people become more open about themselves. Yet in many organizations, people are encouraged to hide their true feelings. The result is often a weakening of the communication process. Self-disclosure can lead to a more open and supportive environment in the workplace. This chapter focuses on constructive self-disclosure and the conditions that encourage appropriate self-disclosure in a work setting.

Self-Disclosure Defined

Self-disclosure is the process of letting another person know what you think, feel, or want. It is one of the important ways you let yourself be known by others. The primary goal of self-disclosure is the building of strong and healthy interpersonal relationships.

It is important to note the difference between self-disclosure and self-description. **Self-description** involves disclosure of information that is non-threatening, such as your age, your favorite food, or where you went to school. This is information that others could acquire in some way other than your telling them. Self-disclosure usually involves some risk. You are revealing private, personal information that cannot be acquired from another source. Examples include your feelings about working with minorities, job security, and views toward new policies and procedures.

Information given through self-disclosure often improves the quality of communication between two people. For example, you work in a factory and are extremely conscious of safety. You take every precaution to avoid work-related accidents. However, a fellow employee has a much more casual attitude toward safety rules and often "forgets" to observe the proper procedures, endangering you and other workers. You can choose to disclose your feelings to this person or hide your reactions. If you choose to avoid self-disclosure, the other person may never know your true feelings; and a potentially dangerous situation will continue to exist. It is an interesting fact of life that two people can work together for many years and never really get to know each other.

Thinking/Learning Starter

On a sheet of paper, list the names of three people with whom you have worked or gone to school for approximately the same length of time. Now place a check mark next to the person who you feel knows you the best. What type of information have you shared with this person that he or she could not obtain from other sources?

Rewards to Be Gained from Self-Disclosure

Before discussing self-disclosure in more detail, it may be helpful to examine four basic rewards you receive from openly sharing what you think, feel, or want.

1. *Increased accuracy in communication.* Self-disclosure often takes the guesswork out of the communication process. No one is a mind reader; if people conceal how they really feel, it is difficult for others to know how to respond to them appropriately. People who are frustrated by a heavy workload, but mask their true feelings, may never see the problem resolved. The person who is in a position to solve this problem needs to be made aware of it. Others should not have to guess how you feel.

The accuracy of communication can often be improved if you report both facts and feelings. When you self-disclose, the other person receives not only information, but an indication of your feelings. In some organizational settings, the established channels of communication encourage reporting facts, but not feelings. Consider the salesperson who is assigned to a large regional territory. This person corresponds with the sales manager through a series of weekly sales reports. The standard sales report is not a good medium to use to report feelings. Unless these two people get together for periodic face-to-face meetings where feelings can be discussed, communication may break down.

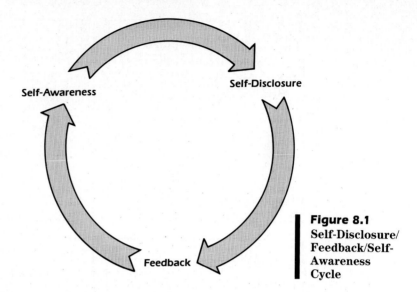

Figure 8.1
Self-Disclosure/
Feedback/Self-
Awareness
Cycle

2. *Reduction of stress.* Sidney Jourard, a noted Swiss psychologist who has written extensively about self-disclosure, feels that too much emphasis on privacy and concealment of feelings creates stress within an individual. Too many people keep their feelings bottled up inside, which can result in considerable inner tension.

Can you recall a time in your life when you were extremely upset over some problem, but did not disclose your feelings to the person who might have been able to solve it? The stress that builds when you avoid self-disclosure can have a harmful effect on your personal health and your performance on the job.

The inner tension you feel may translate into the conclusion, "I am right and the other person is wrong." Over time, if nothing is said between you, your conviction may grow stronger and your inner tension more intense. In most cases, the only way to reduce this tension is to communicate your feelings directly and have the other person try to understand your viewpoint. You may be surprised to hear the person say, "Gee, I didn't know you felt that way. I wish you had come to me sooner."

3. *Increased self-awareness.* Chapter 1 stated that increased self-awareness should be one of the important outcomes of instruction dealing with human relations. Self-awareness is the foundation on which self-development is built. In order to plan an effective change in yourself, you must be in touch with how you behave and how your behavior affects others.[4] People make decisions regarding appropriate behavior based in large part on self-awarenss. Once they are aware of how their behavior affects others, they can choose to change it. Self-awareness increases as you receive feedback from others. The quality of that feedback depends largely upon how much you self-disclose (see Figure 8.1).[5]

To illustrate how self-disclosure can trigger feedback, which in turn increases self-awareness, consider Dana Holden's problem. She is the supervisor of a drafting department, and for several weeks she had felt frustrated by her staff's lack of output. They had been taking too long to complete some projects, and she was being pressured by her boss to get the work done. Finally she decided to schedule a staff meeting to air her concerns.

At the staff meeting, Dana talked about her frustration and invited comments on the problem. One person said reluctantly, "I feel we need to set specific deadlines for each project." Another person said, "Yes, we need deadlines, and you should periodically ask us for progress reports." Dana began to realize that she needed to introduce more structure into her department. After the meeting, she drafted work schedules and report forms, and she discussed them with her staff. The result was greater teamwork and increased productivity.

4. *Relationships grow stronger.* Another reward from self-disclosure is the strengthening of interpersonal relationships. When two people engage in an open, authentic dialogue, they often develop a high regard for the other's views. Often they discover they share common interests and concerns, and these serve as a foundation for a deeper friendship. John Powell, author of *Why Am I Afraid to Tell You Who I Am?*, said about the importance of openness:

> Anyone who builds a relationship on less than openness and honesty is building on sand. Such a relationship will never stand the test of time, and neither party to the relationship will draw from it any noticeable benefits.[6]

Thinking/Learning Starter

Mentally review your previous work experience. Identify at least one occasion when you felt great frustration over some incident, but avoided self-disclosing your feelings to the person in the organization who could have done something about the problem. What factors motivated you not to self-disclose?

The Johari Window:
A Model for Self-Understanding

A first step in understanding the process of self-disclosure is to look at the Johari Window, illustrated in Figure 8.2. This communications model takes

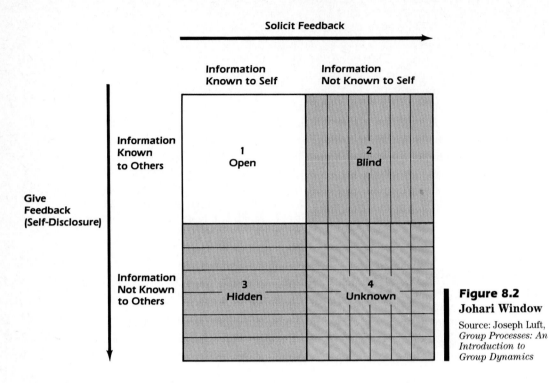

Figure 8.2
Johari Window

Source: Joseph Luft,
Group Processes: An
Introduction to
Group Dynamics

into consideration that there are some things you know about yourself and other things you are not yet aware of. In addition, there are some things that others know about you and some things they are not aware of. The name "Johari" is a combination of the first names of its originators, Joseph Luft and Harry Ingham.

The **Johari Window** identifies four kinds of information about you that affect your communication with others. With the aid of this model, you can explore your potential for increasing your levels of awareness and acceptance through sharing. In other words, the more time and energy you spend hiding information and feelings, the less clearly and effectively you communicate with others.[7] Think of the entire model as representing your total self as you relate to others. The four panes of the window are labeled (1) open area, (2) blind area, (3) hidden area, and (4) unknown area.

1. *Open area.* The **open area** of the Johari Window represents your "public," or "awareness" area. This section contains information about you that both you and others know, and includes information you don't mind admitting about yourself. As your relationship with another person matures, the open pane gets bigger, reflecting your desire to be known. Building a relationship usually involves working to enlarge the open area. The person who possesses

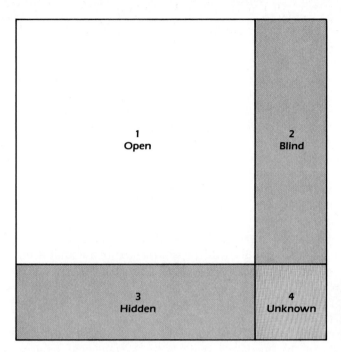

Figure 8.3
Johari Window for a Person with Great Self-Awareness

a great deal of self-awareness and openly shares information and feelings with others will have a Johari Window like the one in Figure 8.3.

2. *Blind area.* The **blind area** consists of information about yourself that others know, but you are not aware of. Others may see you as aloof and stuffy, whereas you view yourself as open and friendly. Or you may view your performance at work as "mediocre," and others see it as "above average." You may consider your dress and grooming practices appropriate for work, but others feel your appearance is not suitable for such a setting. Perhaps you annoy others by frequently pushing your glasses up on your nose with your finger, but are not aware of this mannerism. The more you learn about the information in the blind area, the more you are able to change behavior that may serve as a barrier to improved relations with others.

Building a relationship often involves working to enlarge the open pane and reduce the size of the blind pane. This can be achieved as you become more self-disclosing, thus encouraging others to disclose more of their thoughts and feelings to you. People don't mind giving feedback to a person who is open and willing to share appropriate personal information with them.

3. *Hidden area.* The **hidden area** contains information about you that you know, but others do not. This pane is made up of all those private feelings, needs, and past experiences that you prefer to keep to yourself. These could be incidents that occurred early in life or past work-related experiences you

would rather not share. You should not feel guilty about keeping some secrets. Everyone is entitled to conceal thoughts that are personal and of no concern to others.

4. *Unknown area.* The **unknown area** of the Johari Window is made up of things unknown to you and others. Since you—or anyone else—can never know yourself completely, this area will never disappear. The unknown may represent such things as unrecognized talents, unconscious motives, or early childhood memories that influence our behavior but are not fully understood. Many people have abilities that remain unexplored throughout their lives. A person capable of rising to the position of office manager remains a receptionist throughout his or her career because the potential for advancement is unrecognized. You may possess the talent to become a portrait artist, but never discover it.

Some of the unknown information that is below the surface of awareness can be made public with the aid of open communication. Feedback from others can reduce the size of the unknown pane and increase the size of the open area.

The four panes of the Johari Window are interrelated. As you change the size of one pane, others are affected. At the beginning of a relationship, for example, the open area is likely to be somewhat small. When you start a new job, your relationship with your supervisor and fellow workers might look like the Johari Window in Figure 8.4, in which the open area is very small. As time passes and you develop a more open relationship with the people you work with, the Window in Figure 8.5 might describe your relationship more accurately.

Enlarging Your Open Window

We can take positive steps to develop a larger open window and reduce the size of the other windows. If you want to reduce the blind area, display a receptive attitude that will encourage others to give you feedback. You can also actively solicit feedback from your supervisor and fellow workers in a way that they will feel comfortable in giving it to you. If you want to reduce the hidden area, which contains information you have been keeping from the group, consider disclosing your perceptions, opinions, and feelings. In other words, let the group know where you stand. As you receive more feedback and engage in more self-disclosure, the open window will become larger.[8]

If the open area of your Johari Window is large, you tend to give and receive information about yourself freely. Others see you as honest and trustworthy; they don't have to guess about your intentions. You are always in a position to control the size of the open pane.

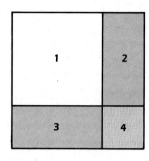

1	2
3	4

Figure 8.4
Johari Window
at the
Beginning of a
Relationship

Figure 8.5
Johari Window
After a Close
Relationship
Has Developed

Thinking/Learning Starter

To test your understanding of the Johari Window, write the term "open," "blind," "hidden," or "unknown" in the appropriate space.

1. _____Gary, a file clerk with a large insurance company, has the potential to become a proficient stenographer. Neither he nor his fellow workers are aware of this latent talent.

2. _____Three years ago, Sara was fired from a job without any explanation from her employer. She has never shared this information with anyone.

3. _____At a recent meeting with her sales manager, Jean expressed doubts about her ability to close sales. The sales manager indicated that he had experienced the same feelings early in his career.

4. _____Jerry sees himself as humorous and entertaining. Fellow workers view his type of humor as vulgar and offensive.

Appropriate Self-Disclosure

At the beginning of this chapter, we stated that the primary goal of self-disclosure should be to build stronger and healthier relationships. This goal can be achieved if you learn how to self-disclose in a constructive way. Appropriate self-disclosure is a social skill that anyone can learn.

As a general rule, seek a balance between disclosing too much and disclosing too little. Gerard Egan, author of several books on interpersonal growth, says self-disclosure can be seen as a continuum, with the overdisclosers at one end and the underdisclosers (or nondisclosers) at the other.

Some people are overdisclosers; that is, they either talk too much about themselves or talk too intimately about themselves in social situations that do not call for that kind of intimacy. Others are underdisclosers, unwilling to let others know anything about them except what can be picked up from observation. They speak little or not at all about themselves. They do not speak intimately of themselves even when the situation calls for intimacy.[9]

He feels that people should strive for the "golden mean" on the self-disclosure continuum, avoiding the extremes of complete concealment and complete openness.

When searching for criteria to determine the appropriateness of self-disclosure in an organizational setting, many factors needs to be considered. How much information should be disclosed? How intimate should the information be? Who is the most appropriate person to share information with? Under what conditions should the disclosures be made? In this section, several criteria that will help you develop your self-disclosure skills are examined.

Use Self-Disclosure to Repair Damaged Relationships

Many strained relationships are unnecessary. They often exist because people refuse to talk about real or imagined problems. Self-disclosure is an excellent method of repairing a damaged relationship. The sales manager for a southern manufacturing firm and the manager of customer accounts maintained a feud for three months because neither person was willing to disclose his or her true feelings. The problems began when a bill was sent to an important customer who had previously paid his account in full. The customer called the sales manager and complained. The sales manager in turn called the manager of customer accounts and accused her of incompetence. As soon as he spoke the words, he was sorry. He had overreacted. The manager of customer accounts, anxious to defend her department, responded angrily with very strong language. She later regretted her lack of self-control. After several weeks, the sales manager visited the manager of customer accounts and said, "Look, I'm sorry for what I said to you. It's clear to me that you run a tight ship, and I should not have reacted to the billing problem with such anger. Please accept my apology." The two managers shook hands, and each returned to work feeling relieved that the problem was solved.

Avoid a Judgmental Attitude

John Powell states that true friendship and mutual respect develop through a process he describes as "gut-level" communication.[10] He says that gut-level communication (emotional openness and honesty) must never imply a judgment of the other person. Emotional candor does not require passing judgment.

Staff meetings are often appropriate settings for self-disclosure on job-related problems. (Photo © Sandra Johnson, 1982)

In many organizations, one employee is put in the position of evaluating the performance of another employee. If the organization uses a formal system of performance appraisal, periodic evaluation may be mandatory. It is during these performance appraisal sessions that a judgmental attitude may surface. The supervisor must assume the dual role of judge and helper. If the supervisor is viewed as being too judgmental, the employee may become defensive and reject helpful suggestions.

How can you apply John Powell's criteria for constructive self-disclosure in a real-world situation? Put yourself in the role of a supervisor counseling a new employee who has been late for work several times. Which of the following statements would be most appropriate?

▶ "Your lack of responsibility has been a real disappointment to me."
▶ "Coming to work late tells me that you are not really interested in this job."
▶ "I'm probably more sensitive than other supervisors about employees coming in late. It means a lot to me to have my staff arrive at work on time."

The last statement does not imply a judgment of the other person's behavior, but it does communicate the supervisor's true feelings about tardiness. Always avoid making statements that can be interpreted as a personal attack. Never say, "I want to talk to you about your mistake" or "You made a mistake."[11]

It is often helpful to preface open communication with some kind of disclaimer to assure the other person that there is no judgment implied. In a situation where you feel another person was too critical of your behavior, you might begin the conversation by saying, "I may be overly sensitive, but the comment you made yesterday did hurt my feelings."

Discuss Disturbing Situations as They Happen

Our reactions to a work-related problem or issue should be shared as soon after the incident as possible. It is often difficult to recapture a feeling once it has passed, and you may distort the incident if you let too much time go by. Your memory is not infallible. The person who caused the hurt feelings is also likely to forget details about the situation.

If something really bothers you, express your feelings. Clear the air as soon as possible so you can enjoy greater peace of mind. Some people maintain the burden of hurt feelings and resentment for days, weeks, even years. The avoidance of self-disclosure usually has a negative effect on one's mental and physical health, as well as performance on the job. Pent-up emotions are one of the most common causes of stress.

Accurately Describe Your Feelings and Emotions

It has been said that one of the most important outcomes of self-disclosure is to make it possible for others to become acquainted with the "real" you. When you accurately describe your feelings and emotions, others get to know you better. This kind of honesty takes courage because of the risk involved. When you tell another person how you feel, you are putting a great amount of faith in that person. You are trusting the other person not to ridicule or embarrass you for the feelings you express.[12]

Too often, people view verbalizing feelings and emotions in an organizational setting as inappropriate. This may seem strange since emotions are so much a part of human behavior. People should not be expected to "turn off"

Total Person Insight	It's unfortunate that we're never really taught how to show emotion in ways that *help* our relationships. Instead, we're usually told what we should *not* do. However, too little emotion can make our lives seem empty and boring, while too much emotion, poorly expressed, fills our interpersonal lives with conflict and grief. Within reason, some kind of *balance* in the expression of emotion seems to be called for.
Gerard Egan	

their feelings the moment they arrive at work. Experiencing feelings and emotions is a part of being human.

What is the best way to report emotions and feelings? Some examples may be helpful. Let's assume you expected to be chosen to supervise an important project, but the assignment was given to a fellow worker. At a meeting with your boss, you might make the following statement:

> "For several weeks I've been looking forward to heading up this project. I guess I didn't realize that anyone else was being considered. Now I not only feel disappointed, but embarrassed."

A fellow worker is constantly borrowing equipment and supplies, but usually fails to return them. This person's actions have caused you a great deal of inconvenience and frustration, and you have decided to disclose your feelings. Here is what you might say:

> "Thanks for taking a few minutes to meet with me. I'm the type of person who likes to keep busy, but lately I've spent a lot of time retrieving tools and supplies you have borrowed. I've been experiencing a great deal of frustration, and decided I should tell you how I feel."

As you report your feelings, be sure the other person realizes that your feelings are temporary and capable of change. You might say, "At this point I feel very disappointed, but I am sure we can solve the problem."

Expressing feelings of anger can be especially difficult for some people. A person brought up in a home where the expression of anger was criticized by parents may later in life avoid letting anger surface. People who are afraid to let someone know they're angry go through life avoiding confrontation. This is unfortunate because everyone should learn how to express anger. Of course, voicing anger by ranting and raving rarely solves anything. The other person will only become defensive and fight back. Neither side wins.

You can learn to express anger in ways that will improve the chances that the other person will receive your message. Some therapists recommend the use of "I" statements. If, for example, a fellow worker is constantly playing practical jokes on you, an appropriate response might be to say, "I really find these jokes irritating. Please leave me alone!" You are reporting your gut-level feelings in a way that is less likely to make the other person defensive.

Select the Right Time and Place

Remarks that otherwise might be offered and accepted in a positive way can be rendered ineffective, not because of what we say, but because of when and where we say it.[13] When possible, select a time when you feel the other person is not preoccupied and will be able to give you his or her full attention. Also, select a setting free of distractions. Telephone calls or unannounced visitors can ruin an opportunity for meaningful dialogue. If there is no suitable place at work to hold the discussion, consider meeting the person for lunch away from the office or talking with the person after work at some appropriate location. If necessary, make an appointment with the person to ensure that time is reserved for your meeting.

Avoid Overwhelming Others with Your Self-Disclosure

Although you should be open, don't go too far, too fast. Many strong relationships are built slowly. (Love at first sight is a rare phenomenon!) The abrupt disclosure of highly emotional or intimate information may drive a wedge between you and the other person. Your behavior might be considered threatening.

Unrestricted "truth" can create a great deal of anxiety in people, particularly in an organization where people must work closely together. To "tell it like it is" with no regard for the sensitivity of the other person may do irreparable damage to a relationship.

As you consider ways to disclose what you think, feel, or want in a constructive manner, remember that you can express yourself in several ways. Thus far, the emphasis has been on the verbal mode of self-disclosure. You can also reveal a great deal through nonverbal self-disclosure. If someone says, "How do you like my new dress?" a note of hesitation in your voice and an expression of doubt on your face may tell the other person you are not very enthusiastic about it. A long pause, or complete silence, following the question will sometimes communicate that you do not know how to phrase your reaction tactfully, or that you hate the dress and prefer to say nothing. The manner in which a verbal message is delivered will also convey other "messages." The emotion in your voice, your eye contact, gestures, and body posture will communicate a great deal about your inner thoughts.

People also self-disclose through actions and symbols. During a political campaign, your preference may be communicated to others by the bumper sticker on your car. The words printed on your T-shirt may tell others what you believe in. The clothing you wear, books you read, music you listen to, how and with whom you spend your leisure time, your hobbies, and other actions communicate information about you to others.

Thinking/Learning Starter

You have reviewed six criteria for constructive self-disclosure. On a sheet of paper, describe at least two situations in which another person violated one or more of these criteria while self-disclosing information to you. Describe your feelings at the time these experiences occurred. What impact did the person's behavior have on your relationship?

Barriers to Self-Disclosure in an Organizational Setting

At this point you might be thinking, "If self-disclosure is such a positive force in building stronger human relationships within an organization, why do people avoid it so often? Why do so many conceal their thoughts and feelings?" To answer this question, you need to examine some of the barriers that prevent people from self-disclosing.

Trust as a Foundation for Self-Disclosure

William Ouchi describes in his book *Theory Z* a unique agreement adopted by members of labor and management at General Motors' Packard Division facility built in Brookhaven, Mississippi. They agreed on a series of principles designed to establish a foundation for long-term success of the plant.[14] The first principle on their list focused on trust: "Without trust, any human relationship will inevitably degenerate into conflict. With trust, anything is possible."

The word **trust** (derived from the German word *trost*, meaning comfort) implies instinctive, unquestioning belief in another person or thing. In a two-person relationship, trust exists when you fully believe in the integrity or character of the other person. When the trust level in an organization is high, employees express faith and confidence in the leadership.

Lack of trust is perhaps the most common—and the most serious—barrier to self-disclosure. Without trust, people usually fear revealing their thoughts and feelings to others—the risks of self-disclosure are too high. When trust is present, people no longer feel as vulnerable in the presence of another person. If the level of trust declines, people tend to raise their defenses out of fear of rejection.

Jack Gibb, in his book *Trust: A New View of Personal and Organizational Development*, states that

> trust makes it unnecessary to examine motives, to look for hidden meanings, to "have it in writing," to have someone—priest, minister, lawyer, therapist, or bureaucrat—intervene between you and me so that we can understand each other or be sure that neither of us is going to hurt the other.[15]

You have confidence in persons you trust and tend to feel open, relaxed, and comfortable in their presence. Gibb also points out that the trust level is the thermometer of individual and group health. When trust is present, people function naturally and openly. Without it, they devote their energies to masking their true feelings, hiding thoughts, and avoiding opportunities for personal growth. Jess Lair, author of *I Ain't Much, Baby—But I'm All I've Got*, describes the effect of trust—or the lack of it—in organizations:

> The more you trust your associates, the more you believe in them, the better they are. The less you believe in them, the worse they are. And yet they are the same people. It's just a difference in what you expect of them.[16]

A Climate for Trust   How does trust grow within an organization? It is more apt to be present when openness is encouraged by people at the top, and information and ideas are freely exchanged. A secure and competent manager will avoid trying to control communications. This person will provide ample opportunity for people to discuss "feelings" as well as "facts." An insecure manager will often attempt to control the nature and the amount of communication that flows throughout the organization. This person deliberately sets up barriers to prevent the natural exchange of feelings, perceptions, and information.

Gibb states that the normal fears people bring to a new job are magnified when they encounter tight controls, veiled threats, and impersonal behavior by supervisory-management personnel. This climate sets the stage for what he describes as the "fear/distrust cycle" (see Figure 8.6).[17] The cycle begins with the management philosophy that people are basically lacking in motivation and cannot be trusted (discussed in Chapter 6 as Theory X). To bring about maximum production, management tries to maintain tight control over employees by initiating a series of strict rules and regulations. As management increases the controls, workers often become more defensive and resentful. The spirit of teamwork diminishes, and everyone in the organization begins talking in terms of "we" versus "they."

When employees display a defensive attitude, management becomes more fearful and less trusting, responding with even tighter controls and more attempts to manipulate members of the work force. The fear/distrust cycle is now a reality and the spirit of teamwork is lost completely. When you assume that someone cannot be trusted, it is surprising how often the person fulfills your expectations!

Thinking/Learning Starter

Recall a situation in which someone created the impression that he or she did not trust you. What did the person do or say to create this impression? How did you react to this behavior?

Role Relationships Versus Interpersonal Relationships

Self-disclosure is more apt to take place within an organization when people feel comfortable stepping outside of their assigned roles and displaying open-

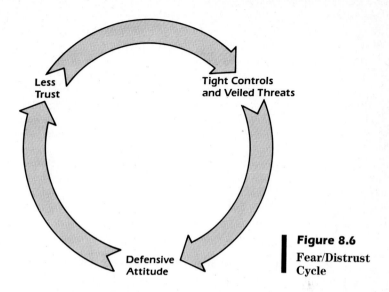

Figure 8.6
Fear/Distrust Cycle

ness and tolerance for the feelings of others. In this society, role expectations are often clearly specified for people engaged in various occupations. For example, some people see the supervisor's role as an impersonal one. Supervisors are supposed to enforce rules and regulations, maintain high production, and avoid getting too close to the people they supervise. The advice given to some new supervisors is, "Don't try to be a nice guy or people will take advantage of you." Yet often the most effective supervisors are those who are approachable, display a sense of humor, and take time to listen to employee problems.

Some newly appointed supervisors may deliberately try to build barriers between themselves and subordinates. They draw a sharp distinction between **role relationships** and **interpersonal relationships.** They are impersonal and aloof, thinking that this is appropriate "role" behavior. Employees usually respond to these actions by becoming defensive or less trusting.

Roles are inescapable, but they need not contribute to the depersonalization of relationships. Role expectations should be clearly stated within an organization, but role differentiation should not lead to a breakdown of interpersonal relations. Each role is played by a person. Others should be able to get to know that person regardless of the role the individual has been assigned.

Familiarity Sets the Stage for Self-Disclosure

Another major barrier to constructive self-disclosure is lack of familiarity. If you don't let others get to know you, they will probably never disclose their feelings, beliefs, and thoughts to you. To the extent that you remain a mys-

Reprinted by permission: Tribune Media Services.

tery, others may decide the risks of self-disclosure are too high.

There is an old saying that "familiarity breeds contempt." Dr. James Carr, management psychologist and public speaker, feels it is time this myth was laid to rest. He states:

> Familiarity breeds contempt? How could it? How could your knowing me intimately make you contemptuous of me unless I had faults that outweighed your own—unless I was contemptible? What do people have to hide when they refuse to let others know them as people?[18]

Dr. Carr also feels that management uses the "familiarity breeds contempt" myth as an excuse for not getting to know the employees they supervise.

> I have long suspected that the "familiarity breeds contempt" premise of leadership was a cop out. It does serve a purpose, you know. By waving your authority, your rank, your degrees or other credentials in the face of your subordinate and holding him at arm's length you can avoid all the bother of knowing him ... or of caring about him. You can prevent his knowing or caring about you as well and thus evade all the responsibility that personal involvement implies.[19]

Dr. Carr raises the issue of teamwork as well. Is it possible to have teamwork without involvement? As we have noted earlier in this text, many employers are organizing employees into teams. When team members are involved in shared decision making and are given the opportunity to work closely with superiors, they generally make a greater commitment to team goals.

Contempt is more apt to surface when people erect barriers that keep others at a distance. It is distance between people and ignorance of their needs, perceptions, and beliefs that give rise to mutual distrust.

Practice Self-Disclosure

If you avoid self-disclosing your thoughts and feelings, you make it harder for others to know the "real" you. You will recall from the beginning of this chapter that self-disclosure involves revealing personal information that cannot be acquired from other sources. This type of information can often improve the quality of your relationships with others.

Do you need to tell others more about your thoughts, feelings, and beliefs? To answer this question, review the statements below. If you tend to agree with most of these items, then you might consider making a conscientious effort to do more self-disclosing.

1. I avoid discussing my concerns even when feelings of anger or frustration build inside me.
2. My relationships with fellow workers tend to be quite formal.
3. In most cases I feel it is best to avoid sharing personal thoughts with coworkers.
4. I feel more comfortable keeping myself under wraps in most work situations.
5. It is best not to discuss a personal problem at work.
6. I avoid giving praise or criticism to deserving coworkers.

It is not difficult to become a more open person if you are willing to practice. If you want to improve in this area, begin by taking small steps. You might want to start with a nonthreatening confrontation with a friend or neighbor. Pick someone with whom you have had a recent minor problem. Tell this person as honestly as possible how you feel about the issue or problem. Keep in mind that your objective is not simply to relate something that is bothering you, but to develop a stronger relationship with this person.

As you gain confidence, move to more challenging encounters. Maybe you feel your work is not appreciated by your employer. Why not tell this person how you feel? If you are a supervisor and one of the people you supervise seems to be taking advantage of you, why not talk to this person openly about your thoughts? With practice you will begin to feel comfortable with self-disclosure, and you will find it rewarding to get your feelings out in the open.

Summary

Open communication is an important key to personal growth and job satisfaction. Self-disclosure, the process of letting another person know what you think, feel, or want, promotes better communication within an organization. Most people want and need accurate feedback from fellow workers and the person who supervises their work.

Constructive self-disclosure can result in many positive rewards to people and organizations. It can pave the way for increased accuracy in communication, reduction of stress, increased self-awareness, and stronger interpersonal relationships.

Everyone can learn how to use self-disclosure in a constructive way. Your goal should always be to approach self-disclosure with the desire to improve your relationship with the other person. You need to describe your feelings and emotions accurately, and avoid making judgments about the other person. Disturbing situations should be discussed as they happen; it is difficult to recapture feelings once they have passed. Select the right time and place to share your thoughts, and avoid abrupt disclosure of highly emotional or intimate information.

A climate of trust serves as a foundation for self-disclosure. In the absence of trust, people usually avoid revealing their thoughts and feelings to others. Self-disclosure is also more apt to take place within an organization when people feel comfortable stepping outside of their assigned roles and displaying openness for the feelings of others.

Lack of familiarity can be a barrier to constructive self-disclosure. To the extent that you remain a mystery, other people may decide the risks of self-disclosure are too high. The old saying that "familiarity breeds contempt" is simply a myth. Too much distance between people can set the stage for mutual distrust.

Key Terms

self-disclosure	hidden area
self-description	unknown area
Johari Window	trust
open area	role relationships
blind area	interpersonal relationships

Review Questions

1. What is the major difference between self-disclosure and self-description?
2. How can self-disclosure contribute to improved teamwork within an organization?
3. List four major rewards to be gained from self-disclosure.
4. Describe how self-disclosure can contribute to increased self-awareness.
5. What is the major difference between the blind area and the hidden area of the Johari Window?

6. What types of interpersonal relationship problems are overdisclosers and underdisclosers likely to encounter?
7. List the guidelines to follow when giving appropriate self-disclosure.
8. In the absence of trust, what major problems can surface in an organization?
9. Describe the fear/distrust cycle.
10. Explain why the old saying "familiarity breeds contempt" is a myth.

Case 8.1

Perceptions of a Black Manager[20]

In the process of collecting information for her book *The Androgynous Manager*, Alice Sargent conducted in-depth interviews with dozens of managers. One of these managers, a black man named Buford Macklin, shared some doubts about the merits of the androgynous style of management.

> If you're conciliatory and try to fit in, then you're homogenized and invisible. Your energy must go to convincing people you're competent. It's never a given, but instead, time and again, it's an uphill battle to prove competence. It's like you're incompetent until you prove otherwise. This means you must be focused and single-minded in your actions. The qualities of androgyny detract from this.

Macklin said that disclosing personal feelings did little to help him climb the management ladder. "It's construed as being soft, indecisive, and unclear. It just does not score the right kind of points to share personal data in the organization with my boss, subordinates, or even colleagues." According to Macklin, style is important. "Credibility requires you to have a strong rational style."

Questions
1. Do you agree or disagree with Mr. Macklin's point of view?
2. In what ways can openness, sensitivity, and concern for people aid Mr. Macklin? In what ways will these behaviors hinder his chances for promotion?

Case 8.2

The Polygraph Issue[21]

To polygraph or not to polygraph? That was the question raised several times during President Ronald Reagan's administration. Alarmed by losses of U.S. secrets to other countries and leaks of information to the press, Reagan turned to the use of lie detectors as part of a strategy for combating espionage. Each time he directed that government employees with access to classified information be subject to polygraph tests, his directive created an uproar in government that persuaded him to rescind it.

In the latest episode, Secretary of State George Shultz declared that "The minute in this Government I am told that I'm not trusted is the day that I leave."[22] Shultz also expressed reservations about the effectiveness of lie detectors, which measure changes in body functions such as breathing rate. Anxiety can cause an innocent subject to appear to be lying; and at least one indicted spy has "passed" a number of polygraph tests.

Another strong opponent of government-wide polygraph testing is Jeane Kirkpatrick, former U.S. Ambassador to the United Nations. She believes that "the institutionalization of distrust may damage the political culture on which democracy rests."[23] Of all forms of government, she noted, democracies have the greatest need for mutual trust. Those who supported the president's directives noted that the unauthorized disclosure of classified information can threaten the security of our nation.

The use of lie detector tests is also at issue in the private sector. Many employees say that a polygraph test is an invasion of their privacy and feel that the experience of taking the test is dehumanizing. Employees also point to the unreliability of lie detector test results. Employers who administer the tests defend them as being necessary and useful. They note that the amount of merchandise and cash stolen by employees has increased in recent years, and lie detector tests help slow this trend. In other cases, they feel that polygraph tests help prevent the selling of technology to competitors.

Questions

1. Do you feel that government employees should be required to take polygraph examinations? Explain your position on this issue.
2. Do you feel that private-sector employees should be required to take polygraph examinations? Explain your position on this issue.

References

1. Daniel Goleman, "Shuttle Tragedy Undermined National Sense of Well-Being," *Roanoke Times & World-News*, February 2, 1986, p. 1. For additional information, see *U.S. News & World Report*, February 10, 1986, pp. 16–21.
2. Adam Clymer, "Most Children Still Enthusiastic About Shuttle, Poll Indicates," *Roanoke Times & World-News*, February 2, 1986, p. A-14.
3. Alice G. Sargent, *The Androgynous Manager* (New York: AMACOM, A Division of American Management Associations, 1981), pp. 189–191.
4. Helen Hall Clinard, *Winning Ways to Succeed with People* (Houston: Gulf Publishing, 1985), p. 200.
5. David W. Johnson, *Reaching Out* (Englewood Cliffs, N.J.: Prentice-Hall, 1981), p. 22.
6. John Powell, *Why Am I Afraid to Tell You Who I Am?* (Chicago: Argus Communications, 1969), p. 77.
7. *Communication Concepts—The Johari Window* (New York: J. C. Penney Company, Inc., Consumer Affairs Department, 1979).
8. Phillip C. Hanson, "The Johari Window: A Model for Soliciting and Giving Feedback," *The 1973 Annual Handbook for Group Facilitators* (San Diego: University Associates, 1973), pp. 114–119.
9. Gerard Egan, *Interpersonal Living—A Skills/Contract Approach to Human-Relations Training in Groups* (Monterey, Calif.: Brooks/Cole, 1976), p. 38.
10. Powell, *Why Am I Afraid*, p. 65.

11. Loren B. Belker, *The First Time Manager* (New York: AMACOM, A Division of American Management Associations, 1978), p. 45.
12. John R. Diekman, *Human Connections* (Englewood Cliffs, N.J.: Prentice-Hall, 1985), p. 63.
13. Hendrie Weisinger and Norman Lobsenz, *Nobody's Perfect—How to Give Criticism and Get Results* (Los Angeles: Stratford Press, 1981), p. 39.
14. William G. Ouchi, *Theory Z* (New York: Avon Books, 1981), p. 158.
15. Jack R. Gibb, *Trust: A New View of Personal and Organizational Development* (Los Angeles: Guild of Tutors Press, 1978), p. 14.
16. Jess Lair, *I Ain't Much, Baby—But I'm All I've Got* (New York: Doubleday, 1969), p. 104.
17. Gibb, *Trust*, p. 192.
18. James G. Carr, "Familiarity Breeds Contempt ... Only If You Are Contemptible," *Pace*, January–February, 1979, p. 15.
19. Ibid.
20. Sargent, *The Androgynous Manager*, p. 164.
21. For more information see *New York Times*, December 23, 1985, p. A-17; *Roanoke Times & World News*, December 30, 1985, p. A-7; *Washington Post*, December 22, 1985, p. A-16.
22. Anthony Lewis, "Abroad at Home," *New York Times*, December 23, 1985, p. A-17.
23. Jeane Kirkpatrick, "Polygraph Produces Aura of Distrust," *Roanoke Times & World-News*, December 30, 1985, p. A-7.

Chapter 9

Learning to Achieve Emotional Control

Chapter Preview

After studying this chapter, you will be able to

1. Explain why employers place a premium on emotional control.
2. Understand the conscious and subconscious influences on behavior.
3. Describe the principles of transactional analysis developed by Dr. Eric Berne.
4. Name the three distinct parts of the personality.
5. Achieve complementary transactions more frequently.
6. Make correct emotional decisions more frequently.

Pitney Bowes is a good example of a company that is striving to balance "high tech" with "high touch." The company's success in marketing mailing systems and sophisticated electronic office equipment requires a blend of innovative technology and excellent customer service. Like most firms in this highly competitive field, Pitney Bowes depends heavily on a staff of well-trained technicians who install and maintain the many types of equipment sold to customers.

Service representatives employed by Pitney Bowes must be highly skilled in the technical aspects of their jobs and possess well-developed human relations skills. When they answer service calls, they must be prepared to repair equipment and, in some cases, respond to the needs of an unhappy customer. When a customer is experiencing downtime because a machine is not working properly, anxiety and frustration may surface. In an effort to help service representatives learn how to deal effectively with impatient or angry customers, the company has adopted a customer relations training program that teaches emotional control. With the aid of this training, representatives are better able to calm angry customers and establish an emotion-free discussion of the problem.[1]

Emotional Control: An Introduction

Much of the happiness we experience comes from the positive emotions that surface when someone recognizes our accomplishments or when we achieve something meaningful. The trust that builds within us when we work with supportive coworkers also produces positive feelings. Just spending time with friends or reading a good book can trigger the emotion of joy. By the same token, much of the unhappiness we experience in our lives comes from negative emotions such as anger, envy, fear, hate, or worry. These are destructive emotions that often serve as barriers to good interpersonal relations. Displaying these emotions at work can damage not only relationships, but one's career as well. In an organizational setting, a premium is placed on a person's ability to control these negative emotions. We live in a society that tends to associate maturity with emotional control.

Destructive emotions can damage our psychological and physical well-being. They destroy peace of mind and often physical health.[2] The starting point in achieving emotional control is to determine the source of emotional difficulties. Why do we sometimes display indifference rather than compassion? Why is it so easy to put down a friend or coworker, and so hard to recognize the person's accomplishments? Why do we sometimes worry about things that will never happen? To answer these and other questions regarding emotional control, it is necessary to study both conscious and subconscious influences on our behavior. We will give only a modest amount of attention to what goes on inside of people and devote most of our attention to what goes on between people.

Conscious Versus Subconscious Influences

Your behavior is influenced by the conscious and subconscious parts of your mind. The **conscious mind** is the mental activity you are aware of and generally control. The ability to recall specific information about a letter typed last week is an example of the conscious part of the mind at work. So is recalling someone's phone number or address.

The **subconscious mind** is a storehouse of forgotten memories, desires, ideas, and frustrations, according to Dr. William C. Menninger, president of the famed Menninger Foundation.[3] He says that the subconscious mind can have a great influence on our behavior.

Although most people cannot remember many of the important things that happened to them during the first years of their lives, these incidents influence their behavior today. For many years, the nature of this influence was discussed in rather vague terms by psychologists and psychiatrists. Sigmund Freud is credited with discovering that different aspects of the subconscious mind influence people's daily thinking and behavior; but Freud and his followers had difficulty explaining the theory to laypeople.

A promising breakthrough in understanding the influence of the subconscious came several years ago with the development of the transactional analysis theory by Eric Berne. This theory of human behavior was explained in his best-selling books *Games People Play* and *What Do You Say After You Have Said Hello?* The practical applications of transactional analysis (TA) were further clarified in the books *I'm OK–You're OK*, written by Thomas Harris, *Staying OK*, by Amy Bjork Harris and Thomas Harris, and *Born to Win*, by Muriel James and Dorothy Jongeward.

Transactional Analysis: An Introduction

In very basic terms, **transactional analysis** is a theory of communication. Without relying on technical language or jargon, TA helps us better understand ourselves and others. It provides a positive tool for achieving emotional control on and off the job. TA also provides a means of understanding and changing an organization. Pan American World Airways has used TA to help customer-contact personnel handle difficult situations. United Telephone Company of Texas used techniques drawn from transactional analysis in a training program geared to help managers become more successful through teamwork. This training enabled managers to adapt their personal reactions to behavior exhibited by others.[4] TA helps people gain insight into their own emotional nature and that of others.

After years of study, Dr. Berne concluded that the brain acts like a two-track stereo tape recorder. One track records events, and the other records the feelings associated with those events. The tape recorder is on all the time from the day of birth.

Picture in your mind's eye a toddling three-year-old walking around his mother's sewing room. He picks up a pair of sharp scissors and begins walking toward the staircase. The mother spots the child and cries, "Tommy, drop those scissors! Do you want to kill yourself?" Tommy's tape recorder records both the event (walking with scissors) and the emotions (fear and guilt). Ten years later, Tommy is taking an art class and his teacher says, "Tommy, bring me a pair of scissors." As he begins to walk across the room, his mind is flooded by the feelings of fear and guilt attached to that earlier childhood event.

If that early experience in the sewing room was traumatic, it may be relived later in life when Tommy is scolded for any reason. A scowling supervisor notices Tommy visiting with a fellow employee and shouts in a shrill voice, "If you don't get back to work, you may be looking for a new job!" The supervisor's tone and expression trigger the emotions associated with being scolded by his mother, and the familiar feelings of fear and guilt return.

Three Parts of Your Personality

People are often not aware of how their behavior looks to others. Sometimes they wonder why they behave the way they do, but more often they wonder why *others* act as they do. Dudley Bennett, author of *TA and the Manager* says:

> To analyze behavior and its motivation, one must first understand that the basic component of behavior is an ego state. An *ego state* is a consistent combination of thought-feelings and related behavior.[5]

Eric Berne discovered, after many years of research, that everyone's personality is composed of three distinct ego states. He used three easily understood terms to describe these sources of behavior: Parent, Child, and Adult.

Parent Ego State   When people are acting, feeling, and thinking as they saw their parents behave, they are said to be in their **Parent ego state**. You acquire the Parent by recording in your brain the way your parents behaved. The name *Parent* was selected by Berne because most of the important tapes are produced when a young person observes and listens to his or her parents or older people who assume a parental role. The tapes inside you include all the dos and don'ts you heard as a child.

Total Person Insight

Dudley Bennett

One of the joys of my work is in helping managers, where it is useful, to think again about their childhood. It is pleasant to re-experience the pains and glories of those early years from the position of concerned understanding. This involves the discovery that grown-ups are actually little boys and girls become large.

▶ "Don't cross the street if cars are coming."
▶ "Do clean off your plate."
▶ "Don't touch the knives. They are sharp and will cut you!"
▶ "Don't talk when Mommy's talking."

For the most part these messages entered your mind unedited. Although most of the messages were spoken for your safety and welfare, the mind was not mature enough to make this distinction. The verbal criticism and physical spanking were often perceived in a negative way. Most people have thousands of do's and don'ts recorded in their subconscious mind. The tapes recorded during those early years are still playing today and account for some of the "I'm not OK" feelings you may experience. On the other hand, you probably received many caresses, hugs, and tender kisses as a child that tended to offset some of the negative aspects of early childhood days.

The Parent has several useful functions. On the job you may be more safety conscious as a result of those early parental warnings. Your protective attitude toward others, and your expression of sympathy can often be traced to early childhood experiences. If you grow up with a strong desire to conserve resources (food, for example), your parents probably deserve part of the credit. A popular and wealthy country-western star with humble beginnings once said: "If you've been without, you learn to share, and to appreciate what you get. You never take it for granted. People sometimes say, 'It must be nice to be able to buy anything you want.' But I can hardly make myself spend $500 on a coat. And to this day, if I've cooked at home, I will not throw anything out, because I can still hear Mama saying, 'You threw that out with all of those children overseas starving to death?'"

In summary, the Parent ego state is two dimensional, as shown in Figure 9.1. When you display a nurturing, caring attitude toward others, you are displaying what can be called the **Sympathetic Parent**. It is the Sympathetic Parent within you that makes it easy to express sincere praise and a caring attitude. The Sympathetic Parent is supportive and protective.

The other dimension of the Parent is referred to as the **Critical Parent**. When you are critical of others, opinionated, and judgmental, you are permitting your Critical Parent to surface. If instructions given on the job are accompanied by a stern look and a booming voice, the person giving these instructions is very likely receiving messages from his or her Critical Parent.

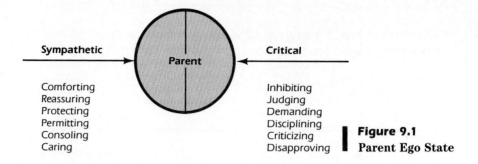

Figure 9.1
Parent Ego State

It is the Critical Parent that causes you at times to be more fault finding than helpful.

Thinking/Learning Starter

Each of the statements below was made by the Sympathetic Parent (SP) or the Critical Parent (CP). In the space provided next to each statement, place the letters SP or CP, depending on which person you think made the statement.

1. _____ "These young workers don't know what hard work is!"
2. _____ "Tom, I'm sorry to learn of your child's illness."
3. _____ "Well, no wonder the adding machine won't work. You put the tape in wrong."
4. _____ "Mary, that's a ridiculous suggestion. You know we can't change store policy!"
5. _____ "Don't feel bad, Tim. Other cashiers have had the same experience."

Child Ego State   As noted earlier, your mental tape recorder records events on one track and feelings associated with those events on another track. It records joy, happiness, and excitement associated with many childhood events. It also records terror, agony, and all the fearful emotions you have experienced.[6]

The Child is the major source of your emotional responses in later years. Persons who display openness, spontaneity, and charm are drawing from their Child. They see nothing wrong with having fun and enjoying life. When a salesperson feels like jumping up and down after closing a big sale, it is the Child that is motivating this behavior. A person who grows up in a home where fun is encouraged and rewarded will find it easy to have fun in later life. Those who grow up in households characterized by negativism and conflict will often find it difficult to enjoy themselves in later years. These people recorded few "fun" tapes as children.

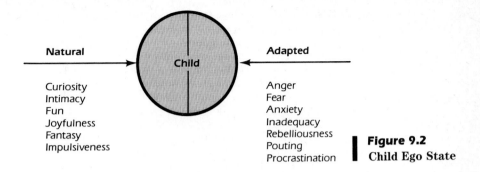

Natural		Adapted
Curiosity	**Child**	Anger
Intimacy		Fear
Fun		Anxiety
Joyfulness		Inadequacy
Fantasy		Rebelliousness
Impulsiveness		Pouting
		Procrastination

Figure 9.2
Child Ego State

The **Child ego state** is also two dimensional, as illustrated in Figure 9.2. Dr. Berne said the Child is exhibited by people in two forms: the Natural Child and the Adapted Child. The **Natural Child** is that part of us that acts as a child naturally would. It is affectionate, impulsive, joyful, and sensuous. Have you ever seen a middle-aged man skip happily along an ocean beach or a young housewife giggle at her birthday party? If so, you saw the Natural Child being expressed. Loud and spontaneous laughter provides yet another clue that the Natural Child is influencing behavior. The Natural Child can also be rebellious, overly aggressive, and unwilling to consider the consequences of feelings and actions.

After birth a child begins to adapt to the demands of others. The behavior results in what Berne calls the **Adapted Child**. This part of the Child ego state is primarily influenced by parents. People frequently learn what they ought to do by being praised or punished. A smile or pat on the back from a parent communicates the idea of approval for doing what is right. The pride you feel today when somebody praises you for your good performance often comes from the Adapted Child. Similarly, the good feeling you get after you've done a job right (particularly if somebody notices or cares) is often a learned feeling.[7]

Angry parental responses convey a sense of punishment for wrongdoing. Most children learn how to avoid pain and how to gain approval during the first few years of life. The young child wants to go to bed when good and ready. When told to go to bed at 8:00 P.M., the youngster demonstrates unhappiness by moving very slowly. A child wants to eat a candy bar just prior to mealtime. The mother says no. The Child responds by displaying a strong outburst of temper. If mother gives in, the child has learned one way to get what he or she wants.

Sometimes the Adapted Child resents complying with the demands of others and does so only grudgingly. The Adapted Child may also feel unsure about himself or herself and therefore procrastinate rather than meet deadlines established by others.

There are pluses and minuses in the Child ego state. It is the Adapted Child that says "please" and "thank you." Taking turns, sharing, and friendliness are other behaviors learned early in life. However, the Adapted Child is often the troubled part of an individual's personality. If during early childhood you discovered that pouting helped you get your way or that a temper tantrum made a great impact on others, you may rely on these childlike behaviors later in life even though some other response is more appropriate.

Thinking/Learning Starter

Each of the statements below was made by the Natural Child (NC) or the Adapted Child (AC). In the space provided next to each statement, place the letters NC or AC depending on which person you think made the statement.

1. _____"This darn machine never works right. I'd like to throw it on the floor and jump on it."
2. _____"Wow! The boss just posted the work schedule, and I get Labor Day off."
3. _____"If the company doesn't provide free parking, let's all walk off the job!"
4. _____"I know why Ken got his raise. He spends all of his time flattering the boss."
5. _____"You'll love the new fall fashions. They are absolutely heavenly!"

Adult Ego State   When people are thinking and acting rationally, when they are gathering data and viewing circumstances with an objective point of view, they are said to be in the **Adult ego state.** Our Adult ego state is free from personal feelings and opinions. It functions like a computer, collecting and processing information from both the Child and Parent. Once this information is gathered, the Adult makes an objective decision. The Adult allows you to *think* about things before you make up your mind. Dorothy Jongeward and Philip Seyer describe the Adult ego state in this way:

> Whenever you are gathering information, reasoning things out, estimating probabilities, and so on, you are in your Adult ego state. While in this ego state you are cool and collected: you make decisions unemotionally. You just want the facts.[8]

The Adult starts to take form during the first year of life. You learn to choose from responses and manipulate your surroundings. Adult data begins to accumulate as you find out for yourself how experience differs from the "taught concept" of life recorded by your Parent and the "felt concept" of life recorded by your Child.[9]

When the Adult is in control, you are more likely to think and act rationally.

Without Adult self-awareness, you tend to be overly influenced by your Parent or Child.

In an organizational setting, the person who has the capacity to process data from their Parent and Child has the greatest potential for emotional control. A person who can handle these messages skillfully is more apt to say and do the right thing. In any organizational situation, circumstances can trigger a response from your Child or Parent that may be inappropriate. When this happens, a relationship may be jeopardized. Consider the following conversation between Thomas Rand, sales representative for Telex Meter Company, and Harold Danville, purchasing agent for a firm that manufactures gas regulators:

Rand: Good morning. My name is Thomas Rand, and I represent the Telex Meter Company. We have a new product that may have application in your plant.

Danville: Several years ago, we did a great deal of business with your firm, but stopped placing orders when your billing department sent us bills for merchandise we didn't purchase. We can't afford to do business with Telex!

Danville has just questioned the integrity of Telex Meter Company. As a representative of this firm, Rand might take the criticism personally. He might be tempted to defend his firm with an angry, childlike response that would probably ruin any chance of continuing his presentation. Instead, he answered with the following statement:

Rand: I must agree that several years ago we did have a short-term problem in our billing department. Due to an increasing volume of business, our staff was unable to handle billing in an orderly and efficient manner. Today we have a modern computerized operation that is virtually error free.

Danville: I'm glad to hear the problem has been taken care of. It was very frustrating to receive a bill for merchandise we didn't order.

Full development of the Adult is achieved in part by training yourself to employ more self-control. When circumstances threaten to trigger an inappropriate response from the Parent or Child, you must use restraint and maintain the composure that defines you as a mature person.

There are times when even a mature Adult is unable to process data from the Parent or Child effectively. When you are under great stress, sick, tired, or extremely disappointed, the Child and Parent may operate as automatic responses. Tapes may replay spontaneously, and the damage is done before the Adult is able to make the right decision. In the stressful world of professional athletics, we often see tempers flare.

Item: John McEnroe was suspended from playing tennis for 42 days at the conclusion of the Stockholm Open-Scandinavian Tennis Championships. He was also fined $2,100 for three counts of misbehavior that included slamming a ball into the stands, calling the umpire a "jerk," and hitting a soft drink can with his racquet.[10]

Item: In the final game of the 1985 World Series, St. Louis Cardinals pitcher Joaquin Andujar was given a 10-day suspension, effective at the opening of the next season, and fined $50 for charging and bumping the plate umpire. He was protesting two consecutive calls.[11]

Item: In words familiar to most Southern stock car racing fans, Dale Earnhardt engaged in some "heavy leaning" near the end of the Miller High Life 400 race held in Richmond, Virginia. On lap 397 of the 400 lap race, Darrel Waltrip passed Earnhardt. Earnhardt apparently turned his car into the rear of Waltrip's car, resulting in a crash involving five of the leading cars. After the race, National Association of Stock Car Racing officials fined Earnhardt $3,000 for unprofessional conduct.[12]

Complementary, Crossed, and Ulterior Transactions

In the language of transactional analysis, each conversation between two people is called a *transaction*. Every social or work-related contact you have with another person involves a series of transactions between ego states. With practice, you can learn to analyze transactions in terms of which ego state (Parent, Adult, or Child) is speaking with which ego state of the other person. Transactions can be classified into three major categories: complementary, crossed, and ulterior.

Complementary Transactions

James and Jongeward defined a **complementary transaction** as one that occurs when a message, sent from a specific ego state, gets the predicted response from a specific ego state in the other person.[13] Let's assume that Randy goes to work Monday morning feeling very depressed. He is having financial problems and is worried about some overdue bills. He says to Harry, a fellow worker, "If things don't improve soon, I may have to find a job that pays more." Harry responds, "I know how you feel, Randy. It sure is hard to get by these days." Figure 9.3 illustrates the complementary nature of this transaction. In this example, Randy hoped to receive a response from Harry's Sympathetic Parent. He received the expected response, so communication will likely continue.

People sometimes bring their problems to work because they have no other outlet. They may seek sympathy from a fellow employee or supervisor

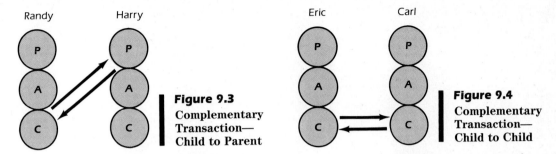

Randy Harry

Figure 9.3
Complementary
Transaction—
Child to Parent

Eric Carl

Figure 9.4
Complementary
Transaction—
Child to Child

because no one else will listen to them. A sensitive person will give an appropriate response.

Complementary transactions may take place between the same ego states, as shown in Figure 9.4. Consider this verbal exchange between Eric, a purchasing agent for a manufacturing firm, and Carl, a salesperson who visits his office. The weather is warm and sunny. Eric makes this statement: "Wow! Look at the weather outside. Let's take the afternoon off and play golf!" Carl responds enthusiastically: "Let's go, my clubs are in my car!" Here we have a complementary transaction between the Child ego state of each person.

In an organizational setting, you may observe many complementary transactions between Adult ego states. Mary, supervisor of data processing, approaches Peter, an employee in the department, and says, "How long will it take to get the data for the annual report?" Peter responds, "I can have it in one week." Figure 9.5 illustrates the Adult-Adult transaction.

Eric Berne said, "The first rule of communication is that communications will proceed smoothly as long as transactions are complementary."[14] A complementary transaction gives a clear message to the other person and prompts a straightforward answer in return. In an organizational setting, complementary transactions are the most productive and result in fewer arguments and hurt feelings.

Crossed Transactions

A **crossed transaction** occurs when the sender of the message does not get the response that he or she expected from the other person. When this

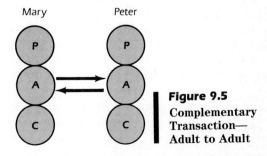

Mary Peter

Figure 9.5
Complementary
Transaction—
Adult to Adult

In a complementary transaction, the message receives the predicted response (Photo by Ellis Herwig, The Picture Cube)

happens, communication and emotional control usually break down. A crossed transaction will create tension between two people. In an organizational setting, it is very important to avoid transactions that result in unnecessary tension or hostility.

To illustrate how crossed transactions develop, return to the conversation between Randy and Harry. Randy says, "If things don't improve soon, I may have to find a job that pays more." Instead of getting the hoped for Sympathetic Parent response, Harry responds with a serious Adult comment: "It may not be possible for you to find another job. Things are pretty tight in the job market right now." You can see in Figure 9.6 how Harry's Adult response did not meet Randy's need for a sympathetic word.

In a typical crossed transaction, the second party is troubled or irritated by the message and responds in a way that surprises and troubles the first party. The result is not effective communication but frustration that may cause the exchange to be terminated. William and his date walked up to the restaurant hostess and said, "We would like a table for two." The hostess said, "The only available table is in the no-smoking section." William's Adult

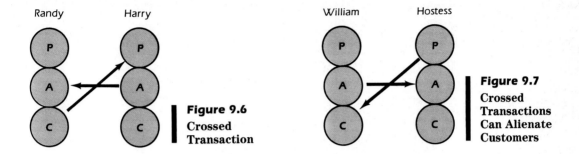

Figure 9.6
Crossed
Transaction

Figure 9.7
Crossed
Transactions
Can Alienate
Customers

responded, "We'll wait until a table is available in the smoking section. We're not in any hurry." The hostess responded in an unfriendly (Critical Parent) manner, "Would you rather smoke than eat?" Figure 9.7 illustrates this crossed transaction that damaged customer relations.

Thinking/Learning Starter

Analyze the possible alternate responses below. Place the letters CT in the space if you feel the response will result in a complementary transaction, or XT if you feel the response will result in a crossed transaction.

1. *Situation A:* One employee says to another, "You don't deserve a raise."
   ___"I know, I just can't seem to do anything right."
   ___"You should talk. Your production is always low."
2. *Situation B:* A secretary says to another employee, "My application for promotion was turned down."
   ___"You think you have problems. Just listen to what happened to me."
   ___"That's too bad. I know you must feel terrible."
3. *Situation C:* A customer says to a store employee, "Can I cash a check for $25?"
   ___"I'm sorry, but we have a $20 limit" (spoken with understanding).
   ___Can't you read that sign on the wall? We have a $20 limit" (spoken with a critical tone).

Ulterior Transactions

An **ulterior transaction** occurs when communication breaks down because the message says one thing but has another meaning; the real meaning is disguised. Ulterior transactions, like crossed transactions, are generally undesirable. In this type of transaction, the second person responds to the hidden meaning of the message rather than to the surface meaning, and the result is an unproductive emotional reaction to the situation.

© 1980 United Feature Syndicate, Inc.

Consider this verbal exchange between Ted, supervisor of the data processing section, and Sarah, office manager. Ted walks into Sarah's office with a frown on his face and says, "Sarah, most of my staff are worn out trying to keep up. If there is no let-up soon, I think we will have a real rebellion on our hands." Ted wants an additional terminal operator assigned to his section but is not discussing his problem in a straightforward manner. He appears to be giving Sarah factual information in an Adult-to-Adult transaction, but he is sending an ulterior message. As illustrated in Figure 9.8, the words themselves seem to be coming from Ted's Adult, but actually his Child is sending a message to Sarah's Parent. Ted may feel resentful because his staff is overworked and he feels Sarah should be taking steps to solve the problem. A more effective approach would be for Ted to say, "Sarah, we are falling behind and I feel you should consider assigning another terminal operator to my section."

Let's consider one more example. Jane walks into a staff meeting fifteen

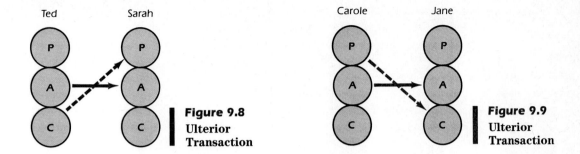

Figure 9.8
Ulterior
Transaction

Figure 9.9
Ulterior
Transaction

minutes late. Carole, her supervisor, points at her watch and says, "I'm glad you were able to make it." Carole has a look of anger on her face. The words appear to be coming from Carole's Adult, but the nonverbal messages (pointed index finger and frown) are coming from Carole's Critical Parent. Figure 9.9 illustrates this ulterior transaction.

Ulterior transactions waste time and often cause a breakdown in relationships. In the first example, Sarah may think, "What is Ted trying to tell me?" or "Why doesn't Ted come to the point and say what's on his mind!" Effective human relations are sidetracked by vague ulterior transactions. Don't make people search for hidden meanings.

Identifying the Source of the Transaction

How can you identify the Parent and Child responses? To pinpoint the source of the transaction, it will be necesssary to consider both verbal and nonverbal aspects of the response. In some cases, nonverbal clues (facial expression, gestures, or tone of voice) may tell us more than words about a person's real attitudes.

When someone speaks, listen closely to his or her tone of voice. A harsh, judgmental tone usually means the Critical Parent is speaking. An impulsive, informal tone probably means a person's Natural Child is talking. If the facial expression communicates disapproval, the source of the message is probably the Critical Parent. If the facial expression communicates excitement, the Natural Child is no doubt speaking. Table 9.1 categorizes nonverbal responses in four areas.

Achieving Greater Emotional Control

William Crockett, a fellow of the NTL Institute, recognized that as human beings we live our lives in two distinct worlds—one of fact and certainty and one of emotions and ambiguity. The world of certainty is that part of our lives that deals with objects and our rational side; our world of ambiguity deals with people and our feeling, or emotional, side—our human world. Too

In one type of ulterior transaction, the message says one thing, but the body language says something else. (Photo by Elizabeth Hamlin, Stock Boston, Inc.)

often we try to handle our human world in the same way that we handle our factual world.[15] In organizational settings, for example, we sometimes observe meetings that follow a very structured agenda. Discussion is limited to "facts," and the group leader discourages the sharing of "feelings." Once the agenda items have been dealt with, the meeting is promptly adjourned. In some situations, staff meetings will be more productive if the group leader provides a forum for discussion of both facts and feelings.

Every occupation requires a certain amount of decision making. Some of these decisions are basic, such as how to organize the content of a memorandum. Other decisions are more complex, for example, how much money to invest in advertising. In some cases, established policies act as guidelines to help you make the correct decision. Many of these decisions can be made in an emotion-free climate. When decisions deal with human issues and problems, however, emotions often enter the picture. With a knowledge and understanding of transactional analysis, you can make the correct emotional decision more frequently.

Emotional Maturity

It is a rare occupation that does not bring the worker into contact with people. The typical receptionist, salesperson, nurse, bank teller, or account executive has contact with hundreds of people every week.

Every encounter involves transactions between people's ego states. Making the correct response to each transaction requires taking charge of your

Table 9.1   Nonverbal Responses in Four Areas

	Parent Ego State	Child Ego State
Tone of Voice	Critical, judgmental, or demanding (Critical Parent)	Affectionate, impulsive, sensuous (Natural Child)
	Comforting, reassuring, protecting (Sympathetic Parent)	Self-centered, rebellious, whining (Adapted Child)
Facial Expressions	Frowns, worried or disapproving looks (Critical Parent)	Excitement, surprise, or wide-eyed looks (Natural Child)
	Concerned, supportive, warm (Sympathetic Parent)	Downcast eyes, quivering lips or chin, pouting (Adapted Child)
Body Gestures	Pointing an accusing finger, hands on hips, or arms folded across chest (Critical Parent)	Spontaneous activity such as laughter, arms moving freely (Natural Child)
	Reaching for, hugging, holding, protecting and shielding from harm (Sympathetic Parent)	Wringing hands, hanging head, withdrawing into a corner (Adapted Child)
Postures	Puffed-up, very proper posture; back straight and shoulders pulled back (Critical Parent)	Jumping up and down, head cocked (Natural Child)
	Open arms protecting from a fall or hurt, arm around shoulder (Sympathetic Parent)	Slouching, or burdened posture (Adapted Child)

emotions. **Emotional maturity** is one of the keys to a satisfying life both at home and at work. Crockett noted that our judgments and decisions are often polluted by our emotions.

> Our emotions may result from our unfulfilled needs for belonging, for feeling important, for recognition or for security. They may result from what seems to be unfair treatment by others. They may result from our fears, hopes and aspirations; or they may come from deeply hidden internal sources of which we are unaware.[16]

Emotional maturity develops as you achieve greater understanding of the emotions that affect your life. This involves becoming well acquainted with the five persons (Sympathetic Parent, Critical Parent, Adult, Natural Child, and Adapted Child) within. Emotional maturity also grows as you learn how

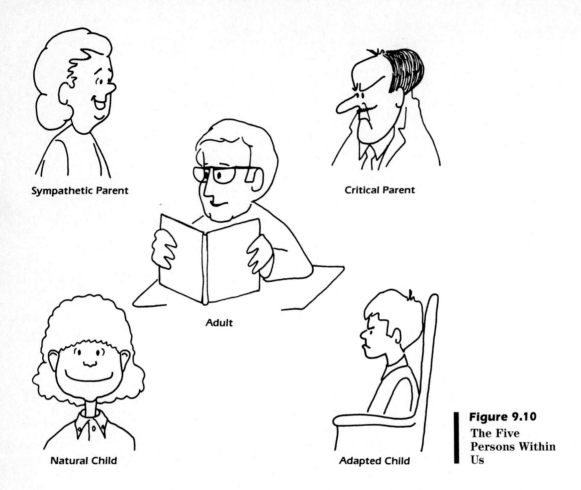

Sympathetic Parent

Critical Parent

Adult

Natural Child

Adapted Child

Figure 9.10
The Five
Persons Within
Us

to spot these five persons within others. To help you build a mental picture of the five persons, let's review the characteristics of each.

Sympathetic Parent   Figure 9.10 provides a caricature of the Sympathetic Parent. This is the type of person who will serve you hot chocolate and marshmallows on a cold day, or will sympathize when you make a mistake in programming and the computer prints all the payroll checks backwards. The Sympathetic Parent will put a hand on your shoulder and offer comfort when you experience a deep disappointment or hurt. This person is supportive, protective, and caring.

Critical Parent   The Critical Parent caricatured in Figure 9.10 always seems to be around when you make a mistake and often makes a judmental comment. The Critical Parent is apt to point a finger at you and say, "Always follow the rules." This person speaks with an "I know best" tone of voice most of the time and likes to voice slogans like "a penny saved is a penny earned." People often become defensive in the presence of the Critical Parent and feel like striking back.

Adult The Adult caricatured in the figure isn't distracted by emotion. Cool and calculating, the Adult can be surrounded by an emotional storm and still make the right decision most of the time. Your Adult is constantly processing data from the other four persons.

Natural Child The Natural Child is the carefree, happy ego state within you. The Natural Child is the impulsive, spontaneous person who says, "What the heck, let's have some fun!" Responses that come from the Natural Child are usually emotionally charged.

Adapted Child The Adapted Child can become the most troublesome part of our personality. If we are overcome by anger or depression when someone criticizes our work, the negative side of our Adapted Child is influencing our behavior. An individual acting from the Adapted Child state may slam doors, sulk, or wait for someone to acknowledge that he or she is "right." The Adapted Child will not want to admit that he or she has made a mistake.

Pushing the Right Button: The Key to Emotional Control

As we saw earlier, your success in dealing with people depends on choosing the correct response to transactions initiated by others. You can't be right all the time, but you can reduce the number of wrong responses through the development of emotional control.

It is helpful to visualize the five persons within us as buttons that appear on an **emotional switchboard**, illustrated in Figure 9.11. When you receive a transaction from another person, you push a button in response. Ideally, you will push the correct button, and a complementary transaction will occur. This happens when our mature Adult processes data from the Parent and Child effectively. As noted earlier, you are less likely to push the correct button when you are ill, tired, under stress, or experiencing great disappointment.

Emotional control is knowing which button to push and when to push it. It requires a great deal of self-discipline, especially in jobs that involve large numbers of personal contacts every day.

The emotional switchboard is always with us. Throughout each day, we must make dozens of decisions about which button to push. Let's suppose that a customer enters the supermarket where you are employed and begins picking up items without a cart. After moving up and down several aisles, the person arrives at your checkout lane with an armload of groceries. A jar of apple jelly, tucked under one elbow, slips out, falls to the floor, and breaks. The customer's face turns bright red.

**Figure 9.11
Emotional
Switchboard**

In this situation, you may receive messages from several of the persons within you. The Sympathetic Parent will tell your Adult that the customer needs a little compassion: "Don't lecture the customer—the person already feels bad enough." The Critical Parent will likely send your Adult a different message: "Make this person clean up the mess. Anyone who shops without a cart needs to be taught a lesson!" Of course, your Natural Child is going to find this situation very funny and tell your Adult to laugh! The Adapted Child may send the Adult still another message: "Oh, nuts. Now someone has to clean up this mess. Why do these accidents always happen in my work area?"

Consider another situation: It was late Friday afternoon and Stephanie was filing the last of several reports that had piled up in her in-basket. She wanted to return to a clean desk on Monday morning. Suddenly her boss, Sandy, ran into the office and said, "Please pull the Hatfield report and make a copy for me. It must go out in the 5:00 P.M. mail." Stephanie looked at the clock and said, "If I hurry I can get to the copy center before it closes at 4:30."

Stephanie arrived at the copy center at exactly 4:30 P.M. The copy center employee on duty said, "Sorry, we're closed. You'll have to come back on Monday." Stephanie felt both angry and frustrated. She knew her boss would be upset if she didn't return with a copy of the report. She also disliked working with people who watch the clock and refuse to do anything extra. Her first impulse was to push her Adapted Child button and say, "If you don't make a copy of this report for me I'll complain to your supervisor." She also considered pushing her Critical Parent button and saying, "If there is anything I can't stand it's a clock watcher. You should be ashamed of yourself!" Instead, she pushed her Sympathetic Parent button and said, "I'm sorry that I didn't get this report to you sooner. It is Friday afternoon, and I know you must be anxious to leave. But I sure would appreciate it if you would make an exception for me. My boss needs this report very badly." The look on her face communicated "help me." The operator took the report from her and began making a copy.

Stephanie pushed the right button (made the correct emotional decision) and avoided an argument with the operator. She also accomplished her objective by obtaining a copy of the report.

Emotional Control Can Be a Challenge

Every day at work you will have to make some difficult decisions. One option is to do only those things that feel good at the moment. In some cases, this will mean ignoring the feelings of customers, patients, fellow workers, and supervisors. Another option is to behave in a manner that is acceptable to those people around you. If you choose this option, you will have to make some sacrifices. Sometimes you must be warm and generous when the feelings inside say, "Be cold and selfish." You may have to avoid an argument when the feelings inside are insisting, "I'm right and the other person is wrong." Getting along with people requires pushing the right button.

Summary

Throughout life your behavior is influenced by the conscious and the subconscious parts of your mind. The conscious part is the mental activity you are aware of and can control. The subconscious part of your mind has been described by William C. Menninger as a "storehouse of forgotten memories." It is mental activity that goes on without your knowledge.

Research conducted by Dr. Eric Berne can help you understand the influence of subconscious mental activity. He developed transactional analysis, a way of analyzing the transactions that take place when two people meet. Dr. Berne discovered that everyone's personality is composed of three distinct parts called ego states: Parent, Child, and Adult. People do not remain permanently fixed in any of these ego states but may fluctuate from one to another depending on the situation.

The contacts you have with people at work involve a series of transactions between ego states. With practice you can learn to analyze transactions and determine which of your ego states (Parent, Adult, or Child) is speaking and which ego state the other person is using.

Transactions between people can be classified into three major categories: complementary, crossed, and ulterior. A complementary transaction is one that occurs when a message, sent from a specific ego state, gets the predicted response from a specific ego state in the other person. A crossed transaction occurs when the sender of the message does not get the response that was expected. An ulterior transaction occurs when communication breaks down because the message says one thing but has another meaning. Making the correct response to each transaction requires considerable control over your emotions. Emotional maturity is an important key to success at work.

Key Terms

conscious mind	Adapted Child
subconscious mind	Adult ego state
transactional analysis	complementary transaction
Parent ego state	crossed transaction
Sympathetic Parent	ulterior transaction
Critical Parent	emotional maturity
Child ego state	emotional switchboard
Natural Child	

Review Questions

1. What is the difference between conscious and subconscious influences on your behavior?
2. How can an understanding of transactional analysis help improve human relations at work?
3. According to Eric Berne, everyone's personality is composed of three ego states: Parent, Child, and Adult. Provide a concise description of each.
4. Describe the two dimensions of the Parent ego state.
5. Describe the two dimensions of the Child ego state.
6. It has been said that our Adult ego state functions like a computer. Explain.
7. Certain mental and physical conditions can make it difficult for your Adult to function effectively. Explain.
8. What are the differences between complementary, ulterior, and crossed transactions? Give examples.
9. Describe the emotional switchboard that is always with us.
10. Why is emotional decision making considered a key to success at work?

Case 9.1

Crossed Transactions in an Emergency[17]

Larry Boff filed a $300,000 damage claim against the city of Dallas, Texas, after ambulances arrived too late to save the life of his sixty-year-old stepmother. Boff called the city's emergency line and requested an ambulance. The result was a heated exchange with nurse Billie Myrick who was assigned to screen incoming calls. A portion of the taped conversation follows:

Myrick: And what is the problem there?

Boff: I don't know, if I knew I wouldn't be ...

Myrick: Sir, would you answer my questions, please? What is the problem?

Boff: She's having difficulty in breathing.

Myrick: How old is this person?

Boff: She's 60 years old.

Myrick: Where is she now?

Boff: She is in the bedroom right now.

Myrick: Can I speak with her, please?

Boff: No, you can't. She seems like she's incoherent.

Myrick: Why is she incoherent?

Boff: How the hell do I know!

Myrick: Sir, don't curse me.

Boff: Well, I don't care. These stupid ... questions you're asking. Give me someone who knows what they're doing. Why don't you send an ambulance out here?

Myrick: Sir, we only come out on life-threatening emergencies.

Boff: Well, this is a life-threatening emergency.

At this point, Boff talked to a supervisor, then Myrick returned to the line. The heated exchange continued, but Myrick refused to send an ambulance. A short time later the woman died. Boff called Myrick again and the recorded transcript ends with these words: "She's dead now. Thank you, ma'am! Would you please send an ambulance? Would you please send an ambulance here?"

Questions

1. What ego state is an emergency telephone operator likely to encounter when answering calls?

2. To avoid a crossed transaction, what button should Billie Myrick have pushed immediately after learning of the need for an ambulance?

3. Early in the phone conversation it appears that Mr. Boff is very angry. In response to a question about the problem, he says: "I don't know, if I

knew I wouldn't be ..." Would things have turned out differently if Mr. Boff had pushed his Adult button at this point?

4. Should persons who are involved in handling emergency phone calls be given the opportunity to study the principles of transactional analysis? Why or why not?

Case 9.2

Breaking the Conference Budget

Helen Hall has been manager of the LaGrande Resort Hotel accounting department for three years. In this position, she supervises a staff of three clerks who handle daily transactions for hotel guests. As manager of the department, she must occasionally meet with guests who feel their bills are not accurate. In most cases, billing problems are handled routinely with no loss of customer good will. However, there are some exceptions.

This morning Glenn Howell, national sales manager for Rider Shoe Corporation, came to the office and requested clarification of his master billing charges. He felt his company had been overcharged for hotel services. Mr. Howell calmly explained his concern:

Glenn Howell: I must confess I don't understand all of the items on my bill. It is about nine hundred dollars more than I expected.

Helen Hall: Well, we seldom make an error, but let me review the charges.

Glenn Howell: Here is the bill. I don't understand why it includes so many individual room charges.

Helen Hall: My records indicate that seventy-three Rider Corporation employees stayed with us for three nights. It looks like a large number of your people used room service for food and beverages. Frankly, I don't think this bill is out of line. (Spoken with a hint of indifference.)

Glenn Howell: I did not authorize these individual purchases. My boss will be furious if I exceed the budget for this conference by nine hundred dollars.

Helen Hall: Mr. Howell, you arranged for seventy-three Rider Corporation employees to register at this hotel. At no time did you request that we restrict room service for these people. Do you expect our staff to refuse service to a registered guest? (Spoken with a hint of anger in her voice.)

Glenn Howell: Look, this is the first time I have been in charge of a national sales conference for our employees. I simply didn't realize that so many people would use room service.

Helen Hall: Next time I would suggest you discuss this matter with your employees prior to the beginning of the conference. (Spoken in a critical tone of voice.)

At the conclusion of the meeting, Mr. Howell walked out of the accounting office with a dejected look on his face. Miss Hall turned to a clerk seated nearby and said, "All sales managers are alike. When it comes to conference planning, they never pay any attention to the important details."

Questions

1. What ego state(s) did Helen Hall rely on during most of her conversation with Glenn Howell?
2. When handling customer complaints, what buttons should Helen Hall use most frequently?
3. If you were director of personnel training for the LaGrande Resort Hotel, what steps would you take to improve Miss Hall's customer relations skills?

Notes

1. Based on personal communication.
2. Allen R. Russon, *Personality Development for Business* (Cincinnati: South-Western Publishing, 1973), p. 51.
3. William C. Menninger and Harry Levinson, *Human Understanding in Industry* (Chicago: Science Research Associates, 1956), p. 29.
4. "Working Together as a Team . . . ," *Training and Development Journal*, June 1982, p. 8.
5. Dudley Bennett, *TA and the Manager* (New York: American Management Association, 1976), p. 1.
6. Jut Meininger, *Success Through Transactional Analysis* (New York: Grosset & Dunlop, 1973), p. 20.
7. Dorothy Jongeward and Philip Seyer, *Choosing Success—Transactional Analysis on the Job* (New York: Wiley, 1978), p. 46.
8. Ibid., p. 11.
9. Thomas A. Harris, *I'm OK—You're OK* (New York: Harper and Row, 1969), p. 29.
10. "McEnroe Accepts 42-Day Suspension After Beating Wilander," *The Courier-Journal*, November 6, 1984, p. D-3.
11. "Joaquin Andujar's Agent May Appeal Fine, Suspension," *Roanoke Times & World-News*, October 31, 1985, p. D-3.
12. "Petty Nabs First Win," *Autoweek*, March 3, 1986, pp. 54–55.
13. Muriel James and Dorothy Jongeward, *Born to Win: Transactional Analysis with Gestalt Experiments* (Reading, Mass.: Addison-Wesley, 1971), p. 24.
14. Eric Berne, *Games People Play* (New York: Grove Press, 1964), p. 30.

15. William J. Crockett, "Our Two Worlds," *Training and Development Journal,* May 1982, p. 60.

16. Ibid., p. 61.

17. "Woman's Death Prompts Probe of Hotline Nurse," *USA Today,* March 7, 1984, p. 6.

Suggested Readings

Harris, Amy Bjork, and Thomas A. Harris. *Staying OK.* New York: Harper and Row, 1985.

Harris, Thomas. *I'm OK—You're OK.* New York: Harper and Row, 1969.

Hollar, Hunter R., and O. C. Brenner. "TA in the Office." *Supervisory Management,* January 1983, p. 14.

James, Muriel, and John James. *The OK Boss.* Reading, Mass.: Addison-Wesley, 1975.

James, Muriel, and Dorothy Jongeward. *Born To Win.* Reading, Mass.: Addison-Wesley, 1971.

Jongeward, Dorothy, and Dru Scott. *Women as Winners.* Reading, Mass.: Addison-Wesley, 1982.

Jongeward, Dorothy, and Philip Seyer. *Choosing Success—Transactional Analysis on the Job.* New York: Wiley, 1978.

Meininger, Jut. *Success Through Transactional Analysis.* New York: Grosset & Dunlop, 1973.

Chapter 10

The Power of Positive Reinforcement

Chapter Preview

After studying this chapter, you will be able to

1. Create awareness of the strong need people have for positive reinforcement.
2. Understand how to use positive reinforcement to improve relationships and reward behavior.
3. List the various forms of positive reinforcement that are applicable in an organization.
4. Explain the use of incentives and awards by organizations.
5. Describe the major barriers to the use of positive reinforcement in an organizational setting.

There is only one thing worse than terminating a flight in Denver and learning that your luggage is in Dallas. That is landing in Denver and discovering that airline officials have no idea of where your luggage is. It was this problem that prompted American Airlines to experiment with a variety of ways to reduce mischecked baggage. These methods ranged from incentives to threats of dismissal or demotion if a ticket agent was caught using improper procedures. None of these methods seemed to work over a long period of time.

One of the most successful attempts to deal with the problem of mischecked baggage was developed by Mike Hoffman, an American Airlines supervisor. He decided to use a strategy called positive reinforcement. In very simple terms, Mike's approach involved a review of an agent's performance and emphasizing what the person had done correctly. This approach is based on the belief that behavior that is followed by positive consequences will be repeated. During the duration of the experiment, he avoided threats, punishments, and criticism. Of course, he did not ignore mistakes. When a mistake was noticed, Mike's approach was simply to review the correct procedure and encourage the employee to perform it correctly. His approach was consistently positive. Employees soon realized that he was not trying to catch them doing something wrong. He was trying to catch them doing something right!

At the beginning of the experiment, he established a base line using the previous month's performance. Then, he held a staff meeting where employees could review their past performance and jointly establish monthly goals. As the weeks passed, he noticed a reduction in the number of mischecked bags. With one exception, the staff reached its goal for six straight months. During one of these months the staff received recognition for a perfect record—zero mischecks.[1]

Personal and Organizational Growth Through Positive Reinforcement

Positive reinforcement is an important key to improved human relationships. Jack Taylor, author of *12 Basic Ideas About People*, noted that the most successful human relations spring from words and actions that evoke responses from the positive side of the emotional scale. People who understand the power of positive reinforcement and are able to employ positive reinforcement strategies are more likely to achieve success on and off the job.

According to psychologist Erik Erikson, recognition is key to the development of what he called ego identity. *Ego identity* is the individual's inner idea of him or herself—who the individual is, what he or she stands for, and what he or she wants out of life.[2] The psychological ingredient of recognition contributes to the development of ego identity; it is as vital to the mind as a nutritious diet is to the body.

Positive reinforcement can also be an inexpensive way to increase organizational effectiveness. Dr. Bruce Baldwin, psychologist and consultant, believes that positive feedback is the most cost-effective way to help an organization run smoothly and improve productivity at all levels.[3] A major component of productivity is employee satisfaction. Employees who feel unappreciated will not perform to the best of their ability. In the absence of positive feedback, the organization assumes the posture of a negative entity to its employees because most information received emphasizes what is wrong rather than what is right. In such an organizational climate, employees become progressively demoralized and defensive because their work is not appreciated.

Several studies have pointed out that upper management and supervisors frequently do not understand employee reward preferences. Managers and supervisors often say that pay or monetary rewards, job security, and good working conditions rank highest as reward preferences. However, when employees are surveyed, a different picture develops. Professor Kenneth Kovach, professor of business administration at George Mason University, gave a list of ten morale-building factors to a group of supervisory personnel with instructions to rank them in order according to what they felt their employees wanted.[4] This same list was then given to their employees, who were instructed to rank the items according to their perspective. The results of this survey, shown in Table 10.1, indicate that "full appreciation of work done" ranks very high among employees. When employee reward preferences are not in harmony with management's reward system, problems arise.

There is also evidence that positive reinforcement improves communication throughout an organization. Studies conducted by Dr. C. B. Stiegler and others found that positive feedback creates a less stressful climate, which results in improved interpersonal communication:

> Positive reinforcement (PR) involves "putting people at ease" in interpersonal communication. Whether one is speaking with, writing to, or listening to another person or persons, PR serves to put people at ease, thereby facilitating open communication. By reducing business pressures, PR results in a freer flow of information, both vertically and horizontally, which in turn increases efficiency.[5]

This chapter discusses the impact of positive reinforcement on both individual and group behavior. The various types of positive reinforcement are examined in detail, and you will learn why so many people have difficulty giving positive feedback to others. A special section is devoted to awards and incentive programs currently used by a variety of organizations.

Table 10.1 Ten Morale-Building Factors

What Managers Think Employees Want	What Employees Really Want
1. Good pay	1. Interesting work
2. Job security	2. Full appreciation of work done
3. Promotion and growth	3. Involvement
4. Good working conditions	4. Good pay
5. Interesting work	5. Job security
6. Tactful discipline	6. Promotion and growth
7. Loyalty to employees	7. Good working conditions
8. Full appreciation of work done	8. Loyalty to employees
9. Help with personal problems	9. Help with personal problems
10. Involvement	10. Tactful discipline

Source: Reprinted, by permission of the publisher, from "Why Motivational Theories Don't Work" by Kenneth Kovach, p. 56, *S.A.M. Advanced Management Journal*, Spring 1980. © 1980 by Society for Advancement of Management, a division of American Management Associations, New York. All rights reserved.

Our Need for Positive Reinforcement

How strong is the need to receive positive reinforcement from others? Psychologist William James believed that the craving to be appreciated is a basic principle of human nature. Mark Twain, the noted author, answered this question by saying he could live for three weeks on a compliment. He was willing to admit openly what most people feel inside. Many have a deep desire for personal recognition but almost never verbalize these thoughts. You never hear about a group of workers going to management and saying, "If we don't receive more positive recognition, we will quit!" However, attitude surveys indicate that a majority of employees feel inadequately recognized.

Few people have the strength of ego to subsist upon self-esteem alone. Most are very dependent upon **positive feedback** from others. Kenneth Blanchard and Spencer Johnson, authors of *The One Minute Manager*, stress the importance of "catching the employee doing something right" and engaging in "one minute praisings."[6] Without this positive feedback, employees suffer from a sense of incompleteness.

Support from Maslow

The hierarchy of needs developed by Abraham Maslow (see Chapter 6 for a discussion of this concept) provides additional support for the use of positive reinforcement in an organizational setting. In part, the need for security (a

DUFFY   **by Bruce Hammond**

second-level need) is satisfied by positive feedback from an approving supervisor, manager, or fellow employee. You are apt to feel more secure when someone recognizes your accomplishments. A feeling of belonging (a third-level need) can be satisfied by actions that communicate "You are part of the team." One employee reported that he felt like a member of the team when the manager of the firm said, "I want you to become more familiar with our business. Let's review this year's sales reports together."

It would seem to be almost impossible to satisfy the esteem needs (fourth level) without positive feedback. Self-esteem is not static in most cases. It may diminish in a work environment where accomplishments receive little or no recognition.

Thinking/Learning Starter

Recall a situation in your life when you accomplished something important, but no one seemed to notice. Remember the feelings that surfaced inside of you. Did you experience disappointment? Hurt? Anger? Feelings of inadequacy? Why do you think your accomplishments were ignored?

Support from Berne

In the previous chapter, you learned the fundamentals of transactional analysis (TA). TA is a simplified explanation of how people communicate. Eric Berne's research also provided new evidence that most people have a strong need for recognition, or "strokes."

The word *stroking* is used to describe the various forms of recognition one person gives another. Strokes help satisfy the need to be appreciated. A **physical stroke** may be a pat on the back or a smile that communicates approval to someone. **Verbal strokes** include words of praise and expressions of gratitude.

Eric Berne said that stroking is necessary for physical and mental health. He found that infants who were deprived of physical strokes (hugs, caresses, and kisses) began to lose their will to live. As people grow into adulthood, they are willing to substitute verbal stroking for physical stroking. Adults still need and want physical stroking, but they will settle for words of praise, incentive awards, and other forms of recognition.

A stroke can be positive or negative. Positive strokes, called "warm fuzzies" in TA language, include such behaviors as listening with genuine attention, smiling, or simply saying "thank you" sincerely to a customer who has just made a purchase. Negative strokes, sometimes called "cold pricklies," produce "I'm not OK" feelings inside of people. A negative stroke may take the form of sarcasm, failure to remember the name of a regular customer, or making fun of another person's appearance.

Stroke Deficit: A Common Condition

Claude Steiner, author of *TA Made Simple*, says that most people live in a state of **stroke deficit**. They survive on a less-than-ideal diet of strokes like people who never have enough to eat.[7] Some individuals are so hungry for positive recognition they will ask for strokes. The following statements, made by an ad layout employee working for a large newspaper, may reveal the need for positive feedback:

▶ "Did you see my appliance ad on the sports page?"
▶ "I heard that the Reed's Department Store ad I prepared attracted a store full of people."
▶ "I've been thinking of entering some of my ads in the annual newspaper ad competition. Do you think my work is good enough?"

A person who is really starved for recognition may say or do things that damage relationships with others. The individual who doesn't receive enough positive strokes may engage in exaggerated self-criticism. The newspaper employee described above might make these statements:

▶ "None of my ads look good. I think I'll quit this job."
▶ "The department manager must hate my work. He hasn't commented on any of my ads for weeks."

No one enjoys working around people who constantly fish for compliments or who spend a lot of time finding fault with themselves. Both of these behaviors may indicate the need for more positive reinforcement.

Forms of Positive Reinforcement

You have no doubt heard of employees who worked thirty or forty years for an organization but did not receive any significant form of recognition until retirement. The traditional gold watch, or some other token of appreciation, was given to the worker on his or her final day. Times have changed. Most progressive organizations recognize that positive reinforcement should be provided at various intervals throughout the employee's career. Continuity is one key to a successful program of positive reinforcement.

Variety is another important element of the successful positive reinforcement program. Everyone needs to become aware of the many different ways to give positive recognition to other people. Without variety, attempts to give recognition may seem mechanical and insincere. In this section, you will be introduced to a wide range of PR strategies.

Confirming and Disconfirming Behaviors

Evelyn Sieburg uses the term **confirmation** to describe a whole series of behaviors that have a positive, or "therapeutic," effect upon the receiver.[8] She uses the term **disconfirmation** to describe those behaviors that arouse in the receiver negative feelings about his or her identity and self-worth. In most cases, confirmation behaviors develop feelings of self-worth in the mind of the worker and may be reflected in increased productivity, less absenteeism, and greater interest in work. Disconfirmation behaviors tend to have the opposite effect.

To understand the wide range of possible confirmation behaviors that may exist in a work setting, let's follow a new worker throughout the first year on the job. Mary Harper graduated from a local community college where she completed a legal assistant program and obtained a position with a large law firm.

Upon arriving at work, she was greeted warmly, given a tour of the office complex, and introduced to the people with whom she would be working. A highlight of the tour was a stop at the president's office where she met the founder of the firm. The president briefly reviewed the history of the firm and extended a warm welcome.

The orientation included a review of the firm's policies and procedures handbook and training that helped her learn how to use the firm's data retrieval system. As she demonstrated competence in using the equipment, the supervisor made comments such as, "Well done ... you're a quick learner" and "Good job ... you're doing fine."

During the first coffee break, she was surprised to see a notice on the bulletin board that said, "Please welcome Mary Harper to our office." This notice reminded other workers that a new person had joined the staff. The bulletin board announcement also made it easier for everyone to remember her name.

THOMAS, THOMAS, and ROYAL
DENVER, COLORADO

August 11, 1986

Ms. Mary Harper
Legal Assistant
Thomas, Thomas, and Royal
144 Walnut Street
Denver, CO 80204

Dear Mary:

You have now completed one year with our firm,
and I want you to know we are very pleased with
your work. Ms. Williams, your supervisor, has
kept me posted; and your performance to date is
certainly praiseworthy.

I notice that you have not missed a single day's
work in your first year. We appreciate such
dedication.

Best wishes for continued success with our firm.

Sincerely,

Stephanie Thomas

Stephanie Thomas
President

ST:br

Figure 10.1
**A Letter Can
Give Positive
Reinforcement**

As the weeks passed, Mary Harper was given positive reinforcement on several occasions. She received positive feedback from fellow workers as well as her supervisor. When she had a problem, her supervisor proved to be a good listener. After six weeks, she was given a formal performance review by her supervisor. Another review followed six months later. These performance reviews helped her become aware of her strengths and of some areas that needed improvement. Because of the professional way her supervisor handled these reviews, Mary always came away with a desire to do better. At the end of the first year, Mary received a letter from the president of the firm (see Figure 10.1).

Would you enjoy working in this organizational setting? Chances are your answer is yes. A host of confirming behaviors gave Mary support during her first year on the job. These confirmations included the following:

Praise   Praise is one of the easiest and most powerful ways to make an employee feel important and needed. The person who receives the praise knows that his or her work is not being taken for granted. When handled correctly, praise can be an effective reinforcement strategy that ensures repetition of desired behaviors.

Courtesy   The poet Tennyson once said, "The greater the man, the greater the courtesy." When Mary Harper reported to work she was welcomed in a courteous manner and introduced to people throughout the office. Even the president of the firm was not too busy to greet the new employee. Courtesy really means to be considerate of others in little things, showing respect for what others revere, and treating everyone, regardless of position, with consideration. You display courtesy when you refuse a request gracefully and remain calm under pressure.

Empathetic Listening   As noted in Chapter 2, everyone likes to spend time with a good listener. Listening to another person's thoughts and feelings can be a powerful reinforcer. **Empathetic listening** means putting yourself in the other person's shoes and looking at problems from his or her viewpoint.

Positive Written Communication   Most people respond positively to notes and letters that express appreciation. However, this form of positive reinforcement is used all too infrequently in organizations. Mary Harper will probably keep the letter written to her by the president and may show it to friends and relatives. A letter of appreciation can have considerable impact on employee morale and can improve interpersonal communication within the organization.

Thinking/Learning Starter

Chances are you owe somebody a thank-you note. Think about events of the past six months. Has someone given time and effort to assist you with a problem? Make a list of at least three people who deserve a thank-you note. Pick one, write that person a note of appreciation, and mail it today.

Performance Review   Mary Harper, like most other employees, wants to know if her work is satisfactory. Feedback from a respected supervisor during the **performance review,** especially positive feedback, can be very rewarding. Donald Schuster, director of management development and train-

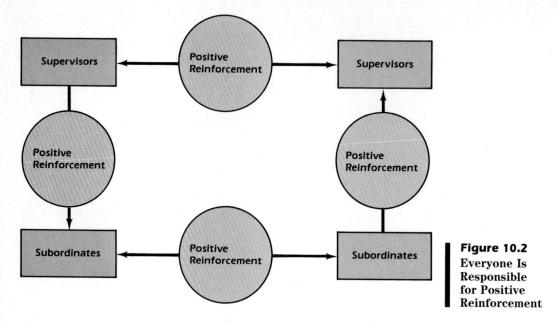

Figure 10.2
Everyone Is
Responsible
for Positive
Reinforcement

ing at World Color Press, uses the term *performance recognition* to describe
an approach in which supervisors motivate employees with meaningful personal recognition.[9] He feels performance recognition should be the primary
focus of the performance review because it results in more open communication between supervisor and subordinate.

Positive Reinforcement: Everyone's Responsibility

Too often we think of positive reinforcement as the responsibility of supervisors and managers. This view is much too narrow. As shown in Figure 10.2,
everyone in the organization has opportunities to recognize the accomplishments of others. Persons who hold supervisory and management positions
can frequently benefit from positive reinforcement initiated by subordinates.
We should also recognize the accomplishments of fellow workers.

The authors of *How to Manage Your Boss* state that "subordinates too
often wait until they have something negative to report before giving the
boss feedback." Catching the boss doing something good and rewarding him
or her is a far more effective way to change behavior than criticizing or
complaining.[10]

Awards and Incentives

Every year nearly $8 billion worth of incentives and awards are given by
business firms throughout the United States. This money is spent on color
TVs, vacation trips, rings, plaques, pins, certificates, and a host of other items.

Total Person Insight

Jan Hartman

I think you must treat other people as you want to be treated. If you do that, you will get along better, earn their respect, and lessen the aggravations in your relationships. Emphasizing the positive aspects of a person and that person's work will get you much better results than harping on the negative.

One of the primary purposes of **awards** and **incentives** is to encourage desired employee behaviors. They are used to

1. Reward behavior that helps reduce or prevent accidents.
2. Reduce absenteeism.
3. Reward years of service with an organization.
4. Improve sales.
5. Build morale.
6. Improve quality control.
7. Increase learning in training programs.
8. Improve customer relations.

The use of awards and incentives is by no means a new movement. John H. Patterson, founder and head of The National Cash Register Company from 1884 to 1922, used a variety of incentive programs to motivate his sales force.

Lowe's Companies, Inc., the nation's largest home center chain, sponsors a recognition program for sales and management excellence. The Lowe's ring is given as an award. (Photo courtesy of Lowe's Companies, Inc.)

Table 10.2 Employee Recognition at Silo Inc.

No one is treated like a number at Silo, a large television, audio, and appliance chain serving several western states. Management is continually looking for new ways to recognize its employees. Here are some of the methods currently in use:

1. *Upcoming Birthdays.* On the first day of each month, the names of employees who will be celebrating their birthdays that month and the actual date of the birthday appear in a memorandum sent to all employees. Around the middle of the month, the entire staff enjoys ice cream and a giant-sized cake adorned with the names of that month's celebrants.

2. *Employee Suggestions.* A monetary reward is given to employees who suggest ways to improve company operations. Award winners are recognized in written correspondence that is circulated throughout the company.

3. *Performance.* Employee-of-the-month awards are given to personnel throughout the organization who display outstanding performance. Individual stores are also recognized for achieving sales goals. At the end of the year, employees select an employee-of-the-year who is the recipient of a vacation package to a resort area.

Sales personnel earned merchandise or travel awards when their performance exceeded a fixed goal. Many of Patterson's ideas are still popular today.

Incentive plans that recognize a variety of employee behaviors are also growing in popularity (see Table 10.2). Many other organizations are adopting recognition and reward programs to achieve a variety of goals.

Item: In Europe, Mercedes-Benz was concerned that dealers' mechanics were forgetting what they had learned in company-sponsored training programs.[11] To solve this problem, they developed a post-training program that connected incentives to retention and application of newly acquired information. Once each month for the first three months following service schools, mechanics received a ten-question review test. Those who filled out the test form earned merchandise prize points for doing so. Those who answered the questions correctly received additional points. To test application skills, a hands-on item was included with the ten pencil-and-paper items. A six-month follow-up of this incentive program found that mechanics who participated in the program performed better than they had at the end of service school.

Item: Gary Wood, manager of one of the Holiday Inns in Nashville, Tennessee, implemented a customer service program that involved the use of "praising coupons." A book of praising coupons was given to each guest when they checked into the hotel. The guest was asked to write on the back of a coupon the name of the employee who provided good service and turn in

Bob Halferty (center) received a $7,500 award for an idea he submitted to the Maytag Employees' Idea Plan. Halferty developed a way to refurbish a machine part instead of purchasing expensive replacements. (Photo courtesy of The Maytag Company)

the coupon at the manager's office. In this situation, the customer was encouraged to "catch employees doing things right." This program recognized employees who provided good service to guests.[12]

Item: At Eastman Kodak, employees can receive cash awards for introducing money-saving ideas. One employee felt cameras should be loaded with batteries, film, and flash bulbs just prior to filling dealers' orders. As a result, customers are now provided with the freshest possible batteries and film. And the company realized tremendous cost savings since less storage space is required and investment in batteries and flash bulbs is delayed. The employee won a $50,000 award for the idea.[13]

Awards and incentives can serve as the backbone of suggestion systems. To draw more ideas from employees, many companies are using merchandise awards in addition to, or in place of, the traditional cash award. Cost-saving ideas from employees save business firms millions of dollars each year. Figure 10.3 shows a typical suggestion form used by many businesses.

Although the popularity of award and incentive programs is growing, the movement is not without its critics. One concern is that incentives treat the symptom, not the problem. For example, a firm may use trading stamps or

JOHN DEERE COMPONENT WORKS

SUGGESTION FORM

"THANKS FOR YOUR SUGGESTION"

SUGGESTION NO. DO NOT WRITE HERE.	DATE FILL IN THIS BOX.	DATE REC. DO NOT WRITE IN THIS BOX.

EMPLOYEE NO.	SALARIED DEPT.	SHOP DEPT.	SHIFT	JOB CLASSIFICATION	NAME LAST	FIRST	INITIAL

ARE YOU WILLING TO DISCUSS YOUR IDEA WITH AN EVALUATOR?

☐ NO ☐ YES ☐ IN PRIVATE ONLY

DO YOU OBJECT TO PUBLICITY IF AN AWARD IS PAID?

☐ NO ☐ YES

Please read the Suggestion Plan rules which are printed on the back of this form.

In submitting this suggestion I agree to all provisions of the Suggestion Plan rules and procedures as shown on the back of this form.

This form must be signed by all parties.

YOUR SIGNATURE AND DATE

Describe your suggestion fully. If necessary, use another sheet of paper and attach it to this form. Enclose a sketch if possible. The Suggestion Administrator or your supervisor will be glad to help you with any problems you may have in filling out this form.

PART NO.	OPER. NO.	MACH. NO.	L.G.	DEPT.	FIXT., FORM OR TOOL NO.

PRESENT METHOD OR CONDITION

SUGGESTED IMPROVEMENT

Figure 10.3
Typical Suggestion Form

Source: John Deere International, Moline, Illinois

cash incentives to reduce absenteeism. The problem may have its roots in poor working conditions or poor supervision. In this example, the incentive program may reduce absenteeism but fail to cure the real problem.

Some critics also say that incentive programs often reinforce the wrong behavior. The salesperson who is set on winning a trip to England may sell a customer a product he or she does not really need. In this case, the incentive has reinforced an undesirable behavior.

Another concern expressed by critics is that the effect of an incentive program may be temporary. They say the positive feelings that accompany winning the TV set or trophy are often short-lived.

Although these criticisms are valid in some cases, it is possible to design incentive programs that will have long-range benefits to the organization and individual employees. A well-designed program can help an organization achieve a variety of goals in such areas as reduced expenses, improved customer service, and increased sales.

Planning the Incentive Program

The key to successful incentive programs is careful planning and implementation. Programs must be administered fairly or some eligible employees will not participate. Any confusion about what behaviors will be rewarded can demotivate employees. The following guidelines should be observed when designing and implementing an incentive program:

1. *Spell out requirements carefully before the program begins and make rules easy to understand.* A written description of the incentive program should be given to every employee who is eligible. It's often a good idea to introduce new programs at meetings or conferences so that employees will have an opportunity to raise questions and discuss items that are not clear.

2. *Administer the award program fairly.* Once the rules have been established, employees must be confident that they will be adhered to.

3. *Provide meaningful rewards.* If the rewards are not significant or if there are not enough of them, little interest in the program will develop. If achieving the award is too difficult, some employees may not even try. If rewards are too easily attained, participants will not be motivated to do their best.

4. *Awards should be given with great fanfare.* When awards are given in an unenthusiastic manner or insincerely, the award will have little impact.

Charles Alden, manager of Special Projects at 3M's Audio/Video Products Division, states that incentive programs should stimulate motivation. Every element of the program should be judged in light of two questions. First, does the incentive program offer real potential for greater self-realization, or is it just another obligation? Second, will it result in increased social recognition and greater confidence in personal worth for the achievers?[14]

Although most programs are designed within the organization, some companies are turning to consulting firms that specialize in recognition, award, and incentive-motivation program design. The E. F. MacDonald Co. of Dayton, Ohio, Jostens Inc. of Minneapolis, Minnesota, and O. C. Tanner Company of Salt Lake City, Utah, represent three such firms.

Removing Barriers to Positive Reinforcement

The material in this chapter is based upon two indisputable facts about human nature. First, people want to know how well they are doing and if their work is satisfactory; second, they appreciate recognition for a job well done. Performance feedback and positive reinforcement can satisfy these important human needs. People often say they prefer negative feedback to no feedback at all. "Don't leave me in the dark" is a common plea (spoken or unspoken) of the American worker.

You will remember from Chapter 3 that behaviors resulting in satisfying consequences for the individual are more likely to be repeated. Positive reinforcement is one way to ensure that desirable behavior is repeated.

Yet, if all these things are true, why isn't PR used more frequently? If it is such a good way to improve human relations, why are so few people willing to give recognition to others? Some of the most common barriers will be discussed in this section.

Preoccupation with Self

One of the major obstacles to providing positive reinforcement is preoccupation with oneself. The term **narcissism** is often used to describe this human condition. Narcissism is a Freudian term based upon the mythical youth who wore himself out trying to kiss his own reflection in a pool of water.

Some social critics feel that the tendency to become preoccupied with oneself became more prevalent during the 1970s. As noted in an earlier chapter, one writer labeled this period the "me decade." Many of the books published during this period communicated the theme "look out for Number One!" Here are a few examples:

1. *The Art of Selfishness* by David Seabury
2. *Winning Through Intimidation* by Robert Ringer
3. *Winning with Deception and Bluff* by Sydney Schweitzer
4. *Power! How to Get It, How to Use It* by Michael Korda
5. *Pulling Your Own Strings* by Wayne Dyer

There is certainly nothing wrong with taking charge of your life and making more of your own decisions. Nor should you apologize for pursuing your own goals as long as you don't walk over other people in the process. However, you need to avoid the kind of self-centeredness that prevents you from recognizing the accomplishments of others.

Sydney Harris, in his book *Winners and Losers*, makes some interesting comments about behaviors that contribute to our success or failure in life. Here are just a few concise comments from his book:

> A *winner* is sensitive to the atmosphere around him; a *loser* is sensitive only to his own feelings.
>
> A *loser* feels cheated if he gives more than he gets; a *winner* feels that he is simply building up credit for the future.
>
> A *winner* acts the same toward those who can be helpful and those who can be of no help; a *loser* fawns on the powerful and snubs the weak.
>
> A *winner*, in the end, gives more than he takes; a *loser* dies clinging to the illusion that "winning" means taking more than you give.[15]

Misconceptions About Positive Reinforcement

Positive reinforcement is not used by some people simply because they have misconceptions about this human relations strategy. One misconception is that people will respond to positive feedback by demanding tangible evidence of appreciation. "Tell people they are doing a good job and they will ask for a raise" seems to be the attitude of some managers. Actually, just the opposite response will surface more often than not. In the absence of intangible rewards (such as praise), workers may demand greater tangible rewards.

A few managers seem to feel they will lose some of their power or control if they praise workers. Yet if managers rely on power alone to get the job done, any success they might achieve will no doubt be short-lived.

A final misconception is the belief that "employees are hired to do a job, and they don't deserve any rewards beyond the paycheck." One part of this statement is correct. Employees *are* hired to do a job. However, it is the manager's responsibility to let them know if the job is being performed correctly. If they are doing a good job, why not reinforce that behavior with a little praise? The manager who operates from the viewpoint "We never bother anyone around here if they are doing their job" has fallen into a trap. Essentially, this person is saying, "My people are not going to get any recognition unless they fail to do their jobs."[16]

The "Too Busy" Syndrome

When you are under a great deal of pressure to get the job done and work is piling up on your desk, it's easy to postpone sending a congratulatory or thank-you note or phoning someone simply for the purpose of saying thank-you. Managers often complain that they don't have time to assess the strengths

---

INFRA-DYNAMICS, INC.
BINGHAMTON   HOUSTON   PALO ALTO

May 19, 1986

Ms. Patty Morrison, Manager
Process Control Division
Plant Number Five
126 James Avenue
Binghamton, NY 13901

Dear Patty:

Once again it gives me pleasure to recognize you
and your staff for outstanding performance in the
area of safety. You folks have maintained a perfect
record throughout the past twelve months.

Congratulations to you and all of your employees
for your contributions to this important job
responsibility. All of us here at the home office are
proud of you. Keep up the good work!

Sincerely,

Ralph Plazio

Ralph Plazio
Vice President
Production and Quality Control

RP:br

Figure 10.4
A Thank You or Congratulatory Letter Reinforces Desirable Behavior

of their people, let alone plan and deliver some type of recognition. The key to solving this problem is planning. Managers need to set aside time for this important area. A consciously planned PR program will ensure that recognition for work well done is not overlooked. One approach might be to set aside time each day to work on performance feedback and positive reinforcement activities, such as the letter in Figure 10.4. In other circumstances, immediate, on-the-spot commendation of a behavior is more appropriate. In

Table 10.3 One Minute Praisings

The one-minute praising works well, say authors Kenneth Blanchard and Spencer Johnson, when you

1. Tell people *up front* that you are going to let them know how they are doing.
2. Praise people immediately.
3. Tell them what they did right—be specific.
4. Tell them how good you feel about what they did right, and how it helps the organization and others who work there.
5. Stop for a moment of silence to let them *feel* how good you feel.
6. Encourage them to do more of the same.
7. Shake hands or touch people in a way that makes it clear that you support their success in the organization.

Source: Chart on page 101 in *The One Minute Manager* by Kenneth Blanchard, Ph.D., and Spencer Johnson, M.D. Copyright © 1981, 1982 by Blanchard Family Partnership and Candle Communications Corporation. Abridged and adapted by permission of William Morrow & Company and McBride Literary Agency.

The One Minute Manager, the authors point out that positive feedback need not take long. They suggest the simple plan outlined in Table 10.3.

Not Identifying Commendable Actions

There are numerous opportunities to recognize the people you work with. However, it is possible to get in a rut and end up saying "thanks" automatically, without really noticing what employees do. By exercising just a little creativity, you can discover many actions that deserve to be commended.

Assume you are the manager of a large auto dealership. One of the key people within your organization is the service manager. This person schedules work to be performed on customers' cars, handles customer complaints, supervises the mechanics, and performs a host of other duties. If you want to give your service manager performance feedback and positive recognition, what types of behavior can you praise? Table 10.4 (p. 258) lists some examples.

The approach to positive reinforcement, of course, should be tailored to the requirements of the job. Positive reinforcement strategies designed for a sales staff may not work in a machine shop. For the shop, workers might be rewarded for performing preventive maintenance or spotting potential machine problems and calling maintenance to have equipment repaired.

Everyone needs to become more aware of the many behaviors that provide an opportunity for positive recognition. It's easy to add variety to your positive reinforcement program!

Table 10.4 Job Performance Behavior to Be Reinforced

1. *Performance Related to Interpersonal Relations*
   a. Empathy for customer needs and problems
   b. Ability to handle customer complaints effectively
   c. Ability to keep all employees well informed
   d. Cooperation with supervisory personnel in other departments
   e. Ability to maintain a sense of humor
   f. Recognition of the accomplishments of employees
   g. Effective supervision of employees

2. *Personal Characteristics*
   a. Honesty in dealings with people throughout the organization
   b. Punctuality
   c. Does not violate policies and procedures
   d. Maintains emotional stability
   e. Maintains a neat appearance
   f. Uses good judgment
   g. Alert to new ways to do the job better

3. *Management Skills*
   a. Avoids waste in the use of supplies and materials
   b. Maintains accurate records
   c. Spends time on short- and long-range planning
   d. Takes steps to prevent accidents
   e. Delegates authority and responsibility
   f. Maintains quality control standards

Not Knowing What to Say or Do

You can also show appreciation for work well done in a great variety of ways. It's a good idea to avoid saying or doing the same thing over and over again. There are many words and phrases that communicate approval. Here are several examples of different expressions you can use to show appreciation:

▶ "Good thinking!"   ▶ "You are improving."
▶ "I'm pleased."   ▶ "Super!"
▶ "Terrific!"   ▶ "This is is the best yet!"

▶ "Excellent idea."   ▶ "Please continue."
▶ "How true."   ▶ "Great!"
▶ "Good answer."   ▶ "Beautiful!"
▶ "Thank you."   ▶ "Fine."
▶ "Perfect!"   ▶ "Keep up the good work."

Of course, you can express appreciation without using verbal communication. There are many nonverbal expressions of approval:

▶ Eye contact
▶ Nodding agreement
▶ Grinning
▶ Laughing happily
▶ Pat on the back
▶ Moving closer to someone
▶ Clapping hands

▶ Signaling okay
▶ Smiling
▶ Thumbs up
▶ Firm handshake
▶ Placing a hand on someone's shoulder

And finally, you can give recognition to others through some type of action. Here are some activities that show approval.

▶ Ask an employee for advice.
▶ Ask an employee to demonstrate the correct performance or procedure.
▶ Ask an employee to serve as chairperson of a committee.
▶ Compliment the work of another person.
▶ Display an employee's work.
▶ Recognize the work of an employee at a staff meeting.
▶ Ask an employee to explain a complex procedure.

Lack of Appropriate Role Models

Most employees tend to look to organizational leaders for clues regarding what is acceptable behavior. The leaders provide a role model for everyone else. If the store manager in your neighborhood supermarket is aloof, seems indifferent to the needs of employees and customers, and generally displays a negative attitude, the store's supervisors are apt to imitate this behavior. After all, if the boss behaves this way, it must be all right. Pretty soon the grocery clerks, baggers, and cashiers—who look to the supervisors for guidance—get the message: Customer relations is not important. Getting along with coworkers isn't important. Providing positive reinforcement for one another is not important.

The people at the top are always in the spotlight. Their actions are constantly being watched by the people they supervise, and their attitudes are contagious!

Do other factors support a program of positive reinforcement? Yes, this human relations strategy flourishes in a supportive environment. Within the organization, there should be respect for each person regardless of job title, duties performed, or earnings. The prevailing climate within the organization should also be positive. People must feel good about the organization, its leadership, and other employees. Positive reinforcement almost comes naturally in a positive work environment. On the other hand, positive reinforcement will almost never flourish in a negative organization.

Summary

People usually feel good when their accomplishments are recognized and become upset when work well done is ignored. Positive reinforcement, when used correctly to reward accomplishments, is a powerful motivator. Everyone needs to receive personal recognition and to feel important.

Although many studies indicate that positive reinforcement is an important employee reward preference, often ranked higher than monetary rewards and job security, many people seem unable or unwilling to say thank you for a job well done. Confirming behaviors need to be used in organizational settings more often. Praise, simple courtesy, being a good listener, written thank-you notes, and incentives and awards represent some of the ways people can reinforce another's behavior.

Preoccupation with self is a major obstacle to providing positive reinforcement to others. Self-centered persons are more apt to overlook the accomplishments of other people. Another obstacle is the view that "employees are hired to do a job, and they don't deserve any rewards beyond the paycheck." Some managers say a busy schedule does not allow time to give recognition to others. These and other barriers tend to minimize the use of positive reinforcement.

Key Terms

positive reinforcement

positive feedback

physical stroke

verbal stroke

stroke deficit

confirmation

disconfirmation

empathetic listening

performance review

awards and incentives

narcissism

Review Questions

1. What evidence is there to support the contention that positive reinforcement is a major employee reward preference?
2. What is the difference between a positive stroke and a negative stroke?
3. What are some behaviors a person might display that would indicate the presence of a stroke deficit?
4. How can one's identity and self-worth be influenced by confirmation behaviors? Disconfirmation behaviors?
5. In a typical organizational setting, what are some confirmation behaviors that might have a positive or "therapeutic" effect on an employee?
6. What are some of the major arguments for and against the use of incentives and awards?
7. Define the term *narcissism*.

8. What are some common misconceptions about positive reinforcement?
9. What are some employee behaviors that might be recognized by a supervisor or manager? List at least five different performance-related behaviors.
10. Why is it important for top management to use positive reinforcement strategies?

Case 10.1

Toyota Uses Perks to Sell Parts[17]

In the early 1980s, a significant change in buying habits surfaced among automobile owners. People began keeping their present autos longer. This led to a boom in sales of auto parts and services, and competition in the auto aftermarket became fierce. Toyota Motor Sales USA's Parts and Service Division noted that an increasing number of parts managers were being approached by auto-parts salespeople who sold non-Toyota products. To counteract these sales efforts, the company decided to inaugurate an incentive program to reward dealers for staying with Toyota parts and for making a concerted effort to sell more of them.

Feldman Consulting, a firm specializing in the development of incentive programs, was hired to design and administer the program. The Feldman staff developed *Discovery IV*, a one-year promotion in four segments involving dealers and service and parts managers, plus tie-in promotions for consumers. Participating dealers were offered trips for two to Hawaii in a four-month contest entitled Discover Paradise.

Points were awarded in three ways:

1. By increasing customer-paid transactions.
2. By improving customer relations.
3. By running at least one tie-in co-op ad each month. The co-op ads, directed to Toyota owners, emphasized that their car maintenance would be cheaper in the long run if they started using Toyota parts and service.

More than 90 percent of Toyota's more than eight hundred dealers participated in the program. The results of this incentive program were quite dramatic. During the last three months of the Discover Paradise contest, sales of parts and service more than doubled those of the same period of the previous year.

Questions

1. What are some of the factors that contributed to the success of this incentive program?
2. Some critics of incentive programs believe that incentives treat the symptom, not the problem. Is the Toyota Motor Sales USA's Parts and Service Division likely to face this problem?
3. What other types of organizational problems might be solved with an incentive program similar to the one developed for Toyota?

Case 10.2

Mary Kay Is Having a Party[18]

Mary Kay Ash started Mary Kay Cosmetics Inc. in 1963, as much to give women a chance to "be somebody" as for any other reason. Two decades later the firm had a sales force of almost 200,000 (of which 99 percent were women), working under 4,000 regional sales directors. The firm markets its products directly to consumers at "parties" in which a sales representative meets with up to five potential customers. The representative, called a beauty consultant, teaches potential customers how to use and care for their skin with Mary Kay products and then takes orders for the products.

A part-time beauty consultant can earn upwards of $50 in commissions at a sales party, and full-time employees of the company earn over $25,000 per year. But money isn't all they earn. Top salespeople are rewarded with diamond rings, mink coats, vacations, shopping sprees, and pink Cadillacs. Consultants also work for a Mary Kay "ladder of success" pin, whose rungs are filled with sapphires or diamonds as succeeding sales goals are met. Everyone connected with the firm can recognize a top salesperson from her pin. And these gifts are usually presented in a hall packed with applauding salespeople and sales directors.

Each regional sales director holds regular two-hour Monday night meetings for prospective and experienced consultants. The director leads the meeting but also stands as a model for the others; she has risen in the organization as a result of her success as a consultant. The meeting itself is structured to build and maintain motivation, teach new sales skills, and reward performance. The first hour is devoted mainly to an orientation for prospective consultants, while experienced hands exchange selling ideas or receive advanced training in a separate area.

Recruits and veterans get together for the second hour. Soon after it begins, the director describes and praises the sales accomplishments of various consultants who are at the meeting. The group stands, applauds perhaps, sings, and offers congratulations to those who did well. In a way, everyone at the meeting experiences their accomplishments. Then the group sets its sales goals, which are reinforced and encouraged by the director. Individual consultants may also voice their personal selling goals. If a consultant has not met such a publicly stated goal, there is no negative feedback. Instead, other experienced consultants offer suggestions on how to reach that objective.

Questions

1. Which forms of positive reinforcement are practiced in the Mary Kay organization, and by whom?
2. Would the approach used by Mary Kay Cosmetics work in other marketing-oriented firms?

Notes

1. Saul W. Gellerman, *Motivation and Productivity*, audio-tape (San Diego, Calif.: University Associates).
2. "The Power of Recognition," *The Royal Bank Letter*, published by the Royal Bank of Canada, Vol. 66, No. 5, 1985, p. 1.
3. Bruce A. Baldwin, "Positive Feedback as Incredible Information," *Pace*, May-June 1982, p. 13.
4. Kenneth Kovach, "Why Motivational Theories Don't Work," S.A.M. *Advanced Management Journal*, Spring 1980, p. 46.
5. C. B. Stiegler, "Know Others—Make Your Communication Work with Positive Reinforcement," *Management World*, May 1976, p. 10.
6. Kenneth Blanchard and Spencer Johnson, *The One Minute Manager* (New York: Morrow, 1982), p. 43.
7. Claude Steiner, *TA Made Simple* (San Francisco: Transactional Pubs, 1973), p. 6.
8. Evelyn Sieburg, "Confirming and Disconfirming Organizational Communication," in *Communication in Organizations*, ed. James L. Owen, Paul A. Page, and Gordon I. Zimmerman (St. Paul, Minn.: West, 1976), p. 130.
9. Donald V. Schuster, "Performance Recognition: The Power of Positive Feedback," *Training*, January 1985, p. 72.
10. Christopher Hegarty with Philip Goldberg, *How to Manage Your Boss* (New York: Rawson, Wade, 1980), p. 125.
11. "E. F. MacDonald Links Motivation and Incentives," *Training/HRD*, April 1981, p. 62.
12. *Putting the One Minute Manager to Work*, p. 54.
13. "Incentive 'Carrots': Make Them Large and Plentiful," p. 8. Adapted with permission from the February 1981 issue of *Training*, The Magazine of Human Resources Development. Copyright 1981, Lakewood Publications, Minneapolis, MN, (612) 333–0471. All rights reserved.
14. Charles L. Alden, "Incentives Can Unlock Self-Motivation," *Sales and Marketing Management*, March 6, 1981, p. 92.
15. Sydney J. Harris, *Winners and Losers* (Niles, Ill.: Argus Communications, 1968), pp. 53, 61, 105, 117.
16. Thomas J. Von der Smase and Herbert E. Brown, "Authentic Motivation: How Psychological Touching Works," *Supervisory Management*, February 1979, p. 20.
17. "Toyota Sells Parts with Perks," *Sales and Marketing Management*, September 13, 1982, pp. 106–110.
18. For more information, see *Business Week*, March 28, 1983, p. 130; *Marketing & Media Decisions*, December 1982, p. 59; and Douglas M. Brooks and Kathy Bristow, "Monday Night Motivation at Mary Kay Cosmetics," *Mirrors of Excellence* (monograph), Robert Houston, ed., 1986, pp. 45–48.

Suggested Readings

Baldwin, Bruce A. "Positive Feedback as Incredible Information." *Pace*, May-June 1982, pp. 11–13.

Blanchard, Kenneth, and Spencer Johnson. *The One Minute Manager*. New York: Morrow, 1982.

Cushing, David. "When and How to Use Incentives in Training." *Training/HRD*, April 1981, pp. 57–66.

Elmers, Robert C., George W. Blomgren, and Edward Gubman. "How Awards and Incentives Can Help Speed Learning." *Training/HRD*, July 1979, pp. 83–86ff.

"Employee Recognition: A Key to Motivation." *Personnel Journal*, February 1981, pp. 103–107.

King, Dennis. "Rewarding Can Be Rewarding." *Supervisory Management*, January 1985, pp. 32–33.

Renken, Henry J. "An Employee-Incentive Program Can Be the Answer to Increased Productivity." *S.A.M. Advanced Management Journal*, Spring 1984, pp. 8–12.

Strang, T. Scott. "Positive Reinforcement: How Often and How Much." *Supervisory Management*, January 1985, pp. 7–9.

Tylczak, Lynn. "The Concept of Value Management." *Pace*, July 1985, pp. 51–53.

Zemke, Ron. "What Makes Suggestion Systems Work?" *Training/HRD*, July 1979, p. A–13.

Chapter 11

Developing Positive First Impressions

Chapter Preview

After studying this chapter, you will be able to

1. Explain the importance of a positive first impression in an organizational setting.
2. Discuss the factors that contribute to a favorable first impression.
3. Distinguish between assumptions and facts.
4. Define *image* and describe the factors that form the image you project to others.
5. List the three things that influence your choice of clothing for work.
6. Understand how manners affect first impressions.

What do high school students in Beverly Hills, California, have in common with management personnel employed by Hughes Aircraft, Mobil Oil, Textron, and many other corporations across America? They are studying manners in the classroom. And the goals of these new educational programs are not greatly dissimilar.

Students enrolled in the new courses offered by Beverly Hills High School emphasize the proper way to shake hands, speak to foreign dignitaries, dress properly for all occasions, and make formal introductions. Judi Kaufman, whose consulting firm was chosen to design the new program, points out that many students lack the basic social skills needed to achieve career success.[1]

Kaufman's firm, Communication Development Associates, has taught manners to executives of several major corporations. The program places emphasis on doing the right thing at the right time, especially important when people meet for the first time. You never have another opportunity to make a good first impression.

A growing number of organizations are giving new attention to the old adage, "first impressions are lasting impressions." Research indicates that initial impressions do indeed tend to linger. Therefore, a positive first impression can set the stage for a lasting relationship. A negative first impression can serve as a barrier to building good personal and customer relations.

A major goal of this chapter is to identify important factors that contribute to a positive first impression. Upon completion of this chapter, you will possess increased confidence in your ability to create a positive first impression in a variety of work and social settings.

The Primacy Effect

The tendency to form impressions quickly at the time of an initial meeting illustrates what social psychologists call a **primacy effect** in the way people perceive one another. The general principle is that first impressions establish the mental framework within which a person is viewed, and later evidence is either ignored or reinterpreted to coincide with this framework.[2]

Martha Kelly met a middle-aged man at an outdoor cookout. He was wearing cutoff blue jeans and an old pair of worn-out sneakers. He had had several drinks and tended to interrupt people and monopolize any conversation. Throughout the afternoon, people avoided him whenever possible. About two weeks later, Martha stopped at a drug store to get a prescription filled. To her surprise, the pharmacist was the same man she had met at the cookout, only now he was dressed in a neatly tailored white jacket, blue shirt, and pin-striped tie. Although he projected a very professional image in dealing with his customers, Martha left the store and went to another pharmacy to get her prescription filled. The positive impression communicated on this day was not strong enough to overcome her first, negative impression.

The Four-Minute Barrier

When two people meet, their potential for building a relationship can be affected by many factors. Within a few moments, one person or the other may feel threatened, offended, or bored. Leonard and Natalie Zunin, coauthors of *Contact—The First Four Minutes*, describe what they call the **four-minute barrier.**[3] In this short period of time, human relationships will be established, reconfirmed (in the case of two former acquaintances meeting), or denied. It is during the first few minutes of interaction with others that people's attention spans are at their greatest and powers of retention at their highest.

Why four minutes? According to the Zunins, this is the average time, demonstrated by careful observation, during which two people in a social situation make up their minds to continue the encounter or to separate. They say the four-minute concept applies to both casual meetings and ongoing contacts, such as husbands and wives meeting at the end of a day.

The way you are treated in this world depends largely on the way you present yourself—the way you look, the way you speak, the way you behave.[5] Although human contact is a challenge, you can learn to control the first impressions you make on others. The key is to become fully aware of the impression you communicate to other people.

Thinking/Learning Starters

To test the practical application of the Zunins' theory in a real-life setting, let's examine it in the context of your past experiences. Review the questions below and then answer each with yes or no.

1. Have you ever gone for a job interview and known instinctively within minutes that you would or would not be hired? _____ Yes _____ No
2. Have you ever met a salesperson who immediately communicated to you the impression that he or she could be trusted and was interested in your welfare? _____ Yes _____ No
3. Have you ever entered a restaurant and developed an immediate dislike for the waiter or waitress after a few opening comments? _____ Yes _____ No
4. Have you ever entered a business firm and experienced an immediate feeling of being welcome after the receptionist spoke only a few words? _____ Yes _____ No

First Impressions in a Work Setting

In a work setting, the four-minute period in which a relationship is established or denied is often reduced to seconds. The examples below help illustrate the effect these immediate first impressions can have in a variety of work situations.

Paula rushed into a restaurant for a quick lunch—she had to get back to her office for a 1:30 P.M. appointment. The restaurant was not crowded so she knew she would not have to wait for a table. At the entrance of the main dining area was a sign reading "Please Wait to Be Seated." A few feet away, the hostess was discussing a popular movie with one of the waitresses. The hostess made eye contact with Paula, but continued to visit with the waitress. About twenty more seconds passed, and Paula began to feel anxiety build inside her. She tried to get the hostess's attention, but the hostess did not respond. After another ten seconds had passed, Paula walked out of the restaurant.

Terry had completed his business in Des Moines, Iowa, and decided to rent a car for a trip to Omaha, Nebraska. He dialed the number of a popular rental car agency and was greeted by "May I help you?" spoken in a very indifferent tone of voice. Terry said that he wanted to rent a compact car and drive it to Omaha. The agency employee replied irritably, "You can't rent a compact car for out-of-town trips. These cars can only be used for local travel. You'll have to rent a full-sized car." Terry felt as though the employee didn't want his business and was criticizing him for not knowing the company's rental policy. He told the employee he would call another rental agency. The entire conversation lasted only thirty-seven seconds.

Sandy and Mike entered the showroom of a Mercedes-Benz dealer. They noticed two salespeople seated at desks near the entrance. One salesperson was dressed in a well-tailored gray suit and white shirt, with a blue tie highlighted by subtle stripes. The other salesperson was wearing a dark green suit, yellow shirt, and a patterned brown tie. The suit, made of polyester fabric, had long ago lost its shape. The salesperson wearing the dark green suit walked over to Sandy and Mike and asked, "May I be of assistance?" Mike said, "We're just looking today." After a few moments, they left the showroom. On the way to their car, Sandy said, "I can't believe someone selling a $40,000 automobile would dress like that." "I agree," Mike said.

In each of these examples, the negative first impression was created in less than sixty seconds. The anxiety level of the restaurant customer increased because she was forced to wait while two employees talked about a personal matter. The rental car employee antagonized a potential customer by using a tone of voice that was offensive. And the car salesperson apparently was not aware of the fact that people will make judgments about others that are based solely on appearance. Unfortunately, these employees are probably not fully aware of the impression they communicate to customers.

Total Person Insight	If people aren't quickly attracted to you or don't like what they see and hear in those first two to four minutes, chances are they won't pay attention to all those words you believe are demonstrating your knowledge and authority. They will find your client guilty, seek another doctor, buy another product, vote for your opponent or hire someone else.
Janet G. Elsea	

Assumptions Versus Facts

The impression you form of another person during the initial contact is made up of assumptions and facts. Most people tend to rely more heavily on **assumptions** during the initial meeting. As the Zunins state, people live in an assumptive world:

> When you meet a stranger, and sometimes with friends, much of the information you get is based on assumption. You form positive or negative feelings or impressions but you must realize that only superficial facts can be gathered in four minutes. Depending on assumptions is a one-way ticket to big surprises and perhaps disappointments.[6]

Cultural conditioning, especially during the early years, leads you to form impressions of some people even before you meet them. People often stereotype entire groups. Here are a few of the common **stereotypes** that still persist in our society:

▶ "Fat people are always jolly."
▶ "Italians are highly emotional."
▶ "Football players are dumb."
▶ "Chess players are all intellectual giants."
▶ "Men wearing moustaches are villainous."

These are just a few of the assumptions that some people perceive as facts. With the passing of time some assumptions tend to lose support as factual information surfaces. Fewer people today support the idea that all married couples should have children, and women are no longer viewed as unacceptable candidates for executive positions. However, people rarely reach the point in life where they are completely free of assumptions. In fact, the *briefer* the encounter with a new acquaintance, the greater the chance that misinformation will enter into your perception of the other person.

The Image You Project

Image is a term used to describe how other people feel about you. A positive image can set the stage for success whereas a negative image may set the stage for failure. In many respects, the image you project is very much like a picture puzzle, as illustrated in Figure 11.1. It is formed by a variety of factors including clothing, hair style, facial expression, tone of voice, and the way you treat other people. Although a wide variety of things contribute to the impression you create in the minds of others, each is under your control.

Why be concerned about your image? Because many studies indicate that the image you project can be as important to job success as your skills. Put another way, your ability to get a job and advance to positions of greater responsibility will often depend on the impression you communicate to others.

Surface Language

As noted earlier, we form opinions about other people based on both facts and assumptions. Unfortunately, assumptions often carry a great deal of weight. Many of the assumptions you develop regarding other people are based upon what the Zunins describe as "surface language." **Surface lan-**

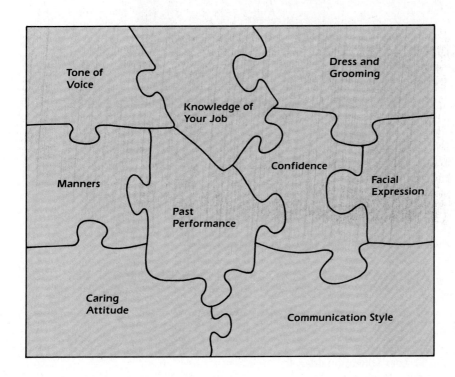

Figure 11.1
Factors That Form Your Image

In a work setting, the image you project can be important to job success. (Photo by Rob Nelson, The Picture Group)

guage is defined as a pattern of immediate impressions conveyed by appearance. The clothing you wear, your hair style, the fragrances you use, the jewelry you display—all combine to make a statement about you to others.

According to many writers familiar with image formation, clothing is particularly important. John T. Malloy, author of *Dress for Success* and *The Women's Dress for Success Book*, was one of the first to acknowledge publicly the link between professional accomplishments and wardrobe. According to his research, what you wear immediately establishes your credibility and likability.[7] Egon Von Furstenberg, author of *The Power Look*, says that discrimination on the basis of appearance is a fact of life in the business world.[8] Perhaps the strongest statement made about the importance of clothing in image formation comes from William Thourlby, author of *You Are What You Wear—The Key to Business Success:*

> When you step into a room, even though no one in that room knows you or has seen you before, they will make ten decisions about you based solely on your appearance. They make many more, but you can be assured that they will make these:
>
> 1. Your economic level
> 2. Your educational level
> 3. Your trustworthiness

4. Your social position
5. Your level of sophistication
6. Your economic heritage
7. Your social heritage
8. Your educational heritage
9. Your success
10. Your moral character

> To be successful in almost any endeavor, you must be sure that these decisions about you are favorable, because in that first impression you make—you are what you wear.[9]

Thourlby points out that clothing and appearance are among the most important criteria we use to judge people. In addition, he notes that people judge your appearance long before they judge your talents. You should therefore take your wardrobe seriously. Physical attractiveness, a strong determinant of first impressions, can be enhanced by your choice of clothing.

Thinking/Learning Starter

Try to recall at least one time in your life when you experienced discrimination based on your appearance. Was it your clothing, hair style, or something else that triggered the other person's reaction?

Selecting Your Career Apparel

Large numbers of people employed in the business community wear uniforms. Some employees, such as the Hertz rental car sales representatives, wear a uniform that was especially designed for their particular job. The mechanics at your neighborhood garage may also wear a special uniform. Today more and more people are getting into uniforms to go to work. According to psychologists, people who serve the public—especially those who are part of a group—often work best in uniform.[10] Wearing the same uniform seems to create a sort of bond between coworkers. Thus, a uniform can make at least a small contribution to building esprit de corps at your local McDonald's restaurant or Holiday Inn motel.

A growing number of organizations are seeking advice about **career apparel** from image consultants. Since 1978—the first year of its publication—the *Directory of Personal Image Consultants* has grown from a listing of 37 personal-improvement specialists to 256 in the 1984–1985 edition. An image consultant is someone who helps ensure that all elements of the visible person—speech, dress, body language, and manners—match the inner tal-

These two employees of Lowe's Companies, Inc. are wearing approved uniforms developed for the company by Unitog Business Clothing Company. (Photo courtesy of Lowe's Companies, Inc.)

ents and aspirations of that person. Each year more than $100 million is spent on image consulting in the United States.[11]

The uniforms worn by UPS employees, airline reservation clerks, and the employees at your local restaurant might be classified as special-design career apparel. Some work uniforms are designed by top talents in the fashion industry. In addition to special-design uniforms, there is another type of career apparel, less formal and somewhat less predictable, worn by large numbers of people in our labor force. Here are some examples:

1. A woman lawyer representing a prestigious firm would be appropriately dressed in a gray or blue skirted suit. A dress with a suit jacket would also be acceptable. She should avoid cute, frilly clothing that might reduce her credibility.

Wearing a uniform can create a bond among employees. These uniforms are typical of those worn by chefs who are employed in fine restaurants. (Photo courtesy of the Culinary Institute of America)

2. A male bank loan officer would be appropriately dressed in a tailored gray or blue suit, white shirt, and tie. This same person dressed in a colorful blazer, sport shirt, and plaid slacks would be seen as too casual in a bank setting.

3. A female receptionist at a prominent accounting firm would be appropriately dressed in a skirt and blouse. This same person would be inappropriately dressed if she showed up for work wearing designer jeans, a sweater, and sandals.

4. A mechanic employed by an auto dealership that sells new cars would be appropriately dressed in matching gray, tan, or light green shirt and pants. The mechanic would be inappropriately dressed in jeans and a sport shirt.

Selecting the correct clothing for a career can be difficult—for both men and women. The rules are usually unwritten and quite subtle. One psychologist who took an in-depth look at the subject made this observation:

> This whole business of dress and grooming is actually playing upon unconscious expectations and assumptions about the significance of clothing. For example, the man who's wearing a dark, three-piece suit projects to others that he's a conservative, predictable individual, while the man with frayed cuffs, or unshined shoes, is just naturally going to come off as careless and sloppy.[12]

The key idea presented here is **unconscious expectations.** Everyone has certain opinions about what is appropriate in terms of dress. Throughout life, we become acquainted with bank loan officers, nurses, police officers, and others employed in a wide range of occupations. We form mental images of the apparel common to each of these occupations. When we encounter someone whose appearance does not conform to our past experiences, we feel uncomfortable. Although today's public is more tolerant in matters related to dress, people still have certain expectations.

In general, three things will influence your choice of clothing for work: (1) the products or services offered by your employer, (2) the type of person served, and (3) the desired image projected by your organization.

Products and Services Offered   Store A sells casual clothing such as blue jeans, corduroy slacks, multicolored shirts, and sweatshirts. Store B sells expensive suits, dress shirts, ties, and other accessories. You would not expect the employees working at Store A to wear a suit to work. Casual clothing, similar to that sold by the store, would be very acceptable. However, the employees working at Store B should dress up to meet the expectations of the clientele served. The customer who purchases an expensive suit will expect the salesperson to be dressed in a conservative manner. This person should wear clothing similar to that sold by the store.

Type of Person Served   What are the expectations of your firm's customers and clients? This is always a key question when you are selecting career apparel. Consider the real estate firm that employs two sales teams: one team sells houses in urban areas and the other sells rural property, primarily farms. The urban home buyer expects to do business with someone who is conservatively dressed—casual clothing won't do. The farmer, on the other hand, is apt to feel uncomfortable when dealing with someone who is dressed up (suit and tie, for example). A more casual outfit may represent appropriate apparel for these employees.

Desired Image Projected by the Organization   Lowe's Companies operates a chain of 295 retail home-center stores. The company is attempting to project the image of an "upscale" discount retailer. The attractive stores are stocked with quality merchandise at competitive prices. Each employee wears neatly tailored apparel that was designed to complement the store image. The dress program was initiated to ensure that all employees present to customers a consistent professional look. (See photo on p. 274.)

Thinking/Learning Starter

Assume that you are planning to purchase: (1) a life insurance policy, (2) a Rolex wrist watch, and (3) eyeglasses. What types of career apparel would you expect persons selling these products to wear? What grooming standards would you recommend?

Wardrobe Engineering

The term **wardrobe engineering** was first used by John T. Malloy to describe how clothing and accessories can be used to create a certain image. This concept was later refined by William Thourlby, Jacqueline Thompson, Emily Cho, Susan Bixler, and other noted image consultants. In recent years, hundreds of books and articles on dress and grooming have been written. Although these authors are not in complete agreement on every aspect of dress, they do agree on a few basic points regarding your wardrobe.

1. *When meeting someone for the first time, you make an impression even before you open your mouth.* People judge your appearance before they know your talents! Keep in mind that nonverbal communication is the first and greatest source of impressions in direct, face-to-face interactions, and clothing is a major part of the nonverbal message you send to a new acquaintance.

2. *Establish personal dress and grooming standards appropriate for the organization where you wish to work.* Before you apply for a job, try to find out what the workers there are wearing. If in doubt, dress conservatively. If you find out the dress code is more relaxed, you can adjust to it later. When you actually begin work, identify the most successful people in the organization and emulate their manner of dress.

3. *Dress for the job you want, not the job you have.*[13] If you are currently a secretary and want to become the office manager, don't continue to dress like a secretary. Employees can communicate with their clothing that they are satisfied with their position. Emily Cho, author of *Looking Terrific*, says that the right wardrobe can transform a person from being part of the corporate scenery to being in the forefront. Some employers say they can walk into a business firm and see who is ready for a promotion.

4. *Avoid wearing the newest dress fad in a business or professional setting.*

Reprinted by permission: Tribune Media Services.

In most cases the world of work is more conservative than college, the arts, or the world of sports. If you are a fashion setter, you might be viewed as unstable or lacking in sincerity. To be taken seriously, avoid clothing that is too flashy!

Women generally have more latitude than men in selecting appropriate attire, but they should still exercise some caution in choosing their wardrobe. In some cases, women are entering positions formerly dominated by men. They need to be taken seriously, and the wardrobe they select can contribute to this end.

5. *When you select a wardrobe, consider regional differences in dress and grooming standards.* Geography is a factor in how people should dress. What may be suitable apparel for a receptionist working in New York City may be inappropriate in Des Moines. Pay attention to local customs and traditions when establishing your personal dress and grooming standards.

6. *The quality of your wardrobe will influence the image you project.* Money spent on career apparel should be viewed as an investment with each item carefully selected to look and fit well. A suit or dress purchased off the rack at a discount store may save dollars initially, but can cost you more if it doesn't help you get that promotion you want. Clothing purchased at bargain prices often wears out quickly. The less money you have, the more concerned you should be about buying quality clothing.

7. *Selection of a wardrobe should be an individual matter.* Diane Harris, a North Carolina–based image consultant who knows the rules about career dress for men and women, says, "Effective packaging is an individual matter based on the person's circumstances, age, weight, height, coloring, and objectives."[14] Don't just duplicate what appears to be appropriate dress selected by others in your field.

Getting a job, keeping a job, and getting a promotion depend to some degree on your wardrobe. Therefore, research your wardrobe as carefully as you would research a prospective employer. Although the practice of judging people solely by what they wear should not be encouraged, you need to recognize that people often are prejudiced regarding physical appearance. Make sure that your appearance helps you create a positive first impression.

Facial Expression

After your overall appearance, your face is the most visible part of you. Facial expressions are the cue most people rely on in initial interactions. They are the "teleprompter" by which others read your mood and personality.[15]

Studies conducted in nonverbal communication show that facial expressions strongly influence whether you like or dislike someone. The expression on your face can quickly trigger a positive or negative reaction from those you meet. How you rate in the "good-looks" department may not be nearly as important as your ability to communicate positive impressions with a pleasant smile.

If you want to identify the inner feelings of another person, watch the individual's facial expressions closely. A frown may tell you "something is wrong." A smile generally communicates "things are OK." Everyone has encountered a "look of surprise" and "a look that could kill." These facial expressions usually reflect the inner emotions of others more accurately than their words.

In many work settings, a cheerful smile is an important key to creating a positive first impression. On the other hand, a deadpan stare (or frown) can communicate a negative first impression to others. If you find it hard to smile, take time to consider the reasons. Are you constantly thinking negative thoughts and simply find nothing to smile about? Are you afraid others might misinterpret your intentions? Are you fearful that a pleasant smile will en-

Facial expressions and gestures are important factors in creating the type of first impression you want. (Photo © Sandra Johnson, 1981)

courage communication with people with whom you would rather not spend time?

If you seldom smile or stopped smiling a long time ago for some reason, you may find it helpful to rehearse this basic skill in front of the mirror. With practice you can learn to smile without inhibition.

Your eyes are also an important part of the facial expression you communicate to others. Ralph Waldo Emerson said, "The eyes of men converse as much as their tongues, with the advantage that the ocular dialect needs no dictionary, but is understood the world over." Eyes can communicate unspoken messages. One of the quickest ways to communicate the message "I'm not listening" to another person is to avoid eye contact. In some situations, lack of eye contact may say to others, "I cannot be trusted." Like smiling, the ability to maintain eye contact with people often requires practice.

Your Voice

Several years ago a Cleveland-based company, North American Systems, developed and marketed Mr. Coffee, which makes a cup of coffee quickly and conveniently. Some credit the quick acceptance of this product to an effective advertising campaign featuring baseball Hall of Famer Joe DiMaggio. He came across to the consumer as an honest, sincere person. When Joe DiMaggio said Mr. Coffee worked and made good coffee, people believed him.

Your voice can project confidence, enthusiasm, sincerity, and optimism to others. Each of these qualities helps create a positive impression. The tone of your voice, the rate of speed at which you speak (tempo), and the volume of your speech contribute greatly to the meaning attached to your verbal messages. In the case of telephone calls, voice quality is critical, because the other person cannot see your facial expressions, hand gestures, and other body movements. You can't trade in your current voice for a new one. However, you can make your voice more pleasing to other people and project a positive tone.

While there is no ideal voice for all business contacts, your voice should reflect at least these five qualities: confidence, enthusiasm, attention, optimism, and sincerity. Assess your own speaking voice and determine if small changes will increase your effectiveness in dealing with people. With today's inexpensive cassette tape recorders, it is easy to find out how you sound to others. To evaluate the quality of your voice, tape your conversation with another person. Play back the tape and rate yourself according to the five qualities listed.

Your Handshake

When two people first meet, the handshake is usually the only physical contact. The handshake can communicate warmth, genuine concern for the other person, and strength. It can also communicate aloofness, indifference, and weakness. The message you send the other party via your handshake will depend on a combination of these factors:

1. *Degree of firmness.* Generally speaking, a firm handshake will communicate a caring attitude, whereas a weak grip communicates indifference.

2. *Degree of dryness of hands.* A moist palm is not only unpleasant to feel, it can communicate the impression that you are nervous. A clammy hand is likely to repel most people.

3. *Duration of grip.* There are no specific guidelines about the ideal duration of a grip. However, by extending the handshake, you can often communicate a greater degree of interest and concern for the other person.

4. *Depth of interlock.* A full, deep grip is more apt to convey friendship and strength to the other person.

5. *Eye contact during handshake.* Visual communication can increase the positive impact of your handshake. Maintaining eye contact throughout the handshaking process is important when two people greet each other.

Most individuals have shaken hands with hundreds of people, but have little idea whether they are creating positive or negative impressions. It is a good idea to obtain this information from those coworkers or friends who will express candid opinions. Like all other human relations skills, the handshake can be improved with practice.

Manners

At the beginning of this chapter we noted that many people are returning to the classroom to study manners. At least some of the renewed interest in manners may have been stimulated by the writings of Letitia Baldrige, author of the *Complete Guide to Executive Manners*. It is her view that "good manners are cost effective."

A study of manners (sometimes called etiquette) reveals a number of areas that potentially could serve as barriers to making a positive first impression. Jonathan Swift recognized the importance of good manners when he said, "Good manners is the art of making people comfortable. Whoever makes the fewest people uncomfortable has the best manners." Making people feel comfortable is at the heart of good human relations. Good manners is a universal passport to positive relationships and respect.

One of the best ways to develop rapport with another person is to avoid behavior that might be offensive to that individual. Although it is not possible to do a complete review of this topic, some of the rules of etiquette that are particularly important in an organizational setting are covered here.

1. *When establishing new relationships, avoid calling people by their first names too soon.* Jacqueline Thompson says that assuming that all work-related associates prefer to be addressed informally by their first names is a serious breach of etiquette.[16] Use titles of respect—Miss, Mrs., Ms., Mr., or Dr.—until the relationship is well established. Too much familiarity can breed irritation. When the other party says "Call me Susan" or "Call me Roy," it's all right to begin using the person's first name. Informality should develop by invitation, not by presumption.

2. *Avoid obscenities and offensive comments or stories.* In recent years, standards for acceptable and unacceptable language have changed considerably. Obscenity is more permissible in everyday conversation than it was in the past. However, it is still considered inappropriate to use foul language in front of a customer, a client, or, in many cases, a fellow worker. According to Bob Greene, syndicated columnist, an obscenity communicates a negative message to most people.

> What it probably all comes down to is an implied lack of respect for the people who hear you talk. If you use profanity among friends, that is a choice you make. But if you broadcast it to people in general, you're telling them that you don't care what their feelings might be.[17]

Never assume that another person's value system is the same as your own. Foul language and off-color stories can do irreparable damage to interpersonal relations.

3. *Do not express strong personal views regarding issues that may be quite controversial.* It is usually not a good idea to express strong political views when you are trying to establish a good relationship with customers or clients. When dealing with the public it is also best not to wear pins or buttons that identify a personal association with a political group. Personal beliefs regarding religious issues should also be avoided. There is seldom a "safe" position to take in the areas of politics or religion.

4. *Never smoke in the presence of a fellow employee, customer, or client unless you are sure he or she will not be offended.* The practice of smoking is viewed with disapproval by a growing number of people. More organizations are restricting smoking to designated areas only. Some people are allergic to smoke and others simply dislike the odor. People who do not smoke will appreciate your consideration for their comfort.

5. *Avoid making business or professional visits unless you have an appointment.* Walking into someone's office without an appointment is generally considered rude. A good rule of thumb is always to make an appointment in advance and arrive promptly. If you are late, quickly voice a sincere apology.

6. *Express appreciation at appropriate times.* A simple thank you can mean a lot. Failure to express appreciation can be a serious human relations blun-

der. The secretary who works hard to complete a rush job for the boss is likely to feel frustrated and angry if this extra effort is ignored. The customer who makes a purchase deserves to receive a sincere thank you. You want your customers to know that their business is appreciated.

7. *Be aware of personal habits that may be offensive to others.* Sometimes an annoying habit can be a barrier to establishing a positive relationship with someone else. Chewing gum is a habit that bothers many people, particularly if you chew gum vigorously or "crack" it. Biting fingernails, cracking knuckles, scratching your head, and combing your hair in public are additional habits to be avoided.

Letitia Baldrige says that in the field of manners, "Rules are based on kindness and efficiency." She also believes that good manners are those personal qualities that make life at work more livable.[18] A knowledge of good manners permits us to perform our daily work with poise and confidence.

Summary

People tend to form impressions quickly at the time of the initial meeting, and these first impressions tend to be preserved. Leonard and Natalie Zunin describe the four-minute barrier as the average time people spend together before a relationship is either established or denied. In an organizational setting, the time interval is often reduced to seconds. Positive first impressions are important because they contribute to repeat business and greater customer loyalty.

The impression you form of another person during the initial contact is made up of assumptions and facts. When meeting someone for the first time, people tend to rely more heavily on assumptions. Many of your assumptions can be traced to early cultural conditioning. Assumptions are also based on surface language. The Zunins describe surface language as a pattern of immediate impressions conveyed by appearance. The clothing and jewelry you wear, your hair style, the fragrances you use all combine to make a statement about you to others.

Egon Von Furstenberg, author of *The Power Look*, contends that discrimination on the basis of appearance is still a fact of life. The clothing you wear is an important part of the image you communicate to others. Three things tend to influence your choice of clothing for work: (1) the products or services offered by the employer, (2) the type of person served, and (3) the desired image projected by the organization.

In addition to clothing, research indicates that facial expressions strongly influence whether you like or dislike someone. The expression on your face can quickly trigger a positive or negative reaction. Similarly, your voice, handshake, and manners also contribute to the image you project when meeting others.

Key Terms

primacy effect

four-minute barrier

assumptions

cultural conditioning

stereotype

image

surface language

career apparel

unconscious expectations

wardrobe engineering

Review Questions

1. What is the impact of positive first impressions on repeat business and customer loyalty?
2. Define the term *primacy effect.*
3. What is the significance of the four-minute barrier described by Leonard and Natalie Zunin? Does this concept apply to work as well as to social settings?
4. Why do people tend to rely more heavily on assumptions than facts during the initial meeting?
5. Why should career-minded people be concerned about the image they project? What factors contribute to the formation of one's image?
6. What are some of the major decisions people make about others based on career apparel?
7. What are the three things that will influence your choice of clothing for work?
8. What is meant by the term *unconscious expectations*?
9. Describe the type of speaking voice that will increase one's effectiveness in dealing with people.
10. Jonathan Swift and Letitia Baldridge have voiced strong support for the study of manners. What reasons do they give for developing an understanding of good manners?

Case 11.1

Is Career Apparel a Good Investment?[19]

A few years ago the Bank of Virginia decided to invest $250,000 in new wardrobes for their tellers. More than 600 tellers, men and women, were outfitted in its 120 Virginia branches. The new career apparel selection for women included an eleven-piece mix-and-match wardrobe worth approximately $700 in the retail market. Men were allowed to choose from a 15-item collection that was equally costly.

Bank officials emphasized that they did not want to recommend a single "uniform" for everyone. Each teller was allowed to take an individual approach to selecting professional banking apparel. The tellers chose their own fashions and colors from Fashion Star Inc., a company that specializes in career apparel. Skirts, blouses, sweaters, blazers, and other items were available in a variety of colors suitable for a bank setting. In most cases, no two tellers appear in identical ensembles on a given day.

The decision to invest a quarter of a million dollars in new wardrobes for tellers was made after the bank conducted a research study to determine what customers wanted in the way of customer service. They responded that they wanted professional service, consistency, and friendly treatment. Bank officials believed that tellers with a consistent professional look would project a more positive image.

Questions

1. If you were a member of the Bank of Virginia board of directors, would you vote for or against the decision to purchase new wardrobes for tellers? Explain your answer.
2. In this chapter we have cited three factors that should influence the choice of clothing for work. Do you think that Bank of Virginia has followed these guidelines?
3. What other types of organizations might consider adopting the wardrobe plan initiated by Bank of Virginia?

Case 11.2

Gender Etiquette in Organizations[20]

Many of the rules of social etiquette arose from the traditional concept of chivalry, in which gentlemen were viewed as the protectors of ladies and were expected to accord them an extra measure of respect. Much of that social etiquette was carried over into the workplace, at a time when most organizations would not consider employing a woman for any position higher than secretary. As a result, business etiquette used to require, among other things, that:

1. Before entering an elevator, men wait until all women present have entered. Before leaving an elevator, they wait until all women who wish to exit have done so.

2. Men stand up when a woman enters the room or office they are in, and continue to stand until she is seated.
3. Women do not offer to shake hands with men when they meet.
4. Women precede men when they are walking together, and men carry women's packages.
5. Men open doors for women. If necessary, a woman walking ahead of a man waits for him to catch up and open the door.
6. Men pay for women's restaurant meals, whether they are social or for business purposes.
7. Men generally greet women with a compliment about their appearance.

Nowadays, however, many women are working side by side with men, and those women do not want to be treated differently because of their gender. Yet many men feel that it is "improper" to treat women otherwise. They may go through contortions trying to open an office door for a woman while holding two attaché cases and an overcoat, but they feel that it must be done. The situation is just as awkward for women, who find it difficult to refuse such treatment without appearing to be discourteous or even pushy.

The problem seems to be one of finding a middle ground—an organizational etiquette that preserves courtesy without distinguishing between male and female organization members. A number of solutions have been offered, but none of them has been fully accepted. Almost all observers agree, however, that gender-based etiquette is out.

Questions

1. Instead of gender, what would be a more rational (and nonsexist) basis for rules of manners in an organizational setting? Explain your answer.
2. Would it be appropriate to offer employees a short course or seminar that is designed to update their knowledge of the new business etiquette?

Notes

1. Thomas D. Elias, "Learning Manners in Beverly Hills," *Roanoke Times & World-News*, March 7, 1986, p. PC-1.
2. Zick Rubin, "The Rise and Fall of First Impressions—How People Are Perceived," in *Interpersonal Communication in Action*, ed. Bobby R. Patton and Kim Fiffen, II (New York: Harper & Row, 1977), p. 150.
3. Leonard Zunin and Natalie Zunin, *Contact—The First Four Minutes* (New York: Ballantine Books, 1972), p. 5.
4. Janet G. Elsea, *The Four-Minute Sell* (New York: Simon and Schuster, 1984), p. 9.
5. Jacqueline Thompson, *Image Impact* (New York: Ace Books, 1981), p. 8.
6. Zunin and Zunin, *Contact*, p. 17.
7. John T. Molloy, *Dress for Success* (New York: Peter H. Wyden, 1975); and John T. Molloy, *The Woman's Dress for Success Book* (New York: Warner Books, 1977).

8. Egon Von Furstenberg, *The Power Look* (New York: Holt, Rinehart & Winston, 1978), p. 5.

9. William Thourlby, *You Are What You Wear—The Key to Business Success* (Kansas City: Sheed Andrews and McMeel, 1978), p. 1.

10. Anita Porter, "What a Difference a Uniform Makes," *TWA Ambassador*, June 1978, p. 18.

11. "Image Consulting Looks Better All the Time," *Training and Development Journal*, September 1984, p. 10.

12. Gerald Egan, "Dressing for Success in Richmond," *New Dominion Lifestyle*, September 1977, p. 24.

13. "Does What You Wear Tell Where You're Headed?" *U.S. News and World Report*, September 25, 1978, p. 59.

14. Dave Knesel, "Image Consulting—A Well-Dressed Step Up the Corporate Ladder," *Pace*, July-August, 1981, p. 74.

15. Elsea, *The Four-Minute Sell*, p. 34.

16. Thompson, *Image Impact*, p. 131.

17. Bob Greene, "Why Must We Say Things Like . . . and . . . ?" *Roanoke Times & World-News*, April 27, 1980, p. 7.

18. Letitia Baldrige, *Letitia Baldrige's Complete Guide to Executive Manners* (New York: Rawson Associates, 1985), p. 13.

19. Mary Bland Armistead, "Banking on a Look," *Roanoke Times & World-News*, September 12, 1981, p. C-1.

20. For more information, see *The Wall Street Journal*, March 24, 1986, p. 31D; *Working Woman*, January 1985, p. 86; and Letitia Baldrige, *Letitia Baldrige's Complete Guide to Executive Manners* (New York: Rawson Associates, 1985) pp. 39–46.

Suggested Readings

Baldrige, Letitia. *Letitia Baldrige's Complete Guide to Executive Manners*. New York: Rawson Associates, 1985.

Carnegie, Dale. *How to Win Friends and Influence People*. New York: Pocket Books, 1964.

Darling, Sharon K. "Dress to Win." *Pace*, March 1986.

Elsea, Janet G. *The Four-Minute Sell*. New York: Simon and Schuster, 1984.

Martin, Judith. *Common Courtesy: In Which Miss Manners Solves the Problem That Baffled Mr. Jefferson*. New York: Atheneum, 1986.

Molloy, John T. *Dress for Success*. New York: Peter H. Wyden, 1975.

Molloy, John T. *Live for Success*. New York: Morrow, 1981.

Molloy, John T. *The Woman's Dress for Success Book*. New York: Warner Books, 1977.

Thompson, Jacqueline. *Image Impact*. New York: Ace Books, 1981.

Thourlby, William. *You Are What You Wear—The Key to Business Success*. Kansas City: Sheed Andrews and McMeel, 1978.

Zunin, Leonard, and Natalie Zunin. *Contact—The First Four Minutes*. New York: Ballantine Books, 1972.

IV

If We All Work Together...

Chapter 12

Team Building: A Leadership Strategy

Chapter Preview

After studying this chapter, you will be able to

1. Explain the importance of teamwork in an organizational setting.
2. List six characteristics of an effective work team.
3. Explain those behavioral science principles that support team building.
4. Describe two of the most important dimensions of supervisory leadership.
5. Describe how members of a work group can contribute to team building.

"It was the worst night of my life." That was the reaction of John P. McCain, a personnel executive at Northern Telecom, after spending the night 100 feet above the earth on top of a rock. There was barely enough room for McCain and the nine other members of his "class," who spent the night huddled together, buckled to a metal ring that was staked to the rock. Two small steps in any direction, and McCain would have found himself walking on air.

Every year thousands of executives like McCain are sent by their firms to participate in such rugged outings. They may navigate rafts through whitewater rapids, ride horseback over wilderness trails, or spend several days together in the woods. These people are not on company-paid vacation; they are participating in vigorous management development programs administered by such organizations as Outward Bound and Boston University's Executive Challenge. Most return to their jobs with increased self-confidence, an awareness of the importance of one's perspective on a problem, and a strong appreciation of teamwork.

One group of twelve Federal Express executives was put aboard an open thirty-foot boat on the coast of Maine and told to sail it to an island that could just be seen on the horizon. It took them a full day to get over their anger at their firm and each other, and to figure out how to sail the boat. But when the experience was over, they were a more cohesive unit, able to work much more effectively with their manager.[1]

Team Building: An Introduction

Can the element of teamwork make a difference between the successful and unsuccessful operation of an organization? Yes, there is evidence that a leadership style that emphasizes **team building** is positively associated with high productivity and profitability. Problems in interpersonal relations are also less common where teamwork is evident. Team building ensures not only that a job gets done, but that it gets done efficiently and harmoniously. This style of leadership seems better suited to the needs of today's better-educated employees.

There is also evidence that team building can have a positive influence on the physical and psychological well-being of supervisory-management personnel. As one author explains, "Team building isn't just a good idea, it's a necessity of biological life. A belief in team work actually results in measured reduction of medical symptoms for managers."[2]

Increased levels of synergy is another positive outcome of teamwork. *Synergy* is evident when the total effort is greater than the sum of the individual efforts. Mathematically speaking, synergy suggests that two plus two equals five. Or, it is the interaction of two or more parts to produce a greater result than the sum of the parts taken individually.[3] Teamwork synergy is encouraged at 3M and many other progressive companies.

Discovery of the Team Concept

Emergence of the team idea came with the now classic Hawthorne studies. You will recall from Chapter 1 that this research was conducted by a group of Harvard professors at the suburban Chicago plant of the Western Electric Company. The research team initially tested the hypothesis that work output is directly related to the amount of light in the work area. This research was an outgrowth of stimulus-response theory that indicates people will respond directly to external stimuli and, if you can control the stimuli, you can control the individual effort.[4] The results of the initial research proved to be puzzling. Production output constantly increased, even when lighting decreased. After an in-depth study of all factors, the research team found that work output was a function of something more than work conditions. They generally agreed that the most significant factor was the develoment of a sense of group identity, a feeling of mutual support, and the cohesiveness that came from increased worker interaction.

Elton Mayo, one of the original researchers, noted that the Hawthorne experiment showed it was possible to take a random collection of employees and build them into a highly productive team. Mayo pointed out that certain factors were present that developed a spirit of teamwork:

1. The supervisor (chief observer) had a personal interest in each person's achievement.
2. He took pride in the record of the group.
3. He helped the group work together to set its own conditions of work.
4. He faithfully posted the feedback on performance.
5. The group took pride in its own achievement and had the satisfaction of outsiders' showing interest in what they did.
6. The group did not feel they were being pressured to change.
7. Before changes were made, the group was consulted.
8. The group developed a sense of confidence and candor.[5]

Thinking/Learning Starter

Review your work experience and try to recall situations where the supervisor took a personal interest in members of your work force. What was the impact of this situation on members of the group?

McGregor's Influence

In the late 1950s, a book by Douglas McGregor, entitled *The Human Side of Enterprise,* presented convincing arguments that management had been ignoring certain important facts about people. He said that managers often failed to recognize the potential for growth and fulfillment characteristic of most workers. McGregor emphasized that "unity of purpose" is the main distinguishing characteristic of many productive work units. When a work group shares common goals and a common commitment, it accomplishes more.

In *The Human Side of Enterprise,* McGregor discussed several characteristics of an effective work team.[6]

1. The atmosphere of the workplace tends to be informal, comfortable, relaxed. There are no obvious tensions. It is a working environment in which people are involved and interested. There are no signs of boredom.
2. There is a lot of discussion about work-related issues, and virtually everyone participates; but their contributions remain pertinent to the task of the group. If the discussion gets off the subject, someone will bring it back in short order.
3. The task or the objective of the group is well understood and accepted by the members. There will have been free discussion of the objectives at some point, until the goals are formulated in such a way that the members of the group can commit themselves to achieving them.
4. The members listen to each other! The discussion does not jump from one idea to another unrelated one. Every idea is given a hearing.
5. There is disagreement. The group is comfortable with this and shows no signs of having to avoid conflict or to keep everything on a plane of sweetness and light.
6. People freely express their feelings as well as their ideas both on the problem and on the group's operation. There is little avoidance, and there are few "hidden agendas."

In summary, McGregor recommended a humanistic and supportive approach in dealing with people. Management's role is to provide an environment in which every worker's potential can be released.

The Managerial Grid

In the early 1960s, Robert R. Blake and Jane S. Mouton authored a popular book entitled *The Managerial Grid.* As illustrated in Figure 12.1, the **Managerial Grid**® is a model based on two management style dimensions: concern for people and concern for production. Where work is physical, concern for production may take the form of number of units produced per hour or

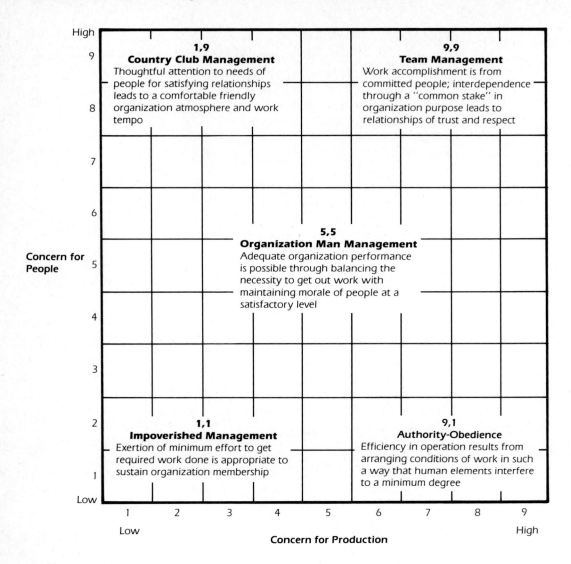

Figure 12.1
Managerial Grid®

Source: Robert R. Blake and Jane Srygley Mouton, *The New Managerial Grid*

the time needed to meet a certain production schedule. In a sales organization, concern for production will take the form of sales volume. Concern for people can be reflected in the way a supervisor views work conditions, compensation, recognition for a job well done, and job security. It can also be revealed in the way a supervisor views safety conditions for subordinates. The Grid helps to clarify how these two dimensions are related and establishes a uniform language for communication about management styles and patterns. Although there are eighty-one different leadership styles within the Grid, five encompass the more important differences among managers. Blake and Mouton developed descriptive names for each.[7]

Impoverished Management (1,1). People with this orientation might be classified as "inactive" managers. They display little concern for people or production. These managers give very little of themselves and expect little from others. This is a "let's-get-by-as-best-we-can"[8] style.

Country Club Management (1,9). Low concern for production and high concern for people characterizes this management orientation. These managers take steps to prevent unhappiness and dissension. The "country club" type manager is eager to accommodate, to avoid being seen as aggressive or demanding. This style wants to keep unhappiness in the work group at a minimum.

Authority-Obedience Management (9,1). This is a task-oriented style of management, with much attention placed on getting the job done. Managers with this orientation display concern for production, not people. People are seen as instruments of production. To this style of manager, achieving performance or production goals is essential, regardless of the human cost.

Organization Man Management (5,5). Managers with this style display moderate concern for both people and production. A limited amount of participative management is practical. This person is primarily concerned with maintaining existing conditions in the organization. The "organization man" manager is more likely to act in accordance with traditions and be satisfied with modest performance.

Team Management (9,9). This is a "proactive" style of management. Persons with this orientation display a high concern for both people and production. They recognize that results are achieved through people. The team manager rewards the contribution of ideas and recognizes accomplishments. Open communication is encouraged, and every effort is made to keep people well informed. The team manager tries to bring out the best in people.

Blake and Mouton have devoted over twenty years to the study of the team-building leadership style. They maintain that this style is the one most positively associated with productivity and profitability, career success and satisfaction, and with physical and mental health:

> Managers come in all sizes, shapes and philosophies. Some are gung ho for production and ride roughshod over everyone and everything. Some con-

centrate on being "nice guys" and create a country club atmosphere at the expense of accomplishment. Still others live by the rules, take their cues from the boss, and play it safe. Some talented few [9,9 team builders] have discovered the secret of involving others, and use the team approach to building organizational effectiveness.[9]

Blake and Mouton use the term "One Best Style" to describe the 9,9 orientation. They feel this leadership style can be applied effectively in almost any type of organization. This style, according to the authors, achieves production "through a high degree of shared responsibility, coupled with high participation, involvement and commitment—hallmarks of teamwork."[10]

Dr. Jay Hall, author of *The Competence Process*, completed a large-scale research project that supports the work of Blake and Mouton.[11] He studied several thousand managers—their personalities and management styles and patterns. The high-achieving managers had a deep interest in both people and productivity. Results indicate that high-achieving managers also rely heavily on the participative ethic, whereas low and moderate achievers avoid involving their subordinates in decision making. He concludes:

> The portrait of the Achieving Manager which emerges from our study is that of an individual employing an integrative style of management, wherein people are valued just as highly as accomplishment of production goals, . . . wherein candor, openness, sensitivity and receptivity comprise the rule in interpersonal relationships rather than its exception, . . . wherein participative practices are favored over unilaterally directive or lame duck prescriptive measures.[12]

Hall suggests that production goals and people's needs are equally important. He believes that to be a successful supervisor or manager, you must be supportive of other people and create opportunities for them:

> Most people put forth their best efforts when they are collaborators in the enterprise before them. When they can see that their needs and objectives are best met by achieving the goals of their organization, most people are willing to give whatever effort is required.[13]

Thinking/Learning Starter

Think about the managers you have worked for or managers you have observed over the years. How much concern did each one display toward people? Toward production? Assign each manager one of the five style-classification names developed by Blake and Mouton.

Behavioral Science Principles Support Team Building

In almost every field of study there are a few universal principles (sometimes called fundamentals) that are supported by research evidence. A principle can be thought of as a general guideline that is true regardless of time, place, or situation. These principles, or fundamental laws, provide guidance for sound decision making.

In the field of human relations there are several principles—based on the behavioral sciences—that support the team-building leadership style. Blake and Mouton developed a list of these principles and applied them to the art of management.[14]

1. *Shared participation in problem solving and decision making is basic to growth, development, and contribution.* As noted previously, people tend to be more productive and effective when they can identify with the goals of the organization. When people are encouraged to participate in making decisions that affect them, they develop an identity and a sense of control over their destiny. Those employees who never get the opportunity to make such decisions develop a feeling of "powerlessness." They become passive and avoid opportunities to make contributions to the organization. There is one other important reason why management should involve employees in problem solving and decision making—people tend to support what they help to create!

Trust and open communication foster teamwork. (Photo by Christopher Morrow, Stock Boston, Inc.)

2. *Mutual trust and respect undergird productive human relationships.* Trust is a catalyst. When trust exists within an organization, a spirit of teamwork is more likely to exist. As trust ebbs, people are less open with each other, less interdependent, and less willing to work as a team. When trust is present, people find it easier to develop open and personal relationships with others. Jack Gibb, author of *Trust—A New View of Personal and Organizational Development*, said, "When I trust myself, trust you, and trust the process, my behavior becomes personal, regardless of other factors in the situation."[15]

3. *Open communication supports mutual understanding.* Everyone has a need to communicate. People are naturally curious and interested in what is happening within the organization. The mutual sharing of thoughts, opinions, and knowledge promotes a deeper bond among people, a greater spirit of teamwork.

4. *Conflict management by direct problem-solving confrontation promotes personal health.* A primary goal of team building is to provide a natural forum for conflict management. Conflict can be costly to an organization. It tends to distract employees, to cause them to lose sight of organizational goals. In addition, conflict can drain people of the energy they need to perform their regular duties. Conflict produces stress, and stress is a major contributor to physical exhaustion. (Chapter 13 discusses conflict management in detail.)

5. *Responsibility for one's own actions stimulates initiative.* As humans grow and mature, they become less dependent on others and seek more control over their own lives. Generally adults tend to develop a deep psychological need to be viewed by others as a self-directing person. When an adult is not permitted to be self-directing, resentment and resistance build. What is the message for supervisory-management personnel? Give employees expanded responsibility and authority so they have the opportunity to grow and develop. When employees can perform tasks on their own, learn from their mistakes, and learn to make their own decisions, they usually experience greater job satisfaction.

Total Person Insight

Trust implies accountability, predictability, reliability. It's what sells products and keeps organizations humming. Trust is the glue that maintains organizational integrity.

Warren Bennis and
Burt Nanus

Team-Building Guidelines for the Supervisor

Thus far a strong case has been made for the team-building leadership style. It will be helpful now to focus on *how* to build teamwork. This section discusses ways that supervisory-management personnel can become team builders. Later in this chapter, you will see how employees can contribute to the team-building process.

The wide range of supervisory-management positions may cause you to ask: Do these positions have much in common? Will team-building strategies work in most situations? The answer to both of these questions is yes. A great majority of successful supervisory-management personnel have certain behavior characteristics in common. Two of the most important dimensions of supervisory leadership—consideration and structure—have been identified in research studies conducted by Edwin A. Fleishman at Ohio State University.[16]

Consideration

The quality of **consideration** reflects the extent to which a supervisor's or manager's relationships with subordinates are characterized by mutual trust, respect for the subordinates's ideas, consideration of their feelings, and a certain warmth in interpersonal relationships. The supervisor-subordinate relationship is characterized by a climate of good rapport and two-way communication.

Consideration is important because every person holding a supervisory position must be able to establish a three-way relationship. That is, they must be able to build rapport (1) with the person who supervises their work, (2) with those supervisors who hold similar positions at the same level (horizontal relationships), and (3) with the subordinates who look to the supervisor for guidance and direction. The quality of these relationshps has a direct bearing on a supervisor's overall success. Consideration is the equivalent of "concern for people" on the Managerial Grid.

Structure

The quality of **structure** reflects the extent to which a supervisor is likely to define and direct his or her role and those of subordinates toward goal attainment. Managers who incorporate structure into their leadership style will actively direct group activities through planning, setting goals, communicating information, scheduling, and evaluating performance. People who work under the direction of a highly structured supervisor know what is expected of them. Structure is the equivalent of "concern for production" on the Managerial Grid.

It is interesting to note that the dimensions of consideration and structure are independent. A supervisor may be well qualified in one area but lack competence in the other. The good news is that anyone can consciously work to develop competence in both areas.

Improving Consideration Skills

Sydney Harris, noted newspaper columnist and author, once said that people have become superbly sophisticated in the management of machines but remain primitive in the management of people. If his observation is correct, then managers have a great deal of unfinished business ahead of them. To improve the dimension of consideration, the following practices can be adopted.

Recognize Accomplishments   When individual achievements are overlooked, supervisors miss a valuable opportunity to improve job relationships with subordinates. People need recognition for good work, regardless of the duties they perform or the position they hold. Of course, recognition should be contingent on performance. When recognition is given for mediocre performance, the supervisor is reinforcing a behavior that is not desirable. If an employee feels unappreciated, that person will not perform to the best of his or her ability.[17]

Provide for Early and Frequent Success   There is an old saying that "nothing succeeds like success." A supervisor should provide each employee with as many opportunities to succeed as possible. The foundation for accomplishment begins the first day the employee reports to work. Robert D. Mulberger, president of the Snelling and Snelling Employment Service Group, a division of the world's largest private employment service, says, "The most effective method a company can use to insure the success of its new employee—its new investment—is timely, practical communication."[18] Supervisors and managers should review job duties and responsibilities, organizational policies and procedures, and any other pertinent information early in the relationship. No worker should have to rely on office gossip or the advice of a perennially dissatisfied employee for answers to important questions. Then once the orientation is complete, initiate an ongoing training

---

Total Person Insight

Ernest A. Fitzgerald

It is a wise person who searches for the best in other people. People who do this form lasting friendships and discover friends who are dependable. They also achieve positions of leadership more readily than other folk. Always look for the best, not the worst; concentrate on the positives, not the negatives; and look for the victories, not the defeats, in the people around you.

NAME: Sue Perez

DATE HIRED: 1/8/86

BIRTHDAY: 4/24/59

HOBBIES: Tennis and archery

FAVORITE MUSIC: Country-Western

SPECIAL INTERESTS: Active in the local Red Cross

COMMENTS: *Sue is interested in supervision.*

Figure 12.2
Employee Information Card

program that covers all facets of the new employee's job. Keep in mind that, in the absence of formal training, the employee may make mistakes that could have been avoided. Early success will build employee morale, which will set the stage for future growth and development.

Individualize Supervision   Everyone likes to be treated as an individual. Each person wants to feel important and personally significant. A supervisor should take time to get to know each person individually. Learn the names of spouses and children. Find out what employees do during their leisure time. Ask about their families and inquire about individual family members from time to time. Find out each employee's birth date and say "happy birthday!" on the appropriate day. Some supervisors record significant information about each of their workers on a series of file cards (see Figure 12.2). These cards are updated as new information is obtained. A card file is especially helpful if you find it difficult to remember important facts about your employees.

Establish a Climate of Open Communication   A climate of open communication contributes greatly to the team-building process. An effective work group uses the communication process to iron out differences of opinion, share ideas, and generally keep one another informed. Communication is closely linked to employee morale—and morale is directly linked to productivity. Therefore, efforts to improve the communication process represent a good use of the supervisor's time and energy.

How can a supervisor create a climate where open communication takes place? Remember, communication is a dialogue or mutual exchange of information between two people. Both people have the opportunity to speak, express ideas, and share opinions. The supervisor who wants to foster a climate of open communication will schedule periodic meetings where employees can exchange ideas or discuss problems with one another and their supervisor.

Periodic meetings represent a form of "team maintenance." Without such meetings, the work group may become less cohesive, less committed to a common goal. Some of the most effective meetings in organizations feature a two-dimensional agenda. One focuses on "facts" and the other focuses on "feelings." Most work groups periodically need to discuss work schedules, production problems, new product introductions, and related areas. For the most part, these are "fact" oriented topics. A group should also set aside time to discuss "feelings." At this time group members are encouraged to freely express their feelings regarding existing or potential problem areas. During this part of the meeting there should be no "hidden agendas." Conflicts are resolved and tensions are reduced.

At Electro Scientific Industries, a maker of precision electronic instruments and systems, employees form small groups and meet with the company's president each spring in what they call "Going Well/In the Way" meetings. Each employee is encouraged to discuss openly both good and bad aspects of his or her work. Such meetings allow both facts and feelings to be expressed, and help employees feel that their contributions to the team effort are recognized.[19]

The quality circle concept, used extensively in Japan, provides a somewhat formal method of keeping the lines of communication open with workers. When small groups of employees join together to discuss quality and production problems, the results are often quite surprising. Quality circles often resolve problems that have baffled the engineers and managers. At the Toyota Motor Sales' Takaoka, Japan, plant, quality circles have produced thousands of suggestions for improvement each year, and most are put into practice.[20]

Thinking/Learning Starter

Assume you are the manager of the bookkeeping department at a small commercial bank. Three of your employees are responsible for check sorting and listing. These employees keep personal and commercial accounts up to date. A fourth employee handles all inquiries concerning overdrafts and other problems related to customer accounts. On a sheet of paper, list five specific behaviors that would contribute to development of the supervisory-management quality described as *consideration.*

"I pledge allegiance to the Drooly Burger and to the company for which it stands—one corporation, indivisible, with employment and profit for all." (© by Vietor)

Improving Structure Skills

The supervisor who incorporates structure into his or her leadership style will play an active role in directing group activities. The team builder gives the group direction, establishes performance standards, and maintains individual and group accountability. To develop the dimension of structure, the following practices can be used:

Clearly Define Goals Members of the group must possess a clear idea of what goals need to be accomplished. Supervisors who are successful in motivating employees usually provide an environment in which appropriate goals are set and understood. From time to time, goals should be reviewed and discussed at group meetings. In the absence of periodic review, group members may lose sight of what needs to be accomplished. A highly effective work group is aware of its progress toward goal attainment. Frequently such a group will stop to examine how well it is doing and determine what factors may be interfering with goal achievement.

Encourage Individual Goal Setting People tend to know their own capabilities and limitations better than anyone else. In addition, personal goal setting results in a commitment to goal accomplishment.[21] The authors of *The One Minute Manager* agree, noting that "one minute goal setting" is one of the most significant keys to effective management[22]

Some supervisors and managers are using a formal approach to goal setting called management by objectives (MBO). Management by objectives is an approach to planning and evaluation in which specific targets are established for a specific period of time. Ideally, the personal goals of the individual employee mesh with the overall goals of the organization. At a date set in advance, the supervisor meets with each subordinate, and together they agree upon targets of performance. Depending on the type of organization, the targets might be the following:

1. Increased sales
2. Completion of a written report
3. Reduction in expenses
4. Improved accuracy
5. Increased production
6. Reduction of absenteeism or tardiness
7. Improved cleanliness

At the end of the established time period, a review of accomplishments is conducted. Hopefully, the involvement of the employee in setting performance goals results in a higher degree of commitment toward achieving the objectives.

The manager of a large men's wear store used MBO to achieve rather dramatic gains in sales and profits. At the beginning of the new year, he met individually with the four full-time salespeople. He asked each person to review his or her past sales efforts and set new goals in two important areas: (1) overall sales volume and (2) multiple sales. (In a multiple sale, the customer buys a related item in addition to the basic purchase, for example, a new tie to go with a suit.)

New goals were established for a three-month period. The manager could have established a longer time, but he wanted employees to see the results of improved performance as quickly as possible. At the end of three months, the manager reported that all salespeople had increased their sales level compared to the same period for the previous year. In addition, all employees achieved the target goals they had set. A decision was made to establish a new set of goals for the next three-month period.

Provide Relevant Feedback Often   Feedback should be relevant to the task performed by the employee and should be given soon after performance. Feedback is especially critical when an employee is just learning a new job. The supervisor should point out improvements in performance, no matter how small. Always reinforce the behavior you want repeated.

Criticize Poor Performance   As a supervisor, you must correct the person who does not measure up to your standards of performance. When members of the group are not held accountable for doing their share of the work,

Effective teamwork on the job is the result of efforts by supervisors and employees. (Photo © Jerry Howard 1982, Positive Images)

group morale may suffer. Other members of the group will quickly observe the poor performance and wonder why the supervisor isn't taking corrective action.

To achieve the best results, focus negative feedback on behavior, not the employee as an individual. A person can make a mistake and still be a valuable employee. Correct the person in a way that doesn't create anger and resentment. Avoid demoralizing the person or impairing his or her self-confidence so much that it becomes difficult to restore. Never criticize or correct individuals in front of other people. Find a quiet place where you can talk about the problem calmly.

Structure Versus Control

Many times supervisors and managers confuse control with structure, states Mardell Grothe, training program design consultant to the National Tooling Machining Association. He says, "Structure is good. It means laying out very clearly what you want and when you want it done and letting the persons react. Control is trying to dictate *how* it should be done from moment to moment." When structure is present, employees know what is to be done, but realize that they have some latitude in how to complete the task. Today's better educated and better informed employees appreciate structure but usually react negatively to too much control.[23]

Thinking/Learning Starter

Assume the role of supervisor of a shipping department at a manufacturing plant. Your staff includes three dock workers who load rail cars and trucks, a fork lift operator who assists with the movement of large portable platforms (pallets), and a dispatcher who maintains records of all products shipped. On a sheet of paper, list five specific behaviors that would help you develop the supervisory-management quality described as *structure*.

Situational Leadership

In recent years we have seen the emergence of a new leadership model. The **Situational Leadership Model**, developed by Paul Hersey and his colleagues at the Center for Leadership Studies, offers an alternative to the Managerial Grid. Robert Blake and Jane Mouton, creators of the Grid, describe this new model:

> The only major challenge to the Grid since it was first published in 1962 has come from those who believe in situationalism. Situationalism means you choose your Grid style to fit the situation; there is no one best way to lead.[24]

Before we discuss the differences between "one best way to lead" and situational leadership, let's discuss the similarities between the two. Both models are based on two nearly identical dimensions. Paul Hersey says that the behaviors displayed by effective managers in the Situational Leadership Model can be described as *task* behavior and *relationship* behavior. He offers the following definitions:

> *Task behavior* is defined as the extent to which the leader engages in spelling out the duties and responsibilities of an individual or group. The behaviors include telling people what to do, how to do it, when to do it, where to do it and who's to do it. *Relationship behavior* is defined as the extent to which the leader engages in two-way or multi-way communication if there is more than one person. The behaviors include listening, encouraging, facilitating, providing clarification, and giving socioemotional support.[25]

Task behavior, concern for production, and structure really mean the same thing. And relationship behavior, concern for people, and consideration do not really differ. In essence, the situational leader and the person who uses the 9,9 team management style rely on the same two dimensions of leadership. Both use task behavior (concern for production) and relationship behavior (concern for people) to influence their subordinates.

What is the major difference between these two leadership models? Hersey says that when attempting to influence others, you must (1) diagnose the readiness level of the follower for a specific task, and (2) provide the appropriate leadership style for that situation.[26] In other words, given the specific situation, you must decide how much task behavior and how much relationship behavior to display. Space does not permit an in-depth comparison of situational leadership with the 9,9 team manager style. However, we can point out that it is not possible to become a situational leader without first developing task behavior (structure) and relationship behavior (consideration). Therefore, mastery of the 9,9 team management style is prerequisite to becoming a situational leader.

Team-Building Guidelines for Employees

Rensis Likert, noted author and business consultant, has said that members of an effective work group are skilled in all the various leadership and membership roles.[27] Each member assumes an active part in helping the group achieve its mission. This means that every member of the work group can and should be a team builder. Each person should work to improve relationships with fellow employees and their supervisor. In this section, you will learn some ways to "manage" your boss.

The idea that you should manage your boss may sound a little unusual at first. But it makes a lot of sense when you consider the advantages of assuming this responsibility. When the subordinate and the boss are both working to maintain a good relationship, conflict is less likely to surface. The boss-subordinate relationship is not like the one between a parent and a child—the burden for managing the relationship should not and cannot fall entirely on the one in authority.

When you take time to manage your boss, he or she will become more effective in performing his or her job. In many cases, managers are no greater than the combined competence of the people they supervise. Some employees don't realize how much the boss needs their assistance and support.

How do you go about managing your boss? Here are three general considerations.[28]

Develop an Understanding of Your Boss

To work effectively with another person, you have to understand the individual's strengths, weaknesses, work habits, communication style, and needs. As a new employee, spend time studying your boss. Try to determine his or her goals and pressures. What is the person trying to accomplish? Does your boss enjoy casual meetings to discuss business matters, or formal meetings with written agendas? In terms of communication style (see Chapter 5), is the person Supportive, Emotive, Reflective, or a Director?

Tom Eastman went to work for a large wholesale firm after graduation from college. In terms of communication style, he was Emotive. His boss, Rich Hagger, was a Reflective. Rich liked to take his time making decisions, gathering all available information and weighing it carefully before he took a position. Tom was making contacts with several large accounts and frequently needed approval from Rich before quoting a price on large orders. Tom would often rush into Rich's office unannounced, pour out a lot of facts and figures, and then ask for an immediate decision. Rich would usually say, "Give me time to think about it." Tom never fully understood his new boss's work style, and over a few months, the relationship became more and more strained. Tom finally left the company and went to work for another firm.

Tom did not understand that his relationship with Rich required mutual support. He could have worked harder to meet the needs of his new boss. For example, Tom might have made an appointment before each visit and provided the boss with advance information. He might have displayed more patience, letting Rich have more time to make decisions.

Assess Your Own Strengths

The boss represents only one-half of the relationship. Developing an effective team also means reflecting on your own strengths, weaknesses, work habits, communication style, and needs. What personal characteristics might impede or facilitate working with your boss? As one author put it, the most important issue related to your adaptability to your boss's style is your own style.

> If you are a reader, you'll have to make a significant adjustment if your boss is a listener. If you're systematic, you may become very frustrated with and even underestimate the competence of an intuitive boss. The burden of assessment and adjustment falls more on you than on your boss. In any confrontation, after all, it is you who have more to lose by misjudgment than your boss.[29]

Suppose that, in order to avoid conflict, you almost never disagree with your boss—even when the boss is obviously wrong. Are you making a contribution to his or her growth and development? Obviously not. There are times when you must be your own person and say what is on your mind.

Develop and Maintain a Relationship

Once you understand yourself and your boss, it is usually possible to establish a good working relationship. But you may need to adjust your style to your boss's preferred method of conducting business. If he or she likes to be involved in decisions, provide an opportunity for input. If your boss prefers to review information before face-to-face meetings, by all means make some type of written correspondence available. If your boss is extremely busy, use his or her time wisely. For example, you might talk business over lunch.

To achieve success within an organization, you need to establish and manage relationships with everyone on your work team. This includes the boss!

Summary

Teamwork ensures not only that a job gets done, but that it gets done efficiently. Therefore, the element of teamwork can often make the difference between the profitable and unprofitable operation of an organization. The team-building leadership style is effective because it is suited to the needs of most of today's employees.

An effective work team tends to be informal and relaxed with no obvious tensions. People are involved, interested, and anxious to participate in solving work-related problems. An effective work group also has clearly understood goals and objectives.

Two important dimensions of supervisory leadership contribute to team building. One of these qualities, *consideration*, reflects the extent to which a supervisor maintains relationships with employees that are characterized by mutual trust, respect, and rapport. The other quality, *structure*, reflects the extent to which a supervisor is likely to direct group activities through planning, goal setting, communication, scheduling, and evaluation.

Members of an effective work group should assume effective leadership and membership roles. Each helps the group achieve its mission. Everyone assumes the role of team builder!

Employees are in a unique position to give guidance and support to their supervisor or manager. Most bosses need this assistance and support in order to achieve success. To manage your boss, it is first necessary to understand him or her. Next, you must assess your own needs and try to identify personal characteristics that might impede or facilitate a working relationship. And finally, work hard to develop and maintain a relationship.

Key Terms

team building

Managerial Grid

impoverished management

country club management

authority-obedience management

organization man management

team management

consideration

structure

Situational Leadership Model

Review Questions

1. In what ways did the Hawthorne studies contribute to emergence of the team-building concept?
2. In the book *The Human Side of Enterprise,* Douglas McGregor discusses several characteristics of an effective work team. What was his view on conflict?
3. Describe the two management style dimensions of the Managerial Grid developed by Robert R. Blake and Jane S. Mouton.
4. How does the impoverished management leadership style differ from the team management leadership style?
5. List and describe at least two behavioral science principles that support team building.
6. What are some of the behaviors displayed by supervisors who are strong in the area of consideration?
7. What are some of the behaviors displayed by supervisors who are strong in the area of structure?
8. Briefly describe the formal approach to goal setting called management by objectives. What targets of performance might be established jointly by employee and supervisor?
9. Provide a brief description of situational leadership. What are the major similarities between the Situational Leadership Model and the Managerial Grid?
10. Describe three major considerations that should guide you in any attempt to manage your boss.

Case 12.1

Building Trust at Quad/ Graphics[30]

In mid-1969, Harry Quadracci found himself in a very uncomfortable position. He was the labor negotiator for a large Wisconsin printing company in the throes of a bitter fourteen-week strike. In addition to the serious labor problems, he also found himself in the middle of a conflict between the printing company's high-level management and the board of directors regarding the best way to end the strike. Finally, he quit and formed his own printing company, Quad/Graphics, Inc. His goal was to develop a modern printing plant and to introduce a different style of labor relations.

He purchased state-of-the-art, full-color printing presses and housed the new equipment in a former warehouse in a rural area near Milwaukee. Today, the company prints over 100 different magazines and catalogs.

From the very beginning, Quadracci took steps to develop good relations with his employees. An ex-lawyer, he structured his company like a typical law firm. He describes his employees as "partners," and like the typical law firm, Quad/Graphics is mostly owned by the partners. He maintains a strong aversion to organizational charts, job descriptions, time clocks, and committing policies and practices to paper. He believes communication with employees should be "personal, vocal, and spontaneous." He likes to meet with his partners in small groups to discuss his philosophy.

Quadracci believes that a successful business is based on trust. He feels that people will give more to the company if they are not under tight controls. To demonstrate his faith in the work force, he sponsors the "Spring Fling and Management Sneak" each year. All managers leave the plant to have meetings and then enjoy a tour of the Milwaukee Art Museum. For a full day, normal printing operations continue without the presence of managers.

The absence of rigid work rules means that everyone in the plant is expected to make more decisions on his or her own. It is expected that decisions will benefit not only the company but other members of the work team. This positive regard for others is summarized in one of the statements that appears in *Trust in Trust at Quad/Graphics:*

> We all trust in each other: we regard each other as persons of equal rank; we respect the dignity of the individual by recognizing not only the individual accomplishments, but the feelings and needs of the individual and family as well; and we all share the same goals and purposes in life.[31]

Questions

1. What major steps did Quadracci take to build a spirit of teamwork at Quad/Graphics.
2. When a company does not develop job descriptions or put policies and practices in writing, what are the primary risks?
3. Do you feel Quadracci's unique approach can be applied to management in other organizations such as hospitals, retail stores, or public schools?

Case 12.2

Influencing the Boss

One year ago Ken Folley told his friends that he had obtained the perfect job. He was hired to serve as administrative assistant to Brian McCulla, president of McCulla Advertising Services. MAS, which was founded by Mr. McCulla about twenty-five years ago, is a leader in the field, and Ken relished the idea of working with a successful entrepreneur who had developed his own business. Someday Ken wanted to open his own advertising agency, and he knew that working with a leader in the field would be a golden opportunity.

When Ken started, Brian McCulla was 58 years old and wanted to become less active in the day-to-day operations of the business. He wasted no time in delegating a variety of duties to the new assistant. Ken became involved in activities ranging from budget preparation to public relations. These duties brought him into contact with Karen Hall, manager of customer services, and Lloyd Andrews, manager of production. Karen Hall's major responsibility was to develop new accounts and service old accounts. Lloyd Andrews supervised graphic artists and layout specialists who prepared camera-ready copy for local papers and print shops.

Ken was on the job only a short time when he began to realize that a great deal of friction existed between Karen Hall and Lloyd Andrews. When critical deadlines had to be met, personnel from customer services often bypassed Lloyd and went directly to members of his staff for assistance. Karen had not discouraged this practice because she believed that "missed deadlines meant lost business." Lloyd felt this hurt his authority as a team leader, and he complained to Brian McCulla about the situation. Unfortunately, Mr. McCulla did not see the problem as serious and has never taken any action.

Ken dislikes the tension that exists between these two key people and has decided to take action to correct the problem. He has made an appointment with Mr. McCulla and has decided to discuss two points during the meeting:

1. The problem is serious and needs to be addressed by the person who supervises the two department heads. A spirit of teamwork will never prevail unless the problem is corrected. If Mr. McCulla takes no action, he may be perceived as an ineffective manager.
2. An effective way to handle the problem is to bring Karen Hall and Lloyd Andrews to Mr. McCulla's office for a meeting. The problem will be discussed by all parties and, hopefully, a solution will be identified.

Questions

1. Should Ken Folley try to solve this problem, or should he avoid getting involved? If he does get involved, what background information should he learn about Mr. McCulla prior to the meeting?
2. What is your opinion of Ken's suggested approach to handling the problem? What additional steps might Mr. McCulla take to solve the problem and establish a greater spirit of teamwork?

Notes

1. William C. Symonds, "A School of Hard Rocks," *Business Week*, March 3, 1986, pp. 128–129; Walter Kiechel III, "Executives on Retreat," *Fortune*, April 1, 1985, pp. 185, 188; Elizabeth Peer, "Outward Bound for Execs," *Newsweek*, October 25, 1982, pp. 110–111.

2. Gordon Lippitt, Ronald Lippitt, and Clayton Lafferty, "Cutting Edge Trends in Organization Development," *Training and Development Journal*, July 1984, p. 62.

3. "Synergy: Or, We're All in This Together," *Training*, September 1985, pp. 64 and 65.

4. William G. Dyer, *Team Building: Issues and Alternatives* (Reading, Mass.: Addison-Wesley, 1977), p. 7.

5. Ibid., p. 9.

6. Adapted from a list in Douglas McGregor, *The Human Side of Enterprise* (New York: McGraw-Hill, 1960), pp. 232–235.

7. From *The New Managerial Grid*, by Robert R. Blake and Jane Srygley Mouton. Houston: Gulf Publishing Co. Copyright © 1978, p. 11. Reproduced by permission.

8. Thomas L. Quick, *Understanding People at Work* (New York: Executive Enterprises Publications Company, 1976), p. 121.

9. Robert R. Blake and Jane S. Mouton, "Should You Teach There's Only One Best Way to Manage?" *Training/HRD*, April 1978, p. 24.

10. Robert R. Blake and Jane Srygley Mouton, "How to Choose a Leadership Style," *Training and Development Journal*, February 1982, pp. 41–42.

11. Reported in Ron Zemke, "What Are High-Achieving Managers Really Like?" *Training/HRD*, February 1979, p. 35.

12. Ibid., p. 36.

13. Jay Hall, *The Competence Process* (The Woodlands, Texas: Teleometrics International, 1980), pp. 220–221.

14. Adapted from a list in Blake and Mouton, "Should You Teach," p. 25.

15. Jack R. Gibb, *Trust—A New View of Personal and Organizational Development* (Los Angeles: Guild of Tutors Press, 1978), p. 45.

16. These two dimensions can be measured by the *Leadership Opinion Questionnaire* developed by Edwin A. Fleishman and available from Science Research Associates, Inc., Chicago, Illinois.

17. "Employee Recognition: A Key to Motivation," *Personnel Journal*, February 1981, p. 103.

18. Robert D. Mulberger, "The New Employee ... Insuring a New Investment," *Pace*, May-June 1981, p. 28.

19. Robert Levering, Milton Moskowitz, and Michael Katz, *The 100 Best Companies to Work for in America* (New York: New American Library, 1985), p. 102.

20. "Adapting Japanese Management to American Organizations," *Training and Development Journal*, September 1982, pp. 9–10.

21. Dean R. Spitzer, "30 Ways to Motivate Employees to Perform Better," *Training/HRD*, March 1980, p. 51.

22. Kenneth Blanchard and Spencer Johnson, *The One Minute Manager* (New York: William Morrow and Company, 1982), p. 27.

23. "The Trouble with Kids," *INC*, January 1983, p. 63.

24. Robert R. Blake and Jane Srygley Mouton, "Deeper Truths About Effective Leadership," *BNAC Communicator*, Winter, 1981, pp. 1 and 2.

25. Paul Hersey, *The Situational Leader* (Escondido, Calif.: The Center for Leadership Studies, 1984), pp. 29 and 30.

26. Ibid., p. 57.

27. Rensis Likert, *New Patterns of Management* (New York: McGraw-Hill, 1961), p. 166.

28. Adapted from John J. Gabarro and John P. Kotter, "Managing Your Boss," *Harvard Business Review*, January-February 1980, pp. 92–100.

29. Donald Sanzotta and Lois Drapin, "Getting Along with the Boss," *Supervisory Management*, July 1984, p. 16.

30. Levering, Moskowitz, and Katz, *The 100 Best Companies to Work for in America*, pp. 295–299.

31. Ibid., p. 298.

Suggested Readings

Anthony, William P. *Managing Your Boss*. New York: AMACOM, a Division of American Management Associations, 1983.

Blake, Robert R., and Jane S. Mouton. "How to Choose a Leadership Style." *Training and Development Journal*, February 1982, pp. 38–47.

Blake, Robert R., and Jane S. Mouton. *The New Managerial Grid*. Houston: Gulf Publishing, 1978.

Dyer, William G. *Team Building: Issues and Alternatives*. Reading, Mass.: Addison-Wesley, 1977.

Gabarro, John J., and John P. Kotter. "Managing Your Boss." *Harvard Business Review*, January-February 1980, pp. 92–100.

Hegarty, Christopher, with Philip Goldberg. *How to Manage Your Boss*. New York: Rawson, Wade Publishers, 1980.

Hersey, Paul. *The Situational Leader*. Escondido, Calif.: The Center for Leadership Studies, 1984.

Chapter 13

Conflict Management

Chapter Preview

After studying this chapter, you will be able to

1. List some of the major causes of conflict in a work setting.
2. Explain the three basic conflict management strategies.
3. Understand why labor unions are formed and understand their role in managing labor-management conflicts.
4. Explain collective bargaining and grievance procedures.
5. Discuss the current challenges facing unions and management.

Violence erupted eight months into a recent strike at the Geo. A. Hormel meat packing plant in Austin, Minnesota, when more than thirty demonstrators clashed with police. Seventeen strikers were arrested, including James Guyette, head of Local P-9 of the United Food and Commercial Workers (UFCW).

Union members were demanding a rollback in previous wage concessions, as well as a guarantee that all strikers would get their jobs back. Company officials maintained, however, that the union's demands were unrealistic. Falling consumer demand and a shrinking meat supply were diminishing profits in the meat packing industry—and threatening some companies' survival.

To complicate matters further, national leadership of the UCFW condemned P-9's militancy as "suicidal" and attempted to take over the local and appoint new officers. If they succeeded in their attempt, they would face major problems in winning the loyalty of the striking workers and getting at least some of their jobs back.[1]

The conflict at Hormel was particularly complicated as it centered around three groups: management, national union officials, and the local union leadership. Yet every organization experiences conflict of some kind. An organization requires a diverse group of people to come together to work toward common goals. Each person brings to the job a unique set of skills, values, attitudes, and behaviors. But while employees must work together, they are seldom able to choose their boss, coworkers, or subordinates. Under such circumstances, conflicts can develop between individuals who must work together but would prefer not to.

Other unions joined striking Hormel meatpackers during a prolonged strike at the Austin, Minnesota plant. The National Guard was present to ensure peace at the plant. (Photo by Steve Woit, The Picture Group)

Conflicts can happen at all levels within an organization. A personal conflict between two assembly-line workers can lead to poor productivity. A dispute between two supervisors can lead to a work slowdown and several missed delivery dates. An executive staff meeting may erupt into a heated debate over budget cuts between the financial director and the marketing manager.

Groups within an organization may discover similar grievances and present a unified effort toward satisfying their needs. Women trainees in a midwestern bank filed a class action suit, charging the bank with discriminatory practices in pay scales and management training programs. Unions in the recession-plagued industrial North fight to retain jobs and workers' benefits. Their efforts are hampered by the long-standing distrust between employees and management.

Conflict, whether between individuals or groups, is common in organizations regardless of their size and function. The consequences of conflict can range from minor inconvenience to major losses of productivity and revenue. The effects of internal organizational conflict are often reflected in the outside world as well. Hawaii's government officials estimated the strike by 5,000 United Air Lines pilots in 1984 cost the state's tourism industry as much as $100 million a day.

The amount of conflict within organizations is increasing as the United States shifts from a heavy industrial base to a service-oriented, high-tech economy. Thus, the need for managers and employees to become skilled in conflict-management techniques is becoming even more important as the work environment becomes more turbulent and uncertain. In this chapter, you will learn some of the causes of conflict in the workplace, strategies for resolving disagreements and disputes, and the role of unions in employee-management conflicts.

Anger: The Root of Most Conflict

Everyone experiences the healthy emotion of anger from time to time. **Anger** is a form of communication that indicates that a problem needs to be addressed.[2] Few of us have learned to handle anger in constructive ways. Some of us experience too much of it, and others suppress it and try to deny their feelings. It's no wonder, then, that so many relationships at work and at home are damaged because of the inability to deal with anger effectively.

Most psychologists agree that the first step in using anger constructively is to acknowledge it as a healthy, everyday emotion. The key, however, is to control the behavior that may result from those angry feelings. Instead of immediately lashing out at the person who made you angry, you can walk away from the situation and give yourself time to cool down. Or you can silently repeat to yourself a phrase that will help you control your behavior, such as, "I can't help the way I feel right now, but I can help the way I act." By controlling your behavior, you can diffuse the situation.

Conflicts in organizations can be caused by anger, breakdowns in communication, prejudice, and other factors. Allowing anger and other strong emotions to subside before attempting to deal with the conflict allows all people involved to confront the problem rationally. **Confrontation**, a systematic process of resolving conflicts together with other people, is the most effective way to handle conflict when you must continue to relate with the people involved.[3] Working out conflict in adaptive ways, sometimes referred to as conflict resolution or conflict management, can enhance human relationships and deepen trust. Managing conflicts in ways that produce two winners is a powerful way to earn the respect and trust of others. We will explore this win/win strategy later in this chapter.

Conflict Within the Work Setting

In an American Management Associations study, corporate executives and managers indicated they devote 24 percent of their working time to conflict management. School and hospital administrators, mayors, and city managers estimate conflict resolution commands nearly 49 percent of their time.[4] Conflict is a common social phenomenon. Yet it can be managed and channeled

Studies reveal that managers spend about 24 to 49 percent of their time dealing with conflict. (Photo © A. de Andrade, Magnum Photos, Inc.)

into useful purposes when people understand the nature and causes of most disputes that arise in the workplace.

Conflict: An Everyday Affair

Conflict can be defined as people's striving for their own preferred outcome which, if attained, prevents others from achieving *their* preferred outcome, resulting in hostility and a breakdown in human relations.[5] Differences, disagreements, and competition generate conflict when the people involved try to deny each other the right to satisfy their own needs. For example, a manager may not allow employees to take part in decisions that affect them. Conflict also occurs when change is imposed or introduced without adequate preparation and involvement of those affected by the change.[6]

However, conflict should not be regarded as a solely negative experience. In fact, some amount of difference of opinion is necessary for creative thinking and true innovation. The heart of effective management lies not in trying to eliminate conflict—an impossible task—but in turning the energy released to constructive ends. Creatively managed, conflict can shake people out of their mental ruts and give them new frameworks, new assumptions, and new points of view. Harlan Cleveland, a long-time observer of organizations, states:

> One of the executive's tasks is to maintain an adequate degree of tension within the organization so that all possible points of view are weighed before important decisions are made. No executive wants staff members that are so bored with the company's work or so similar in function that they never argue with each other or with the boss.[7]

However, if an organization does not have sophisticated methods of managing and maintaining an "adequate degree of tension," conflict can quickly become destructive. It can undermine morale, divert energy from important tasks, decrease productivity by disrupting cooperative action, create suspicion and distrust among employees, and emphasize the differences among individuals and groups.[8]

Total Person Insight

Gordon Lippitt

The rapid changes of the twentieth century have increased human conflict to the point that our sensibilities toward each other are becoming numb. The human capacity for adaptation may be working against our social relationships as we passively accept conditions that are not conducive to the effective resolution of interpersonal differences. Just as we adapt to bad air, tasteless food, polluted water, congested cities, and loud noise, we are also becoming callous and indifferent to the factors in our environment that are setting us at one another's throats.

Causes of Conflict

A variety of factors contribute to conflict among people within organizations. Some of the major causes of disputes or disagreements include the following:[9]

Breakdowns in Communication The greatest source of conflict in organizations is the misunderstanding that often results from ineffective communication. A survey conducted by Opinion Research Corporation, a subsidiary of Arthur D. Little, reported that over 50 percent of employees interviewed cited a lack of communication as the root cause of sagging morale and declining productivity. Nearly 70 percent felt that management had lost touch with the workers, and middle managers reported they felt locked out of the decision-making process.[10]

Many companies have experienced conflict arising from poor communication when introducing computer technology, robotics, or some other form of high technology without adequate staff preparation and training. When economic conditions result in widespread layoffs, competition for the few remaining jobs can create bitter conflicts among employees and between employees and management. Effective communication can help reduce the fear associated with the lack of job security during changing economic times.

Values Clashes You studied in Chapter 7 how differences in values can cause conflicts between generations, among men and women, and among people with different ethnic, racial, and cultural backgrounds. But values clashes can also occur when an individual's expectations are not met by the organization.

In the past ten years, we have made impressive progress as a society in affirming the concept of work as a basic human right and as a means of fulfilling our potential. As a result, many people in both blue-collar and white-collar occupations enter their jobs expecting they will be involved in decisions to a much greater extent than most organizations allow. Also, the civil rights movement created expectations of advancement and opportunity for minorities that organizations may not always be able to meet. Instead of fulfilling their potential, many people find themselves in restrictive jobs with little to say about the nature and pace of their work.

Our society encourages people to get an education, to think for themselves, and to grow. But many jobs do not allow people to make decisions or to be enterprising and creative. Conflict results, and workers either scale down their expectations—and their output—or push their supervisors with demands.[11]

Work Policies and Practices Interpersonal conflicts can develop when an organization has arbitrary and confusing standards for promotions, wages, benefits, and organizational politics involved in getting ahead. In the Opinion Research Corporation survey, a majority of workers reported that they felt their wages and pay increases were unfair. They saw little correlation between job performance and economic reward.[12] When employees discover that another worker doing the same job is making more money or being promoted faster, conflict may result. Cost-of-living increases, health benefits, workers' compensation, and other benefits are often the causes of union-management conflicts.

Personality Clashes People who are detail-oriented may have difficulty working productively with people who make quick decisions and expect immediate results. People who need a great deal of reassurance before beginning a project may have problems dealing with people who work independently. These conflicts can range from minor disagreements to serious breakdowns in human relations.

Personality clashes are an important source of conflict within organizations. And, as one author notes, they are becoming an even greater source of conflict as our society grows.

> Never before in history have people been required to interact with so many other people. The sheer numbers of people that we have to relate to in the modern organization is a new phenomenon. So, more than ever before, we need an effective way of understanding and working with a wide variety of people.[13]

Adversary Management Under adversary management, a supervisor may regard employees and even fellow managers as "the enemy" to be watched closely and outmaneuvered. This type of management makes it difficult to give or receive constructive criticism. Employees resent this style of supervision and will find ways to resist it. Conversely, some employees distrust and resent anyone in a position of authority. Workers who distrust authority may resist changes or suggestions proposed by management, be suspicious of any gestures of good will, and criticize organizational policies and procedures. Such negative attitudes can affect others and disrupt the team spirit of a group.

Thinking/Learning Starters

1. Remember the last time you were angry with another person. How did you handle the situation? Did you repress your anger? Express it? Confront the other person? What were the results? Could you have handled the situation in a more productive mannner? Explain.

2. Identify some of the causes of conflict in an organization in which you worked as an employee or volunteer. What types of conflict seemed to cause the most trouble among people?

Strategies for Dealing with Conflict

When a difference of opinion has progressed to open conflict, various **conflict management** strategies will be needed to resolve the issue. A conflict is viewed as resolved when all opposing parties are satisfied with the outcome.[14] If any party is dissatisfied, the conflict will probably arise again in the future.

Some of the most common approaches used to resolve conflict include withdrawing from an actual or potential dispute, smoothing it over, compromising, forcing a solution on others, and confronting the situation directly. These and other approaches can be grouped into three basic conflict management strategies:

1. *The win/lose strategy.* This approach eliminates the conflict by having one individual "win" over the other.
2. *The lose/lose strategy.* This approach eliminates the conflict by having both individuals "lose" something.
3. *The win/win strategy.* The conflict is eliminated when all parties accept a mutually satisfying solution arrived at through a step-by-step, problem-solving process.

Win/Lose Strategy   There are times when the **win/lose strategy** may resolve a conflict situation. It will depend on how severe the problem is and what results are desired from the solution. Although this approach may solve the conflict on a short-term basis, however, it usually does not address the underlying causes of a problem. When someone wins and someone loses, the loser is likely to resent the solution. In one sense, this approach simply sows the seeds for another conflict. The strategy can be applied in several ways.

The manager can become an autocrat. He or she decides on the solution, and states that it is final. No feedback or discussion is permitted from those involved in the dispute; a mandate settles the matter.

Second, the manager can threaten the security of the others involved if they refuse to accept the solution. "Either do as I say, or find a job somewhere else!" is one way to put it. This approach effectively stifles opposition and puts an end to any debate.

Third, the manager can ignore any arguments or suggestions from others in the conflict. They are treated as "nonpersons" who have nothing to say about how the situation is resolved. If they are ignored persistently enough, they will give up and the manager will have "won."

Fourth, take a vote: majority rules. Unless the vote is unanimous, someone will be on the losing side.

When might the win/lose strategy be used? It can serve in situations where two factions simply cannot agree on any solution—or may not even be able to talk to one another. A long-standing feud among workers may also be an

"This might be tougher than we planned on." (© by Vietor)

instance where a solution may need to be imposed on all parties concerned. In such cases, the concern is not so much to maintain good human relations as it is to ensure that the work gets done.

When want immediate results

Lose/Lose Strategy   Everyone loses when the the **lose/lose strategy** is used. Despite the negative overtones, one of the methods listed below can be called upon to eliminate conflicts—again, depending on the results desired. Basically, this strategy can be accomplished in three ways.

Both parties are asked to compromise. Each person involved must "give in" to the others. When the sacrifices are too great, everyone may feel too much has been given.

An arbitrator decides the conflict. This process often means that a solution is imposed on the disputing parties. However, the arbitration process may take from each side as much as it gives in the effort to reach a final settlement.

Going by the rules will also resolve a conflict, but it may not take into consideration the people problems involved. If a worker requests more flexible working hours because he or she must arrange child care, the manager may settle the issue by quoting the company rules: everyone starts at nine and leaves at five, no exceptions.

The lose/lose strategy can be applied when there is little time to find a solution through discussion and mutual problem solving, or when neither side can come to an agreement. Union-management disputes, for example, may be submitted to arbitration for a settlement. Or citing the company policy manual can cut short a debate that threatens to disrupt a critical work schedule. However, the basic problem may persist. Lose/lose strategies seldom address causes.

Results of the Win/Lose and Lose/Lose Strategies   Most of us are surrounded by the results of the win/lose and lose/lose strategies. Consider, for instance, the conflict between one person's desire to smoke cigarettes and another's need for clean air. Either the smoker quits smoking or the nonsmoker breathes polluted air. The smoker wins, and the nonsmoker loses. Or, the smoker enjoys a rare cigarette in a small smoke-filled room or goes outside. In this case, the nonsmoker wins and the smoker loses. Yet both conflict participants lose comfort and the pleasure of a pleasant human relationship. Each time a cigarette is smoked—or not smoked, in deference to the nonsmoker—the conflict is renewed.

In general, these strategies create a "we versus they" attitude among the people involved in the conflict rather than a "we versus *the problem*" approach. We versus they (or "my way versus your way") means that participants focus on whose solution is superior instead of working together to find a solution that is acceptable to all concerned. In the win/lose and lose/lose strategies, each person tends to see the issue from his or her viewpoint only and does not define the problem in terms of mutual needs and goals. In general, the emphasis is on finding short-term solutions to an immediate problem. These strategies do not attempt to define the end result to be attained by that solution, nor do they attempt to determine the basic causes of the conflict. The Hotel Roanoke in Roanoke, Virginia, lost more than $1.5 million in the three years before a strike by employees. Management needed to operate with fewer full-time and more part-time employees in order to maintain appropriate levels of staff during the erratic ups and downs of the hotel business. Employees wanted the scheduling practices of the past continued as well as more job stability. During the conflict resolution period, breakage of dishes and loss of silverware were very high. Hotel guests complained of discourteous service by employees, yet hotel managers were afraid to discipline staff. Some young hotel managers feared the strength of the veteran union leader. Finally, blood and urine tests were proposed to determine whether drugs or alcohol was causing the employees' behaviors. In the end, employees, employers, and hotel guests were all losers. Everyone lost perspective of the real issues at hand and began reacting to the people rather than the problem.

Win/Win Strategy   The basic purpose of the **win/win strategy** is to fix the problem—not the blame! Those who use this strategy listen to all sides, define the basic issues, and create an atmosphere of trust among everyone involved. Everyone must believe that the problem will be settled on the merits of the case rather than through political or personal influence. The leader or mediator of the win/win process should be flexible, sensitive, patient, and calm. It is this person's responsibility to ensure that no one feels threatened or humiliated. The result of the win/win strategy will be a solution to the problem that caused the conflict, one that all parties can accept and that will enhance good human relations and help increase productivity: a win/win situation. Table 13.1 cites the assumptions of the win/win strategy.

Almost everyone can improve his or her skills in this basic principle. Fighting to win has become an extension of the competitive skills we learn to

Table 13.1 Assumptions of the Win/Win Strategy

Given these assumptions and the opportunities to act on them, if sufficient information and needed material are available, conflicts can be resolved to meet the needs of all involved.

1. People want to work together.
2. People can work together to solve mutual problems.
3. People respect each other's right to participate in decisions that affect them.
4. People respect each other's integrity.
5. People respect each other's capabilities.
6. People, working in the same organization, share the common goals of the group.

Source: Adapted by permission of the publisher, from "Managing Conflict," a cassette by Donald H. Weiss, © 1981 by AMACOM, a division of American Management Association Communications. All rights reserved.

succeed in life. However, every time there is a clear winner in a conflict situation, there are actually two losers. The winner has become a powerful victor, and the loser a resentful victim. The self-esteem of both is damaged and interpersonal trust is diminished. Try to put aside your competitive urges and your pride and attempt to open a sincere dialogue with the other person. By striving to protect the self-esteem and self-respect of the other, you will build mutual trust. You will feel better about yourself and your relationships.

Thinking/Learning Starters

1. Which of the three conflict management strategies would you say is used most often in organizations today? What do you feel are the end results of this strategy?
2. Describe the human relations atmosphere in an organization where win/lose or lose/lose strategies are consistently applied.

The Conflict-Resolution Process

An effective conflict-resolution strategy, such as the win/win approach, rarely results from a confrontation and general discussion. It takes a concentrated, organized effort. The conflict resolution process involves three key elements: attitude adjustment for all parties involved, an effective leader, and a plan of action for the discussion.

Attitudes Toward Conflict Resolution

Conflict triggers everyone's emotional responses. One of the first steps toward solving a problem is to channel that emotional energy toward constructive ends by adopting the right attitudes.[15] Each person involved in the process should strive to adopt these positive attitudes.

1. Accept anger and conflict as healthy responses that allow the opportunity to share opinions and get things done. You may get some feedback that you may not like, and you may need to grow and accept needed changes. Personal growth is sometimes painful.
2. Believe that there is a win/win solution to the problem and focus on the positive results you expect from the solution.
3. Understand that either party could compete with the other, but because a mutually acceptable outcome is so important, each side will choose to cooperate.
4. Remember that all participants are entitled to their opinions. Everyone's opinions must be respected regardless of level of experience, personality, communication style, or position in the organization.
5. Believe that a difference of opinion is healthy and beneficial, not an attack on an idea or a person.
6. Maintain an attitude of patience. Impatient people get things started. Patient people get things done.

If emotions get out of control and the discussion becomes aggressive, be willing to disengage from the conflict-resolution process. Remember, everyone involved becomes particularly vulnerable when changing anger into conflict resolution. Sometimes it is necessary to back away from the confrontation to regain your perspective. Then, when you meet again, the focus can return to solving the problem by dealing with the issues, not the emotions.

Conflict Resolution: The Leader's Role *have an effective leader*

According to Gordon L. Lippitt, former professor of behavioral science at George Washington University, leadership in resolving organizational conflict constructively requires empathy and equality, but not neutrality.[16] A neutral position recognizes neither side; the problem is simply unresolved. An empathetic leader, on the other hand, recognizes the emotions and ideas of both sides without necessarily agreeing completely with either. Equality means that everyone will feel that he or she is being treated with equal respect and consideration.

A sensitive leader also will realize that there are many reasons why people are hesitant to deal with conflict openly. They may feel anxious about confronting others. They may have any one of a number of fears: of losing the acceptance of the group if they talk about their true thoughts and feelings; of taking risks; of solving one problem only to create another, more serious one; of violating what has been termed "group think"—the tendency of people to conform to whatever others in a group think or feel. As a result, the leader needs to foster a cooperative, nonthreatening environment in which to deal with conflicts.

The leader can help depersonalize the conflict so that neither party judges the other. By focusing the dispute on the facts and basic issues, the effective leader allows everyone to view the conflict more objectively and find points of common agreement. A good rule of thumb, Lippitt states, is for leaders to look coolly at the issues and warmly at the people involved.[17]

Conflict-Resolution Discussion Outline

Most organizations have found value in having a discussion outline to follow when dealing with emotional conflicts. A discussion outline helps everyone stay focused on solving the problem, saves time, and preserves the self-esteem of all involved (see Figure 13.1).

Step 1: Define the problem. The saying "a problem well defined is half solved" is not far from the truth. It is surprising how difficult this step can be. Everyone involved needs to focus on the real cause of the problem, not the symptoms or results. At this stage, let everyone write a one- or two-sentence definition of the problem. By allowing everyone to define the problem, the real cause of the conflict will often surface.

Here's an example. Robert was habitually late for work at a small data processing department. Because Margarita's work depended on Robert's, she usually found herself rushing in the afternoon to finish her work on time, often staying after hours to meet her deadlines. Nor surprisingly, a longstanding conflict developed between the two. In a meeting with their supervisor, the real source of the conflict surfaced. Robert's alcoholism was causing him to be late for work. Once this problem was identified, Robert was referred to a treatment program for alcoholics, and his work habits began to improve.

Step 2: Collect facts and opinions. Once the group has defined the basic problem, the next step is to gather the facts and opinions needed to understand the situation. What is the situation? What happened? Who is involved? What policies and procedures are involved? Make sure you point out what was done right along with the behaviors that caused the problem. It is at this stage that the discussion might become bogged down. Some groups may put off solving the conflict until "all the facts are in." They procrastinate until the conflict becomes a crisis. You may not be able to get all the facts in a particular case; but as long as you have the major points and opinions, keep the process moving.

Step 3: Consider all solutions proposed. Now that the problem has been defined and the facts surrounding it brought out, the group should brainstorm all possible solutions. It is important to remember that you are not looking for one final solution but for creative ideas about solving the problem. Allow no one to evaluate, judge, or rule out any proposed solution, no matter how

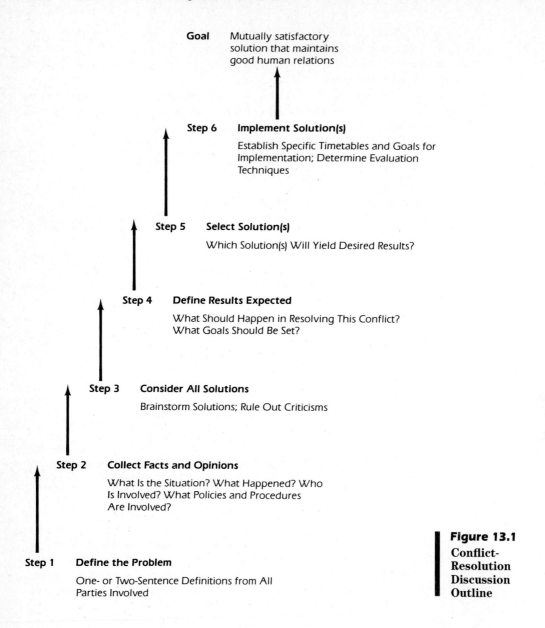

Goal Mutually satisfactory
solution that maintains
good human relations

Step 6   **Implement Solution(s)**

Establish Specific Timetables and Goals for
Implementation; Determine Evaluation
Techniques

Step 5   **Select Solution(s)**

Which Solution(s) Will Yield Desired Results?

Step 4   **Define Results Expected**

What Should Happen in Resolving This Conflict?
What Goals Should Be Set?

Step 3   **Consider All Solutions**

Brainstorm Solutions; Rule Out Criticisms

Step 2   **Collect Facts and Opinions**

What Is the Situation? What Happened? Who
Is Involved? What Policies and Procedures
Are Involved?

Figure 13.1
**Conflict-
Resolution
Discussion
Outline**

Step 1   **Define the Problem**

One- or Two-Sentence Definitions from All
Parties Involved

unorthodox or improbable it may seem. This approach will encourage the group to tap their creative energies without fear of ridicule or criticism.

Step 4: Define the expected results. Obviously, not all solutions to a problem are feasible or desirable. How does the group eliminate poor solutions and settle on the most appropriate ones? Part of the process involves focusing on the desired goals: what end results should follow from solving this problem? What does the group want to see happen?

Step 5: Select the solution(s). Which solutions will give the desired results? In light of the goals the group has set, one—or perhaps two or three—of the solutions will stand out as the most appropriate. The group can then systematically select the best solutions to achieve the desired goals.

Step 6: Implement the solution(s). Establish timetables for the solution(s) to be implemented and provide some way to evaluate the results. Make a point to discuss with others how things are going on a regular basis. Even the best solutions can fail unless all involved make the attempt to follow through.

Thinking/Learning Starters

1. Why is it so important to have the proper attitudes before entering into the problem-solving sequence?
2. Quite often conflict resolution breaks down at step 2 of the discussion outline—collecting facts and opinions—and step 3—considering all solutions. Why do you think this happens? What can be done to prevent the breakdown?

Organized Labor's Approach to Conflict Management

Although many conflicts among coworkers can be managed through effective human relations and conflict-resolution techniques, conflicts between employers (management) and employees (labor) tend to be more complex. As management holds more power than labor, there may be little communication regarding worker needs and grievances.[18] The struggle to balance this power and therefore improve communication between management and labor is one of the main reasons employees often choose to organize into a union or employee association. The employees are able to speak with one voice to bring their grievances and needs to the attention of management.

Employee Associations

Employee associations, sometimes called federations, are usually groups of employees who do not identify with the traditional labor movement. White-collar workers (such as accountants, lawyers, and salespeople) and pink-collar workers (such as secretaries and female clerical workers) may join local organizations of their peers. These employee associations tend to have local or state organizational structures, and they serve several purposes. They can pressure management to gain benefits for members as well as fulfill some of the social and professional needs of their members.

During the 1970s, many of these associations entered into collective bargaining with employers on more substantive issues such as working conditions, wages, contracts, retirement and fringe benefits, and the like. Public service employees and teachers also have used strikes to force city officials to meet with their representatives and talk about their association's concerns. These employee groups have responded to the recession of the 1980s in much the same way as traditional unions. They have either increased their activity to prevent layoffs, wage reductions, and cuts in benefits, or they have retreated from a more militant stance and agreed to wage and benefit concessions. In the future, as more workers enter white-collar and professional ranks and as the economy improves, the number of employee associations is likely to increase. These organizations may become more militant in their efforts to represent workers' needs.

Labor Unions

Whereas employee associations tend to be locally organized, **labor unions** are more likely to have a national as well as regional base, such as the International Brotherhood of Electrical Workers (IBEW), Retail Clerks International (RCI) or the United Auto Workers (UAW). Many people believe that unions have organized most of the work force in this country. In fact, labor unions represent only about 19 percent of the American work force, less than the number represented in the 1940s (see Table 13.2). Much of the reason for the decline in union membership lies in the fact that white-collar professions have grown at an ever-increasing rate, whereas blue-collar

Table 13.2 Union Membership: 1930–1985

Year	Percent of Nonagricultural Work Force
1930	11.6%
1935	13.2
1940	26.9
1945	35.5
1950	31.5
1955	33.2
1960	31.4
1965	28.4
1970	27.3
1975	25.5
1980	21.9
1985	18.8

Source: U.S. Bureau of Labor.

Table 13.3 National Labor Relations Act of 1935 (Wagner Act)

Section 7. Employees shall have the right to self-organize, to form, join, or assist labor organizations, to bargain collectively through representatives of their own choosing, and to engage in concerted activities for the purpose of collective bargaining or other mutual aid or protection.

professions have remained relatively stable or declined in number. Traditionally, white-collar workers have not been oriented toward the labor movement, although this situation may change in the coming years. Already, the AFL-CIO, the Service Employees International Union (SEIU), and the American Federation of Federal, State, County, and Municipal Employees (AFSCME) have been actively organizing clerical workers and flight attendants.

Labor unions were given the legal right to organize and represent workers by the National Labor Relations Act of 1935, also called the **Wagner Act** or labor's Magna Carta, and the Labor-Management Relations Act of 1947, also known as the **Taft-Hartley Act.** These two laws spell out the rights and obligations of both unions and management, as shown in Tables 13.3 and 13.4.

Before these laws came into effect, individual employees were virtually powerless against management. If a worker was injured, had a complaint about working conditions, became ill and couldn't work, or had trouble keeping up with the production schedule, he or she could be fired and replaced. Employers could initiate cuts in pay, extend the working hours, speed up production, or replace men with women and children who would work for lower wages. Employees could fight back by walking out or refusing to work. But employers often outwaited them or brought in other workers to break the strike. Unions helped employees gain an equal share of power in order to bargain with management. The real significance of the Wagner Act lay in

Table 13.4 Key Provisions of Labor-Management Relations Act of 1947 (Taft-Hartley Act)

1. Enabled the United States attorney general to request an eighty-day court injunction (so-called cooling-off period) to prevent strikes that "imperil the national health and safety."
2. Outlawed the closed shop, secondary boycotts, sympathy strikes, and jurisdictional strikes.
3. Outlawed featherbedding (an employer's having to pay for services not performed).
4. Prevented the charging of excessive initiation fees or dues.
5. Prevented the refusal of labor to bargain in good faith with management.
6. Permitted states to outlaw union-shop contracts, which require workers to join a union (states can pass so-called right-to-work laws).

the fact that for the first time the right of the union to speak for its membership and engage in collective bargaining was legally recognized and enforced.

Not all union-management relations are hostile. Perhaps one of the best examples of a positive working relationship between union and management is the Maytag company. "The company is very good to employees in terms of being fair. We have had a good understanding with the company," says Harvey Jackson, vice-president of UAW Local 997, which represents production-line workers at Maytag's Iowa headquarters.[19] Not many companies hear such enthusiasm from their union officials. Wages, benefits, and incentives rank among the most generous in the appliance industry. Moreover, jobs at Maytag are hard to get because there is very little employee turnover. As Maytag's example shows, management and union leaders can function effectively in an organization when there is a willingness to cooperate.

However, if the two sides mistrust one another or try to gain an unfair advantage, conflicts become difficult to resolve in a win/win fashion. As newspaper reports of labor disputes indicate, this situation is all too common. Labor and management often accuse each other of not bargaining in good faith.

Two of the most important tools unions possess for resolving labor-management conflicts are collective bargaining and the grievance procedure.

Collective Bargaining

At its best, **collective bargaining** works much like the win/win strategy. Labor and management define the issues, establish their goals, and decide on their rights and privileges. The results are stated in a written agreement or contract, approved by the union members and the management team. At its worst, collective bargaining resembles the lose/lose strategy. Labor makes unreasonable demands, and management holds out until lack of production forces the company into bankruptcy.

The overwhelming majority of contracts are settled without the need for strikes or other pressure tactics by either side. Generally, management and labor are able to settle their differences at the bargaining table. The process of collective bargaining is similar to the conflict-resolution discussion outline discussed earlier. To begin with, both sides should operate in an atmosphere of trust and candor. If the meeting is characterized by suspicion on either side, negotiations will be much more difficult. Second, both sides must have a clear understanding of the problems or issues to be discussed. Is the problem wages, overtime, seniority rules? The facts and figures supporting the demands of labor and management must be accurate and reflect the latest changes, for example, in the cost of living or the company's profits and losses. Finally, both sides should have in mind what end results they want to achieve and what solutions they feel will achieve them. Would management like to see production increased by 10 percent? Does labor want management's right to require overtime modified in some way?

The actual process of negotiation requires considerable skill on the part of labor and management representatives or it can quickly degenerate into a win/lose or lose/lose situation. The attitude must be, "The more I gain, the more *you* gain also." In bargaining, each side should try to express its objectives in terms of how they will benefit the organization as a whole. The emphasis should be on solving the problem rather than debating who is right or wrong, whose demands are legitimate, and which side has the better solution.

If labor and management cannot settle their conflicts through collective bargaining, they may submit their disputes to arbitration or mediation. There are two types of arbitration: voluntary and compulsory. **Voluntary arbitration** indicates that both sides have willingly submitted their disagreements to a neutral third party, and they want to work together to solve their problems. The arbitrator's decision must be accepted by both sides. **Compulsory arbitration** means that the government has decided the labor-management dispute either threatens national health and safety or will damage an entire industry. Government arbitrators dictate a solution that is binding on both sides and can be enforced in a court of law.

Mediation, on the other hand, carries with it no binding authority. The mediator is simply a neutral third party who listens to both sides and suggests solutions. Both parties are free to reject or accept the solution as they see fit.

If either side refuses to negotiate or will not return to the bargaining table, several pressure tactics can be used to force either labor or management into negotiations. Labor may employ strikes, work slowdowns, picketing, boycotts, and the like. Management may use court injunctions, media campaigns, lockouts, and public pressure to force workers to negotiate. Labor's pressure tactics are aimed at production and, if successful, can hurt the company's financial picture. Management seeks to undermine the solidarity of the union and split the membership, weakening its power base. However, when these tactics are used, the result is usually a win/lose or lose/lose situation.

One of the more well-known instances of such a situation involved the air traffic controller's union, PATCO, and the Federal Aviation Administration (FAA). After unsuccessful attempts to negotiate with FAA officials on issues of worker health and safety, the union called a general strike in August 1981; 11,400 employees walked off the job. The government retaliated by firing the striking workers and decertifying the union, depriving it of the right to represent employees. A "no-strike" clause in the employment contract gave the government the right to fire any strikers. Yet one year later, some of the same employee-management conflicts surfaced with the new air traffic controllers, causing problems on the job.

A task force investigating the PATCO strike, while condemning the union's harassment of management and nonstriking workers, concentrated on the FAA's "rigid and insensitive" management. Supervisors, the task force found, were autocratic and heavy-handed, tended to ignore human relationships, and treated employees as part of the machinery.

Three years after President Reagan dissolved PATCO, the AFL-CIO launched a formal drive to organize the new air traffic controllers. The American Air Traffic Controllers Council is the united voice of supervisors, workers who did not strike in 1981, and newly trained controllers. Because the original cause of the PATCO walkout was ineffectively addressed, the 14,300 current employees feel they need a united voice to bargain with their employer, the FAA.

Grievance Procedures

Collective bargaining produces a working document for conflict management between labor and management. In general, the document covers three areas: (1) binding provisions for wages, duration of the contract, and fringe benefits; little or no changes are anticipated in this section; (2) contingency clauses that govern actions taken by labor or management regarding new conditions that may arise in the future; items like changes in operating procedures, transfers, and training programs fall into this category; (3) grievance procedures, established to handle disputes over interpretation of contract provisions or new situations not covered by the contract.

Individual workers can start the **grievance procedure** by filing a complaint with a shop steward or union representative who will then approach the company supervisor. For example, in one plant, employees wanted to seal off a row of windows with aluminum foil. The sun pouring in through the windows added to the heat given off by machinery and raised the temperature in the room to 115 degrees. The superintendent refused, saying he had no allowance in the budget for such an item. The employees brought their complaint to their shop steward.

If the grievance cannot be settled at this level, it goes up the union and company ladder, as shown in Figure 13.2, until it is resolved or put to a mediator or arbitrator for a decision.

Most unionized companies have a grievance committee comprised of five employees who may offer their advice, counsel, and support at any step in the procedure. A company plagued by grievances should take a closer look at the human relations environment in the organization. The grievance procedure offers a formal, systematic approach to conflict management. No agreement or contract can possibly cover or anticipate all situations that are likely to cause problems. As a result, building in flexibility through the grievance procedure ensures that workers have a "court of appeals" after the contract is ratified.

When Unions Are the Problem

Although unions help resolve conflicts between management and labor, at times they may be the *cause* of the conflicts as well. Instead of protecting workers' interests and making sure that management recognizes the needs of employees, the union can become an obstacle to its own membership. In

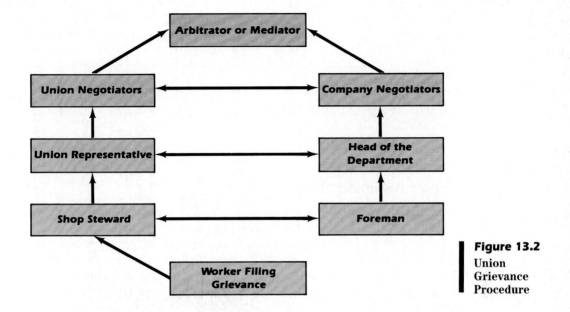

Figure 13.2
Union
Grievance
Procedure

some cases, unions may set an unofficial "quota" on production. Members cannot surpass this quota—even if they want to work harder—without being ostracized by their coworkers.

Also, the division of trade or craft workers can be carried to extremes. In one construction project, electricians would not work in the same area where plumbers were putting in pipes. If either crew had picked up the tools of the other or accidentally damaged the pipe or wiring in some way, the union representatives were prepared to call a work stoppage. Each group had to have sole access to the site at any one time.

Unions can cause conflict within an organization if they try to unionize workers who do not want to belong to a labor organization. The resulting conflicts can disrupt production, cause property damage, and may even result in injuries to workers or organizers. The company may be forced to take the issue to court, an expensive and time-consuming process. In many states, right-to-work laws prohibit unions from establishing closed shops in which employees must become union members in order to work for a company.

In some areas, unions can be the bitterest opponents of equal employment opportunity because of the scarcity of jobs and the competition for work. The government has had to force some unions to accept minorities and women into their apprenticeship and training programs.

Overall, however, unions often serve a valuable function in organizations. They provide a check on management's power to dictate the conditions of employment to workers. Many unions have helped ensure safer working conditions, higher pay, more equitable treatment of women and minorities, and provided a means to resolve labor-management conflicts through collective bargaining and grievance procedures.

Thinking/Learning Starters

1. What can be done to help prevent collective bargaining from becoming a lose/lose or a win/lose situation?
2. What are the purposes of grievance procedures?
3. What benefits can employee associations and labor unions provide for their members?

Union's Declining Strength

These are hard times for organized labor. Public support for unions is at an all-time low. In 1965, 71 percent of people surveyed in a public opinion poll said they approved of labor unions. In 1981, the percentage had dropped to 55. Today it is well under 50 percent.[20] Union members themselves are often the unions' biggest critics. In the past five years, workers in 4,446 collective bargaining units have petitioned the National Labor Relations Board for decertification. These workers contend that their unions no longer represent a majority of the employees. In the past, unions could deliver a unified vote for the Democratic nominee for president of the United States. But in 1984, almost half the voting union members voted for Ronald Reagan instead of Walter Mondale, the candidate the union had endorsed.

As the American work force shifts from a manufacturing to a service economy, the traditional labor unions are losing their strength. Organized labor lost its influence in the construction industry, where four out of five workers are now nonunion. And jobs are being eliminated in the steel, automotive, appliance, and building trades. But in other industries where jobs are more likely to be found, such as health care, food service, entertainment, and communications, the picture is improving. Membership in the American Federation of Federal, State, County, and Municipal Employees is increasing, as it is in unions representing hospital workers and food and restaurant employees. Yet despite the increased support of unions among some white-collar and government employees, unions overall have lost membership because of the declining number of blue-collar workers, their traditional source of strength.

In addition to a changing economy, the influx of computerized information has had a dramatic negative effect on the strength of unions. For generations, large organizations with 50,000 employees or more had to deal with their work force as a mass entity. It was the only way to keep track of them. But with the incredible flexibility of computers, employees can now be better treated as individuals. At American Can, for example, an employee can now select a specific combination of salary, pension, health benefits, flextime, job sharing, and job objectives. This is one of the key reasons unions are losing ground in the new computer-rich society. The idea for organizing a union was for everyone to be treated the same. Today's employees want to be treated as individuals.[21]

Many journalists, politicians, labor leaders, and corporate executives agree that unions' bargaining position has been weakened by the National Labor Relations Board (NLRB). The NLRB is as much a focus of controversy now as it was during the Great Depression, when industrial unions fought for survival. Since its formation in 1935, the NLRB has processed 766,000 complaints of unfair labor practices and issued 46,000 decisions. The agency has established an administrative process and legal framework for labor relations. Recently, however, the NLRB has allowed companies to move operations from union to nonunion plants in order to cut labor costs. It has drastically reduced the rights of union leaders over their striking members; for instance, the NLRB ruled that unions cannot place restrictions on rank-and-file members who withdraw from union membership. In 1985 the Supreme Court upheld a decision barring labor leaders from disciplining rank-and-file members who quit the union during a strike and went back to work, leaving their colleagues walking the picket line. Many employees now reflect the attitude that a union is only as good as it is convenient.

When Management Is the Problem

On the other hand, management is facing an equally grim picture. Sagging productivity, reduced consumer spending, and increased foreign competition mean that organizations must find ways to make operations as efficient and cost effective as possible. Often the quickest way to reduce costs is to lay off workers and negotiate reductions or freezes in wage and benefit increases. In construction, for example, companies are seeking to hold down wages, institute lower overtime pay, and continue the trend toward a ten-hour day, four-day work week.[22] In drastic situations, some organizations are moving their entire production facilities to foreign countries in order to take advantage of cheaper, nonunion labor. Yet these cost-cutting measures alienate workers, making it difficult to motivate them to achieve badly needed increases in production.

Despite management's problems, it is clear that they need to establish programs that recognize employees as individuals and show more concern about intangibles such as employee dignity and recognition of worth. This is especially important when it is impossible to increase wages and benefits.[23]

Union and Management: Conflict or Cooperation?

The problems facing unions and management point up the need for reaching mutually satisfying solutions. Yet, in many instances, the traditional adversary relationship between labor and management in this country is making cooperative action difficult.

When negotiations over wage cuts and concessions broke down, TWA flight attendants struck the financially troubled corporation. (AP/ Wide World Photos)

Item: Phelps Dodge copper mine was hurt by foreign competition from copper producers, losing $74 million in the early 1980s. Other U.S. copper producers, also facing foreign competition, offered their unions three-year wage freezes that left a cost-of-living increase intact. The unions accepted. But Phelps Dodge insisted on eliminating the cost-of-living adjustment, and employees voted to strike. Despite its past paternalistic practices, which had earned it the nickname "Mother Dodge," Phelps Dodge hired all new non-union employees and ordered striking union members to vacate company housing and, in effect, leave town.[24]

Item: U.S. Steel, struggling to regain a foothold in the world market, has been able to gain the cooperation of union leaders but not of rank-and-file workers. Years of management insensitivity toward labor has made employees distrust both U.S. Steel management and their own union officials. Following weeks of effort in the mid-1980s, the company decided to close twenty-four unprofitable plants, eliminating nearly 15,500 jobs.

Yet the adversarial relationship is not universal. William Ouchi, author of *Theory Z*, points out that in such countries as Japan, West Germany, Sweden, and France, government, labor, and management work in much closer harmony. He urges unions and management in the United States to adopt a more cooperative model in organizations:

> A democratic style of management will and should win the trust of its employees. Instead of sabotaging the union, a patient management will discover that the union recognizes the need for more flexible work rules in order to provide higher productivity and job security. Indeed, in a healthy setting, the union provides a company with a ready-made conduit through which to communicate with employees; to organize them and explain benefit plans; to integrate educational, social, and recreational activities.[25]

Lee Iacocca, head of Chrysler Corporation, agrees:

> Japanese labor unions work very closely with mangement. Each side understands that its fate is bound up in the other guy's success. The relationship between labor and management is one of cooperation and mutual respect. That's a far cry from the antagonism and mutual suspicion that has long been the tradition in our country.[26]

Ouchi states that both management and unions must be convinced of the value of creating a productive working relationship. Unions and organizations that fail to work for change together will lower productivity and eventually drive the union and/or the company out of existence. As the president of Local 1014 at U.S. Steel's Gary, Indiana, plant observed, "We should be working as partners, not adversaries; and we should share in the decision making to increase efficiency."[27]

Tentative steps in the direction of a union-management partnership have already been taken by some unions and organizations. Ford Motor Company, in a landmark agreement with the UAW in 1982, gained union concessions on wages and benefits in exchange for more direct union involvement in managerial decision making. Lee Iacocca appointed Douglas Fraser, retiring president of the United Auto Workers, to the board of directors of Chrysler. When he appointed Fraser, Iacocca said that he believed government, labor, and managment have to work together.

Union members may be skeptical about too close a marriage between labor and management leaders, but they are generally in favor of the union having a strong voice on the board. Many expect to catch up on their recent wage concessions as they help the company profits increase. Although organized labor took a beating in negotiations over pay, benefits, and work rules, it emerged from the recession with new roles and powers that many companies have long held to be the exclusive domain of management. To an extent not seen before, a small but growing number of unions are now in a position to influence decisions about product developments, plant closings, compensation, and corporate leadership. The United Steelworkers, for example, has reversed its longstanding opposition to employee ownership and is aggressively helping its members to buy total or partial ownership in plants that otherwise would be closed. Through seats on boards of directors, labor leaders are also gaining access to financial information. In such cases, union members are actively soliciting new business for their plants. Involving union leaders in business decision making is a major breakthrough that has great potential for improving the competitive edge of companies.

There is a growing consensus that labor-management collaboration, more flexible work rules, board representation, stock ownership, and profit sharing for workers are reducing tensions and making fundamental changes in the way in which workers relate to their employers.

> In sharing information about business, as well as profits and stock, employees become more than mere wage takers. They become engaged with the place they work. They feel part of the enterprise and put forward their best effort. That can only be for the better.[28]

Whether companies and unions can lay aside their traditional adversary relationships and work together to solve their mutual problems remains to be seen. Unions will continue to focus on ensuring job security and retraining for workers, keeping wages and benefits equal to or above the rate of inflation, avoiding costly strikes, and protecting workers who must be laid off. Management will seek to hold costs down, increase productivity, gain government protection of domestic industries against foreign competition, and make operations more efficient. It is clear that labor and management must seek problem-solving strategies to manage their many conflicts creatively.

Summary

The healthy emotion of anger is at the root of many conflicts. Even though anger can be expressed in nonproductive ways, you can choose to turn your anger into energy that helps find solutions to problems in ways that lead everyone to feel good.

Conflict in organizations can arise over breakdowns in communication, values conflicts, work policies and practices, personality clashes, and adversarial management. There are several approaches for dealing with conflict, which may be grouped into three basic strategies: win/lose, lose/lose, and win/win. In general, the win/win strategy requires skilled leadership, the development of proper attitudes on the part of all involved, and the use of structured conflict resolution discussions. Using the win/win strategy not only can resolve a conflict but can preserve good human relations.

Conflict between employers and workers can be handled by employee associations and labor unions negotiating with management. Employee associations are often organized on a local level and may serve social as well as professional purposes. Labor unions are usually organized on a national level and help balance the power between labor and management. Both employee associations and unions can engage in collective bargaining. This process defines the rights and privileges of both sides and establishes the terms of employment in a contract or other type of legally binding document. If neither side can agree on issues, they can submit their disputes to arbitration or mediation for settlement. Whereas arbitration is binding on both parties, the mediator's decision can be accepted or rejected by either side. Conflicts that arise after a contract has been negotiated can be handled through the grievance procedure.

Both unions and managment are facing complex problems that involve productivity, job security and worker training, and the preservation of the quality of work life that employees enjoy. Both sides are attempting to cope with the new challenges of high technology and changing economic conditions. As a result, there is an increased need for cooperative action between the two groups. Unions and management in many companies are facing these challenges in creative ways.

Key Terms

anger
conflict confrontation
conflict management
win/lose strategy
lose/lose strategy
win/win strategy
employee associations
labor unions

Wagner Act
Taft-Hartley Act
collective bargaining
voluntary arbitration
compulsory arbitration
mediation
grievance procedure

Review Questions

1. What are some of the major causes of conflict in an organization?
2. Name at least five conflict areas you might encounter when working with other people.
3. What attitudes do participants need to develop before entering into a conflict-resolution process?
4. Explain the win/lose, lose/lose, and win/win strategies and describe the results obtained when each strategy is used to resolve conflicts.
5. List the six steps in the conflict-resolution process and briefly explain each one.
6. What is the basic reason labor unions and employee associations are formed?
7. Explain the difference between arbitration and mediation.
8. What evidence do you see in news reports, newspapers, magazines, and so on, of cooperation between unions and management to resolve their conflicts? In what ways are the two sides not cooperating with each other?

Case 13.1

Labor-Management Conflict at Hormel[29]

Workers at the Geo. A. Hormel & Company meat-packing plant in Austin, Minnesota, went out on strike in August 1985. The strike was part of a dispute that began almost a year earlier, but it has brought only added conflict.

Hormel, like other meat-packing firms, has been faced with a decreasing demand for its products. To keep their costs down, Hormel cut the base wages of its union employees—without negotiating the cut with union officials. Part of the cut was restored through arbitration, and Hormel offered to restore almost all of the remainder when a new labor contract was signed. Union members at other Hormel plants accepted the new contract, but those at the Austin plant did not. At issue were plant safety and job security, as well as wages. A strike resulted, and the plant was shut down.

Some twenty-one weeks later, in January 1986, Hormel reopened the plant. Some union packers returned to work, and Hormel's personnel department began to take applications for employees to replace the strikers. At one point, Hormel needed the help of the Minnesota National Guard to break through a blockade of the plant by union picketers, so employees could get to work.

The Austin union, Local P-9 of the United Food and Commercial Workers, sent striking members to picket other Hormel plants. About a week after the Austin plant was reopened, Hormel fired hundreds of packers in Texas, Nebraska, and Iowa for refusing to cross the picket lines set up at their plants by Local P-9.

Violence had been expected by many observers. It came in May 1986, when hundreds of strikers fought with police outside the Austin plant. The parent union, the UFCW International, had long considered Local P-9's strike to be "mass suicide," given conditions in the industry. Now its president began proceedings to take over Local P-9 and appoint a new union leadership. But even that may not be enough to end the strike or get the strikers working again.[27]

Questions

1. What seem to be the strengths of each side of this dispute? What is your assessment of the balance of power between Local P-9 and Hormel?
2. Who were the winners and losers in this conflict?
3. What would a win/win solution look like? Is such a solution possible? Why or why not?

Case 13.2

The Battle of the Secretaries

The "battle" had reached a crisis point at McKnight & Company, a medium-sized management consulting firm. The dispute centered on whether executive secretaries could accept work from consultants. According to company policy, executive secretaries worked only for officers of the firm. Their responsibilities were more administrative than clerical. Consultants' work was usually handled by typists and clerks. But a recent decline in business had hit the company hard, and several typists had been laid off.

Now business was picking up, and Ron Talbot, a consultant, had more work than the typing pool could handle. He found that other consultants were in the same predicament, so they asked the executive secretaries to help out. One of the officers immediately objected: "I need my secretary to do research, handle correspondence, and make client contacts. I don't want her tied up doing someone else's typing." Ron pointed out, "That may be true when you're in town, but most officers are on the road half of every month. There's no reason why the secretaries can't help then—they hardly have anything to do." The officers refused to back down.

The debate grew more intense until finally Ron and the other consultants took their problems to Chuck Allison, head of the office. In a memo they stated, "We recommend either hiring more typists or changing the policy regarding executive secretaries. We need more help." Allison considered the problem a minor one. He responded, "Company policy states that executive secretaries report to officers only. I agree with this policy. At this point we cannot afford to hire extra help for at least six months. Typists and clerical personnel should be requested to work overtime and on weekends, if necessary, until more help can be hired." Allison felt this solution settled the matter.

Questions

1. Which of the three conflict-management strategies did Allison use? What do you think will be the results of this solution?
2. Is it possible to achieve a win/win solution in this case? Why or why not?
3. The secretaries involved could write to 9 to 5, the National Association of Working Women, and the Service Employees International Union for help and advice on handling the situation. How would these associations benefit McKnight & Company's secretarial staff? How would they benefit the management staff requesting changes in the secretarial work rules? If you were Allison, what would you do if the secretaries began to organize themselves with the help of one of these organizations?

Notes

1. "Standoff at Hormel," *Fortune*, May 12, 1986, p. 9.
2. Bruce Baldwin, "Angry Interactions: Conflict and Compatibility in the Combat Zone," *Pace*, p. 11.

3. Robert Chasnoff and Peter Muniz, "Training to Manage Conflicts," *Training and Development Journal*, January 1985, p. 49.

4. Gordon Lippitt, Ronald Lippitt, and Clayton Lafferty, "Cutting Edge Trends in Organization Development," *Training and Development Journal*, July 1984, p. 60.

5. Rensis Likert and Jane Gibson Likert, *New Ways of Managing Conflict* (New York: McGraw-Hill, 1976), pp. 7–8.

6. Donald H. Weiss, *Managing Conflict* (New York: AMACOM, 1981), p. 11.

7. Harlan Cleveland, *The Future Executive: A Guide for Tomorrow's Managers* (New York: Harper & Row, 1979), pp. 17–29.

8. Gordon Lippitt, "Managing Conflict in Today's Organizations," *Training and Development Journal*, July 1982, pp. 67–74.

9. K. Albrecht, *Stress and the Manager* (Englewood Cliffs, N.J.: Prentice-Hall, 1979), pp. 273–274.

10. "Study Finds Most Workers Unhappy in Their Firms," *Chicago Tribune*, December 13, 1982, pp. 1–2.

11. Perry Pascarella, *New Achievers* (New York: The Free Press, 1984), p. 25.

12. "Study Finds Most Workers Unhappy," p. 2.

13. Robert Bolton and Dorothy Grover Bolton, *Social Style/Management Style* (New York: American Management Association, 1984), p. 6.

14. Likert and Likert, *New Ways of Managing Conflict*, p. 8.

15. Alan Filley, *Interpersonal Conflict Resolution* (Glenview, Ill.: Scott, Foresman, 1975), pp. 60–69.

16. Lippitt, "Managing Conflict," p. 70.

17. Ibid.

18. Peter Drucker, *Managing in Turbulent Times* (New York: Harper & Row, 1980), p. 201.

19. Robert Levering, Milton Moskowitz, and Michael Katz, *The 100 Best Companies to Work for in America* (New York: New American Library, 1985), pp. 212–213.

20. James J. Kilpatrick, "Hard Times for Organized Labor," *The Washington Post*, July 2, 1985.

21. John Naisbitt, *Megatrends—Ten New Directions Transforming Our Lives* (New York: Warner Books, 1982), p. 43.

22. "A Year of Settling for Less—And Breaking Old Molds," *Business Week*, December 20, 1982, pp. 72–73.

23. "Unions in the Office: What Do Women Want?" *Management Technology*, September 1983, pp. 68–69.

24. Paul Taylor, "Trouble in Paradise: The Ultimate Company Town Torn Apart by Strike," *Roanoke Times & World-News*, December 18, 1983, p. G-4.

25. William Ouchi, *Theory Z: How American Business Can Meet the Japanese Challenge* (Reading, Mass.: Addison-Wesley, 1981), pp. 97–100.

26. Lee Iacocca with William Novak, *IACOCCA* (New York: Bantam Books, 1984), p. 322.
27. "U.S. Steel's Get-Tough Policy," *Business Week*, August 30, 1982, pp. 73–74.
28. Carey English, "Companies Learn to Live with Unions in Board Rooms," *U.S. News and World Report*, January 30, 1984, p. 63.
29. For more information, see *Fortune*, May 12, 1986, p. 9; *Fortune*, March 3, 1986, p. 9; *U.S. News & World Report*, February 17, 1986, p. 49; *Roanoke Times & World News*, January 28, 1986, p. A-2; and *The Wall Street Journal*, January 14, 1986, p. 47.

Suggested Readings

Blake, Robert, and Jane Srygley Mouton. *Solving Costly Organizational Conflicts.* Jossey-Bass, Inc., Publishers, 1984.

Drucker, Peter. *Managing in Turbulent Times.* New York: Harper & Row, 1980.

Filley, Allan C. *Interpersonal Conflict Resolution.* Glenview, Ill.: Scott, Foresman, 1975.

Gordon, Thomas. *Leadership Effectiveness Training (L.E.T.).* New York: Wyden Books, 1977.

Kelly, Joe. *How Managers Manage.* Englewood Cliffs, N.J.: Prentice-Hall, 1980.

Kennedy, Gavin. *Managing Negotiations.* Englewood Cliffs, N.J.: Prentice-Hall, 1982.

Likert, Rensis, and Jane Gibson Likert. *New Ways of Managing Conflict.* New York: McGraw-Hill, 1976.

Naisbitt, John. *Megatrends—Ten New Directions Transforming Our Lives.* New York: Warner Books, 1982, Chapter 2.

Robert, Marc. *Managing Conflict from the Inside Out.* Austin, Texas: Learning Concepts, 1982.

Roseman, Edward. *Managing the Problem Employee.* New York: AMACOM, 1982.

Simmons, John, and William Mares. *Working Together.* New York: Alfred A. Knopf, 1983.

V

Special Challenges in Human Relations

Chapter 14

Coping with Personal and Professional Life Changes

Chapter Preview

After studying this chapter, you will be able to
1. Describe work-related changes.
2. Understand why individuals resist change.
3. Summarize ways of actively adapting to change.
4. Explain how individuals can counteract stress.
5. Describe how organizations can manage stress in their employees.

On a quiet Sunday morning in September 1985, one hundred years of American industrial history crumbled to dust in just six seconds. Corning Glass Works, located in Corning, New York, dynamited its 135-foot silica mixing tower, the core of a century-old manufacturing complex built to mass-produce the world's first incandescent light bulbs. The antiquated facility, which had produced hundreds of millions of light bulbs for Corning, was being leveled as the company moved its light bulb production facilities to Brazil.[1]

The brief explosion was Corning Glass Works's admission that it could no longer make money on light bulbs made in America. Corning is, of course, one of many companies forced to make a radical break with the past in order to survive. Eastman Kodak Company has reduced its worldwide work force by 10,000 employees. Foreign competition is threatening the survival of entire U.S. industries such as steel, shoes, and textiles. In order to compete with low-priced foreign goods, companies must initiate drastic cost-cutting measures. In some cases, cost reduction is achieved by closing unproductive plants or by reducing the work force. About two million manufacturing jobs have been eliminated during the past ten years. High-tech industries, far from absorbing these displaced workers, have been laying off thousands of workers themselves.

To remain competitive, many companies are moving away from old methods of doing business toward offices and factory systems that utilize computers, robots, and other forms of technology. The workplace is changing so rapidly that experts estimate 100,000 robots will be in use by 1990. Experts also estimate that by 1988 nearly 60 percent of the American work force will be linked to electronic work stations.[2]

Work-Related Changes

How will these changes affect you in the years ahead? Although the future is difficult to predict, it is possible to anticipate certain conditions that will necessitate changes in your life. If present trends continue, you can expect to experience a series of work-related transitions. There are at least three different kinds of transitions related to a person's life as a worker."[3]

1. *Trying to change jobs or careers because of personal dissatisfaction with present job.* In this category are some 25 million people in America. Put another way, about one out of every four workers is (secretly or openly) contemplating a career or job change. The fact that about 30 percent of all workers wind up in a different occupation every five years indicates that many people do indeed move to different jobs.

2. *Trying to hold on to a job that is rapidly changing.* According to many observers, the United States is now making the transition from the industrial

age into the information/service age.[4] The next decade or two may result in as much change in the way Americans work as the industrial revolution fostered only a century ago. More companies are investing in robotics and automated equipment. Word processing centers are replacing the traditional typing pool. To some observers, computer technology is the harbinger of a brighter and more secure future. Others see serious consequences of spending long hours with machines. Craig Brod, author of *Technostress*, notes that "the computer in many situations is generating very little interesting work, except for executives or research and development workers."[5] He also points out that the computer provides neither variety nor balance. Later in this chapter we will discuss a unique form of anxiety that people develop when they must learn to accept and use computers.

In addition to technological changes in the workplace, we are observing a changing work climate that often results when a larger organization merges with a smaller one. Mergers have become commonplace in America, and there is no reason to believe that this trend will change in the near future. Changes in job descriptions due to the arrival of a new management team can create high levels of stress.

3. *Unemployed but trying to obtain a job.* Between 15 and 20 million adults are estimated to be in this transition category in an average year. These people are either going to work for the first time or trying to re-enter the work force after being fired, quitting, or taking time out for whatever reason.

The movement from being an unemployed worker to an employed worker is often a long and difficult journey. Many of the people who lost jobs in auto, steel, and other "smokestack" industries must first be retrained before they can search for a new job. If the new job is in the service sector, the

---

Total Person Insight

Craig Brod

We have come to expect from people the perfection, accuracy, and speed to which computers have made us accustomed. Busy following standardized procedures and ultralogical reasoning in order to interact with computers, we have begun to think of conversation as data transfer and memory as a search procedure. We already are beginning to speak like machines: "I need more data" or "I can't access that." The directory-assistance operator, the bank teller, the ticket agent, the librarian have all become computer operators with whom we "interface." As we grow more and more impatient with human imperfection and variation, we move further and further away from the very essence of our own humanity.

worker will very likely take a cut in pay. Coping with the demands of a new job and learning to live on less income present a major challenge to most people.

Many organizations are beginning to pay more attention to the dynamics of personal transition and their effects on both human and corporate productivity. It has been estimated that nearly $80 to $90 billion is lost annually because of changes that make employees unproductive. Job loss, demotion, transfer, or being passed over for promotion can create real crises in our lives.

Change and the Individual

A **transition** can be defined as the experience of being forced to give up something and face a change. Much more than we previously thought happens to people who are in transition. In recent years we have learned that life transitions are like little deaths, and most organizations are full of them.

Anticipating Change

In the past two hundred years, much of the world has experienced an acceleration in the rate of change. Events happen more rapidly than people can absorb and adjust to them. Alvin Toffler, in his book of the same name, called this process **future shock.** Each generation in the twentieth century has grown up with products, technological advances, and discoveries unknown to the previous generation. And the pace of change in the near future shows little sign of slowing down.

In a world moving as fast as ours, change will continue to be a fact of life, and organizations and individuals will have to accept its inevitability. With that firmly in mind, we can begin preparing to manage the transitions.

Once the inevitability of change has been accepted, it often can be anticipated. Just as organizations develop strategic plans that seek to minimize risk and maximize success, you can begin developing contingency plans that focus on anticipated changes in your career. Some of the most common careers and anticipated changes in the number of workers needed are listed in Figure 14.1 You can anticipate change in your profession by watching developments in your field, projecting current trends or research, talking with others, and regularly reading professional publications. Anticipating change can help you adjust to the future. The mental game "what if?" is a useful tool to visualize various possible scenarios. What if you were offered a job in another city? What if you discovered a position you always wanted would be available next week? The game helps develop your capacity to create

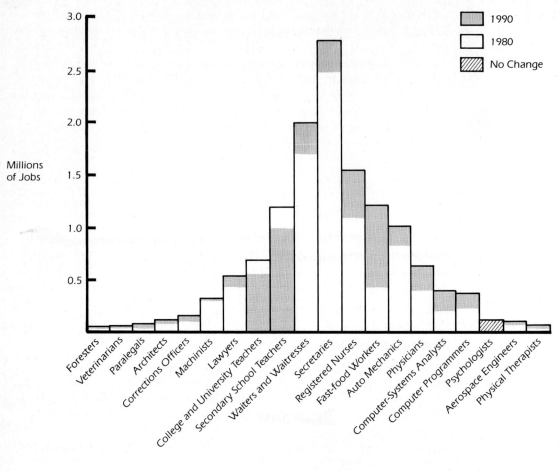

Figure 14.1
Where the Jobs Will Be Found in 1990
Source: U.S. Bureau of Labor Statistics

options and plan what steps to take should various opportunities or setbacks actually occur.

Why We Resist Change

Few of us like our lives to be disturbed in any fundamental way. Usually, the greater the degree of change, the stronger the resistance from those affected by it or those who must implement it. Understanding the factors that make change stressful and so often unwelcome can help us better cope with life's transitions. In this section we review several reasons why people resist change.

Feelings of Inadequacy   When people must learn new skills, accept more responsibility, or take on challenges that stretch their abilities, they are apt to feel inadequate to handle the change. Usually resistance is based more on a lack of self-confidence than on a lack of ability. Carl Wolf of Chase Econometrics Interactive Data Corporation introduced personal computers into his company by letting his employees take them home. After they got accustomed to using the new equipment, the workers lost their fear of computers and began using them at work.[6] A good manager can help workers overcome their lack of self-confidence and encourage them to try new projects and learn new skills.

Personal Security Threatened   Personal security—physical or psychological—is one of everyone's basic needs. Substantial changes in how your work is performed may leave you wondering if you will be laid off or asked to do more work for the same pay. If you perceive the change as a demotion or loss of status, you may feel your worth as a person is being diminished. When executive secretaries in an insurance firm were formed into a word processing center, they lost their status as private secretaries—they now worked for several bosses instead of only one. They were afraid that some of them would be let go as the office became more automated, and their productivity dropped considerably. Changes that threaten security inevitably cause problems in employee motivation and morale.

Fear of the Unknown   Fear of the unknown is a common reaction to new situations. When changing economic conditions threaten the stability of an organization, the grapevine begins to spread rumors. At John Deere, a major farm implement manufacturer, the farm crisis of the mid-1980s exerted tremendous pressure on employees' lives. Daily conversations reflected employees' concerns. Will there be a layoff? How many will go this time? Will I be on the list, or will I survive another cut? If I do survive, will my job responsibilities be the same? Family and professional lives remain in limbo until the answers are known, and tension is high as employees consider the possibilities and options. Management can help alleviate this fear by maintaining good communication—explaining in detail what the changes mean and how they will affect each employee.

Lack of Trust   Sometimes resistance to change is not directed at the change itself but at those who introduce it. The degree of openness and trust between management and employees often determines how readily change is accepted or opposed. Management may feel that employees should not be involved in the planning stages or in decisions about how and when changes should take place. Employees may not believe what management tells them. As a result, an organization can quickly become a rumor mill. This lack of trust may mean that change is forced on employees, leaving in its wake reduced productivity, resentment, and even greater distrust of management.

Inability to See the Larger Picture   If employees are not included in the entire process of change from the beginning, they quite often cannot see beyond their own attitudes and opinions or understand the change in terms of the goals and needs of the organization. For example, a new method for shipping deliveries may inconvenience you as an individual but help the company control costs and reduce operating expenses. If you are helped to understand how the change will improve the overall organization, you probably will support it.

Changes often happen more rapidly than expected, and there may not always be time for someone to explain them to you and help you cope with the new situation. Be ready to accept change and notice the positives of the situation as soon as possible. Perhaps there will be times when you hear of a new technique from a colleague in another organization or read in a trade journal about a more effective way to complete a task. When you see this trend toward a change, mentally prepare yourself for it.

Adapting to Change

For an individual or an organization, adapting to change is basically a matter of attitudes and adjusting established values to new situations. Most changes involve some type of loss, but they can also offer new opportunities.

The Values Test   Many people, when confronted with sudden changes, lose sight of their basic values and make decisions on impulse. Yet values can act as guidelines for dealing with change. A young manager who has always valued close family and community relations may receive an offer to work overseas or relocate in another region of the country. An engineer who values a small-company working environment may be tempted by offers of a sizable salary increase to join a multinational firm. Such changes can create values conflicts. Throughout your career, you will need to clarify your value priorities to determine whether changes will lead you to your personal or professional goals.

The same principle holds true for organizations. A small service company may build its reputation on personalized service to customers. As the company grows, its staff increases; and it is more difficult to maintain the same level of attention to customer needs. The changes brought on by growth conflict with the values on which the company was founded. On the other hand, some organizations must adjust outmoded values to accomplish a change. A reluctance to computerize operations may be based on a value of doing

A large number of Americans are being retrained for new jobs. This displaced worker is learning new skills for a high-tech position. (Photo by Richard Sobol, Stock Boston, Inc.)

things "in a personal way," but not computerizing could be disastrous for the organization's future financial goals.

Active Adaptability   When faced with an unexpected or possibly threatening situation, human beings—like animals—react with the **fight or flight syndrome**. Adrenalin pours into the bloodstream, the heart beats faster, breathing accelerates—the body is poised to fight or run. Unlike animals, however, human beings have a third choice: the ability to adapt consciously to change. Not only are people capable of choosing their responses to a situation, they can also think about the consequences of their choice. The ability to analyze possible choices and consequences *before* acting is called **active adaptability**.

The key to active adaptability is the realization that change can be constructive, even if the initial event appears to be a negative one. A machinist laid off from work at first believed he would never find another job. His skills were no longer needed, and his future seemed lost in the shuffle of factory closings. After a few weeks, however, he decided to take a chance and enroll in a federally funded training program. Eventually, he became a writer and consultant on skilled craft work, a job he found more satisfying than his old one.

Many workers find job placement counseling and training the key to active adaptability. As noted at the beginning of this chapter, Corning Glass Works had to close some of its plants and transfer operations overseas in order to remain competitive. Despite these closings, Corning's reputation has remained good. The company started a comprehensive placement program that helped workers find jobs elsewhere. Others were enrolled in school for retraining.

The need to adapt to change is also creating new demands for adult learning, much of it related to job and career. In a study funded by the Exxon Education Foundation, it was found that of 1,500 adults interviewed, almost 56 percent cited job and career changes as the reason for enrolling in adult education courses. Many adults had to learn new information in order to get jobs, keep them, or advance in them. Some found they had to return to the classroom in order to leave their jobs or make the successful transition from unemployment to employment.[7]

Active adaptability not only helps individuals and organizations adjust to change but can strengthen human relations as well. As employees face change head on, they find positive ways of adapting and adjusting. This feeling of being in control, rather than being controlled by the change, builds the individual's self-esteem. Positive self-esteem helps promote teamwork among coworkers as they face change together.

Thinking/Learning Starters

1. What changes have you had to cope with in your personal and work life? What is your basic attitude toward change?
2. Have you had to adjust your values when confronted with major changes in your life? How did you adapt to these changes?
3. What changes do you anticipate facing in the next three to five years? How can you prepare for these changes?

Change and the Organization

In most organizations, change is often necessary for survival. In this sense, change is not a matter of simply reshuffling top management or altering a product line. Rather, it entails reshaping the culture of an organization to make it more competitive, more efficient, and better able to adapt to an environment in constant flux.

Conditions Necessitating Change

An organization should consider changing when one or more of the following conditions arise:[8]

1. *The organization is in a highly competitive industry and a quickly changing environment.* Organizations that pay close attention to customer needs and believe in the value of adapting to those needs can maintain a competitive edge. They have created a corporate culture open to the evolutionary process of change; they have institutionalized the ability to adapt. For example, Intel Corporation, a computer chip manufacturer in Santa Clara, California, signed a revolutionary pact with IBM to establish close supplier-purchaser ties as a way to meet the Japanese challenge in the computer industry. Although there is always the risk that IBM will swallow up Intel, Intel managers feel confident they can control change and maintain their integrity as a separate company.

2. *The organization is mediocre or failing.* A company that is losing money, and its best employees, will need to make radical changes to survive. Lee Iacocca turned Chrysler Corporation around by emphasizing quality construction, customer service, and attention to consumer tastes. Frank Borman, who took over Eastern Air Lines at a critical time in that company's financial history, attempted the same turnaround. For ten years, labor and management made major concessions. In 1986, however, Eastern was taken over by Texas Air Corporation, Borman resigned the chairmanship, and employees prepared for another round of changes.

3. *The organization is on the verge of becoming very large.* When a company is growing rapidly toward stability and success, it may also begin to acquire the trappings of a bureaucracy in terms of formal policies and systems. As a result, the original values that maintained the company during its earlier, entrepreneurial years may be threatened. Hewlett-Packard has experienced the process of such a transition. The decentralized management that HP forged over the years—although responsible for the company's early success—also resulted in overlapping products, lagging development, and a piecemeal approach to key markets as the company grew. John Young, head of HP, has the difficult task of keeping the spirit of entrepreneurship alive while at the same time orchestrating the company's new direction into the computer field.[9]

4. *The environment undergoes a fundamental change, and the organization is driven by traditional values.* "Traditional values" in this sense means that management believes what worked in the past is bound to work in the

future, regardless of change. Some airlines that competed well in a regulated environment suddenly found themselves in a deregulated situation. The auto industry assumed that consumers would always value the large American car, symbol of affluence and a high standard of living. Many small and medium-sized oil companies geared their corporate culture to the world's continuing demand for energy, never suspecting that within a short time there would be an oil glut on the market. Adherence to traditional values can bring an organization to the brink of disaster quickly in a rapidly changing environment. Traditional values may need to be adjusted to allow the organization to respond to market and competitive conditions.

Change Causes Stress

Most of the changes in our life, regardless of how beneficial, can cause tension or stress. **Stress** is typically defined as any action or set of circumstances under which an individual cannot respond adequately or can only respond at the cost of excessive wear and tear on the body.[10] Under stress, we are in a state of imbalance. Stress is the tension we feel when we try to adapt—whether changing jobs, learning to operate a computer, moving into a new home, or getting married—all the while struggling to regain our old equilibrium.

Although most of what is written about stress today focuses on its negative consequences, it's important to realize that some stress is beneficial. Author John Lawrie states that too much stress can sap your energy, undermine your personal life, and ruin your effectiveness on the job. But too little can stall your personal growth and lead to stagnation.[11] Lawrie says that your goal is not to eliminate stress but to determine when you've passed your limits and then do something about it. A review of Table 14.1 can help you determine if you've passed your limits.

Technostress: A New Threat in the Workplace

The computer revolution has created a new form of stress that is threatening the mental and physical health of many workers. Craig Brod, a consultant specializing in stress reduction, uses the term **technostress** to describe a modern disease caused by an inability to cope with the new computer technologies in a healthy manner.[12] Brod notes that technostress manifests itself in two distinct but related ways. First, stress is apt to surface as we struggle to learn how to adapt to computers in the workplace. Adaptation to the new computer technology often provokes anxiety, according to Brod:

> As the rhythm of the workplace speeds up to match that of the computer, the resulting increase in both load and rate of work, aggravated by the reliance on symbols and abstractions that the computer demands, creates

Table 14.1 Life Events Scale for Measuring Stress

Besides on-the-job stress, there are other sources of stress. Thomas Holmes and Richard Rahe, two psychiatrists at the University of Washington Medical School have developed a life events scale that measures the potential for stress-related illness.

To figure your stress potential, add up the points for each item that has occurred in your life in the past year.

Rank Crisis	Points	Rank Crisis	Points
1. Death of a spouse	100	23. Departure of son or daughter from home	29
2. Divorce	73	24. Trouble with in-laws	29
3. Marital separation	65	25. Outstanding personal achievement	28
4. Jail term	63		
5. Death of a close family member	63	26. Spouse's beginning or stopping work	26
6. Personal injury or illness	53	27. Beginning or end of school	26
7. Marriage	50	28. Change in living conditions	25
8. Job firing	47		
9. Marital reconciliation	45	29. Change of personal habits	24
10. Retirement	45	30. Trouble with boss	23
11. Change in health of family member	44	31. Change in work hours or conditions	20
12. Pregnancy	44	32. Change in residence	20
13. Sexual difficulties	39	33. Change in schools	20
14. Gain of new family member	39	34. Change in recreation	19
15. Business readjustment	39	35. Change in church activities	19
16. Change in financial state	38	36. Change in social activities	18
17. Death of a close friend	38		
18. Change to different line of work	36	37. Mortgage or loan less than $10,000	17
19. Change in number of arguments with spouse	35	38. Change in sleeping habits	16
20. Mortgage more than $10,000	31	39. Change in number of family gatherings	15
21. Foreclosure of mortgage or loan	30	40. Change in eating habits	15
		41. Vacation	13
22. Change in work responsibilities	29	42. Christmas	12
		43. Minor violation of law	11

LOW	*MEDIUM*	*HIGH*
(150–200) 37% chance of getting seriously ill in the next two years.	(225–300) 51% chance of getting seriously ill.	(325–375) 80% chance of getting seriously ill in the next two years.

Source: Reprinted with permission from *Journal of Psychosomatic Research*, Vol. 11, Thomas Holmes and Richard Rahe, "The Social Readjustment Rating Scale, Copyright 1967, Pergamon Press, Ltd.

As America makes the transition from the Industrial Age to the Information/Service Age, word processing centers like this one have become more common. (Northwestern Mutual Life photo)

new physical and psychological pressures. Our reaction to these pressures is expressed in the symptoms of technostress.[13]

Michelle, a capable paralegal secretary employed by a law firm, provides a good example of someone who is finding it difficult to adapt to the computer. She prides herself on her fast and accurate work, and sees the firm's recently installed word-processing system as a threat to her arduously acquired skills. Her terminal sits at her desk, unused and ignored, as she continues to use her electric typewriter. She uses the word processor only when her employer insists.[14]

Overidentification with computer technology is the second way that technostress manifests itself. Some workers have adopted a machine-like mindset that reflects the characteristics of the computer itself. Brod notes that some people have too successfully identified with computer technology and have lost the capacity to feel or relate to others.

> Technocentered people tend to be highly motivated and eager to adapt to the new technology. Unwittingly, however, they begin to adopt a mindset that mirrors the computer itself. Signs of the technocentered state include a high degree of factual thinking, poor access to feelings, an insistence on efficiency and speed, a lack of empathy for others, and a low tolerance for the ambiguities of human behavior and communication.[15]

In some cases, spouses have reported that their technostressed partners began to view them almost as machines. The wife of a director of computer services for a large bank recalls that when she first met her spouse he was a warm, sensitive person. Today he has no close friends, and his only recreational activity is watching television. He has no patience for the easy exchange of informal conversation. He displays many of the symptoms of technostress.[16]

Eliminating technostress is always a cooperative venture. Organizational leaders must implement a humane policy regarding the introduction and use of computer technology. They must recognize and plan for the process of adaptation that people will go through. (More will be said about management's role later in this chapter.) To avoid becoming a technocentered person we must engage in some honest self-appraisal. Do those of us who work with computers find it more difficult to deal with humans? Are we losing our sensitivity to the needs and feelings of others? Are we less patient with those around us? We must be alert to the warning signs of technostress.

Warning Signs of Too Much Stress

Because of our ability to adapt to increasing levels of stress, we may not always be aware of the amount of pressure we are under. Over short periods of time, stress is seldom damaging. However, over extended periods and in very intense circumstances, it can be harmful, creating numerous medical problems including lower back pains, headaches, coronary problems, and cancer (see Table 14.2). Among the psychological problems that can result from too much stress are anxiety, depression, irritability, loss of appetite, reduced interest in personal relationships, and paranoia.

Table 14.2 **Physical Warning Signals of Too Much Stress**

Pounding of the heart	Chronic pain in the neck or lower back
Dryness of the throat and mouth	
Chronic fatigue, with no apparent physical cause	Vomiting or nausea, with no apparent physical cause
Trembling and nervous tics	Stomach pain
High-pitched nervous laughter	Decreased or increased appetite
Stuttering and other speech problems not usually apparent	Nightmares
	Overpowering urge to cry or run and hide
Inability to concentrate	
Insomnia	Difficulty breathing
Frequent urination	Constipation
Diarrhea and cramping	Chest pains, with no apparent physical cause
Irregular or missed menstrual periods.	

Stress does not attack only high-powered executives. Although executives may be exposed to more stress-producing situations than others, they generally have the authority to do something about the problems. Employees who are subject to heavy demands but who have the authority to correct problems are often less stressed than those with fewer responsibilities but no authority to implement solutions.

Supervisors need to be aware of the warning signs of too much stress in themselves or in their employees.[17]

1. An increase in working long hours or an increase in tardiness and absenteeism.
2. Difficulty in making decisions.
3. An increasing number of careless mistakes.
4. Problems interacting and getting along with others.
5. Focusing on mistakes and personal failures.

A long-term pattern of such occurrences suggests a person is overly stressed. The psychological and physical disorders that may result can cause low productivity and lost work days.

Thinking/Learning Starter

1. Total your stress potential points on the Life Events Scale for Measuring Stress (Table 14.1). Do you have any of the physical warning signs of stress listed in Table 14.2? List them and explain how you are attempting to counter these symptoms.
2. Identify a friend or colleague who has recently exhibited strange or uncharacteristic behavior. What high-scoring events on the Life Events Scale might he or she have experienced? Are there any items on the scale that might explain that person's behavior? Explain.

Counteracting the Effects of Stress: A Personal Approach

When we are faced with stressful situations, our adrenal glands release **adrenalin** to prepare us for instant action. Heart rate and blood pressure shoot up, and blood rushes to the muscles where it will be needed for a physical fight. In today's world, fighting is rarely an option; the body is prepared for a physical response when such a response isn't possible. Yet it takes time for the body to return to normal. For instance, it takes four to six hours to burn off the adrenalin created in the two to four seconds following a startling noise. The longer the adrenalin remains in the blood stream, the more damage can be done to the heart, blood vessels, and vital organs. Even though

"I'll have to take a rain-check. Things are piling up here." (© by Vietor)

stress causes a physical response, you can take steps to alleviate your body's reactions to it.

Gaining Control   Stress often occurs when people feel they do not have control over their lives. In many cases, planning ahead is all that is needed to avoid a stressful situation. If a deadline is coming up, map a plan of action that will prevent a crisis situation. Structure your long-term goals just out of reach but not so far out of sight that they add stress instead of lead you in the direction you want to go. Too much stress is often the result of a mismatch between your expectations and your current environment. You can regain control by changing either one. Or sometimes you simply have to learn to accept a situation instead of resist. The fact remains, you *can* choose. You can recognize your own limitations, learn when to pull back, and rearrange your schedule to allow for quiet time and activities outside the job. Take control of your life, but eliminate artificial controls such as smoking, drugs, and alcohol. By only dealing with the symptoms and not the causes of stress, these outside controls leave you right back where you started.

Nutrition   The food you eat can play a critical role in helping you manage stress. Health experts agree that the typical American diet—high in saturated fats, refined sugar, additives, caffeine, and even too much protein—is exactly the wrong menu for coping with stress. The U.S. Senate Select Committee on Nutrition and Human Needs has advised cutting down on fatty meats, dairy products, eggs, sweets, and salt. Fatty deposits can build up in the arteries, forming plaque. When stress increases the blood pressure, this plaque can tear away, damaging the arteries. Too much salt or caffeine stimulates the heart. Refined sugar acts first as a stimulant and then a depressant to the central nervous system. The committee encourages greater consumption of fresh fruits, vegetables, whole grains, poultry, and fish. Eating the right foods in the proper balance can replenish the vitamins and minerals the body loses when under stress and can also have a calming effect on your nervous system.

Exercise An effective exercise program can "burn off" the adrenalin and other harmful chemicals that build up in your bloodstream as a result of a prolonged reaction to stress. Most people have a favorite form of exercise: jogging, tennis, golf, racquetball, or walking. Table 14.3 lists some of the most common forms of exercise and the number of calories they burn per hour. However, the effect of exercise on stress is minimal unless the regimen is fairly extensive and regular. No matter how strenuous the program, exercising once a week is just not enough. Exercise at least three times a week for

Table 14.3 Exercise and Weight Control

	Activity	Calories/Hour	Time Needed to Burn 2,000 Calories
Good	Skating (moderate)	345	5 hrs. 48 min.
	Walking (4½ mph)	401	5 hrs.
	Tennis (moderate)	419	4 hrs. 45 min.
	Canoeing (4 mph)	426	4 hrs. 41 min.
Better	Swimming (crawl, 45 yards/min)	529	3 hrs. 47 min.
	Skating (vigorous)	531	3 hrs. 45 min.
	Downhill skiing	585	3 hrs. 25 min.
	Handball	591	3 hrs. 23 min.
	Tennis (vigorous)	591	3 hrs. 23 min.
	Squash	630	3 hrs. 10 min.
	Running (5.5 mph)	651	3 hrs. 4 min.
	Bicycling (13 mph)	651	3 hrs. 4 min.
Best	Cross-country skiing (5 mph)	709	2 hrs. 50 min.
	Karate	778	2 hrs. 34 min.
	Running (7 mph)	847	2 hrs. 22 min.

These figures are for a 152-lb. person. If you weigh more, you'll burn up more calories in the same time; if you weigh less you'll burn fewer.

Source: "New Rx for a Healthier Heart: 2000 Calories of Sweat a Week," *Executive Fitness Newsletter* (Emmaus, Pa.: Rodale Press, 1978). P. EF–243. Reprinted by permission.

An effective exercise program can "burn off" the adrenalin and other harmful chemicals that build up in your bloodstream as a result of prolonged stress. (Photo by Ellis Herwig, The Picture Cube)

at least twenty minutes. Most important, the exercise program you choose must be fun. Otherwise, you will probably abandon it after a few weeks. John Lawrie, president of Applied Psychology, Inc., recommends a "stress recess" at least once a week. This "recess" may or may not include strenuous exercise (he chooses fishing). The object is to remove yourself from the stressors of every day. Once you have determined which activity you will pursue during your stress recess, decide which day of the week it would do you the most good.

Mental Relaxation According to many physicians and human behavior researchers, the stress response to events is one we *learn*. Individuals can *unlearn* this response by acquiring techniques of **mental relaxation**. Dr. Mary Asterita of the Indiana University School of Medicine says, "In the same way you have learned to speed up your biochemical processes when aroused or alerted, you can learn to slow down the processes and return your body to a normal, balanced state."[18]

Relaxation techniques that Dr. Asterita and others recommend to employees include deep, rhythmical breathing, visualization exercises, and guided meditations. They have found that the nervous system cannot tell the difference between a real and a vividly imagined experience. If an individual visualizes a relaxing scene strongly enough, the nervous system will believe that the experience is actually occurring. Blood pressure drops, breathing slows down, and the fight or flight reaction recedes.

The corporate office of Converse Inc. in Wilmington, Massachusetts, is just one of many organizations that provide in-house seminars to teach personnel how to use mental relaxation techniques.[19] Some organizations have special soundproof rooms with slides of quiet scenery projected on a movie screen. Other organizations encourage employees to take classes in yoga or meditation. The programs teach people how to take advantage of the mind's natural tranquilizers.

Emotional Expression   Stress can trigger two of your strongest emotions, anger and fear. These emotions must be given a healthy outlet, especially during times of change. Often you will feel better just by having someone listen to your concerns: everyone needs emotional support and a chance to vent their feelings. The best listeners are usually those who have an understanding of the nature of your work but who are not directly associated with it. In some cases you may want to consult a psychotherapist. Psychotherapy is no longer considered shameful, and it need not be time consuming or expensive. Constructive self-disclosure is often healthy when you discuss situations as they happen and attempt to describe your feelings and emotions accurately. By selecting the right time, place, and listener, ventilating your emotions could offset the detrimental physical effects of stress.

Regardless of your physical condition, stress can harm—and even kill— you when you choose not to take control of your life and your body. Stress can have great effects on your physical and psychological well-being, and you cannot assume that you will be aware of dangerous stress levels as they build up. The long-term effects of stress are much like many cancers that do not make themselves evident until extensive damage has resulted. Some people hold up well under stress for extended periods; others do not. But everyone should make the effort to put stressful situations into their proper perspective.

Thinking/Learning Starter

1. What are you doing personally to counter the effects of the stress you are under right now?
2. Is there something you would like to do but are not doing to help you cope with stress? Why are you procrastinating?

Counteracting the Effects of Stress: An Organizational Approach

Unresolved personal problems will eventually have a serious impact on the job performance and well-being of from 10 to 15 percent of any given work force.[20] Personal and professional life transitions annually affect 16 percent of all full-time workers. Employees experiencing life transitions typically

Table 14.4 National Health Care Expenditures

	Total Expenses (billions)	Percentage of GNP
1960	26.7	5.3
1970	74.7	7.5
1980	248.0	9.5
1983	355.0	10.8
1984	387.4	10.6

Source: *1986 Statistical Abstract of the United States.*

enter into a four- to six-month period of adjustment during which they produce less than half of their usual output. Corporate America is now beginning to pay closer attention to the dynamics of these transitions and the resulting $80 to $90 billion annual losses.[21]

Employee assistance programs (EAPs) have proven to be the most direct, effective, legally acceptable, and humane means of reducing these costs. These programs often include **wellness programs**, such as physical fitness, drug and alcohol abuse prevention and treatment, nutrition, and quality of work life improvement.[22]

Employers are realizing more than ever before that conditions on the job, particularly when they involve major changes in working conditions or in the corporate culture, can cause high levels of stress in employees. In order to reduce losses caused by illness and absenteeism and to increase productivity, many organizations are now beginning to promote actively "wellness programs" to improve the physical and mental fitness of their employees.

American business pays $80 million each year in health-insurance premiums.[23] As Table 14.4 indicates, expenditures on health care costs are steadily rising. However, medical costs of companies offering health and wellness clinics are 25 percent lower than those of companies that do not provide such programs. Wellness clinics also increase employee productivity and reduce absenteeism by as much as 17 percent.[24] The Lockheed Missiles and Space Company estimates that in five years it saved $1 million in life insurance costs through its wellness programs.[25] But wellness programs are not just for giant corporations. The fewer employees a company has, the greater the relative impact of a disabling illness of even one key worker.

Physical Fitness Programs   From jogging trails in small towns to multimillion dollar gymnasiums at major corporate centers, the new emphasis on health and fitness programs in business is not likely to fade. The Control Data Corporation reports that those who do not exercise cost the company $115 more per year in health care costs than those involved in moderate or vigorous exercise. A study by the Canadian Fitness and Lifestyle Project

This fitness center at General Electric's aircraft engine plant has been very popular with employees. (Photo courtesy of General Electric Co.)

showed company fitness programs saved $233 per employee each year. In Dallas, Texas, teachers who enrolled in a fitness program took an average of three fewer sick days per year, at a savings of $452,000 in substitute pay alone.[26] More and more companies throughout the country are instituting physical fitness programs for their employees, not only because employees enjoy them but because they are cost effective.

Item: 10,000 production workers at the General Electric Aircraft Engine Business Group in Evandale, Ohio, are enjoying a new 35,000 square-foot corporate fitness center that features an indoor track, swimming pool, and exercise equipment.

Item: More than half the workers at Westinghouse Elevator Company in Short Hills, New Jersey, participate two or more times a week in the company's fitness program.

Item: Hourly workers as well as executives at Mannington Mills in Salem, New Jersey, are using a new $2 million sports complex and physical fitness center that also provides baby-sitting services for families.

Organizations too small to invest in private physical fitness facilities make arrangements with nearby health clubs where employees can work out, mostly at company expense, and sometimes on company time.

While companies benefit financially, the employees benefit from improved muscle tone, loss of body fat, a more optimistic outlook, improved sleep, increased energy, and decreased stress, as well as a reduced risk of heart disease. For some exployees, enrollment in an exercise program becomes the stimulus for other life changes. They may stop smoking, reduce their alcohol consumption, or start eating healthier foods. And fitness planners believe that the camaraderie and enthusiasm these programs generate help management-employee relations better than any number of memos and conferences ever could.

Drug- and Alcohol-Abuse Programs   Not long ago, people caught drinking or using drugs on the job would be fired automatically. Today, organizations are realizing that pressure on the job can encourage alcohol and drug abuse as workers seek to cope with stress. Norfolk & Western Railway established a preventive program after discovering that alcohol-related problems—absenteeism, accidents, and mistakes—were costing the company nearly $8 million annually. Other organizations employ counselors trained in alcohol and drug abuse control programs to help employees. These sessions concentrate on early detection of stress-related problems and on helping individuals find healthier ways to cope with stress.

According to the National Institute of Alcohol Abuse and Alcoholism (NIAAA), occupational alcoholism programs are among the most successful of all alcoholism programs. The recovery rate of alcoholic workers has been between 50 to 60 percent of cases treated, and many programs report success rates as high as 70 to 80 percent.[27] The National Council on Alcoholism (NCA) has for many years been a leader in employee assistance programs. Approximately three-fifths of the employees referred to an employee assistance program will have alcohol or other drug dependency problems. The remainder are people experiencing unresolved grief, financial or family difficulties, emotional problems, or stress of impending retirement, problems that may lead to alcohol or drug abuse. Currently, over 5,000 organizations have implemented the NCA employee assistance program.

A pattern of changed behavior may indicate that a worker is abusing drugs or alcohol. For instance, a normally calm individual may become angry very quickly. Compared with past performance, the work of alcohol- or drug-dependent employees may become sloppy or erratic. Executives may be reluctant to take on more responsibility. Drug-dependent employees are often late to work or absent on Mondays and Fridays. As drugs are expensive, employees may experience persistent money problems. An unusually high use of health insurance benefits may also indicate a drug or alcohol problem. Once an employee is identified as having a drug- or alcohol-related problem, the EAP usually begins with two steps. First, the employee is referred to the appropriate psychologist or counseling staff. Second, the employee is given one or more warning interviews in which he or she is given the choice of continuing in the EAP (which may consist of individual or peer-group counseling or many other forms of treatment), referral to an outside agency, or accepting the consequences of unacceptable job performance.[28] No matter what the process, however, the employee's confidentiality is always ensured.

A growing number of organizations are offering well-balanced meals in the company cafeteria. (Northwestern Mutual Life photo)

Nutritional Programs   Unless an organization has a full-time food service for all employees, it is almost impossible to monitor the diets of individual employees. Even when the company cafeteria offers well-balanced meals, employees generally eat breakfast and the evening meal at home. While most organizations understand the value of a balanced diet, their options for improving employees' dietary habits are limited.

The most effective way to get employees interested in improving their diets is to provide in-house workshops taught by nutritionists who can teach employees the right way to eat. Keeping individual daily eating logs can show employees how much sugar, salt, and fat they are consuming. Speakers from Weight Watchers, Nutri/System, and other established weight reduction programs can also be of help.

In addition, organizations can remove vending machines that sell candy and other unhealthy snacks and replace them with machines that offer fruit, whole-grain crackers, and other nutritious foods. Coffee pots and coffee machines can dispense only decaffeinated coffee, and fruit juices can replace soda pop. When someone joins the organization, coworkers and managers can make clear that birthday celebrations, holidays, and special occasions do not need to include doughnuts and cakes laden with refined sugar. Researchers estimate that as many as 10 million Americans suffer from reactions to sugar such as fatigue, inability to concentrate, irritability, and anxiety.[29] Health-conscious organizations can help ensure that human relations problems aren't exacerbated by poor nutrition.

Quality-of-Work-Life Programs   A movement designed to achieve a higher quality of work life for employees and increased profitability for employers is underway in America. Employers interested in improving the **quality of work life** strive to create an organization that achieves a satisfactory balance of business, human, and social needs.[30] They believe that workers are human resources to be developed, not simply used. Improving the quality of work life brings employees, unions, and management together for their mutual benefit by involving all in the decision-making process. This involvement gives employees more of a voice in the changes that are occurring around them. The concept of improving the work environment has been discussed for generations. Walter Reuther, former president of United Auto Workers, said in 1960: "I think in addition to earning your bread and butter, that work ought to give you a sense of participation in the creative process."[31] Today, organizations are implementing quality-of-work-life programs at a record rate.

Each organization has its own way of developing its program. Some are very structured and include quality circle or employee participation groups. Others are simpler, offering a suggestion box and providing incentives for ideas that save the company money and reduce worker stress, such as suggestions on how to reduce noise pollution or dangerous working conditions. Quality circles point out that the work is too routine and needs to be varied. For instance, people who work with computers full time often report physical symptoms such as exhaustion, headaches, eye strain, and neck and back pains. Groups might suggest a reduction of uninterrupted work periods, freedom to take short breaks when needed, better office lighting, and adjustable furniture and terminals that will help reduce the side effects of daily computer work. Productivity increases, and the stress of the employee is reduced.

As employees become involved in making changes in their work life, they often lose their resistance to change and the stress that occurs when changes are implemented by management without worker input. The morale and productivity of organizations in the next decade may very well hinge on how well organizations ease employees into these changes.

Summary

Change is a necessary part of individual and organizational growth and development. Accepting this concept is the key to managing change in today's turbulent environment.

People tend to resist change because they feel inadequate to meet the challenge, feel their security is threatened, fear the unknown, mistrust those initiating the change, or lack an ability to see the larger picture. Individuals can actively adapt to change by using their values as a guideline for decision making and achievement of goals.

Any change produces tension or stress. Although many people thrive on stress, too much can cause physical or psychological harm. Technostress, the inability to cope with the new computer technology in a healthy manner, is the newest threat to individuals and organizations. Individuals can counteract the effects of stress by restructuring their life style, eating a balanced diet, exercising regularly, taking time for mental relaxation, and effectively expressing their emotions. Organizations can help employees cope with stress by providing employee assistance programs, including physical fitness, drug and alcohol abuse prevention, nutrition training, and quality-of-work-life improvements.

Key Terms

transition	adrenalin
future shock	mental relaxation
fight or flight syndrome	employee assistance program
active adaptability	wellness program
stress	quality of work life
technostress	

Review Questions

1. What are three work-related changes most employees face?
2. Explain the relationship between technostress and future shock.
3. Explain how people can actively adapt to change.
4. List four of the reasons people resist change.
5. Under what circumstances do many organizations find it necessary to change?
6. List some of the warning signs of too much stress.
7. How can physical exercise and mental relaxation counteract the effects of stress?
8. Describe the most effective way or ways organizations can counteract stress in their employees.
9. Why should organizations try to eliminate worker stress?
10. How can individuals adapt their life-styles to deal with too much stress?

Case 14.1

Bye-Bye Bell System[32]

The biggest organizational change in history took place on January 1, 1984, when the Bell System—also known as AT&T—divested itself of seven regional telephone companies. The regional companies are now separate and independent firms that provide local telephone service. The new streamlined AT&T sells long-distance service and telephone equipment.

AT&T's employees were aware that the breakup was to occur, but few were able to foresee its full effects. Even on the surface, the change was drastic: On January 1, some 600,000 former AT&T employees began working for the new regional companies. Many returned to their workplaces to find that blue or yellow tape had been placed across the floor; those on one side of the tape worked for AT&T, while those on the other side were employed by a regional company. The two groups now wore different identification badges and could not share facilities in the same building; people who had formerly worked together and exchanged work information could no longer do so, by order of the Federal Communications Commission.

At another level, it seemed to many employees that the entire working atmosphere had changed. AT&T had been a stable and profitable firm whose employees were generally well paid and secure in their jobs. But with divestiture came a concern for competitive effectiveness and the bottom line. To reduce operating costs, executive salaries were frozen and AT&T sought wage concessions from its unions; thousands of positions were eliminated through early retirement, normal attrition, and some firing. Reorganizations resulted in increased responsibilities for many managers, entirely new responsibilities for others, relocation for some, and a general uneasiness about what the future would bring. According to one regional executive, the changes and regroupings came so fast that he didn't know who his boss was from one day to the next.

Not only jobs were in jeopardy, but decision-making as well. Before the breakup, regional company executives based their decisions on AT&T policies and guidelines. After the breakup, they were left without any outside guidance at all. Moreover, they were now forced to deal with competition from a variety of new telecommunications firms. Costs, prices, development and production lags, and the market for their products became important considerations—for the first time, in many cases. Some managers found that their previous experience was close to worthless, that they had to work by an almost completely new set of rules.

Two researchers had, coincidentally, been studying stress and stress resistance at Illinois Bell since well before the breakup. They found that anticipation of the divestiture, as well as the change itself, produced a great increase in stress. Those executives who were best able to cope with the change saw it as a challenge. However, many executives believed they were threatened by the change and suffered a variety of mental and physical symptoms.

Questions
1. Which basic characteristics or elements of the AT&T breakup probably gave rise to the most stress? Why?
2. How could AT&T and the regional companies have helped their employees to cope with the change?
3. How could individual AT&T employees have helped themselves to cope with the change?

Case 14.2

Wellness Programs Start Small[33]

Three years ago, Plaskolite, Inc., a medium-sized producer of plastics, began an employee wellness program. At first, the program was mainly a cash bonus plan: bonuses were given to employees who participated actively in sports and to those who didn't smoke. Now the program includes an in-plant weight room and periodic fitness tests, as well as smoking-cessation, weight-loss, and stress-management clinics.

The goal of the program is to reduce the company's medical costs over the long term, by increasing employee fitness. Monetary benefits were not expected for perhaps ten years, when the effects of the program would show up in lower incidences of such "lifestyle diseases" as diabetes and heart attacks. Yet Plaskolite's insurance has already decreased, and the fitness tests show continual improvement. In addition, the firm has found that its wellness program is of help in both recruiting and employee relations. Other organizations with wellness programs have reported that they also have experienced reduced absenteeism, increased morale, and increased productivity.

Most wellness programs involve three stages:

1. An *informational* stage, in which the benefits of fitness are carefully explained to employees
2. A *motivational* stage, in which employees are encouraged to participate in the program
3. A *behavioral* stage, in which employees do participate and find that, as a result, they feel healthier and actually are in better physical shape

The cost of the program, and of each stage, depends on its extent—and that obviously varies from organization to organization. But even the smallest firm can post informational notices regarding wellness, offer small cash bonuses for participation (as Plaskolite did at first), and follow through to ensure that employees' fitness goals are met. (One small firm gives exercise clothing to employees who meet their goals. Another pays part of the cost of health club membership.)

Questions
1. Suppose you were asked to devise an inexpensive wellness program for a real-estate agency with about 25 employees. How would you determine which areas of fitness to work on first?
2. How would you implement the three stages of the program in the areas of (a) physical fitness and (b) smoking cessation?
3. How would you justify the cost of the program to the owner of the agency?

Notes

1. John M. Broder, "Business Undergoing Wrenching Changes," *Roanoke Times & World-News*, December 1, 1985, p. F-5.
2. Craig Brod, *Technostress: The Human Cost of the Computer Revolution* (Reading, Mass.: Addison-Wesley, 1984), p. 2.
3. Richard Bolles, "The 'Warp' in the Way We Perceive Our Life in the World of Work," *Training and Development Journal*, November 1981, p. 22.
4. Jerry Main, "Work Won't Be the Same Again," *Fortune*, June 28, 1982, pp. 58–59.
5. Craig Brod, *Technostress*, p. 5.
6. Theresa Engstrom, "How Do You Change Employees? Let Them Experiment," *Personal Computing*, December 1982, pp. 128–129.
7. "Does Change Trigger a Need for Training?" *Training/HRD*, February 1981, p. 30.
8. Terrence E. Deal and Alan A. Kennedy, *Corporate Culture: The Rites and Rituals of Corporate Life* (Reading, Mass.: Addison-Wesley, 1982), pp. 159–161.
9. "Can John Young Redesign Hewlett-Packard?" *Business Week*, December 6, 1982, pp. 72–78.
10. Vandra L. Huber, "Managing Stress for Increased Productivity," *Supervisory Management*, December 1981, pp. 2 and 3.
11. John Lawrie, "Three Steps to Reducing Stress," *Supervisory Management*, October 1985, pp. 8 and 9.
12. Craig Brod, *Technostress*, p. 16.
13. Ibid., p. 30.
14. Ibid., p. 37.
15. Ibid., p. 17.
16. Craig Brod, "Technostress," *Review*, September 1984, p. 28.
17. Shane Premeaux, Wayne Mondy, and Arthur Sharplin, "Stress and the First-Line Supervisor," *Supervisory Management*, July 1985, p. 37.
18. "Mind Games That Melt Away Stress," *Executive Fitness Newsletter*, November 27, 1982.
19. Linda Standke, "Advantage of Training People to Handle Stress," *Training/HRD*, February 1979, p. 25.
20. Richard Sprague, "The High Cost of Personal Transitions," *Training and Development Journal*, October 1984, pp. 61–62.
21. Ibid.
22. Ibid.
23. Richard H. Lambert, "Good Health Means Good Business," *DIY Retailing*, February 1985, p. 9.
24. Kim Wright Wiley, "Corporate Fitness Programs, Encouraging Employee Health," *Piedmont Airlines*, September 1985, p. 81.
25. Jane Brody, "Companies Promote Better Health Among Employees," *Roanoke Time & World News*, p. C-1.
26. Ibid.

27. Lin Grensing, "Driving Them Away from Drink," *Training*, December 1984, pp. 123-125.

28. Ibid.

29. Stuart Berger, "Food Can Change Your Mood,"*Parade Magazine*, December 23, 1984, p. 13.

30. U.S. Department of Labor, "A Conference on Quality of Work Life: Issues Affecting the State-of-the-Art," May 1984, p. 1.

31. Saul Rubinstein, "QWL, the Union, the Specialist and Employment Security," *Training and Development Journal*, March 1984, p. 82.

32. For more information, see *Across the Board*, July-August 1984, pp. 37–42; *Business Week*, May 13, 1985, pp. 50, 52; and *IEEE Spectrum*, November 1985, pp. 97–103.

33. For more information, see Nation's Business, March 1986, p. 65; *Risk Management*, June 1985, p. 85; and *Inc.*, February 1986, p. 101.

Suggested Readings

Benson, Herbert. *The Relaxation Response*. New York: Morrow, 1975.

Blanchard, Kenneth, D.W. Edington, and Majorie Blanchard. *The One Minute Manager Gets Fit*. New York: William Morrow, 1986.

Brod, Craig. *Technostress: The Human Cost of the Computer Revolution*. Reading, Mass.: Addison-Wesley, 1984.

Drucker, Peter. *Changing World of the Executive*. New York: Times Books, 1982.

Lakein, Alan. *How to Get Control of Your Time and Your Life*. New York: New American Library, 1973.

Mackenzie, R. Alec. *The Time Trap—Managing Your Way Out*. New York: American Management Associations, 1972.

Robbins, Paula. *Successful Midlife Career Change*. New York: American Management Associations, 1980.

Schafer, Walt. *Managing Stress*. New York: International Dialogue Press, 1982.

Sharpe, Robert, and David Lewis. *Stress: How to Make It Work to Your Advantage*. New York: Warner, 1977.

Chapter 15

Coping with Prejudice and Discrimination

Chapter Preview

After studying this chapter, you will be able to
1. Understand how prejudicial attitudes are formed.
2. Realize the impact of prejudice on one's self-concept.
3. Discuss the term *minority* and identify the minority groups who are victims of discrimination.
4. Describe the more subtle forms of discrimination that often surface in an organization.
5. Understand the various levels and the process of discrimination.
6. Identify some of the ways individuals, organizations, and society can combat prejudice and discrimination.

At age 53, Lewis Ellis became the oldest rookie policeman ever to join the Los Angeles police department. New departmental regulations permit older persons to enter the academy. (AP/Wide World Photos)

Lewis Ellis is a fifty-three-year-old grandfather who does one hundred push-ups a day; he is also the oldest rookie policeman ever to join the Los Angeles police department. At his academy graduation ceremony, he joined 117 other cadets averaging half his age. His family led the crowd of seven hundred people in sustained applause. Wayne Ellis, one of his children, said his father's success did not surprise him. He said his father's philosophy has always been "if you want to do something, go ahead."[1]

Today, a fifty-three-year-old person can compete for entrance into the Los Angeles Police Academy. Just a few years ago, departmental regulations would have barred Lewis Ellis or anyone else over age fifty from entry into the academy. A bias against hiring and fully utilizing the skills of older workers still exists in many organizations.

Age discrimination is but one of several forms of prejudice in the working world today. Discrimination can effectively exclude minorities from employment opportunities, higher education, and training programs. Racial or ethnic tension within a work force can affect productivity and undermine team-building efforts.

The Nature of Prejudice

Prejudice means to prejudge. Throughout life we judge people on the basis of inborn traits—race, sex, ethnic background, physical features—and on acquired traits—education, occupation, lifestyle, customs. Attitudes in favor of or against people that are based solely on these traits are prejudices. Rather than treat others as unique individuals, prejudiced people tend to think in terms of stereotypes. **Stereotypes** are widely held beliefs about what various racial and ethnic groups, socioeconomic classes, men, women, people living in a particular geographic region, etc., are "really like."

For example, a white, male, recent Harvard MBA graduate applies for a management position with an ultraconservative eastern organization. Also being interviewed for the job is a black, male, state university graduate with ten years of management experience in a similar organization. The managers interviewing applicants have traditional attitudes toward Harvard graduates and against black people. Actual on-the-job experience of the black man may not outweigh the stereotype of the white, Harvard MBA. Stereotypes can form prejudiced attitudes for or against a person regardless of other elements that prove the stereotype invalid.

Stereotypes are not always negative. They provide some predictability in our lives, reduce the uncertainty of dealing with other people, and shield us from shock because we see others acting as we expect them to.[2] But people often use stereotypes in negative ways. Stereotypes are often based on a kernel of truth, or on real experiences in dealing with others; yet they are resistant to change because people more readily believe information that confirms their stereotypes rather than challenges them. For instance, you may have learned as a child that all minority workers are basically lazy, not serious about a career, or unable to handle executive-level decisions. Your experience with one such worker may reinforce your stereotype, and you may discount or not remember many other experiences that prove the stereotype invalid. Perhaps women in your organization are considered too emotional, unable to do quantitative analysis, or less committed to careers than men. Do you accept this stereotype, or do you challenge yourself to see how the stereotype doesn't always fit reality? Unchallenged stereotypes can hinder employees' ability to collaborate effectively and equally to get a job done. Healthy and productive organizations are possible only when human relations are free from confining stereotypes.

How Prejudicial Attitudes Are Formed

Three major factors contribute to the development of prejudice: contamination, ethnocentrism, and economic conditions.

Contamination   In Chapter 9, the concept of Parent-Child-Adult ego states was introduced as a model for how we learn attitudes and behaviors. **Contamination** is the transactional analysis (TA) term used to describe what happens when these ego states are not kept separate but overlap, or "contaminate," one another.[3] Prejudice is the result of the Parent ego state overlapping the Adult, as shown in Figure 15.1.

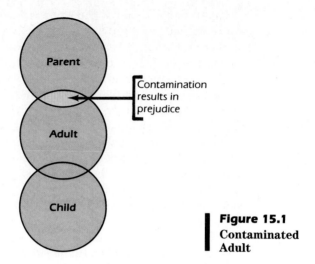

The process of contamination begins when a child learns from family, friends, and others how different racial, ethnic, religious, or other groups are to be treated. The child accepts the attitudes and beliefs of those in positions of authority. The problem arises when the child becomes an adult and also accepts these attitudes and beliefs without testing their validity against experience and new knowledge. This contaminated adult continues to believe what was learned as a child. As noted in Chapter 7, Celanese Fibers, a North Carolina-based firm, held several workshops to help ease racial tensions in the company. Both blacks and whites in the workshops were surprised at the similarity of their parents' messages to them as children. Both parent groups taught their children not to trust members of the other race.[4]

Contamination also occurs when our experience with one person colors our attitude toward that individual's entire group. For example, employees on strike see their company bring in Asian laborers as replacements in order to break the strike. The striking employees are thereafter apt to regard *all* Asians as potential "scabs," or strikebreakers. A manager who finds one younger employee negligent or careless is apt to generalize these attitudes to include all younger workers.

Ethnocentrism The tendency to regard our own culture or nation as better or more "correct" than others is called **ethnocentrism**. The word is derived from *ethnic*, meaning a group united by similar customs, characteristics, race, or other common factors, and *center*. When ethnocentrism is present, the standards and values of our own culture are used as a yardstick to measure the worth of other cultures.

Nearly all societies are ethnocentric to some degree. For example, in the United States and most Western European countries, punctuality in business matters is highly valued. In South America and parts of the Middle East, business appointments are more flexible. A meeting set for five o'clock may not begin until seven or eight. In some Arab countries, business people may have to wait a day or two before an appointment is kept. Americans can easily interpret this trait as an example of other nations' inefficiency rather than as an alternative way of doing business.

Ethnocentrism is often perpetuated by **cultural conditioning**. As children, we are raised to fit into a particular culture. We are conditioned to respond to various situations as we saw others in our culture react. Some cultures value emotional control and avoid open conflicts and discussions of such personal topics as money or values. Other cultures encourage a bolder, more open expression of feelings and values and accept greater levels of verbal confrontation. Tension can result when people's cultural expectations clash in the workplace.

It is natural to enjoy being with others who share similar values, goals, and interests. Every organization, however, brings together individuals from various cultures, and each culture's prejudices are brought into the workplace.

Human relations challenges can arise even when strong cultural differences aren't present in a workplace. Everyone has a basic need to be a part of a group. In a workplace, people can develop strong group identities. Each group tries to maintain its own status and privileges against the intrusion of other groups, or outsiders. Salespeople, for example, may consider their function more important than the work of other groups. Professional groups may consider the support staff—secretaries, mail-room personnel, receptionists—as less skilled and less important to the firm. Such groups often foster a "we" vs. "they" attitude. These groups begin their own cycle of prejudice and discrimination that can harm the effectiveness of an organization.

Economic Factors   When the economy goes through a recession or depression, and housing, jobs, and other necessities become scarce, people's prejudices against other groups increase. If enough prejudice is built up against a particular group, members of that group will be barred from competing for jobs. For example, in the early 1980s a number of relocated Vietnamese tried to establish a fishing community along the coast of Texas. This created conflict with American fishermen who viewed the competition as a threat to their own economic security. Several of the Vietnamese boats were burned, and fights broke out between the two groups. Eventually, the courts intervened, and the two sides reached an uneasy truce.

Today there exists a tremendous increase of Asian and Mexican immigrants competing with Americans for entry-level jobs. Sometimes a union will try to keep these workers out in order to give their members a better chance to obtain employment. If immigrants cannot get into a union, they are not able to compete in more highly paid, union-dominated markets. Each wave of immigrants to the United States has encountered this type of discrimination.

In some cases employers have used prejudice to keep workers divided against one another, allowing employers to keep wages low. Employers who threaten to hire immigrant labor at lower wages keep employees from organizing for better wages and benefits. Low wages and lack of job security in hard economic times produce low employee morale and deepen prejudicial attitudes toward immigrants.

Prejudice based on economic factors has its roots in people's basic survival needs. As a result, it is very hard to eliminate. Until the economy can provide jobs for everyone, competition for work will continue to foster many types of prejudice.

The Impact of Prejudice on Self-Concept

Prejudice damages the self-concept of both the victim and the person who maintains the prejudice. As noted earlier, a person's self-concept affects performance and sets the limits of success and failure. Many victims of continued prejudice tend to hate themselves rather than the group discriminating against them. Wendell Berry, a noted black author, refers to this crippling effect of prejudice as "the hidden wound."[5] He noticed that many blacks tried to imitate white culture as closely as possible while viewing their own group as undesirable.

Today, various ethnic and racial groups recognize the necessity of combating this destructive effect of prejudice on their self-concept. Many black managerial organizations visit inner-city schools to give students a chance to talk with men and women who are successful in the mainstream culture.[6] Positive role models, although not a complete solution to the problem, can inspire others and instill a sense of pride in their own background and heritage.

How is the self-concept of the person maintaining the prejudice affected? Prejudice can create serious conflict within a person if the attitude is at war with a strongly held value or belief. For example, the shop foreman of one plant prided himself on his team-building skills. He firmly believed that all employees deserved an equal chance to prove themselves and to be part of his work team. That is, until a young Chicano worker was hired. The foreman's parents had been prejudiced against Spanish-speaking people, and the old parental attitudes surfaced in the foreman. He found his prejudice at war with his belief in team building. The internal conflict affected his abilities as a team leader; he found he could no longer treat all workers equally. Such internal conflicts can create feelings of guilt and fear and rob an individual of the power to act from inner harmony.

Researchers have found that prejudice is also related to the amount of insecurity, anxiety, and hostility people experience in their lives.[7] People often project onto others what they do not like or cannot face in themselves. The less they are able to "make something of themselves," the more likely they are to be prejudiced against another group. If you use prejudice to bolster a weak self-concept, you avoid confronting your own weaknesses. You lose the chance to grow and achieve your highest potential. Once people understand they have a great deal to gain in terms of an improved self-concept by giving up their prejudices, they are more likely to change their attitudes.

Thinking/Learning Starters

1. What attitudes did you learn from your parents about groups who were different from your own? Did you find these attitudes to be based on fact? Did you accept them as true or question their validity?
2. What groups have you belonged to that gave you a sense of group identity? How did you feel about those who were not in your group?
3. How is the prejudiced person's self-concept affected by the attitudes he or she holds?

Discrimination

Prejudice has been defined as an attitude. **Discrimination** is behavior based on these attitudes. If, as an employer, you believe that overweight people tend to be lazy, that is an attitude. If you refuse to hire someone simply because the person is overweight, you are engaging in discriminatory behavior.

An individual or group that is discriminated against is denied equal treatment and opportunities afforded to the dominant group. They may be denied employment, promotion, training, or other job-related privileges on the basis of race, lifestyle, religion, or other characteristics that have little or nothing to do with their qualifications for a job. In the United States, much discrimination has been directed at minority groups and women.

Targets of Discrimination

A **minority group** is usually defined as a group smaller in number than the dominant one and marked off by some difference in race, religion, ethnic background, or political persuasion. Blacks, Hispanics, native Americans, socialists, various ethnic groups, and religious groups such as Moslems are examples of commonly recognized minorities in this country. Other minorities may be discriminated against because of their lifestyle or some aspect of their physical appearance. Employees who do not fit the proper "image" of an organization may be risking their opportunities for advancement. Since they have few legal options, overcoming or combating this type of discrimination is often very difficult. Although women are not a minority group in terms of numbers, they often suffer some of the same forms of discrimination and prejudice directed at members of traditionally defined minority groups.

Historically, discrimination against minorities and women was not only accepted but in many cases sanctioned by the government as a necessary part of the social and political structure.[8] It was regarded as essential to support the institution of slavery, the many wars against native Americans, and the restrictive immigration laws passed against particular racial and ethnic groups. In the following section, we will take a look at six groups that are often the targets of discrimination.

Discrimination Based on Sex   This type of discrimination—**sexism**—has been, and continues to be, a major issue. The traditional roles women have held in society have undergone tremendous changes in the past two decades. More and more women are entering the work force not only to supplement the family income but to pursue careers in previously all-male professions. Men have also been examining the roles assigned them by society and are discovering new options for themselves. Chapter 16 is devoted entirely to an in-depth discussion of overcoming sexism in organizations.

Ethnic and Regional Discrimination   Ethnic and cultural groups are identified by their language, customs, religion, traditions, and lifestyles. Most major American cities have many types of ethnic neighborhoods—Polish, Greek, German, Jewish, Irish, Italian, and the like.

Discrimination against ethnic groups, while based somewhat on differences in language, customs, religion, and cultural values, has its roots primarily in economic factors. In the late 1800s and early 1900s, waves of immigrants from various ethnic backgrounds came to the United States. Each group competed for jobs and housing with the groups who had come before them and were more established. Since there were seldom enough jobs to go around, prejudice against the newcomers ran high. In Boston, where thousands of Irish immigrants settled, many help-wanted signs warned "No Irish need apply."

Because the United States is so large, regional differences and preferences can be striking. During the 1976 presidential election, regional preferences were most obvious. The national map was almost literally cut in half, with most western states favoring Ford and most eastern and southeastern states favoring Carter (see Figure 15.2).

Discrimination based on regional differences can be intense. During the Great Depression thousands of people left the Texas-Oklahoma-Arkansas dust bowl and migrated west to California in search of jobs. Like ethnic groups, the "Okies" and "Arkies," as they were called, dressed, acted, and talked differently than the native Californians. Prejudice against these outsiders resulted not only in job discrimination but at times in violent conflict. John Steinbeck's classic novel, *The Grapes of Wrath*, is a moving account of this type of discrimination and its effects on people.

Ethnic and regional minorities have a distinct advantage over racial groups in overcoming employment discrimination. Skin color cannot be changed,

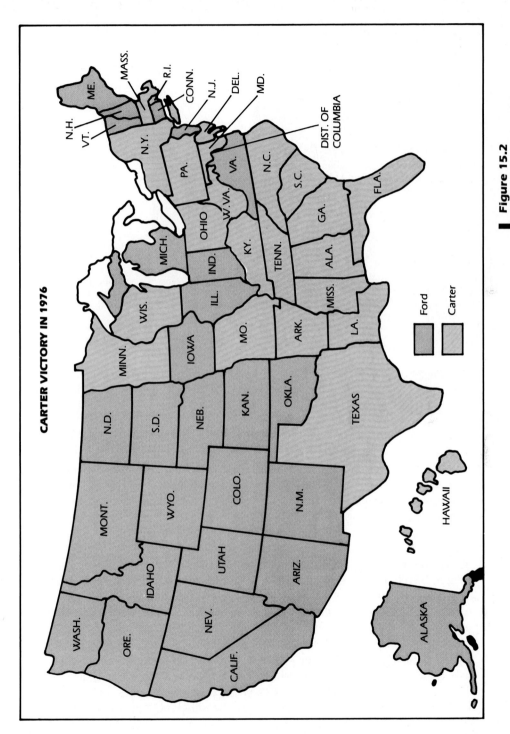

CARTER VICTORY IN 1976

Ford

Carter

Figure 15.2
Regional Preferences During the Carter-Ford Presidential Race, 1976.

Source: AP Wirephoto Chart

Henry Cisneros, popular Hispanic mayor of San Antonio, Texas, provides a good role model for all minorities. His strong work ethic and ability to build personal relationships has contributed to his political success. (Photo courtesy of City of San Antonio)

but people *can* adopt new customs, language, and traditions. Many immigrants accepted the history and traditions of the United States as their own, and some even changed their names to sound more "American." As the differences between immigrants and natives became less distinct, discrimination against them also diminished. (See Figure 15.3 for a comparison of the ethnic make-up of the United States in 1960 and in 1984.)

Religious Discrimination   Even though many of the first settlers came in search of religious freedom, they often refused to grant that same freedom to people of other religions. In this country's predominantly Protestant culture, Catholic and Jewish minorities have been victims of a great deal of discrimination.

Protestant-Catholic wars in Europe left Protestants with a deep mistrust of the Vatican and the power of the pope. The prejudice against Catholics was based not only on theological issues but on the fear that church and state would be too closely aligned. Over the past few decades, much of this prejudice has diminished, although it has not completely disappeared.

Anti-Semitic (anti-Jewish) attitudes constitute one of the oldest forms of religious prejudice in Western culture. For centuries, Jews were forbidden to own property, do business with Christians, marry outside their faith, hold public office, and the like. The few professions left to them included finance, merchandising, farming, and the arts. As with anti-Catholic prejudice, anti-Semitic attitudes have subsided but have not been eradicated.

Racial Discrimination   **Racism** is discrimination based on skin color or other biological traits. This type of discrimination is one of the most difficult to overcome since people cannot change the color of their skin to blend in with dominant groups.

Basically, four racial groups are currently struggling to gain their full place in mainstream U.S. society: blacks, Hispanics, Asians, and native Americans.

Blacks are the largest minority group in the country, numbering some 29 million, or about 12 percent of the total population. As a group they have suffered the most from overt discrimination. Even though the Fourteenth Amendment ended slavery, they continued to be treated as second-class citizens, and the long history of prejudice has created serious inequities in education and employment opportunities for blacks.

Hispanics—Mexican-Americans, Puerto Ricans, Cubans, South Americans, Filipinos, and other Spanish-speaking groups—have also suffered from poor education, lack of job skills, and the language barrier. Many work as migrant farmers or are concentrated in low-paying jobs that offer little opportunity for advancement. Spanish-speaking Americans number approximately 15 million (millions more are in the United States illegally) or about 6.4 percent of the population. By 1990, experts believe that Spanish-speaking Americans will be the nation's largest ethnic group.[9]

In the late 1880s and early 1900s, restrictive immigration laws effectively reduced, and in some cases stopped, the flow of Asians and Pacific islanders into this country. Fewer in number, they posed less of a threat to the dominant culture than did blacks or the Hispanic population. Following the Vietnam War, Asian-Americans flocked to the U.S., accounting for approximately 1.8 percent of the total population by 1985. These 4.1 million new Americans are the latest victims of American prejudices. Asian-Americans are, however, making major strides toward improving their status. Their average income is already higher than the average white family income. They have a lower unemployment rate than whites and are better educated. Among those 25 or older, 32.9 percent complete at least four years of college; the comparable figure for white Americans is 16.2 percent.[10]

At the turn of the twentieth century, native Americans were viewed primarily as an obstacle to westward expansion and as racially and culturally inferior to whites. As the country was settled, many tribes were destroyed and the remainder eventually confined to reservations. Native Americans have made continual efforts to gain control over their political, cultural, and social lives. A new militant spirit among the 1980's generation of native Americans is bringing their struggle for equality to public attention.

The United States Postal Service honored Hispanic Americans with this stamp.

The country's long record of racial discrimination has created gaps in education and employment between whites and minorities that persist to this day. In 1985, 11 percent of Hispanics and 16 percent of blacks—nearly 1 out of 6—were unemployed.[11] The crucial role of employment in securing equal benefits of citizenship has long been recognized. In a report issued by the U.S. Commission on Civil Rights, the commissioners noted:

> The capacity to obtain and hold a "good job" is the traditional test of participation in American society. Steady employment with adequate compensation provides both purchasing power and social status. It develops the capacities, confidence, and self-esteem an individual needs to be a responsible citizen and provides a basis for stable family life.[12]

The courts have also rejected the concept that separate educational facilities for minorities are equal to those for whites and have ordered schools to achieve racially balanced classes. Minorities have long understood the direct link between education and employment. In the 1960s and 1970s, Congress legislated training programs, educational funds, and equal-employment laws to address the problem of discrimination and close the education and skills gap between minorities and whites. Yet, the struggle to overcome the inequities of the past still remains a challenge.

Discrimination Based on Age   **Ageism**, as this form of discrimination is called, can apply to the older worker—forty to seventy—and the younger worker—eighteen to thirty-five.

If you fall into the younger worker category, be aware that employers see two advantages in hiring a young, well-educated employee: (1) young work-

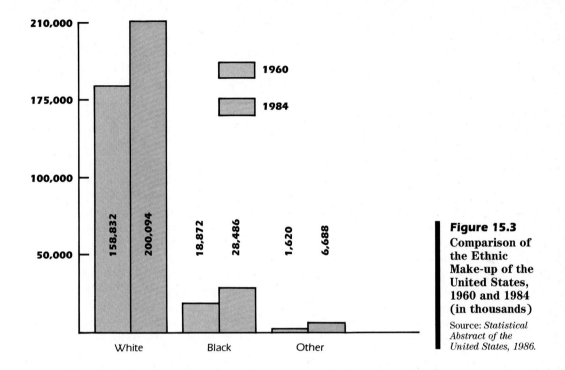

Figure 15.3
Comparison of the Ethnic Make-up of the United States, 1960 and 1984 (in thousands)

Source: *Statistical Abstract of the United States, 1986.*

ers are less expensive to hire than experienced employees, and (2) they tend to be more flexible and willing to learn company procedures. As a result, you increase your chances of employment when you acquire a good education and express your willingness to learn once you are on the job. If employers are reluctant to hire you because of your inexperience, point out that everyone in business begins his or her career with no experience. Someone along the way gives them a chance to prove themselves, and you need the same opportunity.

Older workers between the ages of forty and seventy are protected by law from discrimination on the basis of age. But many employers are reluctant to hire or retrain the older worker. They feel those educated in the 1950s will not understand the technology and methods of the 1990s. Women are particularly hard hit in this age category since many stayed home to raise a family. At age thirty-five to forty, they are returning to the job market after a fifteen- to twenty-year absence. Even though organizations can no longer require mandatory retirement at age sixty-five, employees approaching this age are often victims of potent, more subtle forms of discrimination. They may be laid off, have their workload cut back, no longer be in line for promotion, or given "make work" projects that keep them out of the mainstream of the organization.

When the Mick-or-Mack food store chain fired twenty-five workers in 1983, ten of the fired employees ranging in age from forty-three to sixty-three filed an age discrimination suit against the company. One, a fifty-six-year-old vice president, had been with the company thirty-three years. The fired employees claimed that those with the most seniority were released first, leaving room for newly hired, lower-salaried personnel and part-time youth who received no benefits. An effective cost-cutting measure, but the U.S. District Court ruled in favor of the fired personnel. They were victims of age discrimination.[13]

Employers who resort to this kind of discrimination are missing an opportunity. Studies find that, although it takes older workers somewhat longer to learn new skills and concepts, once the material is learned they tend to be more dependable, stay on the job longer, and show greater critical judgment, insight, and patience. Their loyalty, adaptability, and fidelity often acts as a stabilizing influence on the younger generation.[14]

Many organizations are taking advantage of the experience and maturity of older employees, even those who have officially retired. These workers often answer the need for part-time or temporary help or for expertise that inexperienced and outside help cannot supply. Silvia Corvo, one-time employee of The Travelers Corporation in Hartford, Connecticut, returned to work at age seventy-two as co-director of the company's new retirees' job bank. The Motorola plant in Schaumburg, Illinois, has rehired retirees for the past three years. The company also keeps a permanent pool of clerical workers and employs specialists on call—all over age sixty-five.[15]

The population of older workers will increase by 28 percent between now and the year 2000. As Robert E. Feagles, Travelers' senior vice president for personnel and administration, observes, "As we look down the road, if we are going to run our companies well, we will need the superior talent and resources older workers provide."[16]

Discrimination Based on Physical Disability People with physical disabilities have found it difficult to enter the job market, even though their right to do so is protected by the Rehabilitation Act of 1973. **Handicapped** individuals are defined as those who are mentally retarded, deaf or hearing impaired, speech or language impaired, visually handicapped, seriously emotionally disturbed, orthopedically impaired, or who have other health impairments.[17] When trying to get a job, discrimination often occurs because of public ignorance about the contributions handicapped workers can make. In part, the problem is the lack of access to transportation, buildings, and public facilities. The Department of Labor surveyed over three hundred companies and found 90 percent of them in violation of major laws protecting the right of disabled people to employment in the private sector.[18] The impact on individuals can be tragic.

An exception is the Du Pont corporation. Du Pont's most recent report showed that it employed 2,745 handicapped workers, about 2.4 percent of its work force. Its handicapped employment grew by 89 percent since 1973, while its overall employment climbed 13 percent. Stewart Wiggins is a forty-nine-year-old, blind computer programmer for Du Pont. He uses an Optacon, a small lens that is wired to a device similar to a tape recorder. As the lens is run over a computer printout, Stewart sticks his left index finger into the tape recorder-like device. The lens transmits vibrations that Wiggins has been trained to translate into words. Elrey McCann, a forty-one-year-old research chemist, suffers from multiple sclerosis. As his mobility began to become impaired five years ago, the company gave him his own parking space, installed hand rails along the sidewalks, then purchased a special wheelchair for him and built a special ramp in the parking lot.

The expense of the adjustments Du Pont has made for these and other handicapped employees is minor compared to their productivity and positive influence on other workers. W. J. Schaffers, Wiggins's boss, states, "His attitude is remarkable. He's a tremendous influence on all of us." In job performance, supervisors rated 92 percent of the handicapped workers as average or above, compared with 91 percent for non-handicapped employees. In safety, 96 percent of the handicapped were average or above, while 92 percent of the others were in that category.[19]

At other corporations, however, employers are sometimes frustrated by the lack of a central source of qualified disabled people who possess more than entry-level skills. Traditionally, employers have used state employment agencies and vocational rehabilitation offices to find workers. But the disabled are now seeking private educational and vocational training, and employers may not always know where to look for the graduates of these programs.

As a result of such mutual frustration, many employers believe that disabled people will make the *least* progress in the job market of all protected minorities.[20] They cite as reasons that few of the disabled have more than minimal job skills, federal requirements to make buildings accessible to the disabled are too complex and costly, and the disabled have less political power than other minorities.

Yet Frank Bowe, director of the American Coalition of Citizens with Disabilities (ACCD), a strong advocate for disabled people, believes that the grim picture does not have to stay that way. Bowe feels that firms will find that hiring the handicapped, or "physically challenged," is good business for a number of reasons. It turns tax users into taxpayers, brings badly needed talent and energy into private industry, reassures other employees that if they should become disabled the company understands that their abilities are what count, and satisfies the need of all employees to be valued on the basis of their common human qualities rather than their differences.[21]

Harold E. Krents, a partner in a prominent Washington, D.C., law firm and blind since birth, echoes Bowe's words. He was turned down by over forty law firms after graduating from Harvard Law School before obtaining his present position. His experience taught him the necessity of cooperation among the corporate community, the government, and the disabled worker.

> No one should be employed simply because he or she has a disability. But we all have responsibilities. The corporate community must face this assimilation as a challenge, not a chore. The government must enforce equal employment laws with common sense as well as compassion, for the wrongs of centuries cannot be erased overnight. And finally, we who have disabilities must be prepared to seize the employment opportunities that will finally be open to us.[22]

Subtler Forms of Discrimination

Discrimination based on age, sex, race, ethnic background, or physical disability is prohibited by law. If you feel you are the victim of these types of discrimination, you can take legal action against the organization. But discrimination based on lifestyle, appearance, different values, or some other personal factor is not covered by law. In addition, this type of discrimination is often extremely difficult to prove.

One of the reasons this type of discrimination is so difficult to prove is that employers themselves are often unaware of their prejudices. For instance, height is commonly associated with assertiveness, self-confidence, and an "executive" image. Shorter persons, to compensate, often have to outperform their taller colleagues to create the same impression of confidence and personal ability.

Some employers may discriminate against employees who are single, homosexual, divorced or single parents, or ex-offenders or recovered drug addicts or alcoholics. A woman manager who is divorced may not be hired because other executives' wives may consider her a "threat." Some organizations feel the portly executive does not have the proper image, and often promotions will be withheld as a motivation to lose weight. The list of possible violations of an organization's unwritten code or desired image could be endless. A code or image that is too rigid can be a real obstacle to professional advancement.

Employees may also have their own standards for who is and isn't acceptable. Those who are from another region of the country, speak with an accent, have too much education or too little, or possess some other personal characteristic that marks them as "different" may find themselves victims of discrimination.

What can you do if you discover you are the target of these subtle forms of discrimination? If you wish to stay in the organization, you will need to determine whether the "difference" is something you can change—your weight, the way you dress, your manner of speaking. If the difference is something you cannot—or choose not—to change, you can strive to compensate for it by excelling in your work. Become an expert on the job, and work to increase your skills and your value to the organization. If your future appears blocked, investigate other places where management may be more open and accepting. The important point is that you should refuse to allow discrimination to damage your self-concept or limit your potential.

Thinking/Learning Starters

1. Review the six minority groups discussed in this section. Do you find you have any prejudices against one or more of these groups? If so, how did you acquire your attitudes?
2. Do you feel that understanding the history of these minority groups will make you feel more positive toward them? Why or why not?

Levels of Discrimination

The process of discrimination works on several levels and involves many aspects of our society: individuals, organizations, and structures. The more you learn about how discrimination and prejudice are maintained, the more you can work to overcome these barriers. Our economic, social, educational, and political institutions must be continually examined so that we may understand the roles they play in either maintaining or counteracting the process of discrimination.[23]

Individual Level

Perhaps we are most familiar with discrimination at the individual level. Some people may be openly and intentionally prejudiced, but many act out of unintentional or unconscious prejudiced attitudes and beliefs.

For example, administrators may rely on word-of-mouth recruiting among their friends and colleagues, so that only candidates of the same race and sex learn of potential job openings. Guidance counselors may steer women and minority students away from "hard" subjects such as math and science and into subjects that do not prepare them for higher paying jobs. Personnel officers may believe that women and minorities have certain characteristics that justify hiring them at lower wage levels than white males, regardless of their education or qualifications.

Whether conscious or not, overt or hidden, such actions perpetuate prejudicial stereotypes, deny opportunities to women and minority groups, and maintain discrimination regardless of individual intent.

Organizational Level

Discrimination at this level is often reinforced by well-established organizational rules, policies, and practices. Again, they are not regarded by the organization as discriminatory, but simply as the way the organization does business and carries on its operations.

Discriminatory policies include physical requirements of height and weight that have little, if anything, to do with the job itself. Because of seniority rules in jobs historically held by white males, more recently hired women and minorities are more subject to layoffs and less eligible for advancement. Restrictive employment leave policies, prohibition of part-time work, or the denial of fringe benefits to part-time workers make it difficult for heads of single-parent families to get and keep jobs and meet family needs. Standardized tests or criteria geared to the cultural and educational norms of the middle class or of white males will not yield a fair assessment of minority members' abilities.

These organizational actions protect and maintain the status quo even when no conscious intent to discriminate is present. They are based on the racism and sexism of the past. Often women and minorities are caught in a cycle of actions that tend to limit their chances for success and their opportunities.

Some courts are beginning to uphold such charges of discrimination. As part of a record $42.5 million settlement of a ten-year-old sex and race discrimination complaint, General Motors agreed to hire more women and minorities over the next five years. The settlement established promotion and hiring goals, but most of the money will go toward educational programs for women and minorities and their families. GM agreed to sponsor $15 million in general scholarships, $9 million to train women and minorities for white-collar jobs, $2.2 million on an executive-development program, $6 million on a variety of technical training programs, $1.25 million to develop minority business clients, and twenty-eight endowments of $250,000 to colleges and universities.[24]

Structural Level

Structural discrimination operates at a broader level of society and often involves several institutions such as the educational system, government, and the financial and business communities. It can affect disadvantaged groups in many ways. For example, many businesses owned by women and minorities tend to be small and relatively new. They are less likely to gain needed credit from the financial community or know how to apply for government contracts, the source of revenue for many firms. Because they do not have a record of success with government contracts, contracting officers tend to favor other firms that have had more experience working with government agencies. Several states have recently begun offering seminars to women and minority business owners to help them get government contracts coming into their state. In addition, small business associations in many states have earmarked millions of dollars for loans to women- and minority-owned business enterprises.

Structural discrimination is not limited to a particular time or region and is cumulative in its effects. As a result, it tends to pass on disadvantages from one generation to the next. The basic consequence has been the persistent gap between the status of women and minority groups and that of white males. Since structural discrimination results in fewer qualified women and minorities, employers may be bewildered by charges of sexism and racism when the shortage of qualified applicants appears real. Moreover, they may feel justified in pointing out instances where women and minorities were academically inferior, unmotivated, poor credit risks, and so on, not taking into consideration the interlocking and intertwining effects of structural discrimination. They tend to blame the victim of discrimination instead of examining how their own decisions and actions feed into the overall discriminatory pattern.

Overcoming Prejudice and Discrimination

Prejudice and discrimination, because of their complex nature, must be fought on the individual, organizational, and structural levels. Individuals can learn to gain control over their attitudes and behavior, organizations can work to eliminate past discriminatory patterns, and society can legislate and enforce laws that prohibit conditions that perpetuate inequalities in institutions and communities.

What Individuals Can Do

Three of the most effective means for eliminating, or at least controlling, our own prejudices are decontaminating our minds, developing tolerance, and learning to understand the behavior of others.

Decontamination is basically the process of re-educating yourself to separate the Parent and Adult ego states and substituting past negative experiences and attitudes with more positive ones. Learning why prejudices developed against a particular group reveals how old attitudes are passed from one generation to the next. Education can enable you to appreciate the richness and variety of other cultures and their contribution to the dominant culture. As organizations become more multinational and the work force more multiracial and multicultural, the ability to control your attitudes toward others' differences is becoming essential to career success.

Psychologists and sociologists have found that contact among people of different races, backgrounds, or cultures can break down prejudice when people (1) join together for a common task, (2) meet individuals who shatter stereotypes, and (3) share the same social or economic status. Decontamination also occurs when people strengthen their self-concept and begin to achieve success in their own life. They become less threatened by the progress of others.

Many of the destructive aspects of prejudice can be offset through the development of tolerance and understanding. Tolerant people accept individual differences not only as inevitable but even as desirable. They have a high degree of inner security and can separate important factors from unimportant ones. Understanding, on the other hand, implies a sympathetic awareness on your part of others' beliefs, customs, traditions, and personal differences without necessarily embracing them. Understanding others includes recognizing that each of us is the product of our particular background. An understanding attitude can help you accept the differences of others while maintaining your own uniqueness.

Steps Organizations Can Take

Addressing organizational discrimination must be done on an organization-wide basis. One or two individual departments or managers will have limited impact if the overall management attitude leans toward preserving the status quo. The following basic steps have been found effective over the years.

1. *Make sure top management is committed to the task and vigorously promotes that commitment through the ranks.* The staff will take their cue from the chief executive. If they see him or her promoting tolerance at work yet playing handball at a segregated club, they will question how seriously management is committed to equality. Unless the policy is carried through at every level, it can be sabotaged somewhere along the line. One approach that has worked well in manufacturing plants is to present workshops for foremen and -women and superintendents to teach them how to supervise minority group members—and how to deal with their own prejudicial attitudes.

2. *Review standards for recruiting, hiring, and promotion.* Does the organization recruit where minority students or workers are? Are recruiters trained to deal with people of various cultural, racial, and ethnic backgrounds? Remember that employment tests can be biased in favor of white, middle-class people. Do standards for hiring and promotion reflect a realistic assessment of a candidate's actual abilities? Sometimes standards are lowered to help someone who would not otherwise be hired or promoted. Conversely, standards are sometimes raised to block promotions or hiring. Is this really necessary or fair to all involved?

3. *Establish a means to monitor the nondiscrimination policies and provide top management with regular reports.* Reports should not be a series of numbers quoting how many minority members were hired, but an in-depth

analysis of what positions they filled, their progress, and rate of advancement or turnover. Management needs quality information about how its policies are being carried out and what effect they are having on the organization as a whole.

Changing the Structure: Affirmative Action

Over the past thirty years, various laws and regulations have been passed and federal and state agencies created to help disadvantaged groups gain access to adequate education, training, and employment.

Title VII and the EEOC   Perhaps the single most far-reaching law ever enacted by the federal government in the area of job discrimination is Title VII of the 1964 Civil Rights Act. Title VII prohibits discrimination by employers on the basis of race, color, religion, sex, or national origin. It applies to discrimination in all aspects of employment including recruitment, hiring, promotion, discharge, classification, training, compensation, and other terms, privileges, and conditions of employment.[25]

The agency primarily responsible for enforcing Title VII is the **Equal Employment Opportunity Commission** (EEOC). The EEOC processes charges of discrimination brought by individuals and groups and develops guidelines to help organizations establish and implement affirmative action plans. The number of complaints filed with the EEOC has been rising steadily since 1982. As Figure 15.4 indicates, over 50,000 cases were filed in 1984 alone.

Affirmative action seeks to remedy the effect of past discrimination against minorities and women. Under affirmative action guidelines, employers must identify the discriminatory barriers in their organization that limit minority applicants and employees. They are required to eliminate those barriers and establish whatever programs are necessary to speed the process. Affirmative action programs are mandatory for (1) any organization that contracts with the federal government or receives federal funds, (2) all public employers, and (3) all federal agencies. The **Office of Federal Contract Compliance Programs (OFCCP)** administers the mandatory affirmative action plans; the EEOC oversees voluntary plans.

Successes and Problems   Have affirmative action plans and antidiscrimination legislation worked? Most observers would answer with a qualified yes.

In Chicago, the minority and female share of the police payroll has jumped from 18 to 28 percent since affirmative action was initiated. Forty-one percent of New York City's public employees are minorities and 30 percent are women. More than 40 percent of Denver's civilian workers and 20 percent of the police force come from minority groups. Security Pacific National Bank, a California chain, boosted minority employment from 28 to 36 percent in the last decade; one in five branch managers is now from a minority group.

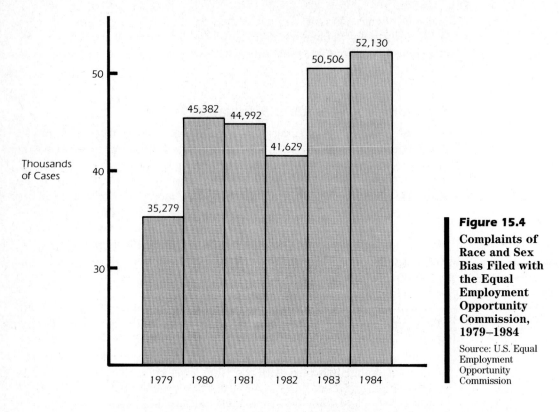

Figure 15.4

Complaints of Race and Sex Bias Filed with the Equal Employment Opportunity Commission, 1979–1984

Source: U.S. Equal Employment Opportunity Commission

New York Telephone has more than doubled its hiring of minorities, to 16.6 percent. The trend is also evident in the professions. In one Los Angeles law firm, there were no female lawyers in the mid-1960s; now, 25 percent of its 200 attorneys are women.[26]

Although it is true that more opportunities have opened for minorities and women, the machinery involved in the process has often hampered attempts to ensure compliance. Contractors who work with the federal government have criticized the excessive and often pointless data requirements, duplication, and contradictions among OFCCP and other federal agencies.

Similarly, representatives of women's and minority groups have cited the ineffectiveness of the OFCCP and EEOC as a critical problem in overcoming discrimination. Inadequate monitoring, lack of readily available and understandable information about federal requirements and procedures, and a general failure to follow up on promises or assurances to those supposed to benefit from the programs were several deficiencies pointed out by employers and minorities alike.

Under the Reagan administration, federal support for affirmative action has declined. In 1985, the U.S. Justice Department asked fifty-one cities and states to dismantle their quota plans as outlined in their affirmative action programs. Virtually every jurisdiction rejected the request. Private firms also seem convinced of the merits of affirmative action goals and timetables. A recent survey of 128 large firms indicated that 95 percent would continue to set hiring and promotion goals, even if the federal government rescinded affirmative action.[27]

Reverse Discrimination   **Reverse discrimination** is another issue that has surfaced as affirmative action programs have been implemented. The term refers to situations in which minorities are favored over whites. A well-qualified white male may not be hired because a company's affirmative action plan calls for a minority member to fill the slot. In 1979, the Supreme Court ruled in the controversial *Bakke* case that the University of California Medical School at Davis had granted preferential treatment to minorities at the expense of "better qualified" whites. The school's quota admissions system was declared unconstitutional.

Yet a few months later in the case of *Weber* v. *Kaiser Aluminum*, the Court ruled in favor of the company's affirmative action program.[28] The program called for a 39-percent representation of black workers in the firm's training sessions. This meant that some black employees were allowed into the program ahead of whites with more seniority. Weber, a white worker, claimed this constituted reverse discrimination. The Court disagreed and ruled that Kaiser had the right to give preferential treatment to black applicants until the company's minority representation goals were reached.

In 1980, the Supreme Court—deferring to the judgment of Congress—approved quotas to guarantee minority-owned businesses a fixed share of government public works contracts. Yet in 1985, the Supreme Court threw out a Memphis, Tennessee, plan that protected the jobs of minority and women firefighters at the expense of white males with more seniority. The justices, by a six-to-three vote, ruled that federal courts may not displace valid seniority plans. This decision may be the most powerful court ruling since the 1964 Civil Rights Act, as it offers a way for some employers to avoid affirmative action plans.

To ensure against charges of reverse discrimination, the EEOC has issued "Guidelines for Affirmative Action." Organizations taking voluntary affirmative action steps in conformity with the guidelines are protected from charges of reverse discrimination that employees might bring. These steps include establishing employment goals that recognize the race, sex, or national origin of employees or applicants; recruitment programs aimed at increasing the number of minorities and women; redesigning jobs to facilitate entry into and advancement within careers; changing biased selection procedures that screen out minorities and women; and providing formal on-the-job training.

A Look to the Future

The debate concerning affirmative action is far from over. The concept and the means for implementing it are likely to be challenged in court many times over the next decades. Yet despite the problems, more organizations are recognizing the inequities that past discrimination has created. A report published by the U.S. Commission on Civil Rights stated:

> We should not blame historically disadvantaged groups for lacking a strong work ethic or for having a different outlook on education. We also cannot blame economic cycles or the age of the population in a particular group. Instead, we must try to end discrimination directly by enforcing the law. The groups involved must not be shortchanged by finding the paths to employment opportunities blocked even when they have acquired education and skills.[29]

The commission also found a surprising theme running through the testimony and statements of government officials, employers, and private citizens. That theme was a widespread desire to oppose all forms of discrimination and eventually, through the cooperation of all concerned, to eliminate it entirely.

Thinking/Learning Starters

1. Have you observed or experienced discrimination at the individual, organizational, or structural levels?
2. What positive effects could affirmative action programs have on human relations between dominant and minority group members? Could there be any negative effects? Explain.

Summary

Prejudice and discrimination are major barriers to effective human relations. Prejudice is an attitude based partly on observation of others' differences and partly on ignorance, fear, and cultural conditioning. Prejudiced people tend to see others as stereotypes rather than as unique individuals.

Prejudicial attitudes are formed through the effects of contamination, ethnocentrism or cultural conditioning, and economic factors. Prejudice can have a harmful effect on both the victim of prejudice and the one who maintains the attitude. If the prejudice conflicts with a major value or is used to bolster a weak self-concept, opportunities for personal growth are restricted in many ways. On the other hand, the victims of prejudice may hate themselves rather than the group oppressing them.

Discrimination is behavior based on prejudicial attitudes. Most minority groups are victims of discrimination. Minorities are those individuals or groups denied equal treatment—particularly in terms of education, employment, housing, and the like. Minority groups protected by law from discrimination include women; ethnic, racial and religious groups; the older and younger worker; and those with physical disabilities. More subtle forms of discrimination not covered by law include differences in lifestyle, values, appearance, and physical characteristics. These differences may violate an organization's "image" of a successful employee or the unwritten code of what is acceptable and unacceptable behavior for employees. Individuals may be effectively blocked from advancement even though they may not know what aspects of the unwritten code they have violated.

The process of discrimination operates on several levels and involves many aspects of society: individuals, organizations, and structures. The effects of such a process are cumulative and tend to perpetuate disadvantages from one generation to the next.

Prejudice and discrimination can be fought by individuals, organizations, and legislation. Laws prohibiting discrimination are a clear message that inequalities must be erased. Organizations can counteract the effects of past discrimination by working to hire and promote minorities. Individuals can reduce their own prejudices by decontaminating their minds and developing the human relations skills of tolerance and understanding. A society in which every individual is judged on his or her merits alone is likely to be stronger both socially and economically.

Key Terms

prejudice	ageism
stereotype	handicapped
contamination	Equal Employment Opportunity Commission
ethnocentrism	
cultural conditioning	affirmative action
discrimination	Office of Federal Contract Compliance Programs
minority group	
sexism	reverse discrimination
racism	

Review Questions

1. Define *prejudice* and *discrimination*. What is the basic difference between these two terms?
2. What are some of the ways people acquire prejudices?
3. Describe the concept of contamination.
4. How does prejudice affect the self-concept of the victim? How does it affect the self-concepts of those who maintain prejudicial attitudes?
5. What determines minority status? What minority groups have been the major targets of discrimination in employment?

6. How can the subtle forms of discrimination hurt an individual's chances to succeed in his or her career?
7. How is the cycle of discrimination maintained?
8. How can tolerance and understanding help overcome the negative effects of prejudice and discrimination?
9. List some of the ways organizations can fight the effects of past discrimination.
10. What are the purposes of affirmative action programs? Explain the term *reverse discrimination.*

Case 15.1

The Mick-or-Mack Dilemma

In 1981 the Mick-or-Mack food store chain was sold to a group headed by former Philadelphia grocery executive Peter McGoldrick. After careful consideration of the profit-and-loss statements and current operating procedures, it became obvious that personnel cuts would be necessary to keep the chain profitable. On a Friday afternoon in January 1983, as employees were clocking out, twenty-five received their termination notices and two weeks' severance pay. They had no warning or opportunity to bargain for cuts in salary or hours, and they received no complaints about the quality of their work.

Company president Conrad Stephanites claimed that he had tried to eliminate unnecessary jobs. However, two of the fired employees had attempted to form a union the previous year, and ten were between forty-three and sixty-three years old. The employees who remained at Mick-or-Mack had little seniority with the company. Many were part-time employees who received no benefits. Several additional part-timers were hired to fill in the gaps.[30]

Ironically, many of the older workers who were fired had kept the union out. "They were the loyal senior workers who made the company what it is," claimed one employee. Yet had the union been successful in organizing the employees, the older workers would probably still have their jobs.

The ten senior employees filed an age-discrimination suit against Mick-or-Mack and won in an out-of-court settlement in July 1985. [31]

Questions

1. If you had been in Mr. Stephanites's position, what would you have done when the home office told you to make the cuts in personnel? What human relations skills could have been used to soften the blow and perhaps eliminate the lawsuit?
2. Apart from legal fees and cash awards to the former employees, what else did the store owners lose?
3. Imagine that you are a younger employee who has been retained by Mick-or-Mack. What would you do? Imagine that you are an older employee released after thirty-three years of service. What would you do?

Case 15.2

The New Employee

Stephanie Samuels had been working as a graphic artist at Devon Ad Agency for two years. Although her record was excellent, she tended to worry about her job. As she and a friend met for lunch in the company cafeteria, Stephanie remarked, "I've really got trouble now."

"What's happened?" her friend asked.

"They hired a new graphic artist in my department—a young German woman. The boss probably wanted someone who would stay until three in the morning and come in every weekend. You know how Germans are—they work all the time. And I'll bet they don't have to pay her much either."

"Is she any good?"

"Oh sure—she's got a degree from one of those European schools so everybody thinks she's a genius."

"Stephanie, I don't know what you're so hot about," her friend protested. "You're a topnotch artist. That ad you and John worked up got nominated for an award last year, remember?"

"And her accent! She could at least learn to speak English better. I don't see why they had to hire a foreigner with all the American artists trying to find jobs. I'll bet the company wants to get rid of their 'expensive' help, like me!"

Questions

1. What seems to be the basis for Stephanie's prejudice against the new graphic artist? Do economic factors play any part in Stephanie's attitude? If so, in what way?
2. How do you think Stephanie could overcome her prejudice?

Notes

1. "Grandfather, 53, Becomes LA's Oldest Rookie Policeman," *Roanoke Times & World-News.*
2. Karen Shepherd, "Why Stereotypes Hurt," *Management World,* January 1985, pp. 41 and 44.
3. Thomas Harris, *I'm OK, You're OK: A Practical Guide to Transactional Analysis* (New York: Harper and Row, 1969), pp. 100–103.
4. Charles M. Kelly, "Confrontation Insurance," *Training/HRD,* August 1981, pp. 91–94.
5. Wendell Berry, *The Hidden Wound* (Boston: Houghton Mifflin, 1970).
6. Bebe Moore Campbell, "Black Executives and Corporate Stress," *New York Times Magazine,* p. 105.
7. Bruno Bettleheim and Morris Janowitz, *Social Change and Prejudice* (London: Collier Macmillan, Ltd., 1964).
8. U.S. Commission on Civil Rights, *Affirmative Action in the 1980s: Dismantling the Process of Discrimination,* Clearinghouse Publication 65 (Washington, D.C.: U.S. Government Printing Office, January 1981), p. 9.
9. Bureau of the Census, U.S. Department of Commerce, *Age, Sex, Race, and Spanish Origin of the Population by Region, Division, and State* (Washington, D.C.: U.S. Government Printing Office, May 1981), pp. 3–5.
10. David A. Bell, "The Triumph of Asian Americans," *The New Republic,* July 15 & 22, 1985, pp. 24–31.
11. Bureau of the Census, U.S. Department of Commerce, *1986 Statistical Abstract of the United States,* 106th ed. (Washington, D.C.: U.S. Government Printing Office, 1986), p. 407.
12. U.S. Commission on Civil Rights, *Unemployment and Underemployment Among Blacks, Hispanics, and Women,* Clearinghouse Publication 74 (Washington, D.C.: U.S. Government Printing Office, November 1982), p. 1.
13. Dwayne Yancey, "Food Store Chain Cuts Off 25; Some Older Workers Claim Foul," *Roanoke Times & World-News,* January 18, 1983, p. B-2.

14. Victoria Kaminski, "Bias Toward Youth Called Training Failure," *Training/HRD*, February 1984, pp. 74–75.

15. "When Retirees Go Back on the Payroll," *Business Week*, November 22, 1982, pp. 112–113.

16. Ibid.

17. "Is Your Language Languishing?" *East Central Communique*, vol. 12, issue 2, 1985, p. 3.

18. U.S. Department of Labor, *Affirmative Action for the Handicapped* (Washington, D.C.: U.S. Government Printing Office, April 1980), p. 102.

19. N. R. Kleinfield, "Du Pont is a Haven for Handicapped Employees," *Roanoke Times & World-News*, April 15, 1984, p. G-6.

20. U.S. Department of Labor, *Affirmative Action for the Handicapped*, pp. 102–103.

21. Ibid., p. 133.

22. Ibid., pp. 8–9.

23. Material in this section was adapted from U.S. Commission on Civil Rights, *Affirmative Action in the 1980s: Dismantling the Process of Discrimination*, pp. 9–15.

24. Patrick Fitzgerald, "GM Bias Pricetag: $42.5M," *USA Today*.

25. U.S. Commission on Civil Rights, *Promises and Perceptions: Federal Efforts to Eliminate Employment Discrimination Through Affirmative Action* (Washington, D.C.: U.S. Government Printing Office, October 1981), p. 17.

26. "Why Drive on Job Bias Is Still Going Strong," *U.S. News & World Report*, June 17, 1985, pp. 67 and 68.

27. Ibid.

28. *"Weber* v. *Kaiser," Time*, April 9, 1979, p. 28.

29. U.S. Commission on Civil Rights, *Unemployment and Underemployment Among Blacks, Hispanics, and Women*, p. 59.

30. Yancey, "Food Store Chain Cuts Off 25," p. B-2.

31. George Kegley, "Mick-or-Mack Suit Charging Age Bias Settled Out of Court," *Roanoke Times & World-News*, July 27, 1985.

Suggested Readings

Affirmative Action for the Handicapped. Washington, D.C.: U.S. Government Printing Office, 1980.

American Indian Civil Rights Handbook. Washington, DC.: U.S. Government Printing Office, 1980.

Dickens, Floyd, and Jacqueline Dickens. *The Black Manager: Making It in the Corporate World.* New York: American Management Associations, 1982.

Promises and Perceptions: Federal Efforts to Eliminate Employment Discrimination Through Affirmative Action. Washington, D.C.: U.S. Government Printing Office, 1981.

Unemployment and Underemployment Among Blacks, Hispanics, and Women. Washington, D.C.: U.S. Government Printing Office, 1982.

Chapter 16

Overcoming Sexism in Organizations

Chapter Preview

After studying this chapter, you will be able to
1. Describe the traditional roles acquired by most men and women.
2. Summarize some of the characteristics of the nontraditional roles men and women are creating for themselves.
3. Understand the effects of sexism on men and women.
4. Discuss methods of coping with sexism in organizations.
5. Explain how these methods can be used to deal with sexual harassment.

History was made recently when a Frontier Airlines 737 jet airplane departed from Denver's Stapleton Airport. Flight 244 was the first U.S. commercial flight with an all-female cockpit crew. The plane was piloted by Captain Emily Warner and First Officer Barbara Cook. One of the officers, Captain Warner, had made history on another occasion. In 1973 she became the first woman pilot for a major U.S. airline. A fifteen-year veteran of a private aviation company, she had tried for six years to get the job of captain.[1]

While the cockpits of commercial airlines are beginning to accept women, the cabins are seeing an increasing number of male flight attendants. About 15 percent of the nation's flight attendants are now males, up from almost none twenty years ago.[2] Although male flight attendants, like other men who enter fields traditionally dominated by women, experience some problems in getting the public to validate their career choices, they appreciate the opportunity never before open to them.

During an era when equal rights is receiving a great deal of attention, many organizations and individuals are making major steps toward eliminating **sexism**—or discrimination on the basis of sex. Sexism limits the opportunities of both men and women to choose the career and lifestyle that best suits their abilities and interests. Like other forms of prejudice, sexism is

Bessie Coleman made history as the first licensed black pilot in the United States. (The Bettman Archive)

Emily Warner made history when she became captain of the first all-female commercial cockpit crew. (Photo courtesy of Frontier Airlines)

based on widely held beliefs about the capabilities, characteristics, and behavior of men and women. Sexual stereotypes can sabotage communication, hinder the achievement of organizational goals, and reduce morale. In this chapter, you will examine some of the changing roles of men and women, the problems facing both sexes on the job, and methods for overcoming sexism that can help you in your own career.

Traditional Sex Roles Are Changing

The women's movement and more recently the men's movement are working to change centuries of tradition regarding the roles of men and women. Over the past twenty years, women have been entering **nontraditional careers,** making choices from a wider range of lifestyles, and participating at political and professional levels undreamed of fifty years ago.

Men are also beginning to examine the **traditional roles** they have always assumed. They are asking if the "strong, unemotional, in-control" image defined by the culture and projected in the media is realistic. Despite his reputation for toughness, the "macho male" is often outlived by his wife. Men are starting to share responsibilities for child rearing and household duties, to desire equal relationships with both men and women, and to question whether success defined as the drive to the top is really the most important factor in life. Many men want to be free to choose careers in traditionally "female" jobs such as retail selling, secretarial work, child care, nursing, and other types of support professions.

All cultures promote different behaviors for boys and girls. Children generally learn these values between three and ten years of age, and they are reinforced throughout the life cycle by teachers, parents, authority figures, and the media. The traditional roles are harmful to both men and women. The expectation that men should be aggressive and unemotional stifles their creativity. And the assumption that women are emotional and weak hinders them in reaching their full potential. While men and women will always be different, their roles can and should be more equal. Changes in work roles and lifestyles are occurring with astonishing rapidity, and no one knows where they will end. One magazine editor observed, "What is happening to all women, men and children in this country is unprecedented, revolutionary. Old stereotypes are being shattered and we have to resist the urge to fashion new, neat images out of the pieces."[3]

Even though changes are accelerating, sexism continues to be a major issue in most organizations and in society. An editorial summed it up this way: "Progress in achieving sex equality has been slower than proponents had hoped, and discriminatory practices and wage differentials still exist."[4]

It will be helpful to examine the traditional roles of both sexes as well as the new picture that is emerging of what a man or woman can be and do.

As discussed in Chapter 15, understanding some of the causes behind prejudice is the first step toward eliminating it. Many of our attitudes toward the opposite sex are based more on cultural conditioning than on fact.

A New View of Women

When a woman chooses to take a nontraditional job or is promoted or hired for a higher-level position within a firm, she must overcome three barriers: her traditional upbringing, the attitudes of her male and female colleagues, and the lack of support systems to help her stay in her job, particularly if she is married and the mother of small children. This section explores the traditional sex role attitudes women are taught, how those attitudes are changing, and the new roles women are creating for themselves.

Conditioned Sexist Attitudes

From their earliest years, women were encouraged to be passive, supportive of others, emotionally expressive, and physically attractive. While being a tomboy was all right during her younger years, a girl was expected to outgrow an interest in sports or "male" pursuits by the time she reached high school age. She often found the traditional image of women reinforced at school. Studies have revealed that elementary textbooks overwhelmingly portrayed girls as less capable than boys, less adventurous, and less inclined to lead or make their own decisions.[5] Instead, they were expected to accept the boys' leadership.

As she grew up, a woman's worth was usually measured by her attractiveness to the opposite sex. If she was highly intelligent or a good athlete, she was encouraged to hide her abilities to avoid scaring away the boys. She was not encouraged to develop her capabilities to the fullest or to think about and plan a career. She would get "just a job" until it was time to marry and have children. Professions women entered included office support work (secretaries, key punch operators, receptionists), teaching (usually below college level), nursing or physical therapy, dental hygiene, and other supportive occupations. If a woman chose to remain single and pursue a career, it was assumed that she could not attract a husband or that she was "unfeminine" in some way.

These conditioned sexist attitudes are hard to break. As men and women attempt to create nontraditional roles, the phrase "We have met the enemy . . . and it is ourselves!" has more meaning than we care to admit. While some women are seeking the education and training to achieve high-salaried jobs, many still are entering traditionally female-dominated occupations. For instance, about two-thirds of working women are employed in service and retail industries or in state and local government. And five of the top ten

Table 16.1 **What's Changed in the Last Five Years?**

Occupation	% Women in the Field		% Point
	1980	*1985*	(Change)
Designer	27.3	52.7	+ 25.4%
Economist	22.9	37.9	+ 15
Health administrator	46.2	57.0	+ 10.8
Psychologist	48.1	57.1	+ 9
Chemist	14.4	23.3	+ 8.9
Architect	5.8	12.7	+ 6.9
Drafter	11.1	17.5	+ 6.4
Attorney	9.4	15.3	+ 5.9
Engineer	2.8	5.8	+ 3

Source: Reprinted with permission from *Working Woman* magazine. Copyright © 1986 by HAL Publications, Inc.

occupations among women are sales or clerical jobs.[6] Yet pay scales in female-dominated occupations tend to be much lower than those in occupations dominated by men.

Fortunately, women are making progress in some areas. There are more women in the work force than ever before, and their number is growing rapidly. Women are increasing their representation in some higher-paying occupations traditionally dominated by men. For instance, as Table 16.1 shows, women in 1985 were 52.7 percent of all designers, a striking increase of 25.4 percent since 1980, when women were only 27.3 percent. And women are now 37.9 percent of all economists, up from 22.9 percent in 1980. Although change is slow in some other fields such as engineering, where only 5.8 percent are women, attitudes toward working women are changing.[7] More women are entering college than ever before, and now represent a majority— 52 percent—of all college students. And women who want to break into nontraditional fields are seeking out the training that will help them gain success in their chosen fields. They are learning to make executive decisions, analyze complex problems, and negotiate for higher salaries, greater job responsibilities, and career advancement opportunities.

Sexual Role Models

Women are less likely to consider a career in business management or administration because they see few female **sexual role models** with whom they can identify. Most executives, salespeople, administrators, and the like are men. The importance of sexual role models was examined recently by the Project on Human Sexual Development, a nonprofit research organization in Massachusetts. Researchers found that what children *see* is far more important than what their parents *tell* them.[8] If children see their mothers in traditional roles, they will tend to identify women as mothers, homemakers, wives. Therefore, even though mothers of girls born after 1960 may encour-

Suzanne Gatchell, a General Motors Executive, is achieving success in the automobile industry which has been historically dominated by men. (Photo © Joyce Ravid)

age their daughters to be assertive and nontraditional, what the daughters see their mothers *doing* will have far more influence than their mothers' words.

As a result of this cultural and social conditioning and the lack of effective, nontraditional role models, many women do not realize the range of opportunities that are open to them. They may continue to seek jobs that offer little potential for advancement or economic gain. If they do achieve higher-level positions, they may have trouble trusting their own judgment, making decisions, and exercising their newly found authority. Women's negative attitudes about their potential can defeat the process of equal employment opportunity before it begins.

New Role Models and Mentors

From childhood on, "tomboy" Linda Gibbs enjoyed working with her hands and helping her father with projects outside the house. Later, when she was divorced and left to support her three children alone, she found out that she

Total Person Insight

Eleanor Maccoby and Carol Jacklin

... it is by no means obvious that attempts to foster sex-typed behavior (as traditionally defined) in boys and girls serve to make them better men and women. Indeed, in some spheres of adult life such attempts appear to be positively handicapping. We suggest that societies have the option of minimizing, rather than maximizing sex differences through their socialization practices.

had little formal training that would qualify her for jobs paying more than the minimum wage. Through job counseling and examination of her skills, she discovered that the skills she had learned from her father could be nurtured and expanded into a nontraditional career she had thought was for men only, carpentry. The vocational school she chose offered programs for **displaced homemakers** like herself in architectural woodworking, fire science, emergency medical technician, electronics, commercial art, small engine repair, automotive mechanics, auto body repair, diesel mechanics, air conditioning and refrigeration, computerized machine and computer-aided drafting, building and contracting, law enforcement and corrections, and professional photography. As often as possible, women graduates already working in nontraditional jobs came to speak to the various groups of students. These role models offered invaluable information and shared their enthusiasm for their career choices.[9]

Linda Gibbs, a carpenter's apprentice, now serves as a role model for other women entering nontraditional jobs. (Photo by Benita R. Van Winkle, courtesy of Daytona Beach Community College)

Many women are choosing not to follow the traditional role models and are instead modeling themselves after successful women in nontraditional fields. The new role model they are creating depicts women as having the ability to

1. Plan a career and prepare for continued advancement.
2. Know what they want and ask for it.
3. Make decisions, live with the consequences, and learn from the process.
4. Realize that with equal rights come equal responsibilities.
5. Seek out opportunities that increase their abilities and status.
6. Develop qualities of cooperation, dependability, self-control, and expertise in some area.

Some successful women have learned androgynous behaviors and are mentoring others. Androgynous behaviors include flexible ways of handling difficult situations to avoid being labeled in stereotypically "feminine" ways. For instance, people in many organizations perceive women as being too emotional. Because men have come to expect women to behave in this way, they sometimes treat the women in their organizations accordingly. Another, newer, stereotype is of the woman manager who is driven to achieve success in the traditional male way. Such women are seen as "barracudas," who will stop at nothing to achieve their goals. These opposing stereotypes limit the effectiveness of women workers. If they are perceived as traditionally "feminine," they may not be taken seriously and their talents may not be utilized fully. Yet if they are seen as serious about their careers, they may be considered abnormal and overly aggressive. Women who have developed androgynous behaviors to cope with these stereotypes can offer necessary support and guidance. Female mentors offer younger women positive role models with which to identify and allow "apprentices" the chance to benefit from their hard-earned experience.

Role Changes Involve Choices

In 1950, only 28 percent of all mothers with children under eighteen had jobs. Today, three out of every four women of prime childbearing age (25–34) are in the work force.[10] Clearly, women are pursuing different lifestyles from their grandmothers' and even their mothers'. These employment patterns are likely to continue as working mothers raise daughters who will follow in their footsteps.

Not surprisingly, women's attitudes and choices regarding marriage and children have changed. More women are delaying marriage or forgoing it altogether to pursue a career that is exciting and challenging to them. Those who do marry realize that their husbands must be secure enough in their own careers to be supportive of their wives' professional life. The right partner can offer companionship, comfort, love, and security.

Similarly, many women are delaying having children during the early years of their marriage while they establish themselves in their field. Today, when they are ready to have children, many of them can choose to remain at home for a short time and then return to their jobs. As women move up the management ladder, companies are offering a wider range of flexible work schedules and child-care options to keep valued employees on the job.

Child Care   It is estimated that by 1990, 10.4 million preschool children will have mothers in the work force, a 23-percent increase from 1980.[11] Nearly 3,000 employers are modifying their policies to accommodate working families by offering options such as on-site day-care centers, financial assistance for day care, maternity leaves for fathers as well as mothers, flexible work hours when a child is home sick, and on-call medical assistance when a child is sick and the parents must go to work or when a parent needs to be away overnight on business. This flexibility, undreamed of ten years ago, opens many more options for working families today.

Providing options for day care helps improve worker morale, absenteeism, and staff turnover. Many corporate executives are realizing the effect providing day care has on their profitability. Companies are examining the options of opening their own day-care centers, subsidizing nearby independent day-care centers, or offering additional cash to employees to help pay day-care costs. Jim Wyllie, president of Nyloncraft, employs 450 people; 85 percent are women. As company officials asked employees about their concerns, they discovered a constant worry about children. Employees' worries about child care seemed to be eroding profits. Turnover at Nyloncraft was 300 percent annually. The estimated cost of training each new employee was $1,500 to $2,000. After building an on-site learning center for children, year-end reports showed that absenteeism had dropped to less than 3 percent.[12]

Flexible Work Schedules   In addition to day-care options, some employers offer employees the option of **job sharing.** For instance, one employee might work every morning, and the other would work every afternoon. Another option that may be available soon is **telecommuting,** which allows employees to work at home at a computer terminal linked to their employer's computer. Data processing, word processing, copy editing, and financial analysis are only some of the tasks that can be completed in such a setting. Companies ranging from J. C. Penney to American Express and from Blue Cross/ Blue Shield to Apple Computer are employing telecommuting right now, while hundreds of other companies are experimenting with the option to determine how they can get involved in this cost-effective employment option.

Other employers are offering flextime to their employees. **Flextime** refers to a policy of replacing the traditional fixed work hours with a more flexible schedule set by employees.[13] Flextime schedules typically include a core time and flexible time. Everyone works during the core time, often 9:30 A.M.

to 3:00 P.M. Employees can choose to work the rest of their hours during the flexible time, for instance, arriving at 7 A.M. and leaving at 3 P.M. or arriving at 9:30 A.M. and leaving at 6 P.M.

A system related to flextime is called the **compressed work week.** Typically, the compressed work week consists of four ten-hour days a week, Tuesday through Friday or Monday through Thursday. Again, employees can adjust their work schedules to fit their lifestyle.

Although many organizations are slow to accommodate working parents, the days of inflexible policies on work schedules and child care are nearing an end. With a positive self-concept and a clear value system intact, the working woman has many choices to make as she pursues her career.

Values and Changing Roles

Most women—particularly those who are heads of single-parent households—work out of economic necessity. Yet Judith Langer, head of Langer and Associates, a New York-based opinion research firm, has found that work also fulfills many of women's self-esteem needs. "The yearning for an identity beyond the traditional family role is so deeply intertwined with economic needs that they can't be separated. Gaining a sense of self is a fundamental part of it."[14]

Making the shift from traditional to new values is not easy. According to Laurie Ashcraft and Elizabeth Nickles, who conducted a survey of 2,400 women nationwide, women go through three stages when leaving the domestic scene and entering the job world.[15] The first is the *realization stage.* A woman begins to get positive messages about herself. Others respond to her favorably when she has done a good job, no one takes her for granted, and she gets the continual and powerful reinforcement of a paycheck. Her self-concept changes, and she feels she can manage it all—home, career, and outside interests. This is frequently described as the honeymoon phase.

The second stage is the *ambivalence period.* In any role change or change in self-concept, there is internal conflict. Women are torn between traditional values and their new role outside the home. They fall prey to the "superwoman syndrome" and believe they should be able to put in a full day's work, take care of their family, and have time and energy left over at the end of the day. Trying to live up to this myth has led to frustration, resentment, and exhaustion. Eventually they come to accept that they have only limited time and energy and need to delegate many of their responsibilities to others.

The third stage is a *transformation time* as these internal conflicts are resolved. Not only are women at this point more secure in their careers, but they look to their jobs as a source of self-fulfillment and status, and not solely to the home. In this stage, the woman has become motivated, acquires objectives and ambition, and is firmly committed to the world of work.

The result of this values shift? Ashcraft and Nickles found that employed women as a group are more self-confident, feel more attractive physically, and are more assertive than those who remain out of the work force. Women are finding that they can break away from the limited roles they have been taught and decide the course of their lives for themselves. The values choices are not easy: balancing the demands of home, career, and outside interests is difficult and takes considerable planning and support. Yet the overwhelming percentage of women surveyed believed the rewards were worth the effort.

Thinking/Learning Starters

1. Women, have your career expectations been limited or expanded by other women you have known? How?
2. How has the traditional woman's role made it difficult for women to succeed in the world of work? Why?
3. Have your own attitudes about what women can be and do changed over the years? If so, in what ways? If not, why?

A New View of Men

Many men are beginning to realize that they have been as rigidly stereotyped in their role as women have been in theirs. Given the fact that the latest statistics indicate most men die *eight to nine years* before their spouses, many wonder if upholding the male image is worth the price.

Conditioned Sexist Attitudes

Boys have been conditioned from their early years to be competitors and to win. They were urged to be tough and aggressive, learn teamwork, select male pastimes like sports and mechanics, and enter a masculine profession such as sales, management, science, engineering, or law. A boy was taught to withstand physical pain and to push his body to the limits.

Above all, he was not to act like a girl, take up interests that were considered feminine, or show any tendencies that could be considered homosexual. A girl could be a tomboy, but a boy could not be a "sissy." If he expressed his frustration, disappointment, or sadness by crying, he could be ridiculed as weak or "feminine." As a result, most men learned to suppress their more sensitive feelings and concentrate on developing their intellectual abilities or physical and athletic prowess.

Whereas a woman's worth was measured in terms of her physical attractiveness, a man's was measured by his ability to compete and achieve his

Table 16.2 Comparison of Traditional and Modern Versions of the Male Sex Role

Traditional Male Sex Role	Modern Male Sex Role
Is validated primarily by physical strength and aggression.	Is validated by economic success, achievement, and power over others, especially in the business world.
Shuns emotional expressions, especially those emotions indicative of weakness and vulnerability.	Expects male to be sensitive and emotionally expressive with women but not with other men.
Approves of emotions that indicate strength and power such as anger.	Discourages emotions such as anger and hostility.
Approves sexual double standard where sex is a male prerogative.	Downplays sexual double standard and expects male to satisfy female's sexual needs.
Supports strong male-male relationships but not of an intimate nature.	Encourages men to seek company of women as emotional and romantic partners.
Views women as inferior to men.	Views women as different but not inferior, although not men's equal in the business world.

Source: From Doyle, James A. *The Male Experience.* © 1983 Wm. C. Brown Publisher, Dubuque, Iowa. All rights reserved. Reprinted by permission.

goals, and by his power to earn high salaries and material benefits. If women have been viewed as "sex objects," perhaps men have been seen as "success objects." A man was under constant pressure to prove himself and keep moving up the ladder. Even though men learned the value of teamwork, they had to keep looking over their shoulder for whoever might be gaining on them. As a result, competition tended to isolate men emotionally from one another.

Men often feel that problems are something that can be solved rationally, without emotion. And they have honed their competitive skills to the point that many are unable to form close relationships with other men—relationships that would allow them to share their inner feelings and talk about their worries and inadequacies. Psychologists have become increasingly aware that we have neglected the stress associated with being male, which often manifests itself through illness, frustration, loneliness, and resentment. Ex-football star Tommy Francisco is a prime example. According to his former coach, Francisco was not considered aggressive as a boy, but with some coaching he "became a tougher person" who excelled at college football. After he graduated from college, he owned an insurance company. Financial and personal problems forced him to give up the firm in 1981, the year in which his wife left him. His self-esteem at an all-time low, Francisco began to drink heavily and abuse drugs. Then, in October 1982, he pleaded guilty

Fathers today are playing an increasingly larger role in their children's lives. (Photo by Richard L. Good)

to charges of armed robbery. When admitted to a psychiatric hospital in 1983, psychiatrists found he felt "despondent, desperate, and hopeless." They claimed he was suffering from "a crazy macho culture" that teaches "to be manly, one cannot ask for help."[16]

As women have begun to challenge the sex roles that have prevented them from living life fully, men, too, have begun to realize that traditional male sex roles have stopped them from participating in all aspects of human experience. The men's movement, although not yet as organized as the women's movement, is beginning to break down traditional sex-role stereotypes and allowing men to develop their full human potential at work and at home.

As men struggle with their own identity, they have the additional challenge of learning to relate to women who are asserting their rights. The tough, unemotional image of men, sometimes referred to as the John Wayne myth, meant that a man always had to be in control—or appear to be in control—of his life and his job responsibilities. He had to be the dominant partner in his relationships with women. He was taught that women had to be provided for and protected, and they, in return, would be supportive of his efforts to succeed. He was given few, if any, guidelines for treating women as colleagues or equals.

These attitudes have been perpetuated through such means as advertising; stereotyped images—the executive, the blue-collar worker, the professional, the scientist, and the like; and the corporate culture of many organizations.

"Herbie, this is all part of becoming a man." (© 1986; reprinted courtesy of Bill Hoest and *Parade* magazine.)

However, as is the case for women, changes in the roles of men are slowly becoming more apparent. Men are appearing in television commercials washing dishes and diapering babies. A Campbell Soup Company spot shows a young husband in the kitchen preparing dinner for his working wife.[17] Such advertising images reflect the reality of many couples' lives and are a sharp departure from the "working husband/homemaker wife" syndrome.

Sexual Role Models

Men, like women, tend to imitate the sexual role model closest to them, usually the father. Their image may be of a man emotionally uninvolved with his family or absent a great deal. The father may tell his son, "it's okay to cry" or "it's all right to share the housework"; but unless the son sees the father doing these things, he is not likely to act on these permissions. In addition, the role models a boy sees in advertisements, in business magazines, and on television often support the aggressive, controlled, commanding male image that he has been taught to accept.

Binds and Double Binds in the Male Role   Herb Goldberg, in his book *The Hazards of Being Male*, points out that the rigid sexual role men accept puts them in several no-win binds.[18] In the *career-ladder bind* the necessity to keep advancing in his career often means a man gives up doing what attracted him into the job in the first place. An engineer promoted to management does little design work or research—he manages others who do it. If he is management material yet stays at a lower level in order to keep doing what he likes, he risks being seen as somewhat "odd" or "peculiar." In the *emotional bind,* if he expresses his feelings more freely on the job, he may be viewed as "erratic." If he holds everything in, he is likely to suffer some type of stress-related illness such as ulcers. Either way he loses.

Goldberg is also alarmed at the harmful effects that maintaining the male image has on the body. Men are taught that it is not masculine to complain about physical aches and pains. They expect their bodies to keep going regardless of the pressures they are under. In addition, bottling up emotions, particularly being unable to cry to release stress or tension, means that the body must absorb a punishing amount of emotional energy without a healthy outlet. As a result, men tend to suffer more than women from hypertension, lung cancer, heart disease, intestinal problems, and alcohol and drug abuse.[19]

As more men come to understand some of the destructive aspects of the traditional male role, they will begin to look for options. Some men have already found them.

Options for Change

Men, like women, now have more choices regarding marriage and family life. Men who share the financial burden equally with their wives or elect not to be the major family breadwinner are freed from some of the more oppressive aspects of the male role. They no longer need to keep climbing the career ladder to meet family expenses or take higher-paying jobs that are less personally fulfilling. Executive psychologists indicate that men who see themselves in an equal partnership with their wives are more productive and effective on the job, have longer and happier marriages, and rear children who can cope more easily with new trends in role expectations. Men who are single may also have an advantage, since more married men are choosing not to transfer or are moving when their *wives* are transferred. A single man can travel, relocate, or move from company to company without disrupting a family member's career or schooling.

Many men seeking a more nontraditional role are placing their relationships with their children on a par with or even above their career goals. They may delay career advancement while their children are young in order to spend more time with them. Some organizations are willing to make special arrangements for fathers as they have for employed mothers. Aetna Life & Casualty allowed David Keene, an assistant vice president in real estate,

Total Person Insight	We, as men, want to take back our full humanity. We no longer want to strain and compete to live up to an impossible oppressive masculine image—strong, silent, cool, handsome, unemotional, successful, master of women, leader of men, wealthy, brilliant, athletic, and "heavy." We no longer want to feel the need to perform sexually, socially, or in any way to live up to an imposed male role, from a traditional American society or a "counterculture."

to work part time and still draw full salary while he stayed home to care for the Keene's adopted child.[20]

However, just as some women have been victims of the "super mom" syndrome, a few men are being caught up in the "super dad" syndrome. Both try to be everything and to do all tasks of a wage earner, parent, and spouse to perfection. Could this be adding more stress to the lives of men just as it has to women? Despite this new and potential drawback, men are now beginning to receive societal "permission" to stay home and raise their children.

Other men who choose to devote the majority of their time to developing a career may put off fathering children or decide not to have a family at all. On the other hand, some single men have been allowed to adopt children. In divorce cases, the courts are beginning to award child custody on the basis of parental qualifications. In some instances, the father may be considered to be the better choice. People are learning that biology alone does not determine who can be a sensitive, nurturing parent.

Values and Role Changes

The man who is tired of always being in control, of not being allowed to express his emotions freely, and who feels he must constantly strive for achievement can now more readily change that image. He can learn to be assertive instead of domineering, to show affection more openly, to ask for help from others, and to define the kind of life he wants to lead. Research indicates that executives who are in touch with their feelings and express them in appropriate ways are proving to their employees that the boss is human, too. The result can be an organization or department where human relations receives top priority along with production.

More men are asking themselves if their career choices reflect what they would like to do or what they were expected to do. They are examining their personal relationships and asking how important it is to marry early in life and have a family or to marry at all.

As men shift from traditional to newer values, they may experience many of the same conflicts women go through when making the change. Also, they may not have the understanding or support of their colleagues, who may be threatened by the change. When Ken Mason, president of Quaker Oats, resigned from his position to pursue private research on the social responsibility of business, many of his friends and colleagues criticized his decision as "abandoning the real world." Mason disagreed, saying, "I'm not impressed with the power of a corporate president. I am impressed with the power of ideas. I have a better chance of developing my ideas now than if I were doing the things presidents have to do."[21] Mason believes that men's concern with more humanistic values—long-term social consequences, relationships on and off the job, and the total environment—will serve business's best interests.

Thinking/Learning Starters

1. Men, do you feel the role options discussed in this section would be beneficial for you? If so, in what way?
2. How has the traditional male role affected men's abilities to relate to others?
3. As a man, have you questioned the validity of the traditional male role? What aspects of that role have you challenged? What aspects do you feel comfortable with?

The Effects of Sexism in Organizations

In addition to the traditionally held sex roles, the long history of sex discrimination has created a number of inequities between men and women in terms of education, salary, employment opportunities, and on-the-job behavior.

Problems Women Face in the Work Force

In 1984 there were 45 million women in the work force. By the year 2000, 64 million women will be working—a 45 percent gain. (See Figure 16.1.) The number of working men will grow only from 62 million to 70 million—13 percent.[22] Women will probably fill two-thirds of the jobs to be created between now and the year 2000. Yet 80 percent of today's working women fill traditional, low-status, low-paying jobs: typing, nursing, waiting on tables, retail sales, cleaning, and so forth.

Statistics show that women are beginning to move into management. For instance, in 1950 there were fewer than 700,000 women managers, officials, and proprietors. In 1982 there were more than 2.5 million. Yet statistics like

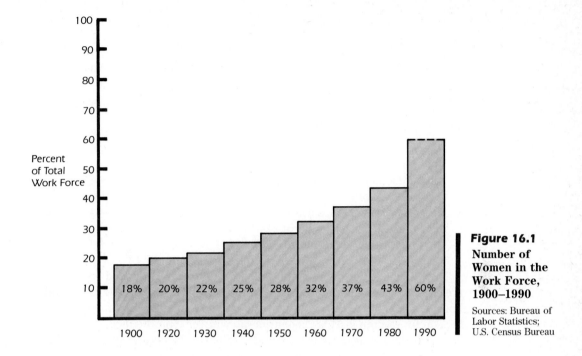

Figure 16.1
Number of Women in the Work Force, 1900–1990

Sources: Bureau of Labor Statistics; U.S. Census Bureau

these do not make evident that many of these managerial jobs are in traditionally female fields such as personnel, public relations, and administration. Such jobs are lower in status and are removed from a clear path to the top and higher salaries.[23] The only Fortune 1000 female chief executive officer is Katherine Graham, who inherited the Washington Post Company.

According to employment projections published by the U.S. Department of Labor, this situation may change as more women enter traditionally male-dominated professions and acquire the education required to compete for such jobs. For example, by 1990, the number of women who are private household workers will decline by 23 percent, while the number in management will increase 20 percent and the number working in the industrial labor market will rise 15 percent.[24] In addition, more women are finding careers in banking, sales, business law, and technical professions.

The Wage Gap

Inequalities in wages between men and women exist for two reasons: (1) women have tended to occupy low-paying jobs, and (2) in many industries and professions, women's labor is not considered as valuable, although women do the same types of jobs as men with the same level of skill and responsibility. In 1965, it was estimated that women as a whole earned 64 cents to every dollar earned by men. By 1985, that figure had slipped to 59 cents. The following comparisons of men's and women's wages were listed in a 1982 Bureau of Labor Statistics Survey.[25]

▶ Male administrators of elementary and secondary schools earned an average of $520 a week, compared to $363 for women.
▶ Male computer systems analysts earned an average weekly pay of $546, while their female counterparts earned a weekly average of $420.
▶ Women held 68.5 percent of the health technician jobs in hospitals and clinics, yet they earned an average weekly wage of $273, compared with $324 for men doing the same work.
▶ Female elementary school teachers earned an average of $68 a week less than males, even though women held 82.2 percent of those jobs.
▶ Men who worked at sales counters, except for those in food establishments, earned an average of $240 a week, while women, who held 76.2 percent of such jobs, earned $195.

The picture is considerably bleaker for minority women and women who are heads of single-parent households. One out of every three female-headed households is living below the poverty level. The median income of families headed by women is $10,802, considerably lower than the median income of husband-wife families, $25,065 annually.[26] The U.S. Commission on Civil Rights has found that a single-parent family's economic status is likely to be worse if the family is non-white. For white, female-headed families, the poverty rate was 27.4 percent. But for black female-headed families, it was 52.9 percent, and for Hispanic female-headed families, 53.2 percent.[27]

Under pressure from the Equal Employment Opportunity Commission (EEOC), affirmative action programs, and various working women's groups, organizations are beginning to adjust their salaries to eliminate the wage gap. But much remains to be done. Those who find themselves victims of wage discrimination have legal recourse through the **Equal Pay Act** of 1963, passed to prohibit inequalities in pay. Organizations who practice such discrimination or who refuse to adjust unequal pay scales can be sued under this act.

The Issue of Comparable Worth

The chairman of the U.S. Civil Rights Commission, Clarence Pendleton, calls it the "looniest idea since looney tunes." A staff lawyer for the National Women's Law Center refers to it as "one of the most important issues facing women." President Reagan finds the idea "harebrained." All are referring to the same subject: the controversial topic of comparable worth. The policy of **comparable worth** would require that women and men be paid equally not only for the same jobs but also for jobs that require the same level of skill, effort, responsibility, and working conditions.[28]

The issue of comparable worth was first raised in 1971 when the state of Washington enacted a law prohibiting sexual discrimination in employment.

The state government took action to comply with the statute. The governor said: "If the state's salary schedules reflect a bias in wages paid to women compared to those of men, then we must move to reverse this inequity." This directive led to a 1974 study examining fifty-nine jobs typically held by males and sixty-two typically held by females. The study developed a hypothetical point system based on four criteria: knowledge and skills, mental demands, accountability, and working conditions. For example, when the jobs of a male truck driver and female laundry worker were compared on the scale, each scored about 100 points. However, the truck driver's earnings were $1,574 a month, the laundry worker $1,114. Based on the study's analysis, state employees filed a discrimination suit against their employer. In December 1983, they won their case. The court ruling ordered the state to end sexual discrimination by raising salaries for approximately 15,000 state workers in predominantly female jobs at an estimated cost of $225 million. It also awarded back pay to workers, at a cost of about $838 million. The ruling had a ripple effect all across the nation. Seven bills were introduced in Congress to introduce comparable worth to the federal government and private industry.

The Washington State ruling was appealed and struck down by the 9th U.S. Circuit Court of Appeals. While admitting that a 20-percent wage gap between women's and men's jobs existed, the court ruled that a wage gap by itself does not show that the state intentionally discriminated against women. Washington state employees have appealed this decision.

Although the final verdict in the Washington suit is not yet in, the case has helped other states reevaluate the wage gap and take steps to alleviate the discrepancies. Minnesota is one of seven states that have voluntarily implemented pay equity or comparable worth programs for state employees and is the first in the nation to require local governments to do the same. In 1983, Minnesota legislators appropriated $21.8 million to increase wages during the following two years for secretaries, nurses, and other employees whose jobs had been identified as underpaid. In 1985, the legislature appropriated another $11.8 million to complete the pay equity increases for 1985–1987. Needless to say, comparable worth is an extremely expensive remedy for an age-old problem. The fact that it involves such large amounts of state tax revenue has caused a great deal of controversy. Table 16.3 indicates some of the arguments for and against comparable worth.

Myths and Realities About Working Women

Many people today believe that the drive for equal rights for working women that began in the early 1970s has succeeded. Although women have made progress in many areas, the barriers to their full participation in the labor force still remain. Many popular myths about working women make the struggle to overcome these barriers more difficult. It is important to note that women as well as men may believe these myths. However, when the

Table 16.3 Comparable Worth: Two Sides of the Issue

Pro	Con
Women are as well educated as their male counterparts and should be paid accordingly.	It is costly. States could go bankrupt by starting comparable-worth plans.
Women will remain in low-paying, dead-end jobs unless comparable-worth plans are adopted.	Many variables, such as supply and demand, affect wages. It would be difficult to legislate and would work against the free market setting wages.
The concept of equal pay for the same job does not go far enough because most men and women do not work in the same jobs.	It is impossible to assign relative values to jobs and any artificial system would be arbitrary and subjective.
Women continue to make less than men. Comparable-worth legislation could redress this.	It invites unwarranted governmental intrusion through federal wage controls on private industry.
Comparable worth is not a new, off-the-cuff idea of the feminist movement. It has been operating for several years in other countries, including Australia, Canada, France, and England.	Women choose the kinds of jobs they do. They are not forced to go into low-paying jobs.
Greater purchasing power by women could be created if women's salaries were brought in line with men's wages.	Women traditionally have accepted less pay for better working conditions. It is a logical trade-off.
Comparable worth does not require immediate pay increases to achieve equity, but calls for reexamining and developing a pay equity process.	Comparable worth is another invention of the women's movement to put down men.

Source: From *Roanoke Times & World News,* May 13, 1984. Reprinted by permission.

beliefs are examined in light of today's realities, much of the justification for sex discrimination disappears.[29]

1. *Women work to earn extra pocket money.* Forty-five percent of all working women are single, widowed, divorced, or separated and must work to provide for themselves and their families. In addition, women who are married contribute, on average, from one-fourth to one-half of the family income. In many families, the wife's earnings are critical to the support of the family, covering medical expenses, schooling, credit payments, and other family-related expenses. With the current number of unemployed male heads of families, many households must now rely totally on the wife's earnings. Thus, inequities in men's and women's pay hurts a family considerably.

"So according to the stereotype, *you* can put two and two together, but *I* can read the handwriting on the wall." (© 1986 Joel Pett in *The Kappan*)

2. *Women earn less because they don't stay in the job market.* The average working woman is in the labor force for twenty-eight years, compared with thirty-eight years for men. In the past twenty years, there has been a marked shift in women's work patterns. Previously, most women worked for only a few years, then dropped out after marrying, and re-entered the market after divorce, widowhood, or when the children had grown. Now, 59 percent of mothers with school-age children work.

3. *Women don't have the education to get ahead.* As of 1980, both men and women had completed a median of 12.8 years of education. Women have shown major progress over the past decade in earning degrees in the medical and legal professions and in many other previously all-male occupations. However, women continue to earn less than men with comparable educational backgrounds.

4. *Unemployment is caused by the influx of women into the labor force.* For women to be the cause of male unemployment, the large number of women who are now in the labor force would have had to take jobs traditionally held by men. In fact, the vast majority of women take clerical jobs in part because they are excluded from many male-dominated fields. Current unemployment rates among men are caused by reductions in blue-collar jobs, especially in manufacturing and construction. In addition, many unemployed men do not have adequate skills to replace working women. If all the women now holding jobs were to leave the work force to make room for all the unemployed men, about 17 million jobs would still remain vacant.

5. *Women are not strong enough or emotionally stable enough to succeed in high-pressure jobs.* A common belief is that women are more vulnerable to drastic swings of mood than men and are physically less able to endure

the daily pressure at top management levels. As a result, they should not be in positions where they can affect the growth and profitability of the company. Research does not support these beliefs, however. In our culture, women are encouraged to express their emotions of fear, anxiety, disappointment, grief, or pain, whereas such emotional expressions are considered a sign of weakness in the traditional male role. Men and women may express their emotions differently, but they are equally emotional.

As American society begins to challenge these outdated myths, companies have discovered that selecting only male candidates for management positions means ignoring about half of the best talent available. Tapping that pool of skills is nothing more than good business. Men and women both are beginning to be comfortable working for and with female managers. In 1965, the *Harvard Business Review* conducted a survey of corporate executives to assess their views of women in business. Only 27 percent indicated they would be comfortable working for a woman, and only 9 percent of the executives said they held "strongly favorable" attitudes toward women executives. The statistics rose to 47 percent and 33 percent respectively when the same survey was conducted in 1985.[30]

Although many of the myths about men's and women's capabilities are being dispelled, some old behaviors and attitudes persist. When women are promoted into a new department, sit on or chair a new committee, or change jobs, they sometimes feel as if they have been plunged into the "dark ages." The weariness feminists feel at the persistence of old stereotypes is called "feminist fatigue" by popular author Ellen Goodman.

> It's like two different cultures living side by side. One culture has been enormously affected by these changes, grown out of rhetoric and into easy living with new ideas and ideals. The other culture remains powerful and pristine in its old ways. One culture understands. The other demands tired explanations or ancient passivity. The constant commute between these two cultures could make anyone come down with a case of feminist fatigue.[31]

Support for Change

Organizations such as the National Organization for Women (NOW), Women Employed, and the National Women's Political Caucus are developing support structures to help women succeed in the job world. These structures include scholarships, student loans, day care centers, counseling, consciousness-raising groups, conferences, career fairs or exhibits, and seminars. In addition, professional associations and organizations, networks, and unions can help women on many levels. They not only combat sex discrimination but pass on job information, facilitate communication among women in the same or similar professions, and help women upgrade their skills. Creating a professional network is one way women are helping other women achieve their career goals.

Thinking/Learning Starters

1. Why do inequalities in wages exist between men and women?
2. After reading the myths and realities of working women, did you find any of your own attitudes about such women challenged? If so, which ones?

Problems Facing Men

Men also encounter resistance when they attempt to break out of their stereotyped roles. The strongest resistance may come from those closest to them: family, coworkers, and friends. The changes a man makes to break away from the traditional masculine role can be threatening to others. In addition, certain myths about men make it difficult for others to accept a man in a nontraditional role. Some of the more common myths include the following:

1. *Men are too ambitious to stay in "female" jobs.* The typical image of a man is someone who enters a job at a lower level and works his way to the top. Employers may be reluctant to hire male clerical workers and support staff because they feel the men won't stay long in these positions. If a man makes it clear he wants to remain in office support work, others may wonder, "What's wrong with him? Can't he find a *real* job?"

2. *Men don't have the patience or manual dexterity to do the work women do.* Many people have been conditioned to believe that women are better at fine, detailed work and men are more skilled with heavy machinery and equipment. Men who have entered secretarial professions are likely to hear such remarks as "He types well, for a man" or "He's almost as good at detail as a woman." Like women in management positions, men in traditionally female jobs find they must prove their right to be there and their ability to do the work.

3. *Men have a natural ability to take charge.* Even if a man pursues a career in a traditionally female job, he may be a victim of the male role in peculiar ways. His female coworkers may elect him unofficial spokesperson for the group when any grievances need to be aired. Or he may discover that he is being given the difficult jobs to do or is viewed as the handyman when a machine breaks down. Many men resent the expectation that they will take charge in a situation that requires leadership, decision-making abilities, or mechanical skill.

4. *Men should always uphold the "male image" on the job.* Men also experience considerable peer pressure to "act like a man" or "pull with the team." A man's desire to drop out of corporate life and work at more low-key jobs or put his family ahead of his career may be threatening to his colleagues. He is likely to find his masculinity questioned or be criticized for not being able to take the pressure. One manager reported that when he began talking about his conflicts and inner doubts about the traditional male role, the other managers stopped eating lunch with him. "I think they were afraid that what I was going through was contagious!"

A man who places personal goals above his job, wants time off to care for a sick child or help out with a newborn baby, or allows himself to express his more "feminine" emotions may be considered by male colleagues to be a weak link in the team. Men in key positions in an organization are particularly vulnerable in this regard. Bill Agee, while an executive at Bendix, had always been described as "brash," "egotistical," or "ruthless"—characteristics considered part of corporate macho. However, when he began accepting the advice of a female company executive, Mary Cunningham, he suddenly found himself labeled as "weak," "hesitant," and "easily influenced." Agee regarded himself as simply a good business person who valued expert advice.[32] Other men who admit to using their intuition, considered a feminine trait, or who gain a reputation of being more emotional than logical may also find they have violated the unwritten code, discussed in the previous chapter, defining what is and isn't acceptable behavior in their particular companies.

5. *Men must provide a high standard of living for their families.* On the surface, this statement seems a natural expression of a man's desire to see that his family is well provided for. Too often, however, this feeling is translated as "keeping up with the Joneses." The necessity to provide his family with the best of everything may keep a man in a high-paying job or profession he doesn't like. He may also feel that he must continue to move up the corporate ladder or increase his earning capacity to maintain or raise his family's standard of living. As a result, family members often do not understand or accept the process a man undergoes when he chooses to create a new role for himself. They fear the loss of status or the privileges the man's income has provided.

Support for Change

Nearly all the men who have struggled to liberate themselves from the stereotyped male role have emphasized, *"don't go it alone."* Men's support groups around the country—the Chicago Men's Gathering, Minneapolis Men's Center, St. Louis Men's Center, the Los Angeles Men's Collective, and the East Bay Men's Center in California—sponsor consciousness-raising groups for men, patterned after women's consciousness-raising sessions. These small groups help men (1) examine the traditional male role, (2) recognize and express their feelings, and (3) support those who are making changes in their lives.

Men's support groups, conferences, and books have also helped men understand how women's struggle for equality is their fight as well. If one sex remains trapped in a rigidly defined role, neither sex can be truly liberated. "Maybe someday," one man said, "we won't talk about men's liberation or women's liberation; we'll talk about *human* liberation."

Thinking/Learning Starters

1. Do you believe men can do as good a job in "female" professions as women? Why or why not?
2. In your opinion, why do many men stress "don't go it alone" when a man is making major changes in his traditional masculine role?

Coping with Sexist Behavior

Traditional attitudes, beliefs, and practices are not changed easily. If you are a man or woman breaking ground into a nontraditional role, you will encounter resistance. In addition, you may be confused about how to act or overly sensitive about the way others treat you. As a result, if you are choosing a new role for yourself, you will need to learn new skills to control your own behavior as well as to confront some of the very real obstacles you will encounter in organizations. Methods for dealing with sexist behavior range from guidelines for a new etiquette through assertiveness training to legal action.

New Organizational Etiquette

As women enter into higher levels of management and men begin to work in support positions, the ways men and women deal with one another undergo subtle changes. Does this require a new set of manners and rules of etiquette? In some cases, yes. The guidelines listed below may help you understand how to act in these new situations.

1. When a woman executive visits a male executive, he should rise from his desk to greet her. When a man enters a woman's office, *she* should rise from her desk.
2. Whoever has a free hand (could be a small woman) should help anyone carrying too heavy a load (could be a large man).

3. The woman who thinks she must "out-macho" the men to be accepted is likely to find she is wrong. The successful woman is assertive (when this behavior is warranted), maintains her sense of humor, and helps men adjust to her presence as a colleague.

4. Men should not assume that a woman doesn't want to talk about sports, cars, or other "masculine" interests. This merely reinforces the "outsider" attitude toward a woman.

5. Women resent being "go-fers." The male in charge of a meeting should not look to the woman to take notes, answer the phone, or type material. Nor should women leap to serve the coffee when someone suggests it's time for a break. All management personnel should rotate clerical duties, such as taking the minutes of a meeting.

6. Whoever arrives first at the door should open it, and whoever stands in the front of the elevator should get off first.

7. A woman in a business situation should open her own car door and light her own cigarettes.

8. Whoever extends an invitation to lunch or dinner should pay the tab.

What about the reverse situation—when a man is breaking into a traditionally female occupation? Some of the etiquette guidelines include the following:

1. Don't assume that the man will automatically know how to fix any machine that breaks down.

2. If something heavy must be moved, ask several people to help. Don't assume the man will always be able to do it.

3. Avoid passing all problem clients or difficult jobs onto the man. He will not necessarily know how to handle them any better than the women.

4. Share routine office duties. Making any exception—men don't make the coffee, go out for sandwiches, and the like—only underscores the fact that he is an "outsider."

5. Make sure that training materials, memos, and so on, use inclusive terms. Do not refer to clerical and secretarial personnel only as "she" or "her."

The new etiquette is basically a way to overcome old stereotypes and traditional ways of setting men and women apart solely on the basis of sex. Today, it is much more a matter of one professional, who happens to be a man, relating to another professional, who happens to be a woman. It is likely that both men and women will feel somewhat awkward at first relating to one another as equal colleagues. By practicing these etiquette skills and adopting a positive, helpful attitude toward each other, men and women can help ease the transition from traditional to nontraditional roles. Both sides will be winners.

Assertiveness Skills

Assertiveness training is becoming more and more popular as a way of teaching men and women to express their thoughts and feelings in appropriate ways and to ask for what they want or need. Often, men and women learn these skills for different reasons. Many women need to overcome a lifetime of conditioning to be passive and wait for rewards or promotions to come their way. Many have suffered in silence when they discovered that someone else doing the same work was receiving more pay. They may have put up with sexual harassment on the job or seen less well-qualified people promoted over them. On the other hand, many men must learn to be less demanding and domineering and more considerate of the needs and feelings of coworkers or subordinates. They can change their aggressive behavior into assertive behavior.

Assertive, aggressive, and passive behaviors are distinctly different. *Assertive* behavior involves standing up for your rights and expressing your thoughts and feelings in a direct, appropriate way that does not violate the rights of others. *Aggressive* behavior means expressing your thoughts and feelings and defending your rights in a way that is usually inappropriate and often violates the rights of others. *Passive* behavior means that an individual fails to express his or her thoughts and feelings and does not stand up for the rights being violated.

Assertive skills can be used to counteract sexist behavior in a way that maintains the integrity and self-respect of both parties. For example, a woman manager is interrupted by a male colleague while giving a report; it is obvious he does not think her work is very important. An assertive response on her part would be, "Excuse me, I'd like to finish what I was saying." She has not attacked the other person but asserted her right to speak. An aggressive response might have been, "Why don't you just wait your turn—are you always so rude?" By attacking the person's character, the woman may have made an enemy. Certainly, she did nothing to change the man's attitude. A passive response would have been to say nothing. If the woman allows herself to be interrupted over and over, she will soon fade into the background of the organization.

Knowing when to be assertive and when to overlook an attitude or behavior depends largely on the situation and how important an issue is to you. As an assertive person, you let others know how their behavior affects you, giving others the opportunity to change that behavior. You are defining your rights as a person. Each individual must determine which rights are important enough to defend when they are violated.

Legal Recourse

Many court decisions have been handed down from the state and federal levels outlawing discrimination on the basis of sex. For example, the courts have recently decided that maternity leave and benefits should be granted to pregnant women in the same way disability leave and benefits are awarded to other employees in the same organizations. As a result, women who choose to combine motherhood and career can have a child, recuperate from the childbirth experience, and return within a reasonable time to their jobs without loss of seniority, position, or income.

We have already discussed some of the controversial court decisions revolving around equal pay for work that involves the same level of skill, effort, and responsibility. Even though the comparable worth issue is still in limbo, the Equal Pay Act of 1963, amended in 1972 and 1974, continues to offer solid support to executive, administrative, professional, and outside sales personnel as well as federal, state, and local government employees. However, employees in some small retail and service establishments are still not covered by the act. If you are ever unsure if you have been discriminated against because of your sex, Title VII of the Civil Rights Act has issued "Guidelines on Discrimination Because of Sex." Examine them, and then take the necessary steps.

Some of the opportunities now open to women—particularly at the executive levels in traditionally male professions—are the result of legal actions filed by individuals or groups. In some cases, men have also resorted to legal action to open professions previously considered all female. In addition, men are more likely to file reverse discrimination charges, discussed in the previous chapter, as they seek to gain entry into affirmative action training and management development programs.

Taking legal action is a big step and often involves months or years of litigation. Yet many of the antidiscrimination laws now in force began when one person or a group of people were willing to pursue their case through the courts. The Equal Rights Amendment may someday be among those laws.

Sexual Harassment

One of the most sensitive areas of discrimination is sexual harassment. Because the subject is often a highly emotional one, the EEOC has published guidelines that help men and women know when they are being sexually harassed. **Sexual harassment** is any unwelcome verbal or physical behavior that meets the following criteria.

1. Your employer or supervisor threatens the security of your job or a potential promotion because you object to his or her comments of a personal, sexual nature; touching and feeling that are definitely sexual in nature; or demands for sexual favors. These behaviors can take the form of being forced to look at sexually explicit pictures, listen to dirty jokes or comments about your body, or offers of promotions or raises in exchange for sexual favors.

2. Withholding of a promotion or pay increase, demotion, or firing because of acceptance or rejection of the conduct.

3. Sexual innuendoes by a supervisor or fellow employees interferes with your work performance or creates a hostile, intimidating, or offensive work environment.

Who are the most frequent targets? They are new employees, people who are on probation in their jobs, and the very young or inexperienced. People who have recently experienced personal crises, such as divorce, are often victims. Women who take what are traditionally considered male jobs are often subject to sexual harassment.

Although sexual harassment is a problem for both sexes, the overwhelming majority of cases affect women. Many organizations ranging from large corporations to universities are now developing programs to help stop sexual harassment. One such program is the "Tell Someone" program at the University of Michigan. The program was the first of its kind to encourage victims of sexual harassment to complain to authorities. Many organizations have their own policies that define sexual harassment, outline procedures for reporting it, and prescribe punitive actions for proven offenders. One city council defined sexual harassment as making sexual comments, innuendoes, insults, jokes, suggestions, or gestures; leering; whistling suggestively; displaying sexually derogatory posters, cartoons, or drawings; touching; pinching; and committing sexual assault. The policy was made part of the city's affirmative action plan.

Employers are developing explicit policies because they could be forced to pay back wages and attorney's fees for an employee who quit or didn't get a promotion because of sexual harassment. Even if there are no direct costs, permitting sexual harassment perpetuates low morale and high turnover, which raises personnel costs. As victims leave the organization, unemployment costs increase. This often happens because employers are not aware they are sexually harassing an employee—the behaviors were never clearly defined.

The Fair Employment Practices Guidelines encourage organizations to:

▶ Circulate a written policy statement, including a clear definition, prohibiting sexual harassment.
▶ Encourage employees to report any complaints. Courts have held an organization liable if an employee was aware of sexual harassment of another employee and didn't report it. The victim and observers need to be encouraged to report each incident.
▶ Discipline offenders swiftly and appropriately.
▶ Protect victims from reprisals by allowing them to remain anonymous.

What should an individual do when sexually harassed? The first step anyone should take, male or female, is to tell the person no. You don't have to be nasty, but you should be firm. Tell them you don't appreciate that kind of comment; you don't like to be rubbed against; or you prefer not to listen to those types of jokes. Talking with your coworkers is often helpful. They can provide emotional support and help document instances of harassment. Chances are, if one person is being harassed, others are too. If the harasser is a coworker, you can speak with your immediate supervisor or union steward and tell him or her what is happening. Ask for assistance in solving the problem. Remember, it is the company's responsibility to be aware of the situation and correct the behavior before legal charges are filed. If the harasser is your supervisor, it is a good idea to speak to someone higher up in the system. Put the company on notice that *they* have a problem. Then, document everything: whom you talked with, when, what actions they took, what they said, what you told them, and what you agreed on. If you decide to file charges with the federal Equal Employment Opportunity Council, you're going to have to be able to substantiate your complaint.

As the problem of sexual harassment receives wider attention, the incidence of court cases is likely to increase. The grounds for filing charges are becoming more liberal and so are the awards. Continental Can Company was ordered by a court to pay $100,000 to an employee who filed suit against a manager in their Denver-based plant.[33] The EEOC hopes that continued court action will discourage the abuse as a whole. Often, however, just threatening legal action may be enough to stop sexual harassment.

Summary

Sexism is discrimination based on widely held beliefs about the abilities, characteristics, and behavior of men and women. The traditional roles assigned to both sexes limit their opportunities to choose a career and lifestyle best suited to their abilities and true interests.

Many men and women are breaking out of these traditional roles. Over the past twenty years, women have entered the job world in increasing numbers and in professions previously considered all-male. They also have a wider range of choices regarding marriage and children than ever before. Through the women's movement, many women are rejecting the old image of "feminine" as passive, illogical, dependent, and totally supportive of others.

Men are also choosing new roles for themselves. They are working to dispel the "John Wayne myth" that men must always be in control, emotionally unexpressive, logical, and achievement oriented. They realize that the rigid male role has had devastating effects on men's health and on their relationships with women *and* other men. Men's liberation groups seek to help men re-examine the traditional role, express their feelings, make changes in their lives, and recognize that women's struggle for equality is their fight as well.

Both sexes face problems because of a long history of sex discrimination. Women are working to close the wage gap and gain access to higher paying jobs. Men have recently begun to enter traditionally female professions and accept more personally rewarding careers even if they do not offer the same material rewards. The policy of comparable worth is a controversial way some have suggested to bridge the wage gap.

Methods for coping with sexist behavior include practicing the new organizational etiquette for men and women, acquiring assertiveness skills, and understanding the legal measures available to individuals who believe they are the victims of sex discrimination. These methods can be used in dealing with the sensitive issue of sexual harassment.

Key Terms

sexism
nontraditional career
traditional role
sexual role model
displaced homemaker
job sharing
telecommuting

flextime
compressed work
  week
Equal Pay Act
comparable worth
assertiveness training
sexual harassment

Review Questions

1. List some of the traditional qualities men and women have been encouraged to develop.
2. What qualities were men and women *not* encouraged to develop?
3. How important are sexual role models in a young man's or woman's life? How do these role models influence others?
4. What are some of the nontraditional choices regarding marriage and children open to men and women today?
5. What are some of the effects of past discrimination against women in organizations?
6. Describe some of the difficulties men encounter when they attempt to change their traditional role.
7. What types of support for change are available to men and women?
8. Describe the difference between assertive, aggressive, and passive behavior. What is the value of assertive behavior?
9. List some of the legal measures taken to eliminate sexism in organizations.
10. How can corporate policies prevent incidents of sexual harassment? What can individuals do?

Case 16.1

Ignorance Is No Excuse[34]

Is an organization responsible for the sexual harassment of one employee by another, even if upper management does not know that the harassment is occurring? That is one of several questions that the U.S. Supreme Court is expected to consider in a case brought by Mechelle Vinson against the Capital City Federal Savings & Loan Association of Washington, D.C.

Vinson, who worked at a branch of Capital City, charged that her boss had continually threatened her job and her life if she did not respond to his sexual advances. A lower federal court found for the defendant, after testimony that Vinson never complained to higher-ups at Capital City. However, an appeals court overturned that decision, declaring that "We didn't know" was not a sufficient defense for employers. The case was then appealed to the Supreme Court; it became the first sexual harassment case to be heard by the Court.

The attorney for Capital City has argued that the Savings & Loan could not be held responsible without being notified in some way. Vinson's lawyer countered by declaring that the bank was indeed liable—that Vinson's boss represented the bank because he was her immediate supervisor.

Questions

1. How would you answer the question that begins this case? Explain your answer.
2. Suppose the Supreme Court rules that organizations are responsible for sexual harassment, even when they don't know it is taking place. How might an organization protect itself against that liability?

Case 16.2

Competition and Comparable Worth[35]

Executives at ZXP Corporation began to look into comparable worth as soon as they heard that New York State was using it to evaluate inequities in state employees' wages. Because its headquarters are in Albany, New York (the state capitol), ZXP competes for employees with many state agencies. Changes in state wage schedules would affect the firm's ability to attract and retain workers.

The managers analyzed ten jobs held predominately by males and ten jobs held predominately by females at ZXP, using four recommended rating criteria. Their findings were amazingly consistent: In every case in which a "female" job and a "male" job were rated comparable or nearly comparable, ZXP was found to pay a lower wage for the "female" job. Moreover, in every case, the ZXP wages were in line with current labor market wages for the area. In other words, other major employers in the Albany area were doing the same thing.

As an example, the mainly "female" job of file clerk and the mainly "male" job of janitor were assigned exactly the same number of worth points in the analysis. Yet ZXP paid file clerks at the base rate of $4.85 per hour and janitors at $6.40 per hour.

Assuming that these results are typical for ZXP companywide, the executives could take any of several actions. Among these are:

1. Do nothing further with the comparable worth analysis. Keep tabs on the labor market and at least match the current market wage for each type of job.
2. Extend the comparable worth analysis to all jobs in the company. Raise wages for those jobs that are far out of line.
3. Extend the analysis to all jobs, but *raise or lower* wages as necessary to provide equal pay for comparable worth, regardless of gender.
4. Ensure that, for each type of job, men and women are treated similarly with regard to hiring and promotion policies, base pay and merit increases, performance appraisals, and the like.

ZXP's management wants to be as fair as it can with the firm's employees, whom they consider to be an important business resource. They expect to pay wages that are high enough to keep qualified employees, but not so high as to make the firm unprofitable.

Questions

1. What problems might be involved in having top executives evaluate the worth of such jobs as janitor and file clerk? How could such problems be eliminated (without adding new ones)?
2. Is comparable worth a reasonable yardstick for determining wage rates? In what ways is it a better or worse yardstick than the "market price" of labor?
3. What, if anything, should ZXP do with regard to its wage schedules and policies? Why?

Notes

1. The People Column, *Roanoke Times & World-News*.
2. Marion A. Ellis, "Flight Attendant Job Still Attracts Hundreds," *Roanoke Times and World-News*.
3. Kate Rand Lloyd, "Stereotypes Don't Pay Today," *Advertising Age*, July 26, 1982, p. M-16.
4. Taken from an editorial by Dr. Gene Bottoms, Executive Director of the American Vocational Association, *Voc Ed*, April 1983, p. 9.
5. Warren Farrell, *The Liberated Man* (New York: Random House, 1974), p. 35.
6. William Serrin, "Women Changing the Workplace, But Limiting Factors Still in Evidence," *Roanoke Times & World-News*.
7. "What's Changed in the Last Five Years," *Working Woman*, January 1985, p. 2.
8. Elizabeth Howland, "Role Models," *Roanoke Times & World-News*, October 4, 1979.

9. Victoria Blanchard and Rose Cherry, "Displaced Homemakers Find Independence," *Voc Ed*, April 1985, pp. 33–35.

10. Peter Francese, "Work-force Growth Fastest for Females."

11. "Flexible Work Hours Seen as Aiding Child-Care," *Roanoke Times & World-News.*

12. Donna Fenn, "The Kids Are All Right," *INC.*, January 1985, pp. 48–54.

13. Philip I. Morgan and H. Kent Baker, "Taking a Look at Flexitime," *Supervisory Management*, February 1984, pp. 37–41.

14. Lori Lesler, "Behind the Wheel of a Quiet Revolution," *Advertising Age*, July 26, 1982, pp. M-11–M-12. Statistics computed by the Bureau of Labor Statistics, U.S. Department of Labor.

15. Laurie Ashcraft and Elizabeth Nickles, "Ads Start to Roll with the Social Punches," *Advertising Age*, July 16, 1982, p. M-24. Used with permission.

16. Debbie Mead, "Francisco Gets 2-Year Term for Robbery," *Roanoke Times & World-News*, January 28, 1984, pp. A-1, A-10.

17. Lesler, "Behind the Wheel," p. M-12.

18. Herb Goldberg, *The Hazards of Being Male* (New York: Nash Publishing, 1976), pp. 96–106.

19. Ibid., pp. 96–119.

20. "Working Around Motherhood," *Business Week*, May 24, 1982, p. 188.

21. Myron Magnet, "Chucking It," *Fortune*, July 27, 1981, pp. 82–86.

22. Adapted from data in Malcolm Morrison, "The Aging of the U.S. Population: Human Resources Implications," *Monthly Labor Review*, May 1983.

23. Gay Bryant, *The Working Woman Report* (New York: Simon and Schuster), 1984.

24. Women's Bureau, Office of the Secretary, U.S. Department of Labor, *Job Options for Women in the 80s* (Washington, D.C.: U.S. Government Printing Office, 1980), p. 3.

25. "Compensation Gap: Women's Pay for Same Jobs Still Lower," *Roanoke Times & World-News*, March 7, 1982, p. A-5.

26. Women's Bureau, *Job Options for Women in the 80s*, p. 5.

27. "Rise in Poor Families Headed by Females Called Alarming," *Roanoke Times & World-News*, April 12, 1983, p. 4.

28. Diana L. Charles, "Comparable Worth: Is It Worth It?" *Training and Development Journal*, November 1985, pp. 63–66.

29. Jacqueline Crawford and Gary N. McLean, *Humanity as a Career: A Holistic Approach to Sex Equity* (Rehoboth, Mass.: Two Oaks Publishing, 1979), pp. 20–22.

30. "More and More, She's the Boss," *Time*, December 2, 1985, pp. 64–66.

31. Ellen Goodman, "Cultural Commuting Is Fatiguing," © 1982, The Washington Post Writers Group.

32. Robert Sam Anson, "Unlimited Partnership," *Savvy*, November 1982, p. 38.

33. Ron Zemke, "Sexual Harassment: Is Training the Key?" *Training/HRD*, February 1981, pp. 22, 27–31.

34. For more information, see *Industry Week*, June 24, 1985, pp. 57–58; *Time*, April 7, 1986, pp. 62–63; and *Business Week*, March 31, 1986, p. 35.

35. For more information, see *Management Review*, September 1985, pp. 40–43; *Advertising Age*, October 3, 1985, p. 60; and *Management Review*, March 1986, pp. 40–43.

Suggested Readings

Alexander, Jan Northup. *The Promotable Woman*. Springfield, Va.: Management Training Systems, 1985.

Brownmiller, Susan. *Femininity*. New York: Linden/Simon and Schuster, 1984.

Bryant, Gay. *The Working Woman Report*. New York: Simon and Schuster, 1984.

Doyle, James A. *The Male Experience*. Dubuque, Iowa: William C. Brown Publishers, 1984.

Elgin, S. H. *The Gentle Art of Verbal Self-Defense*. Englewood Cliffs, N.J.: Prentice-Hall, 1980.

Farrell, Warren. *The Liberated Man*. New York: Bantam, 1976.

Goldberg, Herb. *The Hazards of Being Male*. New York: Signet, 1976.

Hennig, Margaret, and Anne Jardin. *The Managerial Women*. New York: Simon & Schuster, 1977.

Horn, Patrice, and Jack Horn. *Sex in the Office: Power and Passion in the Workplace*. Reading, Mass.: Addison-Wesley, 1983.

Jongeward, Dorothy, and Dru Scott. *Women as Winners*. Reading, Mass.: Addison-Wesley, 1976.

Kleiman, Carol. *Women's Networks*. New York: Lippincott & Crowell, 1980.

MacKinnon, C. A. *Sexual Harassment of Working Women: A Case of Sex Discrimination*. New Haven: Yale University Press, 1979.

Renick, J. C. "Sexual Harassment at Work: Why It Happens, What to Do About It." *Personnel Journal*, August 1980.

Rowe, M. P. "Dealing with Sexual Harassment." *Harvard Business Review*, May–June 1981.

Shapiro, Barry, and Evelyn Shapiro, eds. *The Women Say/The Men Say*. New York: Dell, 1979.

Zemke, Ron. "Sexual Harassment: Is Training the Key?" *Training/HRD*, February 1981, pp. 22–30.

VI

You Can Plan for Success

Chapter 17

Making Your Plan for Improved Human Relations

Chapter Preview

After studying this chapter, you will be able to

1. Understand that effective human relations is a series of *skills* that can be developed and *improved.*
2. Assess your strengths and areas needing improvement in human relations.
3. Improve your ability to work well with others.
4. Develop a plan to improve your human relations skills.

Whenever you encounter a human relations problem, you can handle the situation in one of three ways. You can try to change the other person, try to change the situation, or try to change yourself.

1. *Changing the other person.* "If she would only see things my way ... ," "If his attitude would change ... ," "Things would be great if only the boss weren't so picky. ...." It's tempting to believe that a human relations problem lies entirely with the other person; in that way you do not have to look at your own behavior or accept any responsibility for being part of the problem. Yet every time you insist that another person change to suit your values, attitudes, or needs, it is almost impossible to maintain effective human relations. People will resent your attitude that only *they* have a problem.

2. *Changing the situation.* There may be times when a human relations problem simply cannot be resolved despite all you do. In these cases, it may be better to try to pursue your career elsewhere. However, too often people change their situations to avoid confronting their own shortcomings or accepting responsibility for their behavior. By adopting this approach, you do not solve the problem—you simply take it with you. It won't be long before the same problem crops up again on the new job.

3. *Changing yourself.* This book has reinforced the concept that each individual can control his or her own behavior when dealing with other people. In fact, your own behavior is often the only part of a situation that *is* under your control. As a result, changing yourself seems to be a logical, intelligent approach to many human relations problems. You are accepting responsibility for your actions, feelings, and attitudes in a situation and determining what you need to change. If you make personal growth your objective, you will be able to let go of many negative attitudes and habits without feeling that someone else forced you to do so. You are tapping into your potential and increasing your ability to achieve your personal and career goals. Your changed behavior may cause other people to decide *they* will change, but even if they continue to act in the old way, you are choosing how you will respond to them. You are not letting their behavior dictate your actions and attitudes. In effect, you have set up a win/win situation for yourself.

With the guidance offered in this book, you can put into action specific techniques to modify your behavior. Most of what you have learned will transfer into your everyday life. It will take some work and planning on your part, but real change *is* possible. This chapter is designed to help you make a specific plan for improving your human relations skills—now and in the future as you progress in your career.

Assess Your Human Relations Abilities

Assessment means evaluating; self-assessment means evaluating your strengths and weaknesses and your potential for improvement. You can begin now to

Copyright © 1982. Reprinted by permission of AMACOM and Henry Martin

map your plan for improved human relations by building your skills in this area. But in order to change your behavior, you need to know which characteristics you would like to improve.

The following self-assessment continuums are designed to help you determine your areas of strength and weakness. By evaluating your effectiveness on each of the continuums, you will be able to devise a plan for improving your human relations skills.

This chapter is organized to follow the outline of the book. The final section describes a step-by-step plan to help you develop the skills and attitudes you wish to have. Each chapter is summarized briefly, outlining the human relations skills discussed there. If you have any difficulties with concepts or terms, refer back to the appropriate chapter. The continuums can help you evaluate how well you have mastered the skills. Consider each continuum carefully, and place an X nearest the point that you feel accurately reflects your self-assessment. We suggest you use a pencil the first time through the continuums.

One of the objectives of this type of evaluation is to provide a long-term, progressive assessment of your skills. In approximately six months, we suggest you go through the continuums again, being careful to mark any change in behavior with a different colored pen or pencil. Throughout your career, you can return to these continuums, each time measuring how you are progressing.

The plan outlined in the final section will help you develop or improve those skills you would like to have. This approach is a proven technique for making lasting changes in behavior. We feel it can work well for you.

Do You Understand Yourself?

Attitudes Are Important

In Chapter 3, *attitude* was defined as any strong belief or feeling toward people, situations, or groups. You begin to acquire your attitudes at a very early age from interactions with parents, family, teachers, and friends. Throughout life you continuously develop new attitudes about work, the people you associate with on the job, family life, and the like.

Employee attitudes represent a powerful force in any organization. Workers who treat customers indifferently can lose business for the firm. A casual attitude toward safety rules and regulations may lead to a serious accident. You can usually determine another person's attitude by observing his or her behavior. An employee who regularly arrives at work on time no doubt believes that punctuality is important.

Success in getting along with people depends on your attitude toward yourself and others. To the extent that you possess a strong self-concept (a positive attitude toward yourself), you will find it easier to get along with other people. If you are generally optimistic about your future and possess positive attitudes toward others, you will very likely enjoy considerable success in the area of interpersonal relations.

Do you tend to display positive attitudes toward people?

I am very weak in this area.	I am somewhat weak in this area.	I am strong in this area.	I am very strong in this area.

Although people do not easily adopt new attitudes or discard old ones, attitudes can be changed. People change their attitudes as a result of life experiences. Feedback from others often stimulates people to change. When you have the opportunity to give feedback to others, be sure to balance negative feedback with positive. Always focus your feedback on the *behavior*, not on the person, and avoid making judgments. Try to focus the feedback on specific situations or attitudes. And make sure you give feedback at an appropriate time and place.

Are you able to give other people feedback effectively?

| I am very weak in this area. | I am somewhat weak in this area. | I am strong in this area. | I am very strong in this area. |

If you find your Xs appear on the far left side of either continuum, you may need to re-examine your basic attitudes toward people and your ability to give constructive feedback. See if you can identify specific attitudes in yourself you would like to change. Look over Chapter 3. Can you identify ways to begin changing your attitudes? The chapter also offers guidelines on giving constructive feedback, an important skill on the job.

Building a Positive Self-Concept

Your self-concept is the organized, consistent set of ideas, attitudes, and feelings you have about yourself that influences the way you relate to others. A healthy, positive self-concept is the foundation for a successful career in any field. Your self-concept shapes your personal and career expectations. If you have a positive self-concept, you will *expect* to succeed and you will devise a plan to use your strengths and abilities to their fullest. If you expect to fail, you probably will.

Your current self-concept was developed through the influences of your family members, friends, teachers, and your own life experiences. However, your future self-concept can be shaped by your own efforts and by seeking the help of others. Pygmalions and mentors—people who have identified your potential—can have a positive effect on your self-concept.

People with positive self-concepts are future oriented; they have learned from their past successes and failures. They are able to cope with life's problems and disappointments, and realize that problems need not make them anxious or depressed. They direct their emotions so that they can *act* rather than *react* to situations. In addition, they are able to ask for help and give it to others without feeling threatened by their own weaknesses or others' successes. Because they accept themselves, they accept others as unique, talented individuals eager to develop their potential.

How would you describe your current self-concept?

| I have a very negative self-concept. | I have a negative self-concept. | I have a positive self-concept. | I have a very positive self-concept. |

You cannot change what has happened in the past. But you can change the future by becoming aware of the person you would like to be. It takes time to change, but the effort is well worth it. You can begin to develop a strong self-concept by accepting yourself as you are now, identifying and accepting your limitations as you focus on your positive attributes. If you do something you don't like, hate the activity—not yourself. You can change your behavior by visualizing and rehearsing the results you want. Set goals high enough to be a challenge, but realistic enough so that you can achieve them. Take every experience as an opportunity to learn and to grow, and develop a strong expertise in some area. Remember to reward yourself when you act like the person you are striving to become.

Have you identified ways to improve your self-concept?

Identified but no action taken	Occasional activity toward improved self-concept	Frequent activity toward improved self-concept	Daily activity toward improved self-concept

If you find you rate your self-concept low, you probably have low expectations for your future success. By taking action to change your opinion of yourself, you can use nearly every situation in life to build up your strong points and minimize your weaknesses. Chapter 4 provides a good beginning for improving your self-concept.

Understanding Your Communication Style

The impressions that others form about you are based on what they observe you saying and doing. The pattern of behavior that others observe is your communication style. This style remains relatively stable throughout your life.

The communication style model is formed by combining two important dimensions of human behavior: dominance and sociability. The combination of these two dimensions forms the four communication styles we have labeled emotive, director, reflective, and supportive.

There is no "best" communication style. Each style has its unique strong points. Directors are admired for the determination they display. Reflectives are respected for their emotional control. The outspoken and enthusiastic behavior of the emotive can be very refreshing, and supportives are esteemed for their casual, responsive style.

People tend to make judgments about others based, in part, on their communication style. When two persons who display different styles meet, communication-style bias may surface. This barrier to human relations can be overcome if you are willing to practice "style flexing." Style flexing can be described as a deliberate attempt to change or alter your style in order to meet the needs of the other person.

Total Person Insight	Versatility is the endorsement given us by others. It, too, is an out-in-the-open factor. It reflects how much we are perceived by others as caring about relationships. A person with too little versatility appears to be more concerned with his or her emotions than with those of others.
Perry Pascarella	

Do you practice style flexing when you meet people who display a style different from your own?

| I almost never display this behavior. | I seldom display this behavior. | I display this behavior sometimes. | I display this behavior often. |

If you feel you need to learn more about style flexing, review some of the guidelines discussed in Chapter 5. The ability to adjust your communication style to the different styles of others can be a valuable skill in dealing with the public and with various levels of management.

Identifying Your Motivations

Part of planning your career is determining what motivates you. Motivation can be defined as the internal drive to accomplish a goal. On the job, motivation is what makes you *want* to work harder. When you are strongly motivated, you tend to have a clear idea of what your goals are and how you can accomplish them.

Do you feel you know what your goals are at this point?

| I don't know what I want or what I'm working toward. | I have some idea but I'm still searching. | I have a fairly good idea of my goals. | I know what I want and what I'm working toward. |

Motivation is based on needs. When a need is important to you, you will go through several steps, called a motivational cycle, to satisfy that need. Abraham Maslow and Frederick Herzberg found that the strongest motivators over the long run are higher-order needs such as self-esteem or self-actualization. Lower-order needs—physiological, safety or security, and social needs—tend to motivate people over the short term. Yet most experts have found that *any* need can be a motivating factor depending on the individual.

People with well-developed human relations skills achieve more job satisfaction (Photo by Richard Wood, The Picture Cube)

Right now, do you know what will motivate you to work harder?

I don't know; I haven't thought about my needs.	I'm not sure; I am examining my needs more carefully.	I think I know what motivates me.	Yes, I've determined what my strongest needs are.

McGregor's Theory X regarding human behavior states that people do not really want to work; they avoid responsibility and must be closely supervised. Theory Y is a more optimistic view, which recognizes that work is as natural to people as play. Most employees seek responsibility and can be highly creative in the way they fulfill their job duties. Managers who accept Theory Y are more likely to make an effort to provide a work environment in which employees *want* to give more. Another theory of human behavior, William Ouchi's Theory Z, describes a management style in which employees are treated as a family. Theory Z attempts to satisfy both lower-level and higher-level motivational needs.

As you examine your own attitudes about work, would you say that you are closer to Theory X or Theory Y?

I believe that work is not a satisfying way to express myself.	I don't believe you can expect too much from work.	I believe that work can be somewhat satisfying.	I believe that work can be a way to express myself creatively.

One of the most common problems facing people who are in school and thinking about a future career is a lack of direction—not knowing what they want to do or how they will get there. Taking the time to discover what truly motivates you can help you choose a satisfying career. If you discover that you do not have a clear sense of your strongest needs or how a career can help you express yourself creatively, review Chapter 6. See if you can identify what motivates you most strongly.

Your Value System

A value is the personal worth or importance one assigns to an object or idea. Formed early in life, values are more enduring than attitudes or opinions. Because they represent deep preferences that motivate you, a clear picture of your value priorities can help you to achieve your goals. Terminal values reflect what you would like to accomplish in life before you die. Instrumental values help you control and direct your behavior during your lifetime. An understanding of your priorities can help you make personal and career choices and deal with other people.

Generally, your value system will be oriented toward people, ideas and concepts, or things. Identifying in which of these three categories your values lie will help you choose the type of career that will give you the greatest personal satisfaction. Clarifying your values is extremely important in building good human relations. Values conflicts within yourself or between you and others need to be settled if you are to achieve your goals and maintain good relationships. You will need to determine which values are important in your life and which ones you can and cannot compromise. In addition, your ability to understand other people's value priorities without accepting them as your own will produce a positive atmosphere for establishing good human relations.

To what extent do you now have a clear picture of your value priorities?

My values have not been identified.	My values have been identified, but not prioritized.	My value priorities are somewhat clear.	My value priorities are well established.

Value priorities and motivation go hand in hand. If you can discover what you value, you can establish priorities that will help you choose the best career for yourself and help you stay motivated. If you discover that you do not have a good idea of your strongest values, you can use the values clarification exercises in Chapter 7 or some of the books listed at the end of that chapter. They can help you find out what your highest terminal and instrumental values are at this point in your life.

Do You Understand Others?

Constructive Self-Disclosure

Self-disclosure is the practice of letting other people know what you think, feel, or want. Constructive self-disclosure helps build stronger relationships. People usually get along better when a spirit of openness and honesty exists in the work environment.

Self-disclosure is not the same as self-description. Self-description means sharing routine information that will not threaten you or other people. For example, if one supervisor says to another, "Monday I'll be implementing the new performance appraisal program," he or she is simply describing a planned activity. If the person goes on to say, "Deep down inside I don't feel the new program will work," then self-disclosure is taking place.

When people use constructive self-disclosure, they can increase the accuracy of their communication, reduce stress, increase their self-awareness, and develop better relationships.

How well do you feel you practice constructive self-disclosure?

| I am very weak in this area. | I am somewhat weak in this area. | I am strong in this area. | I am very strong in this area. |

When you share your thoughts and feelings with others, it is important to avoid the extremes of overdisclosure and underdisclosure. Overdisclosure means to talk too much about yourself, or share intimate information in situations that do not call for such openness. Underdisclosure means to share too little information about yourself, even when the situation calls for greater openness.

Can you share information about yourself in appropriate ways, avoiding the extremes of total concealment and complete openness?

| I am very weak in this area. | I am somewhat weak in this area. | I am strong in this area. | I am very strong in this area. |

Don't be discouraged if your Xs are to the left on the continuums. Most people find self-disclosure difficult; they have been taught not to reveal too much of themselves. However, with practice, you can become adept at this communication skill without under- or overdisclosing your thoughts and feelings. You can learn more about improving this skill in Chapter 9.

Learning to Achieve Emotional Control

Negative emotions such as anger, envy, and fear can serve as barriers to good human relations. Yet people often don't understand why they and others feel and behave as they do. The subconscious part of the mind has a great influence on our behavior. One of the easiest ways to develop an understanding of subconscious mental activity is to study transactional analysis, a simplified explanation of how people communicate, developed by Eric Berne. Through transactional analysis (TA), you can learn to achieve emotional control, a skill highly valued by most organizations in our society.

Berne discovered that everyone's personality is composed of three distinct parts he called the Parent, Adult, and Child ego states. People are in their Parent ego state when they act, feel, and think as they saw their parents behave. When you display a nurturing, caring attitude toward others, you are acting like a Sympathetic Parent. However, when you are opinionated or judgmental toward others, you are usually being influenced by your Critical Parent.

How frequently does the Critical Parent surface in your daily transactions with other people?

I display this behavior often.	I display this behavior sometimes.	I seldom display this behavior.	I almost never display this behavior.

When you feel and act as you did when you were a child, you are in your Child ego state. The Natural Child is the part of you that is impulsive, joyful, affectionate, and spontaneous. The Natural Child can also be rebellious and unwilling to consider the consequences of behavior.

Early in life we learn to adapt to the demands of others. This behavior results in what Berne calls the Adapted Child. Some adapted behaviors have a negative impact on others. For example, people who discover as children that pouting or temper tantrums help them get their way may rely on these childlike behaviors later in life.

There are pluses and minuses in the Child ego state. How frequently do you display its negative aspects?

The Adult person within you makes decisions based on information collected from the Parent and the Child. This ego state is like a human computer that processes data fed into it. The Adult helps you look objectively at impulses from the Parent and Child, and can enable you to select an appropriate emotional response in a stressful situation.

Do you use the Adult to solve problems and make emotional decisions in a logical and emotion-free manner?

I almost never display this behavior.	I seldom display this behavior.	I display this behavior sometimes.	I display this behavior often.

Your responses on these continuums can tell you much about how you react to stressful situations or times when you don't get what you want. If you find that you are relying too heavily on your Critical Parent or the negative aspects of your Adapted Child, you may have trouble with your human relations. Selecting the appropriate "button" on your emotional switchboard can help you achieve stronger, more satisfying relations with others. You may want to review Chapter 9 or read some of the books listed at the end of that chapter if you feel you need help in becoming acquainted with the five persons within you.

The Power of Positive Reinforcement

Positive reinforcement is an important key to improved human relationships. Attitude surveys show that positive reinforcement is an important reward preference among most employees. Sincere words of praise and expressions of gratitude serve as a universal tonic that satisfies one of people's most basic needs. Achieving success in the field of human relations requires, among other things, recognizing the accomplishments of others.

Every day you have an opportunity to utilize positive reinforcement strategies. When a new person joins your staff, why not introduce yourself and extend a warm welcome? A simple act of courtesy can contribute greatly to the building of a new relationship. If someone you work with has a problem, how about taking time to listen? Listening to that person's thoughts can be a powerful reinforcer. If someone you work with recently accomplished something important, how about sending that individual a written congratulatory note? A written expression of appreciation is always welcome. Positive reinforcement is everyone's responsibility. When your boss does something good, why not take a few minutes to recognize that behavior?

Do you display confirming behaviors often?

I am very weak in this area.	I am somewhat weak in this area.	I am strong in this area.	I am very strong in this area.

If positive reinforcement is a universal tonic, why is it not used more frequently? Why are some people unwilling or unable to express appreciation to others? One explanation is that they are preoccupied with themselves.

They are overly concerned about their own welfare and pay little attention to the needs of people around them—a behavior called narcissism.

Do you spend too much time thinking about yourself?

I display this behavior often.	I display this behavior sometimes.	I seldom display this behavior.	I almost never display this behavior.

Can you balance a healthy regard for your own affairs with the ability to recognize and reinforce the positive behavior of others? If you discover that you are too preoccupied with your own concerns or have difficulty praising others for their accomplishments, you may want to review some of the reinforcement techniques suggested in Chapter 10.

Developing Positive First Impressions

First impressions are important. A positive first impression can help you get the job you want and prepare you for a promotion. Success in handling initial public contacts can help you advance in your career because this skill is valued by most employers.

The ability to make a positive first impression is an asset in many occupations. (Photo by Larry Lawfer, The Picture Cube)

Total Person Insight	As businesses experience increasing competition, employers' awareness of the importance of public contact is also increasing. Employers realize that customer or client satisfaction is vital to their survival and that pleasant, helpful service contributes to attracting and holding business.
Julia H. Martin Donna J. Tolson	

First impressions develop quickly. Within a few seconds, the person you have contact with may feel threatened or offended, or he or she may feel positive about the encounter. Although making a good first impression is challenging, you can control the impression you communicate to others. The image you project is formed by a variety of factors including tone of voice, personal mannerisms, dress, facial expressions, hair style, and your handshake. Good manners are also an important contribution to a positive first impression.

Do you project the type of image that will create positive first impressions in the career field you have chosen?

I am very weak in this area.	I am somewhat weak in this area.	I am strong in this area.	I am very strong in this area.

An increasing number of self-help books on the market deal with how to create a positive first impression. Many career-minded people do not present themselves to their best advantage, nor do they realize the impression they make on other people. If you feel you are weak in this area, you may want to review some of the guidelines presented in Chapter 11 or study some of the self-help books listed at the end of that chapter.

Do You Work Well with Others?

Team Building: A Leadership Strategy

People who realize that group effort is necessary in order to achieve goals usually make good team members. Effective teamwork makes it possible to get the job done and at the same time permits each team member to maximize his or her own efforts.

An effective team is free of serious tensions. Team members work in an informal, comfortable, and relaxed atmosphere. The tasks to be completed by the group are well understood and accepted by members. Disagreement sometimes occurs, but major conflicts that result in lost productivity are avoided.

All team builders have certain qualities in common. They maintain a deep interest in both people and productivity—employee goals are not ignored in order to achieve production goals. Team builders are open, sensitive, and receptive to the ideas of others. They recognize accomplishments and make every effort to keep team members involved and well informed. The team-building style also emphasizes structure. Planning, setting goals, scheduling, and evaluating activities are key to building a successful team.

How do you assess your team-building skills?

I am very weak in this area.	I am somewhat weak in this area.	I am strong in this area.	I am very strong in this area.

Members of a productive group are skilled in all the various leadership *and* membership roles. Every member helps the group achieve its mission. A team member takes time to improve relationships with fellow workers and the supervisor.

How do you assess your team membership skills?

I am very weak in this area.	I am somewhat weak in this area.	I am strong in this area.	I am very strong in this area.

Some people find they are weak in team-building skills because they lack experience as a team member. For example, a person who has not participated in team sports may bring to the organization fewer team-building skills. If you feel the need to improve in this area, you can begin by reading one or two of the books listed at the end of Chapter 12. You can also gain experience as a team member by volunteering for team projects whenever possible.

Conflict Management

Conflict can be defined as people's striving for their own preferred outcomes, which prevents others from achieving *their* preferred outcomes. It can be caused by anger, breakdowns in communications, values conflicts, and other factors. Conflict causes breakdowns in human relations, which can lead to a decline in productivity and the effectiveness of an organization. Effective human relations skills will help you avoid many potential conflict situations with people at work. However, sometimes you must rely on a more concrete behavior system to resolve major conflicts. Conflict management may be accomplished through win/lose, lose/lose, and win/win strategies. The win/lose and lose/lose strategies focus on a "we versus they" approach and often result in an unsatisfactory resolution. The win/win strategy focuses on fixing the problem, not the blame. All parties involved work together toward a mutually satisfying solution.

Conflict generates negative emotional responses from all involved. Those who use the win/win strategy listen to all sides, define the basic issues, and create an attitude of trust among all involved. The leader or mediator of the process should be flexible, sensitive, patient, and calm. Participants in the conflict-resolution process must accept anger and conflict as healthy responses and as opportunities for personal growth. They need to believe that a positive solution is possible, and understand that finding a mutually acceptable outcome is more important than competing. Participants should respect everyone's opinions, and believe that differences are healthy.

If conflict in an organization continues to go unresolved, the employees can, and often do, form associations or join labor unions in order to balance the power between labor and management. As they organize, their individual voices take on greater power. This delicate balance of power between labor and management must be achieved and maintained so that organizations can move from a "we versus they" relationship into a team effort that leads to goal attainment. When conflict occurs after employees are an organized unit, a step-by-step grievance procedure often can be used for effective conflict management.

When you are involved in a conflict with another person at work, how well can you maintain the proper attitudes for conflict resolution?

I take statements personally, react defensively and emotionally.	I compete rather than cooperate.	I cooperate rather than compete.	I focus on positive outcomes rather than on personal attacks.

Learning to use the win/win approach takes practice. You will need to think about problems in a new way, particularly if you have looked at conflict in a "someone has to win and someone has to lose" frame of mind. By learning the win/win strategy outlined in Chapter 13, you are putting problem-solving on a new level—stressing cooperation rather than competition. You will find that other human relations skills—communication style flexing, constructive self-disclosure, team building, and the like—are all used in effective problem-solving situations.

Can You Meet the Challenge of Change?

Dealing with Change

Change is an inevitable part of individual and organizational growth. Yet people tend to resist change because they feel inadequate or insecure, fear

"And I'm telling you, to get along in this world, you're going to have to learn to bend a little." (Reprinted with permission of Charles Barsotti)

the unknown, mistrust those initiating the change, or lack an ability to see the larger picture. By anticipating and welcoming change, you can maintain a positive attitude and deal effectively with the demands change makes on you and your coworkers. The fight or flight syndrome that many people experience when threatened by change can have a negative impact on good human relations. A strong sense of personal and professional values will provide a standard for judging whether the change will have a positive or negative effect on the individual.

How would you judge your ability and willingness to adjust to change?

| I am very weak in this area. | I am somewhat weak in this area. | I am strong in this area. | I am very strong in this area. |

Any change produces tension or stress. Stress can be physically and psychologically damaging. Individuals should be aware of the warning signs of too much stress and the techniques for reducing stress that can keep themselves healthy and enhance their ability to maintain effective human relations. Management can help reduce stress by providing employee-assistance programs, by making quality-of-work-life improvements, and by giving employees the information they need about proposed changes.

Have you developed good habits of diet, sleep, and exercise to help you handle stress and maintain your positive human relations skills?

I am very weak in this area.	I am somewhat weak in this area.	I am strong in this area.	I am very strong in this area.

Handling change is difficult for nearly everyone. Do you feel you need to learn how to adjust to change and the accompanying stress? If so, the suggestions in Chapter 14 are a good place to start. In addition, you will find many good books on the market dealing with stress and how to handle almost any type of change—particularly on the job.

Coping with Prejudice and Discrimination

Prejudice means to prejudge and represents an attitude toward people who are "different" in some way. Discrimination is action based on prejudicial attitudes. Race, sex, religion, ethnic background, age, physical appearance, disabilities, and lifestyles are several of the factors that might cause people to discriminate against minority groups. Although education, self-awareness, contact among people of various groups, and laws are all helping to reduce the effects of prejudice and discrimination, society still has a long way to go. Affirmative action programs and equal employment opportunity legislation are beginning to give previously disadvantaged employees greater employment opportunities. However, these programs may also result in charges of reverse discrimination. Human relations suffer in any situation in which prejudiced attitudes are out of control.

When you identify a prejudiced attitude in yourself toward another person or group, do you actively try to identify their positive characteristics and exhibit tolerance and understanding toward their "difference"?

I am very weak in this area.	I am somewhat weak in this area.	I am strong in this area.	I am very strong in this area.

Overcoming prejudices in yourself takes determination and a desire not to let such attitudes limit your circle of possible friends and associates. If you feel you need to improve in this area, review the suggestions in Chapter 15. Seek the help of those whom you feel demonstrate attitudes of tolerance and understanding.

Overcoming Sexism in Organizations

During the past decades, women and men have begun to challenge their traditional sex roles. Women have begun to enter careers in larger numbers than at any other time in history, and men are beginning to share responsibilities for child rearing and household duties. More women and men are entering fields traditionally dominated by one sex. Women who are entering traditionally male-dominated fields are getting support from new role models and mentors, and women and men both are learning new ways of interacting with each other on and off the job.

Despite the great progress made in the last decades, many women are still entering low-paying, low-status, traditionally female-dominated occupations. And serious inequities between men's and women's wages still exist. This wage gap is particularly serious for minority women and female heads of single-parent families. Some states are considering comparable-worth legislation to close the wage gap.

This male day care teacher is assuming duties that were once performed primarily by women. (Photo by Elizabeth Hamlin, Stock Boston, Inc.)

Women and men who enter nontraditional occupations should be prepared to handle a variety of human relations challenges. Strong assertiveness skills can help you cope with sexist behavior or sexual harassment. Legal action is an option for dealing with sexism when your rights have been violated, but it should be used as a last resort as it often creates more human relations problems and can threaten your job security. Sexist attitudes will continue to persist for many years to come until inequities between women and men in employment opportunities, pay, and other areas are eliminated. You will need to develop your human relations skills in order to handle sexist behavior in a calm, nonthreatening manner. At the same time, you will need to eliminate your own sexist attitudes.

How skilled are you in using your human relations skills to deal with sexist behavior in a manner that preserves the integrity of both sides?

I am very weak in this area.	I am somewhat weak in this area.	I am strong in this area.	I am very strong in this area.

Developing skills to deal with sexism can be extremely valuable. You want to avoid as much as possible a "men versus women" or "women versus men" attitude. If you feel you need to work on these skills, you can follow up on the suggestions in Chapter 16. In addition, the books listed in the Suggested Readings can offer useful guidelines. Practice your new skills whenever and wherever you can. Remember, you are trying to overcome deeply ingrained attitudes toward the opposite sex in order to view men and women as professional colleagues.

A Plan You Can Follow

After completing the continuums, you should have a good idea of where your strengths and weaknesses lie. Your ultimate goal is to move your Xs as far to the right on each continuum as you can. Although this may seem an ambitious goal, a well-known public speaker on personal growth once remarked, "Shoot for the moon; even if you miss, you'll end up among the stars!"[1]

You have probably identified several areas that you would like to improve. Select what you feel are one or two of the most important ones and focus on developing those skills or attitudes. Avoid trying to change too much too fast. You want to build a record of success.

The technique summarized in Figure 17.1 can be used to help you make the changes you feel are necessary to improve your human relations skills. The six steps of the cycle, described below, are a step-by-step approach

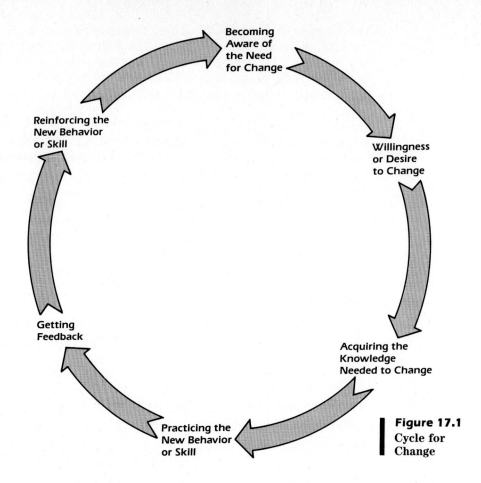

Figure 17.1
Cycle for Change

toward your goal. This technique will work whether you want to develop a skill or change an attitude.

1. Becoming Aware of the Need for Change

The first step toward growth begins with self-awareness. You may discover through this book and your self-assessment what you need to change or improve. Or other people may point out to you what aspects of your behavior or skill level need to be changed. Once you become aware of where you are, you can begin to take steps toward where you want to be.

2. Willingness or Desire to Change

Although awareness is the key to beginning the cycle of change, your attitude toward change is what makes you take action. You can change only when you have the *desire* or *willingness* to plan for and follow through on a program to improve your human relations abilities. Decide for yourself why change needs to be made and what benefits you will gain. Believe that change is possible for you.

3. Acquiring the Knowledge You Need to Change

So far, the process of change has been internal. You are aware of what you want to work on and have decided for yourself what benefits you will gain by changing. Now you will need to seek information, advice, and experience from others. This can mean finding a teacher, joining a group, or gathering sufficient material and teaching yourself.

For example, suppose you decide you need to develop a more positive self-concept. Your first step might be to visit a bookstore and buy a few self-help books such as *How to Be Your Own Best Friend.* You read the books and pick up several good ideas. But you realize that reading is not enough—you need to talk with others who share the same goal. You may enroll in a self-help class, join a consciousness-raising group, or just get together with two or three others who are concerned about improving their self-concept. Some people may choose to see a counselor or therapist when the process of change seems too difficult or when they want an impartial listener. Whatever the method you choose, gain as much "how to" information as you can.

Does this sound like a lot of work? Remember, you've been doing it all your life! Until now, your behavior has been shaped and influenced by what you have learned from parents, teachers, friends, and the media. Now you are choosing to take your development and growth into your own hands. *You* are deciding what will shape and influence your behavior from now on.

4. Practicing Your New Skills

Information is only as useful as you make it. This means that you must *practice* what you have learned in order to change your behavior. If you are a shy person, does this mean you need to volunteer to make a speech in front of several hundred people? Although there is always the rare individual who makes a major change seemingly overnight, most people find that the best and surest way to develop a new skill or attitude is to do it gradually. This is particularly true if you feel a lot of anxiety about changing. Take your time. Allow yourself to ease into your new behavior until you feel comfortable with it. What's the best way to practice? We have pointed out some general guidelines in this book.

In Chapter 4, you learned that the mind has the ability to create an imaginary scene so vividly that your nervous system believes it is real. Visualize yourself acting the way you would like to act, possessing the skill you would like to develop. Spend some time each day doing this exercise. Don't try too hard, just relax and let yourself visualize each scene. This might seem like a child's game, but it works! In fact, experts have found that it is one of the most effective ways of bringing about change.

Second, act as if you already possess the confidence, communication skill, attitude, or whatever it is you want to develop. At first it may seem that you are just fooling yourself and others, but keep at it. At some point you won't notice, and you will no longer be acting; the behavior will be part of you.

Third, find a comfortable, nonthreatening environment in which to practice your new skill or behavior before trying it out at work. Your family or friends might be able to help. Or perhaps the best place is a group or classroom setting where no one knows what your past behavior was like. Many people, for instance, have developed their public speaking skills by joining Toastmasters.

Finally, use whatever self-help aids you need to help you maintain your desire to change. You may find a book that inspires you or a picture that expresses the quality or skill you want to develop.

Above all—be persistent! Change does not happen quickly. It took you many years to learn the old behavior, and it will take time to learn a new way of behaving. However, once you consciously decide to change, your mind will put its marvelous creative power to work for you.

5. Getting Feedback on Your Progress

Whenever you can, ask for feedback as you practice your new skill. You will find that your progress will be much faster than if you use only the trial-and-error method. Everyone has blind spots, particularly when trying out something new. You will often need to rely on the feedback of others to tell you when you are off course or when you have really changed—sometimes you are too close to the process to tell. For example, a friend may point out to you that you seldom accept compliments. Whenever someone praises your work, you mention what you didn't do or what wasn't good about the job. Once you are aware of this tendency, you can practice saying "thank you" and accepting the compliment you rejected before. You can begin to see yourself as a successful person who can accept recognition. Feedback from a friend can help you take another step toward an improved self-concept.

6. Reinforcing Your New Behavior

When you see yourself exhibiting the type of behavior you want to develop— or when someone mentions that you have changed—reward yourself! The rewards can be simple, inexpensive ones—treating yourself to a movie, a bouquet of flowers, a favorite meal, or a special event. This type of reinforcement is vital when trying to improve or develop behavior skills. Don't postpone rewarding yourself until the goal is reached. Intermediate successes are just as important as the final result. As the saying goes, "Success is hard by the yard . . . but a cinch by the inch."[2] As you achieve each inch of your goal, reward yourself.

What happens if you slip and repeat the old behavior? Recognize that occasionally it will happen, forgive yourself, and resolve to act differently the next time. Don't pay any more attention to the negative behavior than you have to. You don't want to feed energy to the old, you want to reinforce the new. Rewarding yourself can help make the cycle of change self-propelling.

The Total Process: How It Works

Colin, the manager of a large department store, had never worked for a woman boss. When Joan was hired as district supervisor, his immediate reaction was, "I can't report to a *woman*!" During the first management meeting, Colin found himself resenting everything Joan did from the way she opened the meeting to her closing remarks. She appeared to sense his attitude, and her questions about his profit picture seemed to be probing for weaknesses. On the way home with another manager, Colin mentioned his belief that women did not belong in management. His colleague replied, "Don't let your sexist attitudes sabotage your career. I have a feeling our supervisor is here to stay."

His friend's remarks jolted him. Sexist? He had never thought of himself as sexist—his attitudes had always seemed the normal way to think. Over the next few days he tried to forget the remark, but his basic sense of fairness would not let him. Finally, he came to the painful conclusion that he *was* prejudiced against women in management. Not only could his attitude undermine his effectiveness as a manager, but it was already causing a breakdown in human relations between himself and Joan. He had to change—but how?

Colin started by reading articles on women in management, their problems, successes, and potential. He began to get a feel for the difficult position most women executives found themselves in when they had to supervise an all-male staff. He talked to other men who had women bosses and found that most of them had great respect for their women managers. Some of them were able to give him practical advice on how to change his behavior on the job. At business conferences, he made a point to spend time with women executives. He discovered that their anxieties and aspirations for their jobs were a lot like his own.

He started practicing the nonsexist behavior he had learned on his own and from others. He asked another manager to give him feedback on his behavior and let him know when his sexist attitudes were showing. Whenever he succeeded in changing his behavior—even slightly—he rewarded himself, sometimes taking in a round of golf after work.

His greatest reward, however, came from Joan. Four months after he had decided to change his attitude, she stopped him on the way out of a meeting and said how much she appreciated his contribution to the discussion. He realized then that at some point along the way, he had become a part of the management team again. Over the next few months, he and Joan created an exciting sales campaign to increase local store profits.

You Can Improve Your Human Relations Skills

Regardless of the skill or attitude you are working to improve, the plan outlined in this chapter *will* work. One of the exciting aspects of this plan is that you are competing against yourself. You set your own standards and goals. You decide what kind of person you want to be. The results can mean not only career advancement or financial benefits but the development of strong, satisfying relationships with others. These relationships may be the key to future opportunities, and you, in turn, may be able to help others achieve their goals.

In the opening chapter of the book, we talked about the total-person approach to human relations. By now, we hope you realize that you are not just another person starting a career. You are a unique combination of talents, attitudes, values, goals, needs, and motivations—all in a state of development. You can decide to tap your potential to become a successful, productive human being, however *you* understand those terms. We hope this book will help you develop your human relations skills and become what you want to be. You can turn the theories, concepts, and guidelines presented here into a plan of action for your own life and career. We wish you the best!

Notes

1. Leo Hauser, *Five Steps to Success* (Minneapolis: Personal Dynamics Institute, 1980).
2. Ibid.

Name Index

Subject Index

Figure Credits Continued

rights reserved. Figure 8.2 from Joseph Luft, *Group Processes: An Introduction to Group Dynamics*, 3rd ed. By permission of Mayfield Publishing Company, Palo Alto, California. Copyright © 1984 by Joseph Luft. Figure 10.3 courtesy of John Deere International, Moline, Illinois. Figure 12.1, The Managerial Grid®, from *The Managerial Grid III*. By Robert R. Blake and Jane Srygley Mouton. By permission of Gulf Publishing Co., Houston, Texas. Copyright © 1985. Used with permission. All rights reserved. Figure 14.1 from the Bureau of Labor Statistics, U.S. Department of Labor. Figure 15.2 adapted from an AP Wirephoto Chart. Figure 15.3 statistics from *Statistical Abstract of the United States 1986*, U.S. Department of Commerce. Figure 15.4 statistics from U.S. Equal Employment Opportunity Commission. Figure 16.1 statistics from Bureau of Labor Statistics, U.S. Census Bureau.

Total Person Insights Continued

ard Egan, *You and Me* (Monterey, Calif.: Brooks/Cole, 1977), p. 73. *p. 217:* Dudley Bennett, *TA and the Manager* (New York: American Management Associations, 1976), p. viii. *p. 249:* Jan Hartman, "How to Learn from Success and Failure," *New Dimensions*, April-May 1984, p. 5. *p. 270:* Janet G. Elsea, *The Four-Minute Sell* (New York: Simon and Schuster, 1984), p. 9. *p. 298:* Warren Bennis and Burt Nanus, *Leaders—The Strategies for Taking Charge* (New York: Harper and Row, 1985), pp. 43–44. *p. 300:* Ernest A. Fitzgerald, "Choosing the Right Window," *PACE*, March 1986, p. 5. *p. 319:* Gordon Lippitt, "Managing Conflict in Today's Organizations," *Training and Development*, July 1982, p. 3. *p. 350:* Craig Brod, *Technostress: The Human Cost of the Computer Revolution* (Reading, Mass.: Addison-Wesley, 1984), p. xx. *p. 412:* Eleanor Maccoby and Carol Jacklin, *The Psychology of Sex Differences*, cited in James Doyle, *The Male Experience* (Dubuque, Iowa: William C. Brown, 1983), p. 88. *p. 421:* Berkeley Men's Center Manifesto, cited in Doyle, *The Male Experience* (Dubuque, Iowa: William C. Brown, 1983), p. 288. *p. 450:* Perry Pascarella, "To Motivate Others Try Versatility," *Industry Week*, May 3, 1982. *p. 457:* Julia H. Martin and Donna J. Tolson, "Changing Job Skills in Virginia: The Employers' View," *News Letter*, vol. 63, no. 6, Institute of Government, University of Virginia, January 1986, p. 2.

Text Credits Continued

ers, Belmont, CA 94002. Reprinted by permission. *p. 77:* "Scandinavian Models of Employee Participation," Knut Haganaes and Lee Hales, *SAM Advanced Management Journal*, Winter 1983, pp. 24–26. Reprinted by permission of the Society for Advancement of Management. *p. 134:* "Imagine Your Way to Success," an address to the National Association for Professional Saleswomen, October 1983. Reprinted by permission of the Foundation for Christian Living. *p. 163:* Frederick Herzberg, "The Managerial Choice: To Be Efficient and To Be Human (Salt Lake City, Utah: Olympus Publishing, 1982), p. 131. Used by permission of Dr. Frederick Herzberg. *p. 153:* Material adapted from "This Is the Answer" by William Baldwin. Reprinted by permission of *Forbes* Magazine, July 5, 1982. © Forbes Inc., 1982. *pp. 166–167:* Levering, Moskowitz and Katz, *The 100 Best Companies to Work for in America*, © 1984, Addison-Wesley Publishing Company, Inc. Reading, Massachusetts. Reprinted with permission. *p. 209:* Alice G. Sargent, *The Androgynous Manager* (New York: AMACOM, a division of American Management Associations, 1981), p. 164. Reprinted by permission of the American Management Associations. *p. 235:* "Woman's Death Prompts Probe of Hotline Nurse," *USA Today*, March 7, 1984. Reprinted by permission. *p. 240:* "Gellerman on Motivation and Productivity," audiotape by Saul Gellerman (San Diego: University Associates, Inc.) Reprinted by permission of the author. *p. 285:* "Banking on a Look," by Mary Bland Armistead, *Roanoke Times & World News*, September 12, 1981. Reprinted by permission. *p. 295:* Adapted from The Managerial Grid III, by Robert R. Blake and Jane Srygley Mouton. Houston: Gulf Publishing Company, Copyright © 1985, p. 12. Reproduced by permission. *pp. 297–298:* Reprinted with permission from the April 1978 issue of *Training*, The Magazine of Human Resources Development. Copyright 1978, Lakewood Publications Inc. Minneapolis, MN. All rights reserved. *p. 311:* Levering, Moskowitz and Katz, *The 100 Best Companies to Work for in America*, © 1984, Addison-Wesley Publishing Company, Inc. Reading, Massachusetts. Reprinted with permission. *p. 415:* Laurie Ashcraft and Elizabeth Nickles, "Ads Start to Roll with the Social Punches," *Advertizing Age*, July 16, 1982, p. M-24. Reprinted by permission of Crain Communications.